THE HISTORY OF THE ENGLISH
CHURCH AND PEOPLE

THE HISTORY OF THE ENGLISH CHURCH AND PEOPLE

Bede

Introduction by Michael Frassetto

BARNES
& NOBLE
BOOKS
NEW YORK

CONTENTS

BOOK II

BOOK III

THE LIVES OF THE HOLY ABBOTS
OF WEREMOUTH AND JARROW

INTRODUCTION

THE *History of the English Church and People* (also known as *The Ecclesiastical History of England*), completed in 731 and possibly revised and updated over the next few years, is arguably the greatest and most influential work of history of the Middle Ages. Written by the Anglo-Saxon scholar and monk, the Venerable Bede, the work is at once a national history and a witness to the greatness of God and His church on earth. An immensely popular work, the *History* contributed to the adoption of the Annus Domini dating system, which Bede used throughout his great work. Although Bede included discussion of numerous miracles in the work, he collected evidence and evaluated sources in an almost modern way that has led many to identify Bede as the "father of English history."

Bede lived in the late seventh and early eighth centuries during what is commonly called the Dark Ages, but as his writings and life demonstrate, this was far from an age of ignorance or cultural darkness. He was a central figure in the Northumbrian Renaissance, one of the many cultural revivals of the early Middle Ages, and his broad reading and elegant Latin demonstrate the high quality that scholarship and literary production could achieve at that time. He composed the *History* near the end of his life with the hope that his readers, of whom there would be many throughout the Middle Ages and beyond, would learn from the example, both good and bad, of its many very human characters. His work focuses on the history of the conversion to Christianity of the people of England and often examines the actions of the leading figures of society—the kings, bishops, abbots, and nuns—who were the key actors in English history. He also reveals the experiences of simple monks and gives us a glimpse of the everyday life of less exalted figures, and, thus, provides a comprehensive picture of the English people in a formative period in their history.

Bede was probably born around the year 673 on lands that belonged to the famous monastery of Wearmouth, which had been founded by Benedict Biscop and which Bede himself would eventually join. He later transferred to its companion monastery of Jarrow and may have been one of the few survivors of a plague that struck the community in 686. He spent nearly his entire life in the monasteries of Wearmouth and Jarrow, seldom venturing beyond its confines. He did make trips to the famed abbey of Lindisfarne and other monasteries in England as well as making visits to the archbishop of York and Ceolwulf, king of Northumbria. He tells us that he became a deacon at nineteen years old and a priest at thirty and that he observed the monastic rule all his life. A conscientious monk, Bede was also a devoted scholar and teacher whose writings had a profound influence on early medieval learning. He wrote numerous commentaries on the books of the Bible and the works of the Fathers. Widely read in both sacred and profane letters, although he knew pagan authors mostly through anthologies, Bede wrote two books on poetry, one of which included a commentary on Latin grammar. Influenced by Isidore of Seville and Pliny the Elder, whose work he read in the original, Bede wrote a book on natural phenomena. An orthodox Christian, Bede was charged with heresy over the contents of his first book on computus, the science of calculating dates of the calendar. His second book on computus, however, became the standard work on the subject in the Middle Ages and was important preparation for his *History*. His final work, a translation into Old English of the Gospel of John, was left unfinished when he died on May 25, 735. By then Bede had achieved great fame and was buried in the porch of the monastery church, later his remains were moved to the main altar. In 1020, his relics were stolen and buried at the shrine of St. Cuthbert in Durham. His relics were allegedly moved to the Holy Land when King Henry VIII shut down the monasteries in England. In 1899, he was declared a Doctor of the Church, and in 1935, Bede was declared a saint.

The *History* was one of the most popular works of the Middle Ages and achieved almost instant acclaim. Indeed, like many of Bede's works, it was a "best seller" in the Middle Ages. Although no copy of the *History* in Bede's own hand is extant today, the earliest copy that exists was compiled within a few years of his death. Almost no important library in the Middle Ages was without a copy of the work or at least a part of it, and more than 150 manuscript copies of the *History* as well as numerous manuscripts with extracts of it are to be found today. Bede's elegant and literate Latin as well as his narrative techniques made the work popular in its original and in translation in the Middle Ages and beyond. The earliest translation into Old English was made during the time of King Alfred the Great in the ninth century. The first modern English translation was made by Thomas Stapleton and was printed by John Laet in Antwerp in 1565. The first printed version of the *History* was made by Heinrich Eggestym in c. 1475, placing it in the ranks of the earliest printed books. It was so popular and widely read that polemicists on both sides of the Reformation and Counter Reformation used it in their religious debates.

Often seen as a lone voice in the early medieval wilderness, Bede was instead the leading scholar of his time and a historian in a long line reaching back to Eusebius in the fourth century. Along with that first great Christian historian, Bede can be listed with Orosius and Cassiodorus in the early fifth century and, closer to his own time, Gregory of Tours, the historian of the Franks of the late sixth century whose work Bede surely knew but did not cite. In Bede's own time, there were a number of annalists and chroniclers, most importantly Fredegar and his anonymous continuator, who told the story of the last kings of the Merovingian dynasty and the founders of the Carolingian line. Along with the chroniclers, there were many hagiographers, the authors of the lives of saints, who contributed to the historical record of the time. Indeed, saints' lives were among the more important sources for the *History*. Bede himself wrote saints' lives, including two versions of the life of St. Cuthbert, and his hagiographical work is often recognized as important preparation for his writing of the *History*. The *Life of St. Germanus*, Stephen of Ripon's *Life of Wilfrid*, and the Whitby *Life of Gregory* were among the saints' lives Bede used in the preparation of his great work, but, as with all the sources he used, Bede did not slavishly copy from the saints' lives but adapted and carefully sifted the material to best suit the narrative he composed.

It is his use of sources that clearly distinguishes Bede from his contemporaries and establishes the *History* as one of the more reliable accounts of early medieval history. Bede's work clearly demonstrates his wide reading and impeccable scholarship. Throughout the work there are traces of the great ancient Latin writer Virgil, whose works Bede probably knew only second hand. The Bible was an even more important source for Bede; references to both the Old Testament and New Testament can be seen throughout the *History*. Along with biblical and pagan sources and the hagiographers, Bede drew from earlier historians and other sources in a critical way that was almost modern. In fact, he was one of the few medieval writers to cite the sources he quoted. For the earlier part of his history, until the time of the mission of St. Augustine of Canterbury, Bede relied on the historians Gildas and Orosius, the *Life of St. Germanus*, and a few other earlier writers. The rest of the work was based on a variety of sources, including a number of documents that the priest Nothelm of London brought back from Rome for Bede or that contacts at Canterbury provided him. At various points of the *History*, Bede cites the full text of letters sent by Pope Gregory I and other popes to the archbishops of Canterbury and various other ecclesiastics in England. He also cites the full text of synodal decrees and other ecclesiastical documents produced by members of the English church. Bede was also an early medieval oral historian; he gathered stories from the many churchmen he knew and included them in the history, often citing the name of the person who told the story and explaining his own relationship with that person.

Bede's *History* tells the story of the conversion and history of early medieval England in five books running from the time of the invasions of Julius Caesar to Bede's own time. It is no coincidence that the work is arranged in five books, recalling the Pentateuch, the first five books of the Bible, because Bede recognized God's hand in the history of the English just as God, according to the Hebrew Scriptures, worked his will through the ancient Israelites. The English may have been seen by Bede as the new chosen people, the new Israel upon whom God bestows his blessings. Indeed, the conquest of the island by the Anglo-Saxon peoples and defeat of the native Britons is presented by Bede as the bestowal of God's rewards and punishments. The Britons were chastised by God for their failure to share the faith with other peoples, and the pagan Anglo-Saxons, invited by the already Christian Britons, were allowed to conquer the natives because of the sins of the Britons and were rewarded further by their own conversion to the Christian faith. The subsequent growth of the English kingdoms, notably Bede's own Northumbria (a region that is the focus of much of the *History*), and the success and failures of the English kings was, for Bede, the result of God's plan.

The purpose of the *History*, as Bede indicates in the preface, was to encourage his readers to do good and to avoid doing evil, and, dedicated to King Ceolwulf, the work fit into the genre of the mirror for princes, which was designed to encourage righteousness and good governance among kings. The narrative contains numerous moral exempla designed to encourage Bede's readers to live good Christian lives. Vortigern's invitation of the Anglo-Saxons, and the Britons' defeat, is the first of many episodes that reveals the penalties for those who do not live according to God's law. The failure of the West Saxons to convert to Christianity led to their downfall, just as the apostasy of other Anglo-Saxon kings led to their destruction by the pagan king Cadwalla. Various monks and priests also provide an example of those who lived sinfully. Bede tells the tale of a monastery that was burned to the ground because of the wickedness of the monks. Bede also provides repeated illustration of the benefits of accepting God's law, most notably in the visions and miracles he describes throughout the *History*. The good Christian king, Oswald, revealed the power of God in the miraculous cures that occurred at the site of his death. Oswald also ended a fatal epidemic after the monks appealed to heaven for help. Saintly bishops and monks also cured diseases, calmed the waters to protect their followers, and were rewarded with visions of their own acceptance into heaven. In this way, Bede demonstrated both the power of God and the rewards for those who lived according to God's law.

Central to Bede's narrative was the decline of the Celtic church in England and the triumph of the church of Rome and adoption of the proper dating of Easter, the latter a particular concern of Bede's considering his own interests in computus. The most renowned anecdotes in the *History* are associated with these two matters. Among these episodes is the tale of Gregory the Great and the Deiran boys, according to which the future pope was inspired to send a mission to convert England because of the angelic faces of the slave boys from the island he saw in the market place in Rome. The mission of Augustine of Canterbury and his reception by and conversion of King Ethelbert of Kent further details the triumph of the Roman church. Another example is Bede's account of the synod of Whitby in 664, which celebrates the acceptance of Roman Christianity and the Roman method of calculating Easter. The victory of Rome was guaranteed at the council when the advocate for Rome proclaimed that the Roman system was that of St. Peter, keeper of the keys to the kingdom of heaven. Bede's *History* thus provides a moving tale of the conversion of the English to Roman Christianity, is intended to provide guidelines for living morally, and is based on an almost modern historical methodology. For these reasons and because of Bede's elegant style and dramatic sense of narrative, his *History* remains one of the most important and popular sources from the early Middle Ages.

Michael Frassetto holds a Ph.D. in history from the University of Delaware and has taught at several colleges He is religion editor at Encyclopaedia Britannica and is the author of *Encyclopedia of Barbarian Europe: Society in Transformation.*

BOOK I

PREFACE

TO THE MOST GLORIOUS KING CEOLWULPH, BEDE, THE
SERVANT OF CHRIST AND PRIEST

I formerly, at your request, most readily transmitted to you the
Ecclesiastical History of the English Nation, which I had newly pub-
lished, for you to read, and give it your approbation; and I now
send it again to be transcribed, and more fully considered at your
leisure. And I cannot but commend the sincerity and zeal, with
which you not only diligently give ear to hear the words of the Holy
Scripture, but also industriously take care to become acquainted
with the actions and sayings of former men of renown, especially of
our own nation. For if history relates good things of good men, the
attentive hearer is excited to imitate that which is good; or if it
mentions evil things of wicked persons, nevertheless the religious
and pious hearer or reader, shunning that which is hurtful and perverse, is the more earnestly excited to perform those things which
he knows to be good, and worthy of God. Of which you also being
deeply sensible, are desirous that the said history should be more
fully made familiar to yourself, and to those over whom the Divine
Authority has appointed you governor, from your great regard to
their general welfare. But to the end that I may remove all occasion
of doubting what I have written, both from yourself and other readers or hearers of this history, I will take care briefly to intimate from
what authors I chiefly learned the same.

. 1

My principal authority and aid in this work was the learned and reverend Abbot Albinus; who, educated in the Church of Canterbury by those venerable and learned men, Archbishop Theodore of blessed memory, and the Abbot Adrian, transmitted to me by Nothelm, the pious priest of the Church of London, either in writing, or by word of mouth of the same Nothelm, all that he thought worthy of memory, that had been done in the province of Kent, or the adjacent parts, by the disciples of the blessed Pope Gregory, as he had learned the same either from written records, or the traditions of his ancestors. The same Nothelm, afterwards going to Rome, having, with leave of the present Pope Gregory, searched into the archives of the holy Roman Church, found there some epistles of the blessed Pope Gregory, and other popes; and returning home, by the advice of the aforesaid most reverend father Albinus, brought them to me, to be inserted in my history. Thus, from the beginning of this volume to the time when the English nation received the faith of Christ, have we collected the writings of our predecessors, and from them gathered matter for our history; but from that time till the present, what was transacted in the Church of Canterbury, by the disciples of St. Gregory or their successors, and under what kings the same happened, has been conveyed to us by Nothelm through the industry of the aforesaid Abbot Albinus. They also partly informed me by what bishops and under what kings the provinces of the East and West Saxons, as also of the East Angles, and of the Northumbrians, received the faith of Christ. In short I was chiefly encouraged to undertake this work by the persuasions of the same Albinus. In like manner, Daniel, the most reverend Bishop of the West Saxons, who is still living, communicated to me in writing some things relating to the Ecclesiastical History of that province, and the next adjoining to it of the South Saxons, as also of the Isle of Wight. But how, by the pious ministry of Cedd and Ceadda, the province of the Mercians was brought to the faith of Christ, which they knew not before, and how that of the East Saxons recovered the same, after having expelled it, and how those fathers lived and died, we learned from the brethren of the monastery, which was built by them, and is called Lasting-ham. What ecclesiastical transactions took place in the province of the East Angles, was partly made known to us from the writings and tradition of our ancestors, and partly by relation of the most reverend Abbot Esius. What was done towards promoting the faith, and what was the sacerdotal succession in the province of Lindsey, we had either from the letters of the most reverend prelate Cunebert, or by word of mouth from other persons of good credit. But what was done in the Church throughout the province of the Northumbrians, from the time when they received the faith of Christ till this present, I received not from any particular author, but by the faithful testimony of innumerable witnesses, who might know or remember the same; besides what I had of my own knowledge. Wherein it is to be observed, that what I have written concerning our most holy father, Bishop Cuthbert, either in this volume, or in my treatise on his life and actions, I partly took, and faithfully copied from what I found written of him by the brethren of the Church of Lindisfarne; but at the same time took care to add such things as I could myself have knowledge of by the faithful testimony of such as knew him. And I humbly entreat the reader, that if he shall in this that we have written find anything not delivered according to the truth, he will not impute the same to me, who, as the true rule of history requires, have laboured sincerely to commit to writing such things as I could gather from common report, for the instruction of posterity.

Moreover, I beseech all men who shall hear or read this history of our nation, that for my manifold infirmities both of mind and body, they will offer up frequent supplications to the throne of Grace. And I further pray, that in recompense for the labour wherewith I have recorded in the several countries and cities those events which were most worthy of note, and most grateful to the ears of their inhabitants, I may for my reward have the benefit of their pious prayers.

CHAPTER I

OF THE SITUATION OF BRITAIN AND IRELAND, AND OF THEIR ANCIENT INHABITANTS

BRITAIN, an island in the ocean, formerly called Albion, is situated between the north and west, facing, though at a considerable distance, the coasts of Germany, France, and Spain, which form the greatest part of Europe. It extends 800 miles in length towards the north, and is 200 miles in breadth, except where several promontories extend further in breadth, by which its compass is made to be 3675 miles. To the south, as you pass along the nearest shore of the Belgic Gaul, the first place in Britain which opens to the eye is the city of Rutubi Portus, by the English corrupted into Reptacestir. The distance from hence across the sea to Gessoriacum, the nearest shore of the Morini, is fifty miles, or as some writers say, 450 furlongs. On the back of the island, where it opens upon the boundless ocean, it has the islands called Orcades. Britain excels for grain and trees, and is well adapted for feeding cattle and beasts of burden. It also produces vines in some places, and has plenty of land and water-fowls of several sorts; it is remarkable also for rivers abounding in fish, and plentiful springs. It has the greatest plenty of salmon and eels; seals are also frequently taken, and dolphins, as also whales; besides many sorts of shell-fish, such as muscles, in which are often found excellent pearls of all colours, red, purple, violet, and green, but mostly white. There is also a great abundance of cockles, of which the scarlet dye is made; a most beautiful colour, which never fades with the heat of the sun or the washing of the rain; but the older it is, the more beautiful it becomes. It has both salt and hot springs, and from them flow rivers which furnish hot baths, proper for all ages and sexes, and arranged according. For water, as St. Basil says, receives the heating quality, when it runs along certain metals, and becomes not only hot but scalding. Britain has also many veins of metals, as copper, iron, lead, and silver; it has much and excellent jet, which is black and sparkling, glittering at the fire, and when heated, drives away serpents; being warmed with rubbing, it holds fast whatever is applied to it, like amber. The island was formerly embellished with twenty-eight noble cities, besides innumerable castles, which were all strongly secured with walls, towers, gates, and locks. And, from its lying almost under the North Pole, the nights are light in summer, so that at midnight the beholders are often in doubt whether the evening twilight still continues, or that of the morning is coming on; for the sun, in the night, returns under the earth, through the northern regions at no great distance from them. For this reason the days are of a great length in summer, as, on the contrary, the nights are in winter, for the sun then withdraws into the southern parts, so that the nights are eighteen hours long. Thus the nights are extraordinarily short in summer, and the days in winter, that is, of only six equinoctial hours. Whereas, in Armenia, Macedonia, Italy, and other countries of the same latitude, the longest day or night extends but to fifteen hours, and the shortest to nine.

This island at present, following the number of the books in which the Divine law was written, contains five nations, the English, Britons, Scots, Picts, and Latins, each in its own peculiar dialect cultivating the sublime study of Divine truth. The Latin tongue is, by the study of the Scriptures, become common to all the rest. At first this island had no other inhabitants but the Britons, from whom it derived its name, and who, coming over into Britain, as is reported, from Armorica, possessed themselves of the southern parts thereof. When they, beginning at the south, had made themselves masters of the greatest part of the island, it happened, that the nation of the Picts, from Scythia, as is reported, putting to sea, in a few long ships, were driven by the winds beyond the shores of Britain, and arrived on the northern coast of Ireland, where, finding the nation of the Scots, they begged to be allowed to settle among them, but could not succeed in obtaining their request. Ireland is the greatest island next to Britain, and lies to the west of it; but as it is shorter than Britain to the north, so, on the other hand, it runs out far beyond it to the south, opposite to the northern parts of Spain, though a spacious sea lies between them. The Picts, as has been said, arriving in this island by sea, desired to have a place granted them in which they might settle. The Scots answered that the island could not contain them both; but "We can give you good advice," said they, "what to do; we know there is another island, not far from ours, to the eastward, which we often see at a distance, when the days are clear. If you will go thither, you will obtain settlements; or, if they should oppose you, you shall have our assistance." The Picts, accordingly, sailing over into Britain, began to inhabit the northern parts thereof, for the Britons were possessed of the southern. Now the Picts had no wives, and asked them of the Scots; who would not consent to grant them upon any other terms, than that when any difficulty should arise, they should choose a king from the female royal race rather than from the male: which custom, as is well known, has been observed among the Picts to this day. In process of time, Britain, besides the Britons and the Picts, received a third nation, the Scots, who, migrating from Ireland under their leader, Reuda, either by fair means, or by force of arms, secured to themselves those settlements among the Picts which they still possess. From the name of their commander, they are to this day called Dalreudins; for, in their language, Dal signifies a part.

Ireland, in breadth, and for wholesomeness and serenity of climate, far surpasses Britain; for the snow scarcely ever lies there above three days: no man makes hay in the summer for winter's provision, or builds stables for his beasts of burden. No reptiles are found there, and no snake can live there; for, though often carried thither out of Britain, as soon as the ship comes near the shore, and the scent of the air reaches them, they die. On the contrary, almost all things in the island are good against poison. In short, we have known that when some persons have been bitten by serpents, the scrapings of leaves of books that were brought out of Ireland, being put into water, and given them to drink, have immediately expelled the spreading poison, and assuaged the swelling. The island abounds in milk and honey, nor is there any want of vines, fish, or fowl; and it is remarkable for deer and goats. It is properly the country of the Scots, who, migrating from thence, as has been said, added a third nation in Britain to the Britons and the Picts. There is a very large gulf of the sea, which formerly divided the nation of the Picts from the Britons; which gulf runs from the west very far into the land, where, to this day, stands the strong city of the Britons, called Alcluith. The Scots, arriving on the north side of this bay, settled themselves there.

CHAPTER II

CAIUS JULIUS CÆSAR, THE FIRST ROMAN THAT CAME INTO BRITAIN

BRITAIN had never been visited by the Romans, and was, indeed, entirely unknown to them before the time of Caius Julius Cæsar, who, in the year 693 after the building of Rome, but the sixtieth year before the incarnation of our Lord, was consul with Lucius Bibulus, and afterwards while he made war upon the Germans and the Gauls, which were divided only by the river Rhine, came into the province of the Morini, from whence is the nearest and shortest passage into Britain. Here, having provided about eighty ships of burden and vessels with oars, he sailed over into Britain; where, being first roughly handled in a battle, and then meeting with a violent storm, he lost a considerable part of his fleet, no small number of soldiers, and almost all his horses. Returning into Gaul, he put his legions into winter-quarters, and gave orders for building six hundred sail of both sorts. With these he again passed over early in spring into Britain, but, whilst he was marching with a large army towards the enemy, the ships, riding at anchor, were, by a tempest either dashed one against another, or driven upon the sands and wrecked. Forty of them perished, the rest were, with much difficulty, repaired. Cæsar's cavalry was, at the first charge, defeated by the Britons, and Labienus, the tribune, slain. In the second engagement, he, with great hazard to his men, put the Britons to flight. Thence he proceeded to the river Thames, where an immense multitude of the enemy had posted themselves on the farthest side of the river, under the command of Cassibellaun, and fenced the bank of the river and almost all the ford under water with sharp stakes: the remains of these are to be seen to this day, apparently about the thickness of a man's thigh, and being cased with lead, remain fixed immovably in the bottom of the river. This, being perceived and avoided by the Romans, the barbarians, not able to stand the shock of the legions, hid themselves in the woods, whence they grievously galled the Romans with repeated sallies. In the meantime, the strong city of Trinovantum, with its commander Androgeus, surrendered to Cæsar, giving him forty hostages. Many other cities, following their example, made a treaty with the Romans. By their assistance, Cæsar at length, with much difficulty, took Cassibellaun's town, situated between two marshes, fortified by the adjacent woods, and plentifully furnished with all necessaries. After this, Cæsar returned into Gaul, but he had no sooner put his legions into winter-quarters, than he was suddenly beset and distracted with wars and tumults raised against him on every side.

CHAPTER III

CLAUDIUS, THE SECOND OF THE ROMANS WHO CAME INTO BRITAIN, BROUGHT THE ISLANDS ORCADES INTO SUBJECTION TO THE ROMAN EMPIRE; AND VESPASIAN, SENT BY HIM, REDUCED THE ISLE OF WIGHT UNDER THEIR DOMINION

In the year of Rome 798, Claudius, fourth emperor from Augustus, being desirous to approve himself a beneficial prince to the republic, and eagerly bent upon war and conquest, undertook an expedition into Britain, which seemed to be stirred up to rebellion by the refusal of the Romans to give up certain deserters. He was the only one, either before or after Julius Cæsar, who had dared to land upon the island; yet, within a very few days, without any fight or bloodshed, the greatest part of the island was surrendered into his hands. He also added to the Roman empire the Orcades, which lie in the ocean beyond Britain, and then, returning to Rome the sixth month after his departure, he gave his son the title of Britannicus. This war he concluded in the fourth year of his empire, which is the forty-sixth from the incarnation of our Lord. In which year there happened a most grievous famine in Syria, which, in the Acts of the Apostles is recorded to have been foretold by the prophet Agabus. Vespasian, who was emperor after Nero, being sent into Britain by the same Claudius, brought also under the Roman dominion the Isle of Wight, which is next to Britain on the south, and is about thirty miles in length from east to west, and twelve from north to south; being six miles distant from the southern coast of Britain at the east end, and three only at the west. Nero, succeeding Claudius in the empire, attempted nothing in martial affairs; and, therefore, among other innumerable detriments brought upon the Roman state, he almost lost Britain; for under him two most noble towns were there taken and destroyed.

CHAPTER IV

LUCIUS, KING OF BRITAIN, WRITING TO POPE ELEUTHERUS, DESIRES TO BE MADE A CHRISTIAN

In the year of our Lord's incarnation 156, Marcus Antoninus Verus, the fourteenth from Augustus, was made emperor, together with his brother, Aurelius Commodus. In their time, whilst Eleutherus, a holy man, presided over the Roman church, Lucius, king of the Britons, sent a letter to him, entreating that by his command he might be made a Christian. He soon obtained his pious request, and the Britons preserved the faith, which they had received, uncorrupted and entire, in peace and tranquillity until the time of the Emperor Diocletian.

CHAPTER V

HOW THE EMPEROR SEVERUS DIVIDED THAT PART OF BRITAIN, WHICH HE SUBDUED, FROM THE REST BY A RAMPART

In the year of our Lord 189, Severus, an African, born at Leptis, in the province of Tripolis, received the imperial purple. He was the seventeenth from Augustus, and reigned seventeen years. Being naturally stern, and engaged in many wars, he governed the state vigorously, but with much trouble. Having been victorious in all the grievous civil wars which happened in his time, he was drawn into Britain by the revolt of almost all the confederate tribes; and, after many great and dangerous battles, he thought fit to divide that part of the island, which he had recovered from the other unconquered nations, not with a wall, as some imagine, but with a rampart. For a wall is made of stones, but a rampart, with which camps are fortified to repel the assaults of enemies, is made of sods, cut out of the earth, and raised above the ground all round like a wall, having in front of it the ditch whence the sods were taken, and strong stakes of wood fixed upon its top. Thus Severus drew a great ditch and strong rampart, fortified with several towers, from sea to sea; and was afterwards taken sick and died at York, leaving two sons, Bassianus and Geta; of whom Geta died, adjudged a public enemy; but Bassianus, having taken the surname of Antoninus, obtained the empire.

CHAPTER VI

THE REIGN OF DIOCLETIAN, AND HOW HE PERSECUTED THE CHRISTIANS

In the year of our Lord's incarnation 286, Diocletian, the thirty-third from Augustus, and chosen emperor by the army, reigned twenty years, and created Maximian, surnamed Herculius, his colleague in the empire. In their time, one Carausius, of very mean birth, but an expert and able soldier, being appointed to guard the sea-coasts, then infested by the Franks and Saxons, acted more to the prejudice than to the advantage of the commonwealth; and from his not restoring to its owners the booty taken from the robbers, but keeping all to himself, it was suspected that by intentional neglect he suffered the enemy to infest the frontiers. Hearing, therefore, that an order was sent by Maximian that he should be put to death, he took upon him the imperial robes, and possessed himself of Britain, and having most valiantly retained it for the space of seven years, he was at length put to death by the treachery of his associate, Allectus. The usurper, having thus got the island from Carausius, held it three years, and was then vanquished by Asclepiodotus, the captain of the Prætorian bands, who thus at the end of ten years restored Britain to the Roman empire. Meanwhile, Diocletian in the east, and Maximian Herculius in the west, commanded the churches to be destroyed, and the Christians to be slain. This persecution was the tenth since the reign of Nero, and was more lasting and bloody than all the others before it; for it was carried on incessantly for the space of ten years, with burning of churches, outlawing of innocent persons, and the slaughter of martyrs. At length, it reached Britain also, and many persons, with the constancy of martyrs, died in the confession of their faith.

CHAPTER VII

THE PASSION OF ST. ALBAN AND HIS COMPANIONS, WHO AT THAT TIME SHED THEIR BLOOD FOR OUR LORD. [A.D. 305.]

AT that time suffered St. Alban, of whom the priest Fortunatus, in the Praise of Virgins, where he makes mention of the blessed martyrs that came to the Lord from all parts of the world, says—

In Britain's isle was holy Alban born.

This Alban, being yet a pagan, at the time when the cruelties of wicked princes were raging against Christians, gave entertainment in his house to a certain clergyman, flying from the persecutors.

This man he observed to be engaged in continual prayer and watching day and night; when on a sudden the Divine grace shining on him, he began to imitate the example of faith and piety which was set before him, and being gradually instructed by his wholesome admonitions, he cast off the darkness of idolatry, and became a Christian in all sincerity of heart. The aforesaid clergyman having been some days entertained by him, it came to the ears of the wicked prince, that this holy confessor of Christ, whose time of martyrdom had not yet come, was concealed at Alban's house. Whereupon he sent some soldiers to make a strict search after him. When they came to the martyr's house, St. Alban immediately presented himself to the soldiers, instead of his guest and master, in the habit or long coat which he wore, and was led bound before the judge.

It happened that the judge, at the time when Alban was carried before him, was standing at the altar, and offering sacrifice to devils. When he saw Alban, being much enraged that he should thus, of his own accord, put himself into the hands of the soldiers, and incur such danger in behalf of his guest, he commanded him to be dragged up to the images of the devils, before which he stood, saying, "Because you have chosen to conceal a rebellious and sacrilegious person, rather than to deliver him up to the soldiers, that his contempt of the gods might meet with the penalty due to such blasphemy, you shall undergo all the punishment that was due to him, if you abandon the worship of our religion." But St. Alban, who had voluntarily declared himself a Christian to the persecutors of the faith, was not at all daunted at the prince's threats, but putting on the armour of spiritual warfare, publicly declared that he would not obey the command. Then said the judge, "Of what family or race are you?"—"What does it concern you," answered Alban, "of what stock I am? If you desire to hear the truth of my religion, be it known to you, that I am now a Christian, and bound by Christian duties."—"I ask your name," said the judge; "tell me it immediately."—"I am called Alban by my parents," replied he; "and I worship and adore the true and living God, who created all things." Then the judge, inflamed with anger, said, "If you will enjoy the happiness of eternal life, do not delay to offer sacrifice to the great gods." Alban rejoined, "These sacrifices, which by you are offered to devils, neither can avail the subjects, nor answer the wishes or desires of those that offer up their supplications to them. On the contrary, whosoever shall offer sacrifice to these images shall receive the everlasting pains of hell for his reward."

The judge, hearing these words, and being much incensed, ordered this holy confessor of God to be scourged by the executioners, believing he might by stripes shake that constancy of heart, on which he could not prevail by words. He, being most cruelly tortured, bore the same patiently, or rather joyfully, for our Lord's sake. When the judge perceived that he was not to be overcome by tortures, or withdrawn from the exercise of the Christian religion, he ordered him to be put to death. Being led to execution, he came to a river, which, with a most rapid course, ran between the wall of the town and the arena where he was to be executed. He there saw a multitude of persons of both sexes, and of several ages and conditions, who were doubtlessly assembled by Divine instinct, to attend the blessed confessor and martyr, and had so taken up the bridge on the river, that he could scarce pass over that evening. In short, almost all had gone out, so that the judge remained in the city without attendance. St. Alban, therefore, urged by an ardent and devout wish to arrive quickly at martyrdom, drew near to the stream, and on lifting up his eyes to heaven, the channel was immediately dried up, and he perceived that the water had departed and made way for him to pass. Among the rest, the executioner, who was to have put him to death, observed this, and moved by Divine inspiration hastened to meet him at the place of execution, and casting down the sword which he had carried ready drawn, fell at his feet, praying that he might rather suffer with the martyr, whom he was ordered to execute, or, if possible, instead of him.

Whilst he thus from a persecutor was become a companion in the faith, and the other executioners hesitated to take up the sword which was lying on the ground, the reverend confessor, accompanied by the multitude, ascended a hill, about 500 paces from the place, adorned, or rather clothed with all kinds of flowers, having its sides neither perpendicular, nor even craggy, but sloping down into a most beautiful plain, worthy from its lovely appearance to be the scene of a martyr's sufferings. On the top of this hill, St. Alban prayed that God would give him water, and immediately a living spring broke out before his feet, the course being confined, so that all men perceived that the river also had been dried up in consequence of the martyr's presence. Nor was it likely that the martyr, who had left no water remaining in the river, should want some on the top of the hill, unless he thought it suitable to the occasion. The river having performed the holy service, returned to its natural course, leaving a testimony of its obedience. Here, therefore, the head of our most courageous martyr was struck off, and here he received the crown of life, which God has promised to those who love Him. But he who gave the wicked stroke, was not permitted to rejoice over the deceased; for his eyes dropped upon the ground together with the blessed martyr's head.

At the same time was also beheaded the soldier, who before, through the Divine admonition, refused to give the stroke to the holy confessor. Of whom it is apparent, that though he was not regenerated by baptism, yet he was cleansed by the washing of his own blood, and rendered worthy to enter the kingdom of heaven. Then the judge, astonished at the novelty of so many heavenly miracles, ordered the persecution to cease immediately, beginning to honour the death of the saints, by which he before thought they might have been diverted from the Christian faith. The blessed Alban suffered death on the twenty-second day of June, near the city of Verulam, which is now by the English nation called Verlamacestir, or Varlingacestir, where afterwards, when peaceable Christian times were restored, a church of wonderful workmanship, and suitable to his martyrdom, was erected. In which place, there ceases not to this day the cure of sick persons, and the frequent working of wonders.

At the same time suffered Aaron and Julius, citizens of Chester, and many more of both sexes in several places; who, when they had endured sundry torments, and their limbs had been torn after an unheard-of manner, yielded their souls up, to enjoy in the heavenly city a reward for the sufferings which they had passed through.

CHAPTER VIII

THE PERSECUTON CEASING, THE CHURCH IN BRITAIN ENJOYS PEACE TILL THE TIME OF THE ARIAN HERESY. [A.D. 307–337.]

WHEN the storm of persecution ceased, the faithful Christians, who, during the time of danger, had hidden themselves in woods and deserts, and secret caves, appearing in public, rebuilt the churches which had been levelled with the ground; founded, erected, and finished the temples of the holy martyrs, and, as it were, displayed their conquering ensigns in all places; they celebrated festivals, and performed their sacred rites with clean hearts and mouths. This peace continued in the churches of Britain until the time of the Arian madness, which, having corrupted the whole world, infected this island also, so far removed from the rest of the globe, with the poison of its arrows; and when the plague was thus conveyed across the sea, all the venom of every heresy immediately rushed into the island, ever fond of something new, and never holding firm to anything.

At this time, Constantius, who, whilst Diocletian was alive, governed Gaul and Spain, a man of extraordinary meekness and courtesy, died in Britain. This man left his son Constantine, born of Helen his concubine, emperor of the Gauls. Eutropius writes, that Constantine, being created emperor in Britain, succeeded his father in the sovereignty. In his time the Arian heresy broke out, and although it was detected and condemned in the Council of Nice, yet it nevertheless infected not only all the churches of the continent, but even those of the islands, with its pestilent and fatal doctrines.

CHAPTER IX

HOW DURING THE REIGN OF GRATIAN, MAXIMUS, BEING CREATED EMPEROR IN BRITAIN, RETURNED INTO GAUL WITH A MIGHTY ARMY. [A.D. 383.]

In the year of our Lord's incarnation, 377, Gratian, the fortieth from Augustus, held the empire six years after the death of Valens; though he had long before reigned with his uncle Valens, and his brother Valentinian. Finding the state of the commonwealth much impaired, and almost gone to ruin, he looked around for some one whose abilities might remedy the existing evils; and his choice fell on Theodosius, a Spaniard. Him he invested at Sirmium with the royal robes, and made him emperor of Thrace and the Eastern provinces. At which time, Maximus, a man of valour and probity, and worthy to be an emperor, if he had not broken the oath of allegiance which he had taken, was made emperor by the army, passed over into Gaul, and there by treachery slew the Emperor Gratian, who was in a consternation at his sudden invasion, and attempting to escape into Italy. His brother, Valentinian, expelled from Italy, fled into the East, where he was entertained by Theodosius with fatherly affection, and soon restored to the empire. Maximus the tyrant, being shut up in Aquileia, was there taken and put to death.

CHAPTER X

HOW, IN THE REIGN OF ARCADIUS, PELAGIUS, A BRITON, INSOLENTLY IMPUGNED THE GRACE OF GOD

In the year of our Lord 394, Arcadius, the son of Theodosius, the forty-third from Augustus, taking the empire upon him, with his brother Honorius, held it thirteen years. In his time, Pelagius, a Briton, spread far and near the infection of his perfidious doctrine against the assistance of the Divine grace, being seconded therein by his associate Julianus of Campania, whose anger was kindled by the loss of his bishopric, of which he had been just deprived. St. Augustine, and the other orthodox fathers, quoted many thousand catholic authorities against them, yet they would not correct their madness; but, on the contrary, their folly was rather increased by contradiction, and they refused to embrace the truth; which Prosper, the rhetorician, has beautifully expressed thus in heroic verse—

"A scribbler vile, inflamed with hellish spite,
Against the great Augustine dared to write;
Presumptuous serpent! from what midnight den
Durst thou to crawl on earth and look at men?
Sure thou wast fed on Britain's sea-girt plains,
Or in thy breast Vesuvian sulphur reigns."

CHAPTER XI

HOW DURING THE REIGN OF HONORIUS, GRATIAN AND CONSTANTINE WERE CREATED TYRANTS IN BRITAIN; AND SOON AFTER THE FORMER WAS SLAIN IN BRITAIN, AND THE LATTER IN GAUL

IN the year 407, Honorius, the younger son of Theodosius, and the forty-fourth from Augustus, being emperor, two years before the invasion of Rome by Alaric, king of the Goths, when the nations of the Alani, Suevi, Vandals, and many others with them, having defeated the Franks and passed the Rhine, ravaged all Gaul, Gratianus Municeps was set up as tyrant and killed. In his place, Constantine, one of the meanest soldiers, only for his name's sake, and without any worth to recommend him, was chosen emperor. As soon as he had taken upon him the command, he passed over into France, where being often imposed upon by the barbarians with faithless treaties, he caused much injury to the Commonwealth. Whereupon Count Constantius by the command of Honorius, marching into Gaul with an army, besieged him in the city of Aries, and put him to death. His son Constans, whom of a monk he had created Cæsar, was also put to death by his own Count Gerontius, at Vienne.

Rome was taken by the Goths, in the year from its foundation, 1164. Then the Romans ceased to rule in Britain, almost 470 years after Caius Julius Cæsar entered the island. They resided within the rampart, which, as we have mentioned, Severus made across the island, on the south side of it, as the cities, temples, bridges, and paved roads there made, testify to this day; but they had a right of dominion over the farther parts of Britain, as also over the islands that are beyond Britain.

CHAPTER XII

THE BRITONS, BEING RAVAGED BY THE SCOTS AND PICTS, SOUGHT SUCCOUR FROM THE ROMANS, WHO, COMING A SECOND TIME, BUILT A WALL ACROSS THE ISLAND; BUT THE BRITONS BEING AGAIN INVADED BY THE AFORESAID ENEMIES, WERE REDUCED TO GREATER DISTRESS THAN BEFORE

FROM that time, the south part of Britain, destitute of armed soldiers, of martial stores, and of all its active youth, which had been led away by the rashness of the tyrants, never to return, was wholly exposed to rapine, as being totally ignorant of the use of weapons. Whereupon they suffered many years under two very savage foreign nations, the Scots from the west, and the Picts from the north. We call these foreign nations, not on account of their being seated out of Britain, but because they were remote from that part of it which was possessed by the Britons; two inlets of the sea lying between them, one of which runs in far and broad into the land of Britain, from the Eastern Ocean, and the other from the Western, though they do not reach so as touch one another. The eastern has in the midst of it the city Giudi.

The western has on it, that is, on the right hand thereof, the city Alcluith, which in their language signifies the Rock Cluith, for it is close by the river of that name.

On account of the irruption of these nations, the Britons sent messengers to Rome with letters in mournful manner, praying for succours, and promising perpetual subjection, provided that the impending enemy should be driven away. An armed legion was immediately sent them, which, arriving in the island, and engaging the enemy, slew a great multitude of them, drove the rest out of the territories of their allies, and having delivered them from their cruel oppressors, advised them to build a wall between the two seas across the island, that it might secure them, and keep off the enemy; and thus they returned home with great triumph. The islanders raising the wall, as they had been directed, not of stone, as having no artist capable of such a work, but of sods, made it of no use. However, they drew it for many miles between the two bays or inlets of the seas, which we have spoken of; to the end that where the defence of the water was wanting, they might use the rampart to defend their borders from the irruptions of the enemies. Of which work there erected, that is, of a rampart of extraordinary breadth and height, there are evident remains to be seen at this day. It begins at about two miles' distance from the monastery of Abercurnig, on the west, at a place called in the Pictish language, Peanfahel, but in the English tongue, Penneltun, and running to the westward, ends near the city Alcluith.

But the former enemies, when they perceived that the Roman soldiers were gone, immediately coming by sea, broke into the borders, trampled and overran all places, and like men mowing ripe corn, bore down all before them. Hereupon messengers are again sent to Rome, imploring aid, lest their wretched country should be utterly extirpated, and the name of a Roman province, so long renowned among them, overthrown by the cruelties of barbarous foreigners, might become utterly contemptible. A legion is accordingly sent again, and, arriving unexpectedly in autumn, made great slaughter of the enemy, obliging all those that could escape, to flee beyond the sea; whereas before, they were wont yearly to carry off their booty without any opposition. Then the Romans declared to the Britons, that they could not for the future undertake such troublesome expeditions for their sake, advising them rather to handle their weapons like men, and undertake themselves the charge of engaging their enemies, who would not prove too powerful for them, unless they were deterred by cowardice; and, thinking that it might be some help to the allies, whom they were forced to abandon, they built a strong stone wall from sea to sea, in a straight line between the towns that had been there built for fear of the enemy, and not far from the trench of Severus. This famous wall, which is still to be seen, was built at the public and private expense, the Britons also lending their assistance. It is eight feet in breadth, and twelve in height, in a straight line from east to west, as is still visible to beholders. This being finished, they gave that dispirited people good advice, with patterns to furnish them with arms. Besides, they built towers on the sea-coast to the southward, at proper distances, where their ships were, because there also the irruptions of the barbarians were apprehended, and so took leave of their friends, never to return again.

After their departure, the Scots and Picts, understanding that they had declared they would come no more, speedily returned, and growing more confident than they had been before, occupied all the northern and farthest part of the island, as far as the wall. Hereupon a timorous guard was placed upon the wall, where they pined away day and night in the utmost fear. On the other side, the enemy attacked them with hooked weapons, by which the cowardly defenders were dragged from the wall, and dashed against the ground. At last, the Britons, forsaking their cities and wall, took to flight and were dispersed. The enemy pursued, and the slaughter was greater than on any former occasion; for the wretched natives were torn in pieces by their enemies, as lambs are torn by wild beasts. Thus, being expelled their dwellings and possessions, they saved themselves from starvation, by robbing and plundering one another, adding to the calamities occasioned by foreigners, by their own domestic broils, till the whole country was left destitute of food, except such as could be procured in the chase.

CHAPTER XIII

IN THE REIGN OF THEODOSIUS THE YOUNGER, PALLADIUS WAS SENT TO THE SCOTS THAT BELIEVED IN CHRIST; THE BRITONS BEGGING ASSISTANCE OF ÆTIUS, THE CONSUL, COULD NOT OBTAIN IT. [A.D. 446.]

In the year of our Lord 423, Theodosius the younger, next to Honorius, being the forty-fifth from Augustus, governed the Roman empire twenty-six years. In the eighth year of his reign, Palladius was sent by Celestinus, the Roman pontiff, to the Scots that believed in Christ, to be their first bishop. In the twenty-third year of his reign, Ætius, a renowned person, being also a patrician, discharged his third consulship with Symmachus for his colleague. To him the wretched remains of the Britons sent a letter, which began thus:—"To Ætius, thrice Consul, the groans of the Britons." And in the sequel of the letter they thus expressed their calamities:—"The barbarians drive us to the sea; the sea drives us back to the barbarians: between them we are exposed to two sorts of death; we are either slain or drowned." Yet neither could all this procure any assistance from him, as he was then engaged in most dangerous wars with Bledla and Attila, kings of the Huns. And, though the year before this, Bledla had been murdered by the treachery of his brother Attila, yet Attila himself remained so intolerable an enemy to the Republic, that he ravaged almost all Europe, invading and destroying cities and castles. At the same time there was a famine at Constantinople, and shortly after, a plague followed, and a great part of the walls of that city, with fifty-seven towers, fell to the ground. Many cities also went to ruin, and the famine and pestilential state of the air destroyed thousands of men and cattle.

CHAPTER XIV

THE BRITONS, COMPELLED BY FAMINE, DROVE THE BAR-
BARIANS OUT OF THEIR TERRITORIES; SOON AFTER
THERE ENSUED PLENTY OF CORN, LUXURY, PLAGUE, AND
THE SUBVERSION OF THE NATION. [A.D. 426–447.]

IN the meantime, the aforesaid famine distressing the Britons
more and more, and leaving to posterity lasting memorials of its
mischievous effects, obliged many of them to submit themselves to
the depredators; though others still held out, confiding in the
Divine assistance, when none was to be had from men. These continually made excursions from the mountains, caves, and woods,
and, at length, began to inflict severe losses on their enemies, who
had been for so many years plundering the country. The Irish robbers thereupon returned home, in order to come again soon after.
The Picts, both then and afterwards, remained quiet in the farthest part of the island, save that sometimes they would do some
mischief, and carry off booty from the Britons.

When, however, the ravages of the enemy at length ceased, the
island began to abound with such plenty of grain as had never
been known in any age before; with plenty, luxury increased, and
this was immediately attended with all sorts of crimes; in particular, cruelty, hatred of truth, and love of falsehood; insomuch, that
if any one among them happened to be milder than the rest, and
inclined to truth, all the rest abhorred and persecuted him, as if
he had been the enemy of his country. Nor were the laity only
guilty of these things, but even our Lord's own flock, and his pastors also, addicting themselves to drunkenness, animosity, liti-
giousness, contention, envy, and other such like crimes, and
casting off the light yoke of Christ. In the meantime, on a sudden,
a severe plague fell upon that corrupt generation, which soon
destroyed such numbers of them, that the living were scarcely sufficient to bury the dead: yet, those that survived, could not be withdrawn from the spiritual death, which their sins had incurred,

either by the death of their friends, or the fear of their own. Whereupon, not long after, a more severe vengeance, for their horrid wickedness, fell upon the sinful nation. They consulted what was to be done, and where they should seek assistance to prevent or repel the cruel and frequent incursions of the northern nations; and they all agreed with their King Vortigern to call over to their aid, from the parts beyond the sea, the Saxon nation; which, as the event still more evidently showed, appears to have been done by the appointment of our Lord Himself, that evil might fall upon them for their wicked deeds.

CHAPTER XV

THE ANGLES, BEING INVITED INTO BRITAIN, AT FIRST OBLIGED THE ENEMY TO RETIRE TO A DISTANCE; BUT NOT LONG AFTER, JOINING IN LEAGUE WITH THEM, TURNED THEIR WEAPONS UPON THEIR CONFEDERATES. [A.D. 450–456.]

IN the year of our Lord 449, Martian being made emperor with Valentinian, and the forty-sixth from Augustus, ruled the empire seven years. Then the nation of the Angles, or Saxons, being invited by the aforesaid king, arrived in Britain with three long ships, and had a place assigned them to reside in by the same king, in the eastern part of the island, that they might thus appear to be fighting for their country, whilst their real intentions were to enslave it. Accordingly they engaged with the enemy, who were come from the north to give battle, and obtained the victory; which, being known at home in their own country, as also the fertility of the country, and the cowardice of the Britons, a more considerable fleet was quickly sent over, bringing a still greater number of men, which, being added to the former, made up an invincible army. The newcomers received of the Britons a place to inhabit, upon condition that they should wage war against their enemies for the peace and security of the country, whilst the

Britons agreed to furnish them with pay. Those who came over were of the three most powerful nations of Germany—Saxons, Angles, and Jutes. From the Jutes are descended the people of Kent, and of the Isle of Wight, and those also in the province of the West-Saxons who are to this day called Jutes, seated opposite to the Isle of Wight. From the Saxons, that is, the country which is now called Old Saxony, came the East-Saxons, the South-Saxons, and the West-Saxons. From the Angles, that is, the country which is called Anglia, and which is said, from that time, to remain desert to this day, between the provinces of the Jutes and the Saxons, are descended the East-Angles, the Midland-Angles, Mercians, all the race of the Northumbrians, that is, of those nations that dwell on the north side of the river Humber, and the other nations of the English. The two first commanders are said to have been Hengist and Horsa. Of whom Horsa, being afterwards slain in battle by the Britons, was buried in the eastern parts of Kent, where a monument, bearing his name, is still in existence. They were the sons of Victgilsus, whose father was Vecta, son of Woden; from whose stock the royal race of many provinces deduce their original. In a short time, swarms of the aforesaid nations came over into the island, and they began to increase so much, that they became terrible to the natives themselves who had invited them. Then, having on a sudden entered into league with the Picts, whom they had by this time repelled by the force of their arms, they began to turn their weapons against their confederates. At first, they obliged them to furnish a greater quantity of provisions; and, seeking an occasion to quarrel, protested, that unless more plentiful supplies were brought them, they would break the confederacy, and ravage all the island; nor were they backward in putting their threats in execution. In short, the fire kindled by the hands of these pagans, proved God's just revenge for the crimes of the people; not unlike that which, being once lighted by the Chaldeans, consumed the walls and city of Jerusalem. For the barbarous conquerors acting here in the same manner, or rather the just Judge ordaining that they should so act, they plundered all the neighbouring cities and country, spread the conflagration from the eastern to the western sea, without any opposition, and covered almost every part of the devoted island. Public as well as private structures were overturned; the priests were everywhere slain before the altars; the prelates and the people, without any respect of persons, were destroyed with fire and sword; nor was there any to bury those who had been thus cruelly slaughtered. Some of the miserable remainder, being taken in the mountains, were butchered in heaps. Others, spent with hunger, came forth and submitted themselves to the enemy for food, being destined to undergo perpetual servitude, if they were not killed even upon the spot. Some, with sorrowful hearts, fled beyond the seas. Others continuing in their own country, led a miserable life among the woods, rocks, and mountains, with scarcely enough food to support life, and expecting every moment to be their last.

CHAPTER XVI

THE BRITONS OBTAINED THEIR FIRST VICTORY OVER THE ANGLES, UNDER THE COMMAND OF AMBROSIUS, A ROMAN

WHEN the victorious army, having destroyed and dispersed the natives, had returned home to their own settlements, the Britons began by degrees to take heart, and gather strength, sallying out of the lurking places where they had concealed themselves, and unanimously imploring the Divine assistance, that they might not utterly be destroyed. They had at that time for their leader, Ambrosius Aurelius, a modest man, who alone, by chance, of the Roman nation had survived the storm, in which his parents, who were of the royal race, had perished. Under him the Britons revived, and offering battle to the victors, by the help of God, came off victorious. From that day, sometimes the natives, and sometimes their enemies, prevailed, till the year of the siege of Baddesdown-hill, when they made no small slaughter of those invaders, about forty-four years after their arrival in England. But of this hereafter.

CHAPTER XVII

HOW GERMANUS THE BISHOP, SAILING INTO BRITAIN
WITH LUPUS, FIRST QUELLED THE TEMPEST OF THE SEA,
AND AFTERWARDS THAT OF THE PELAGIANS, BY DIVINE
POWER. [A.D. 429.]

SOME few years before their arrival, the Pelagian heresy, brought
over by Agricola, the son of Severianus, a Pelagian bishop, had sadly
corrupted the faith of the Britons. But whereas they absolutely
refused to embrace that perverse doctrine, so blasphemous against
the grace of Christ, and were not able of themselves to confute its
subtilty by force of argument, they thought of an excellent plan,
which was to crave aid of the Gallican prelates in that spiritual war.
Hereupon having gathered a great synod, they consulted together
what persons should be sent thither, and by unanimous consent,
choice was made of the apostolical priests, Germanus, bishop of
Auxerre, and Lupus of Troyes, to go into Britain to confirm it in the
faith. They readily complied with the request and commands of the
holy Church, and putting to sea, sailed half way over from Gaul to
Britain with a fair wind. There on a sudden they were obstructed by
the malevolence of demons, who were jealous that such men
should be sent to bring back the Britons to the faith. They raised
storms, and darkened the sky with clouds. The sails could not bear
the fury of the winds, the sailors' skill was forced to give way, the
ship was sustained by prayer, not by strength, and as it happened,
their spiritual commander and bishop, being spent with weariness,
had fallen asleep. Then the tempest, as if the person that opposed
it had given way, gathered strength, and the ship, overpowered by
the waves, was ready to sink. Then the blessed Lupus and all the rest
awakened their elder, that he might oppose the raging elements.
He, showing himself the more resolute in proportion to the greatness of the danger, called upon Christ, and having, in the name of
the Holy Trinity, sprinkled a little water, quelled the raging waves,
admonished his companion, encouraged all, and all unanimously

fell to prayer. The Deity heard their cry, the enemies were put to flight, a calm ensued, the winds veering about applied themselves to forward their voyage, and having soon traversed the ocean, they enjoyed the quiet of the wished-for shore. A multitude flocking thither from all parts, received the priests, whose coming had been foretold by the predictions even of their adversaries. For the wicked spirits declared what they feared, and when the priests afterwards expelled them from the bodies they had taken possession of, they made known the nature of the tempest, and the dangers they had occasioned, and that they had been overcome by the merits and authority of the saints.

In the meantime, the apostolical priests filled the island of Britain with the fame of their preaching and virtues; and the word of God was by them daily administered, not only in the churches, but even in the streets and fields, so that the Catholics were everywhere confirmed, and those who had gone astray, corrected. Like the Apostles, they had honour and authority through a good conscience, obedience to their doctrine through their sound learning, whilst the reward of virtue attended upon their numerous merits. Thus the generality of the people readily embraced their opinions; the authors of the erroneous doctrines kept themselves in the background, and, like evil spirits, grieved for the loss of the people that were rescued from them. At length, after mature deliberation, they had the boldness to enter the lists, and appeared for public disputation, conspicuous for riches, glittering in apparel, and supported by the flatteries of many; choosing rather to hazard the combat, than to undergo the dishonour among the people of having been silenced, lest they should seem by saying nothing to condemn themselves. An immense multitude was there assembled with their wives and children. The people stood round as spectators and judges; but the parties present differed much in appearance; on the one side was Divine faith, on the other human presumption; on the one side piety, on the other pride; on the one side Pelagius, on the other Christ. The holy priests, Germanus and Lupus, permitted their adversaries to speak first, who long took up the time, and filled the ears with empty words. Then the venerable prelates poured forth the torrent of their apostolical and evangelical eloquence. Their discourse was interspersed with scriptural sentences, and they supported their most weighty assertions by reading the written testimonies of famous writers. Vanity was convinced, and perfidiousness confuted; so, that at every objection made against them, not being able to reply, they confessed their errors. The people, who were judges, could scarcely refrain from violence, but signified their judgment by their acclamations.

CHAPTER XVIII

THE SAME HOLY MAN GAVE SIGHT TO THE BLIND DAUGHTER OF A TRIBUNE, AND THEN COMING TO ST. ALBAN'S, THERE RECEIVED SOME OF HIS RELICS, AND LEFT OTHERS OF THE BLESSED APOSTLES, AND OTHER MARTYRS

AFTER this, a certain man, who had the quality of a tribune, came forward with his wife, and presented his blind daughter, ten years of age, for the priests to cure. They ordered her to be set before their adversaries, who, being convinced by guilt of conscience, joined their entreaties to those of the child's parents, and besought the priests that she might be cured. The priests, therefore, perceiving their adversaries to yield, made a short prayer, and then Germanus, full of the Holy Ghost, invoked the Trinity, and taking into his hands a casket with relics of saints, which hung about his neck, applied it to the girl's eyes, which were immediately delivered from darkness and filled with the light of truth. The parents rejoiced, and the people were astonished at the miracle; after which, the wicked opinions were so fully obliterated from the minds of all, that they ardently embraced the doctrine of the priests.

This damnable heresy being thus suppressed, and the authors thereof confuted, and all the people's hearts settled in the purity of the faith, the priests repaired to the tomb of the martyr, St. Alban, to give thanks to God through him. There Germanus, having with him relics of all the Apostles, and of several martyrs, after offering up his prayers, commanded the tomb to be opened, that he might lay up therein some precious gifts; judging it convenient, that the limbs of saints brought together from several countries, as their equal merits had procured them admission into heaven, should be preserved in one tomb. These being honourably deposited, and laid together, he took up a parcel of dust from the place where the martyr's blood had been shed, to carry away with him, which dust having retained the blood, it appeared that the slaughter of the martyrs had communicated a redness to it, whilst the persecutor was struck pale. In consequence of these things, an innumerable multitude of people was that day converted to the Lord.

CHAPTER XIX

HOW THE SAME HOLY MAN, BEING DETAINED THERE BY AN INDISPOSITION, BY HIS PRAYERS QUENCHED A FIRE THAT HAD BROKEN OUT AMONG THE HOUSES, AND WAS HIMSELF CURED OF A DISTEMPER BY A VISION. [A.D. 429.]

As they were returning from thence, Germanus fell and broke his leg, by the contrivance of the Devil, who did not know that, like Job, his merits would be enhanced by the affliction of his body. Whilst he was thus detained some time in the same place by illness, a fire broke out in a cottage neighbouring to that in which he was; and having burned down the other houses which were thatched with reed, was carried on by the wind to the dwelling in which he lay. The people all flocked to the prelate, entreating that they might lift him in their arms, and save him from the impending danger. He, however, rebuked them, and relying on faith, would not suffer himself to be removed. The multitude, in despair, ran to oppose the conflagration; however, for the greater manifestation of the Divine power, whatsoever the crowd endeavoured to save, was destroyed; but what he who was disabled and motionless occupied, the flame avoided, sparing the house that gave entertainment to the holy man, and raging about on every side of it; whilst the house in which he lay appeared untouched, amid the general conflagration. The multitude rejoiced at the miracle, and praised the superior power of God. An infinite number of the poorer sort watched day and night before the cottage; some to heal their souls, and some their bodies. It is impossible to relate what Christ wrought by his servant, what wonders the sick man performed: for whilst he would suffer no medicines to be applied to his distemper, he one night saw a person in garments as white as snow, standing by him, who reaching out his hand, seemed to raise him up, and ordered him to stand boldly upon his feet; from which time his pain ceased, and he was so perfectly restored, that when the day came on, he, without any hesitation, set forth upon his journey.

CHAPTER XX

HOW THE SAME BISHOPS PROCURED THE BRITONS ASSISTANCE FROM HEAVEN IN A BATTLE, AND THEN RETURNED HOME. [A.D. 429.]

IN the meantime, the Saxons and Picts, with their united forces, made war upon the Britons, who, being thus by fear and necessity compelled to take up arms, and thinking themselves unequal to their enemies, implored the assistance of the holy bishops; who, hastening to them as they had promised, inspired so much courage into these fearful people, that one would have thought they had been joined by a mighty army. Thus, by these holy apostolic men, Christ Himself commanded in their camp. The holy days of Lent were also at hand, and were rendered more religious by the presence of the priests, insomuch that the people being instructed by daily sermons, resorted in crowds to be baptized; for most of the army desired admission to the saving water; a church was prepared with boughs for the feast of the resurrection of our

Lord, and so fitted up in that martial camp, as if it were in a city. The army advanced, still wet with the baptismal water; the faith of the people was strengthened; and whereas human power had before been despaired of, the Divine assistance was now relied upon. The enemy received advice of the state of the army, and not questioning their success against an unarmed multitude, hastened forwards, but their approach was, by the scouts, made known to the Britons; the greater part of whose forces being just come from the font, after the celebration of Easter, and preparing to arm and carry on the war, Germanus declared he would be their leader. He picked out the most active, viewed the country round about, and observed, in the way by which the enemy was expected, a valley encompassed with hills. In that place he drew up his inexperienced troops, himself acting as their general. A multitude of fierce enemies appeared, whom as soon as those that lay in ambush saw approaching, Germanus, bearing in his hands the standard, instructed his men all in a loud voice to repeat his words, and the enemy advancing securely, as thinking to take them by surprise, the priests three times cried, Hallelujah. A universal shout of the same word followed, and the hills resounding the echo on all sides, the enemy was struck with dread, fearing, that not only the neighbouring rocks, but even the very skies were falling upon them; and such was their terror, that their feet were not swift enough to deliver them from it. They fled in disorder, casting away their arms, and well satisfied if, with their naked bodies, they could escape the danger; many of them, in their precipitate and hasty flight, were swallowed up by the river which they were passing. The Britons, without the loss of a man, beheld their vengeance complete, and became inactive spectators of their victory. The scattered spoils were gathered up, and the pious soldiers rejoiced in the success which heaven had granted them. The prelates thus triumphed over the enemy without bloodshed, and gained a victory by faith, without the aid of human force; and, having settled the affairs of the island, and restored tranquillity by the defeat, as well as of the invisible, as of the carnal enemies, pre-

pared to return home. Their own merits, and the intercession of
the holy martyr Alban, obtained them a safe passage, and the
happy vessel restored them in peace to their rejoicing people.

CHAPTER XXI

THE PELAGIAN HERESY AGAIN REVIVING, GERMANUS, RETURNING INTO BRITAIN WITH SEVERUS, FIRST HEALED A LAME YOUTH, THEN HAVING CONDEMNED OR CONVERTED THE HERETICS, THEY RESTORED SPIRITUAL HEALTH TO THE PEOPLE OF GOD. [A.D. 447.]

NOT long after, advice was brought from the same island, that certain persons were again attempting to set forth and spread abroad
the Pelagian heresy. The holy Germanus was entreated by all the
priests, that he would again defend the cause of God, which he had
before asserted. He speedily complied with their request; and taking with him Severus, a man of singular sanctity, who was disciple to
the most holy father, Lupus, bishop of Troyes, and afterwards, as
bishop of Treves, preached the word of God in the adjacent parts
of Germany, put to sea, and was calmly wafted over into Britain.

In the meantime, the wicked spirits flying about the whole
island, foretold by constraint that Germanus was coming, insomuch
that one Elafius, a chief of that region, hastened to meet the holy
men, without having received any certain news, carrying with him
his son, who laboured under a weakness of his limbs in the very
flower of his youth; for the nerves being withered, his leg was so contracted that the limb was useless, and he could not walk. All the
country followed this Elafius. The priests arrived, and were met by
the ignorant multitude, whom they blessed, and preached the word
of God to them. They found the people constant in the faith as they
had left them; and learning that but few had gone astray, they found
out the authors, and condemned them. Then Elafius cast himself at
the feet of the priests, presenting his son, whose distress was visible,
and needed no words to express it. All were grieved, but especially

the priests, who put up their prayers for him before the throne of mercy; and Germanus, causing the youth to sit down, gently passed his healing hand over the leg which was contracted; the limb recovered its strength and soundness by the power of his touch, the withered nerves were restored, and the youth was, in the presence of all the people delivered whole to his father. The multitude was amazed at the miracle, and the Catholic faith was firmly planted in the minds of all; after which, they were, in a sermon, warned and exhorted to make amends for their errors. By the judgment of all, the spreaders of the heresy, who had been expelled the island, were brought before the priests, to be conveyed up into the continent, that the country might be rid of them, and they corrected of their errors. Thus the faith in those parts continued long after pure and untainted. All things being settled, the blessed prelates returned home as prosperously as they came.

But Germanus, after this, went to Ravenna to intercede for the tranquillity of the Armoricans, where, being very honourably received by Valentinian and his mother, Placidia, he departed to Christ; his body was conveyed to his own city with a splendid retinue, and numberless deeds of charity accompanied him to the grave. Not long after, Valentinian was murdered by the followers of Ætius, the Patrician, whom he had put to death, in the sixth year of the reign of Marcianus, and with him ended the empire of the West.

CHAPTER XXII

THE BRITONS, BEING FOR A TIME DELIVERED FROM FOREIGN INVASIONS, WASTED THEMSELVES BY CIVIL WARS, AND THEN GAVE THEMSELVES UP TO MORE HEINOUS CRIMES

IN the meantime, in Britain, there was some respite from foreign, but not from civil war. There still remained the ruins of cities destroyed by the enemy, and abandoned; and the natives, who had escaped the enemy, now fought against each other. However, the kings, priests, private men, and the nobility, still remembering the late calamities and slaughters, in some measure kept within bounds; but when these died, and another generation succeeded, which knew nothing of those times, and was only acquainted with the present peaceable state of things, all the bonds of sincerity and justice were so entirely broken, that there was not only no trace of them remaining, but few persons seemed to be aware that such virtues had ever existed. Among other most wicked actions, not to be expressed, which their own historian, Gildas, mournfully takes notice of, they added this—that they never preached the faith to the Saxons, or English, who dwelt amongst them; however, the goodness of God did not forsake his people, whom He foreknew, but sent to the aforesaid nation much more worthy preachers, to bring it to the faith.

CHAPTER XXIII

HOW POPE GREGORY SENT AUGUSTINE, WITH OTHER MONKS, TO PREACH TO THE ENGLISH NATION, AND ENCOURAGED THEM BY A LETTER OF EXHORTATION, NOT TO CEASE FROM THEIR LABOUR. [A.D. 596.]

IN the year of our Lord 582, Maurice, the fifty-fourth from Augustus, ascended the throne, and reigned twenty-one years. In the tenth year of his reign, Gregory, a man renowned for learning and behaviour, was promoted to the apostolical see of Rome, and presided over it thirteen years, six months and ten days. He, being moved by Divine inspiration, in the fourteenth year of the same emperor, and about the one hundred and fiftieth after the coming of the English into Britain, sent the servant of God, Augustine, and with him several other monks, who feared the Lord, to preach the word of God to the English nation. They having, in obedience to the pope's commands, undertaken that work, were, on their journey, seized with a sudden fear, and began to think of returning home, rather than proceed to a barbarous, fierce, and unbelieving nation, to whose very language they were strangers; and this they unanimously agreed was the safest course. In short, they sent back Augustine, who had been appointed to be consecrated bishop in case they were received by the English, that he might, by humble entreaty, obtain of the holy Gregory, that they should not be compelled to undertake so dangerous, toilsome, and uncertain a journey. The pope, in reply, sent them a hortatory epistle, persuading them to proceed in the work of the Divine word, and rely on the assistance of the Almighty. The purport of which letter was as follows:—

"*Gregory, the servant of the servants of God, to the servants of our Lord.* Forasmuch as it had been better not to begin a good work, than to think of desisting from that which has been begun, it behoves you, my beloved sons, to fulfil the good work, which, by the help of our Lord, you have undertaken. Let not, therefore, the toil of the journey, nor the tongues of evil speaking men, deter you; but with all possible earnestness and zeal perform that which, by God's direction, you have undertaken; being assured, that much labour is followed by an eternal reward. When Augustine, your chief, returns, whom we also constitute your abbat, humbly obey him in all things; knowing, that whatsoever you shall do by his direction, will, in all respects, be available to your souls. Almighty God protect you with his grace, and grant that I may, in the heavenly country, see the fruits of your labour. Inasmuch as, though I cannot labour with you, I shall partake in the joy of the reward, because I am willing to labour. God keep you in safety, my most beloved sons. Dated the 23rd of July, in the fourteenth year of the reign of our pious and most august lord, Mauritius Tiberius, the thirteenth year after the consulship of our said lord. The fourteenth indiction."

CHAPTER XXIV

HOW HE WROTE TO THE BISHOP OF ARLES TO ENTERTAIN THEM. [A.D. 596.]

THE same venerable pope also sent a letter to Ætherius, bishop of Arles, exhorting him to give favourable entertainment to Augustine on his way to Britain; which letter was in these words—

"*To his most reverend and holy brother and fellow bishop Ætherius, Gregory, the servant of the servants of God.* Although religious men stand in need of no recommendation with priests who have the charity which is pleasing to God; yet as a proper opportunity is offered to write, we have thought fit to send you this our letter, to inform you, that we have directed thither, for the good of souls, the bearer of these presents, Augustine, the servant of God, of whose industry we are assured, with other servants of God, whom it is requisite that your holiness assist with priestly affection, and afford him all the comfort in your power. And to the end that you may be the more ready in your assistance, we have enjoined him particularly to inform you of the occasion of his coming; knowing, that when you are acquainted with it, you will, as the matter requires, for the sake of God, zealously afford him your relief. We also in all things recommend to your charity, Candidus, the priest, our common son, whom we have transferred to the government of a small patrimony in our church. God keep you in safety, most reverend brother. Dated the 23rd day of July, in the fourteenth year of the reign of our most pious and august lord, Mauritius Tiberius, the thirteenth year after the consulship of our lord aforesaid. The fourteenth indiction."

CHAPTER XXV

AUGUSTINE, COMING INTO BRITAIN, FIRST PREACHED IN THE ISLE OF THANET TO KING ETHELBERT, AND HAVING OBTAINED LICENCE, ENTERED THE KINGDOM OF KENT, IN ORDER TO PREACH THEREIN. [A.D. 597.]

AUGUSTINE, thus strengthened by the confirmation of the blessed Father Gregory, returned to the work of the word of God, with the servants of Christ, and arrived in Britain. The powerful Ethelbert was at that time king of Kent; he had extended his dominions as far as the great river Humber, by which the Southern Saxons are divided from the Northern. On the east of

Kent is the large Isle of Thanet containing according to the English way of reckoning, 600 families, divided from the other land by the river Wantsum, which is about three furlongs over, and ford-able only in two places, for both ends of it run into the sea. In this island landed the servant of our Lord, Augustine, and his companions, being, as is reported, nearly forty men. They had, by order of the blessed Pope Gregory, taken interpreters of the nation of the Franks, and sending to Ethelbert, signified that they were come from Rome, and brought a joyful message, which most undoubtedly assured to all that took advantage of it everlasting joys in heaven, and a kingdom that would never end, with the living and true God. The king having heard this, ordered them to stay in that island where they had landed, and that they should be furnished with all necessaries, till he should consider what to do with them. For he had before heard of the Christian religion, having a Christian wife of the royal family of the Franks, called Bertha; whom he had received from her parents, upon condition that she should be permitted to practise her religion with the Bishop Luidhard, who was sent with her to preserve her faith. Some days after, the king came into the island, and sitting in the open air, ordered Augustine and his companions to be brought into his presence. For he had taken precaution that they should not come to him in any house, lest, according to an ancient superstition, if they practised any magical arts, they might impose upon him, and so get the better of him. But they came furnished with Divine, not with magic virtue, bearing a silver cross for their banner, and the image of our Lord and Saviour painted on a board; and singing the litany, they offered up their prayers to the Lord for the eternal salvation both of themselves and of those to whom they were come. When he had sat down, pursuant to the king's commands, and preached to him and his attendants there present, the word of life, the king answered thus:—"Your words and promises are very fair, but as they are new to us, and of uncertain import, I cannot approve of them so far as to forsake that which I have so long followed with the whole English nation. But because you are come from far into my kingdom, and, as I conceive, are desirous to impart to us those things which you believe to be true, and most beneficial, we will not molest you, but give you favourable entertainment, and take care to supply you with your necessary sustenance; nor do we forbid you to preach and gain as many as you can to your religion." Accordingly he permitted them to reside in the city of Canterbury, which was the metropolis of all his dominions, and, pursuant to his promise, besides allowing them sustenance, did not refuse them liberty to preach. It is reported that, as they drew near to the city, after their manner, with the holy cross, and the image of our sovereign Lord and King, Jesus Christ, they, in concert, sung this litany: "We beseech Thee, O Lord, in all Thy mercy, that thy anger and wrath be turned away from this city, and from the holy house, because we have sinned. Hallelujah."

CHAPTER XXVI

ST. AUGUSTINE IN KENT FOLLOWED THE DOCTRINE AND MANNER OF LIVING OF THE PRIMITIVE CHURCH, AND SETTLED HIS EPISCOPAL SEE IN THE ROYAL CITY. [A.D. 597.]

As soon as they entered the dwelling-place assigned them, they began to imitate the course of life practised in the primitive church; applying themselves to frequent prayer, watching and fasting; preaching the word of life to as many as they could; despising all worldly things, as not belonging to them; receiving only their necessary food from those they taught; living themselves in all respects conformably to what they prescribed to others, and being always disposed to suffer any adversity, and even to die for that truth which they preached. In short, several believed and were baptized, admiring the simplicity of their innocent life, and the sweetness of their heavenly doctrine. There was on the east side of the city a church dedicated to the honour of St. Martin, built whilst the Romans were still in the island, wherein the queen, who, as has been said before, was a Christian, used to pray. In this they first began to meet, to sing, to pray, to say mass, to preach, and to baptize, till the king, being converted to the faith, allowed them to preach openly, and build or repair churches in all places.

When he, among the rest, induced by the unspotted life of these holy men, and their delightful promises, which, by many miracles, they proved to be most certain, believed and was baptized, greater numbers began daily to flock together to hear the word, and, forsaking their heathen rites, to associate themselves, by believing, to the unity of the church of Christ. Their conversion the king so far encouraged, as that he compelled none to embrace Christianity, but only showed more affection to the believers, as to his fellow-citizens in the heavenly kingdom. For he had learned from his instructors and leaders to salvation, that the service of Christ ought to be voluntary, not by compulsion. Nor was it long before he gave his teachers a settled residence in his metropolis of Canterbury, with such possessions of different kinds as were necessary for their subsistence.

CHAPTER XXVII

ST. AUGUSTINE, BEING MADE BISHOP, SENDS TO ACQUAINT POPE GREGORY WITH WHAT HAD BEEN DONE, AND RECEIVES HIS ANSWER TO THE DOUBTS HE HAD PROPOSED TO HIM. [A.D. 579.]

IN the meantime, Augustine, the man of God, repaired to Arles, and, pursuant to the orders received from the holy Father Gregory, was ordained archbishop of the English nation, by Ætherius, archbishop of that city. Then returning into Britain, he sent Laurentius the priest, and Peter the monk, to Rome, to acquaint Pope Gregory, that the nation of the English had received the faith of Christ, and that he was himself made their bishop. At the same time, he desired his solution of some doubts that occurred to him. He soon received proper answers to his questions, which we have also thought fit to insert in this our history—

The First Question of Augustine, Bishop of the Church of Canterbury.—Concerning bishops, how they are to behave themselves towards their clergy? or into how many portions the things given by the faithful to the altar are to be divided? and how the bishop is to act in the church?

Gregory, Pope of the City of Rome, answers.—Holy Writ, which no doubt you are well versed in, testifies, and particularly St. Paul's Epistle to Timothy, wherein he endeavours to instruct him how he should behave himself in the house of God; but it is the custom of the apostolic see to prescribe rules to bishops newly ordained, that all emoluments which accrue, are to be divided into four portions;—one for the bishop and his family, because of hospitality and entertainments; another for the clergy; a third for the poor; and the fourth for the repair of churches. But in regard that you, my brother, being brought up under monastic rules, are not to live apart from your clergy in the English church, which, by God's assistance, has been lately brought to the faith; you are to follow that course of life which our forefathers did in the time of the primitive church, when none of them said anything that he possessed was his own, but all things were in common among them.

But if there are any clerks not received into holy orders, who cannot live continent, they are to take wives, and receive their stipends abroad; because we know it is written, that out of the same portions above-mentioned a distribution was made to each of them according to every one's wants. Care is also to be taken of their stipends, and provision to be made, and they are to be kept under ecclesiastical rules, that they may live orderly, and attend to singing of psalms, and, by the help of God, preserve their hearts, and tongues, and bodies from all that is unlawful. But as for those that live in common, why need we say anything of making portions, or keeping hospitality and exhibiting mercy? inasmuch as all that can be spared is to be spent in pious and religious works, according to the commands of Him who is the Lord and Master of all, "Give alms of such things as you have, and behold all things are clean unto you."

Augustine's Second Question.—Whereas the faith is one and the same, why are there different customs in different churches? and why is one custom of masses observed in the holy Roman church, and another in the Gallican church?

Pope Gregory answers.—You know, my brother, the custom of the Roman church in which you remember you were bred up. But it pleases me, that if you have found anything, either in the Roman, or the Gallican, or any other church, which may be more acceptable to Almighty God, you carefully make choice of the same, and sedulously teach the church of the English, which as yet is new in the faith, whatsoever you can gather from the several churches. For things are not to be loved for the sake of places, but places for the sake of good things. Choose, therefore, from every church those things that are pious, religious, and upright, and when you have, as it were, made them up into one body, let the minds of the English be accustomed thereto.

Augustine's Third Question.—I beseech you to inform me, what punishment must be inflicted, if any one shall take anything by stealth from the church?

Gregory answers.—You may judge, my brother, by the person of the thief, in what manner he is to be corrected. For there are some, who, having substance, commit theft; and there are others, who transgress in this point through want. Wherefore it is requisite, that some be punished in their purses, others with stripes; some with more severity, and some more mildly. And when the severity is more, it is to proceed from charity, not from passion; because this is done to him who is corrected, that he may not be delivered up to hell-fire. For it behoves us to maintain discipline among the faithful, as good parents do with their carnal children, whom they punish with stripes for their faults, and yet design to make those their heirs whom they chastise; and they preserve what they possess for those whom they seem in anger to persecute. This charity is, therefore, to be kept in mind, and it dictates the measure of the punishment, so that the mind may do nothing beyond the rule of reason. You may add, that they are to restore those things which they have stolen from the church. But, God forbid, that the church should make profit from those earthly things which it seems to lose, or seek gain out of such vanities.

Augustine's Fourth Question.—Whether two brothers may marry two sisters, which are of a family far removed from them?

Gregory answers.—This may lawfully be done; for nothing is found in holy writ that seems to contradict it.

Augustine's Fifth Question.—To what degree may the faithful marry with their kindred? and whether it is lawful for men to marry their stepmothers and relations?

Gregory answers.—A certain worldly law in the Roman commonwealth allows, that the son and daughter of a brother and sister, or of two brothers, or two sisters, may be joined in matrimony; but we have found, by experience, that no offspring can come of such wedlock; and the Divine Law forbids a man to "uncover the nakedness of his kindred." Hence of necessity it must be the third or fourth generation of the faithful, that can be lawfully joined in matrimony; for the second, which we have mentioned, must altogether abstain from one another. To marry with one's stepmother is a heinous crime, because it is written in the Law, "Thou shalt not uncover the nakedness of thy father": now the son, indeed, cannot uncover his father's nakedness; but in regard that it is written, "They shall be two in one flesh," he that presumes to uncover the nakedness of his stepmother, who was one flesh with his father, certainly uncovers the nakedness of his father. It is also prohibited to marry with a sister-in-law, because by the former union she is become the brother's flesh. For which thing also John the Baptist was beheaded, and ended his life in holy martyrdom. For, though he was not ordered to deny Christ, and indeed was killed for confessing Christ, yet in regard that the same Jesus Christ, our Lord, said, "I am the Truth," because John was killed for the truth, he also shed his blood for Christ.

But forasmuch as there are many of the English, who, whilst they were still in infidelity, are said to have been joined in this execrable matrimony, when they come to the faith they are to be admonished to abstain, and be made to know that this is a grievous sin. Let them fear the dreadful judgment of God, lest, for the gratification of their carnal appetites, they incur the torments of eternal punishment. Yet they are not on this account to be deprived of the communion of the body and blood of Christ, lest they seem to be punished for those things which they did through ignorance before they had received baptism. For at this time the Holy Church chastises some things through zeal, and tolerates some through meekness, and connives at some things through discretion, that so she may often, by this forbearance and connivance, suppress the evil which she disapproves. But all that come to the faith are to be admonished not to do such things. And if any shall be guilty of them, they are to be excluded from the communion of the body and blood of Christ. For as the offence is, in some measure, to be tolerated in those who did it through ignorance, so it is to be strenuously prosecuted in those who do not fear to sin knowingly.

Augustine's Sixth Question.—Whether a bishop may be ordained without other bishops being present, in case there be so great a distance between them, that they cannot easily come together?

Gregory answers.—As for the church of England, in which you are as yet the only bishop, you can no otherwise ordain a bishop than in the absence of other bishops; unless some bishops should come over from Gaul, that they may be present as witnesses to you in ordaining a bishop. But we would have you, my brother, to ordain bishops in such a manner, that the said bishops may not be far asunder, that when a new bishop is to be ordained, there be no difficulty, but that other bishops, and pastors also, whose presence is necessary, may easily come together. Thus, when, by the help of God, bishops shall be so constituted in places everywhere near to one another, no ordination of a bishop is to be performed without assembling three or four bishops. For, even in spiritual affairs, we may take example by the temporal, that they may be wisely and discreetly conducted. It is certain, that when marriages are celebrated in the world, some married persons are assembled, that those who went before in the way of matrimony, may also partake in the joy of the succeeding couple. Why, then, at this spiritual ordination, wherein, by means of the sacred ministry, man is joined to God, should not such persons be assembled, as may cither rejoice in the advancement of the new bishop, or jointly pour forth their prayers to Almighty God for his preservation?

Augustine's Seventh Question.—How are we to deal with the bishops of France and Britain?

Gregory answers.—We give you no authority over the bishops of France, because the bishop of Arles received the pall in ancient times from my predecessor, and we are not to deprive him of the authority he has received. If it shall therefore happen, my brother, that you go over into the province of France, you are to concert with the said bishop of Arles, how, if there be any faults among the bishops, they may be amended. And if he shall be lukewarm in keeping up discipline, he is to be corrected by your zeal; to whom we have also written, that when your holiness shall be in France, he may also use all his endeavours to assist you, and put away from the behaviour of the bishops all that shall be opposite to the command of our Creator. But you, of your own authority, shall not have power to judge the bishops of France, but by persuading, soothing, and showing good works for them to imitate; you shall reform the minds of wicked men to the pursuit of holiness; for it is written in the Law, "When thou comest into the standing corn of thy neighbours, then thou mayest pluck the ears with thine hand; but thou shalt not move a sickle unto thy neighbours' standing corn." For thou mayest not apply the sickle of judgment in that harvest which seems to have been committed to another; but by the effect of good works thou shalt clear the Lord's wheat of the chaff of their vices, and convert them into the body of the Church, as it were, by eating. But whatsoever is to be done by authority, must be transacted with the aforesaid bishop of Arles, lest that should be omitted, which the ancient institution of the fathers has appointed. But as for all the bishops of Britain, we commit them to your care, that the unlearned may be taught, the weak strengthened by persuasion, and the perverse corrected by authority.

Augustine's Eighth Question.—Whether a woman with child ought to be baptized? Or how long after she has brought forth, may she come into the church? As also, after how many days the infant born may be baptized, lest he be prevented by death? Or how long after her husband may have carnal knowledge of her? Or whether it is lawful for her to come into the church when she has her courses? Or to receive the holy sacrament of communion? Or whether a man, under certain circumstances, may come into the church before he has washed with water? Or approach to receive the mystery of the holy communion? All which things are requisite to be known by the rude nation of the English.

Gregory answers.—I do not doubt but that these questions have been put to you, my brother, and I think I have already answered you therein. But I believe you would wish the opinion which you yourself might give to be confirmed by mine also. Why should not a woman with child be baptized, since the fruitfulness of the flesh is no offence in the eyes of Almighty God? For when our first parents sinned in Paradise, they forfeited the immortality which they had received, by the just judgment of God. Because, therefore, Almighty God would not for their fault wholly destroy the human race, He both deprived man of immortality for his sin, and, at the same time, of his great goodness, reserved to him the power of propagating his race after him. On what account then can that which is preserved to the human race, by the free gift of Almighty God, be excluded from the privilege of baptism? For it is very foolish to imagine that the gift of grace opposes that mystery in which all sin is blotted out. When a woman is delivered, after how many days she may come into the church, you have been informed by reading the Old Testament, viz. that she is to abstain for a male child thirty-three days, and sixty-six for a female. Now you must know that this is to be taken in a mystery; for if she enters the church the very hour that she is delivered, to return thanks, she is not guilty of any sin; because the pleasure of the flesh is in fault, and not the pain; but the pleasure is in the copulation of the flesh, whereas there is pain in bringing forth the child. Wherefore it is

45

said to the first mother of all, "In sorrow shalt thou bring forth children." If, therefore, we forbid a woman that has brought forth, to enter the church, we make a crime of her very punishment. To baptize either a woman who has brought forth, if there be danger of death, even the very hour that she brings forth, or that which she has brought forth the very hour it is born, is no way prohibited, because, as the grace of the holy mystery is to be with much discretion provided for the living and understanding, so is it to be without any delay offered to the dying; lest, while a further time is sought to confer the mystery of redemption, a small delay intervening, the person that is to be redeemed is dead and gone.

Her husband is not to approach her, till the infant born be weaned. A bad custom is sprung up in the behaviour of married people, that is, that women disdain to suckle the children which they bring forth, and give them to other women to suckle; which seems to have been invented on no other account but incontinency; because, as they will not be continent, they will not suckle the children which they bear. Those women, therefore, who, from bad custom, give their children to others to bring up, must not approach their husbands till the time of purification is past. For even when there has been no child-birth, women are forbidden to do so, whilst they have their monthly courses, insomuch that the Law condemns to death any man that shall approach unto a woman during her uncleanness. Yet the woman, nevertheless, must not be forbidden to come into the church whilst she has her monthly courses; because the superfluity of nature cannot be imputed to her as a crime; and it is not just that she should be refused admittance into the church, for that which she suffers against her will. For we know, that the woman who had the issue of blood, humbly approaching behind our Lord's back, touched the hem of his garment, and her distemper immediately departed from her. If, therefore, she that had an issue of blood might commendably touch the garment of our Lord, why may not she, who has the monthly courses, lawfully enter into the church of God? But you may say, Her distemper compelled her, whereas these we speak of are bound by custom. Consider, then, most dear brother, that all we suffer in this mortal flesh, through the infirmity of our nature, is ordained by the just judgment of God after the fall; for to hunger, to thirst, to be hot, to be cold, to be weary, is from the infirmity of our nature; and what else is it to seek food against hunger, drink against thirst, air against heat, clothes against cold, rest against weariness, than to procure a remedy against distempers? Thus to a woman her monthly courses are a distemper. If, therefore, it was a commendable boldness in her, who in her disease touched our Lord's garment, why may not that which is allowed to one infirm person, be granted to all women, who, through the fault of their nature, are distempered?

She must not, therefore, be forbidden to receive the mystery of the holy communion during those days. But if any one out of profound respect does not presume to do it, she is to be commended; yet if she receives it, she is not to be judged. For it is the part of noble minds in some manner to acknowledge their faults, even where there is no offence; because very often that is done without a fault, which, nevertheless, proceeded from a fault. Therefore, when we are hungry, it is no crime to eat; yet our being hungry proceeds from the sin of the first man. The monthly courses are no crime in women, because they naturally happen; however, because our nature itself is so depraved, that it appears to be so without the concurrence of the will, the fault proceeds from sin, and thereby human nature may herself know what she is become by judgment. And let man, who wilfully committed the offence, bear the guilt of that offence. And, therefore, let women consider with themselves, and if they do not presume, during their monthly courses, to approach the sacrament of the body and blood of our Lord, they are to be commended for their praiseworthy consideration; but when they are carried away with love of the same mystery to receive it out of the usual custom of religious life, they are not to be restrained, as we said before. For as in the Old Testament the outward works are observed, so in the New Testament, that which is outwardly done, is not so diligently regarded as that which is inwardly thought, in order to punish it by a discerning judgment.

For whereas the Law forbids the eating of many things as unclean, yet our Lord says in the Gospel, "Not that which goeth into the mouth defileth a man; but that which cometh out of the mouth, this defileth a man." And presently after He added, expounding the same, "Out of the heart proceed evil thoughts." Where it is sufficiently shown, that that is declared by Almighty God to be polluted in fact, which proceeds from the root of a polluted thought. Whence also Paul the Apostle says, "Unto the pure all things are pure, but unto them that are defiled and unbelieving, nothing is pure." And presently after, declaring the cause of that defilement, he adds, "For even their mind and conscience is defiled." If, therefore, meat is not unclean to him who has a clean mind, why shall that which a clean woman suffers according to nature, be imputed to her as uncleanness?

A man who has approached his own wife is not to enter the church unless washed with water, nor is he to enter immediately although washed. The Law prescribed to the ancient people, that a man in such cases should be washed with water, and not enter into the church before the setting of the sun. Which, nevertheless, may be understood spiritually, because a man acts so when the mind is led by the imagination to unlawful concupiscence; for unless the fire of concupiscence be first driven from his mind, he is not to think himself worthy of the congregation of the brethren, whilst he thus indulges an unlawful passion. For though several nations have different opinions concerning this affair, and seem to observe different rules, it was always the custom of the Romans, from ancient times, for such an one to be cleansed by washing, and for some time respectfully to forbear entering the church. Nor do we, in so saying, assign matrimony to be a fault; but forasmuch as lawful intercourse cannot be had without the pleasure of the flesh, it is proper to forbear entering the holy place, because the pleasure itself cannot be without a fault. For he was not born of adultery or fornication, but of lawful marriage, who said, "Behold I was conceived in iniquity, and in sin my mother brought me forth." For he who knew himself to have been conceived in iniquity, lamented that he was born from sin, because the tree in its bough bears the moisture it drew from the root. In which words, however, he does not call the union of the married couple iniquity, but the pleasure of the copulation. For there are many things which are proved to be lawful, and yet we are somewhat defiled in doing them. As very often by being angry we correct faults, and at the same time disturb our own peace of mind; and though that which we do is right, yet it is not to be approved that our mind should be discomposed. For he who said, "My eye was disturbed with anger," had been angry at the vices of those who had offended. Now, in regard that only a sedate mind can apply itself to contemplation, he grieved that his eye was disturbed with anger; because, whilst he was correcting evil actions below, he was obliged to be withdrawn and disturbed from the contemplation of things above. Anger against vice is, therefore, commendable, and yet painful to a man; because he thinks that by his mind being agitated, he has incurred some guilt. Lawful commerce, therefore, must be for the sake of children, not of pleasure; and must be to procure offspring, not to satisfy vices. But if any man is led not by the desire of pleasure, but only for the sake of getting children, such a man is certainly to be left to his own judgment, either as to entering the church, or as to receiving the mystery of the body and blood of our Lord, which he, who being placed in the fire cannot burn, is not to be forbidden by us to receive. But when, not the love of getting children, but of pleasure prevails, the pair have cause to lament their deed. For this the holy preaching allows them, and yet fills the mind with dread of the very allowance. For when Paul the Apostle said, "Let him that cannot contain, have his wife;" he presently took care to subjoin, "But this I say by way of indulgence, not by way of command." For this is not granted by way of indulgence which is lawful, because it is just; and, therefore, that which he said he indulged, he showed to be an offence.

It is seriously to be considered, that when God was to speak to the people on Mount Sinai, He first commanded them to abstain from women. And if so much cleanness of body was there required, where God spoke to the people by the means of a subject creature, that those who were to hear the words of God should not do so; how much more ought women, who receive the body of Almighty God, to preserve themselves in cleanness of flesh, lest they be burdened with the very *greatness* of that unutterable mystery? For this reason, it was said to David, concerning his men, by the priest, that if they were clean in this particular, they should receive the shewbread, which they would not have received at all, had not David first declared them to be clean. Then the man, who, afterwards, has been washed with water, is also capable of receiving the mystery of the holy communion, when it is lawful for him, according to what has been before declared, to enter the church.

Augustine's Ninth Question.—Whether after an illusion, such as happens in a dream, any man may receive the body of our Lord, or if he be a priest, celebrate the Divine mysteries?

Gregory answers.—The Testament of the Old Law, as has been said already in the article above, calls such a man polluted, and allows him not to enter into the church till the evening after being washed with water. Which, nevertheless, spiritual people, taking in another sense, will understand in the same manner as above; because he is imposed upon as it were in a dream, who, being tempted with filthiness, is defiled by real representations in thought, and he is to be washed with water, that he may cleanse away the sins of thought with tears; and unless the fire of temptation depart before, may know himself to be guilty as it were until the evening. But discretion is very necessary in that illusion, that one may seriously consider what causes it to happen in the mind of the person sleeping; for sometimes it proceeds from excess of eating or drinking; sometimes from the superfluity or infirmity of nature, and sometimes from the thoughts. And when it happens, either through superfluity or infirmity of nature, such an illusion is not to be feared, because it is rather to be lamented, that the mind of the person, who knew nothing of it, suffers the same, than that he occasioned it. But when the appetite of gluttony commits excess in food, and thereupon the receptacles of the humours are oppressed, the mind from thence contracts some guilt; yet not so much as to obstruct the receiving of the holy mystery, or celebrating mass, when a holy day requires it, or necessity obliges the sacrament to be administered, because there is no other priest in the place; for if there be others who can perform the ministry, the illusion proceeding from overeating is not to exclude a man from receiving the sacred mystery; but I am of opinion he ought humbly to abstain from offering the sacrifice of the mystery; but not from receiving it, unless the mind of the person sleeping has been filled with some foul imagination. For there are some, who for the most part so suffer the illusion, that their mind, even during the sleep of the body, is not defiled with filthy thoughts. In which case, one thing is evident, that the mind is guilty even in its own judgment; for though it does not remember to have seen any thing whilst the body was sleeping, yet it calls to mind that when waking it fell into bodily gluttony. But if the sleeping illusion proceeds from evil thoughts when waking, then the guilt is manifest to the mind; for the man perceives from whence that filth sprung, because what he had knowingly thought of, that he afterwards unwittingly revealed. But it is to be considered, whether that thought was no more than a suggestion, or proceeded to enjoyment, or, which is still more criminal, consented to sin. For all sin is fulfilled in three ways, viz., by suggestion, by delight, and by consent. Suggestion is occasioned by the Devil, delight is from the flesh, and consent from the mind. For the serpent suggested the first offence, and Eve, as flesh, was delighted with it, but Adam consented, as the spirit, or mind. And much discretion is requisite for the mind to sit as judge between suggestion and delight, and between delight and consent. For if the evil spirit suggest a sin to the mind, if there ensue no delight in the sin, the sin is in no way committed; but when the flesh begins to be delighted, then sin begins to grow. But if it deliberately consents, then the sin is known to be perfected. The beginning, therefore, of sin is in the suggestion, the nourishing of it in delight, but in the consent is its perfection. And it often happens that what the evil spirit sows in the thought, the flesh draws to delight, and yet the soul does not consent to that delight. And whereas the flesh cannot be delighted without the mind, yet the mind struggling against the pleasures of the flesh is somewhat unwillingly tied down by the carnal delight, so that through reason it contradicts, and does not consent, yet being influenced by delight, it grievously laments its being so bound. Wherefore that principal soldier of our Lord's host, sighing, said, "I see another law in my members warring against the law of my mind, and bringing me into captivity to the law of sin, which is in my members." Now if he was a captive, he did not fight; but if he did fight, how was he a captive? he therefore fought against the law of the mind, which the law that is in the members opposed; if he fought so, he was no captive. Thus, then, man is, as I may say, a captive and yet free. Free on account of justice, which he loves, a captive by the delight which he unwillingly bears within him.

CHAPTER XXVIII

POPE GREGORY WRITES TO THE BISHOP OF ARLES TO ASSIST AUGUSTINE IN THE WORK OF GOD. [A.D. 601.]

THUS far the answers of the holy Pope Gregory, to the questions of the most reverend prelate, Augustine. But the epistle, which he says he had written to the bishop of Arles, was directed to Vergilius, successor to Ætherius, the copy whereof follows—

"*To his most reverend and holy brother and fellow bishop, Vergilius; Gregory, servant of the servants of God.* With how much affection brethren, coming of their own accord, are to be entertained, is well known, by their being for the most part invited on account of charity. Therefore, if our common brother, Bishop Augustine, shall happen to come to you, I desire your love will, as is becoming, receive him so kindly and affectionately, that he may be supported by the honour of your consolation, and others be informed how brotherly charity is to be cultivated. And, since it often happens that those who are at a distance, sooner than others, understand the things that need correction, if any crimes of priests or others shall happen to be laid before you, you will, in conjunction with him, sharply inquire into the same. And do you both act so strictly and carefully against those things which offend God, and provoke his wrath, that for the amendment of others, the punishment may fall upon the guilty, and the innocent may not suffer an ill name. God keep you in safety, most reverend brother. Given the 22nd day of June, in the nineteenth year of the reign of our pious and august emperor, Mauritius Tiberius, and the eighteenth year after the consulship of our said lord. The fourth indiction."

CHAPTER XXIX

THE SAME POPE SENDS AUGUSTINE THE PALL, AN EPISTLE, AND SEVERAL MINISTERS OF THE WORD. [A.D. 601.]

MOREOVER, the same Pope Gregory, hearing from Bishop Augustine, that he had a great harvest, and but few labourers, sent to him, together with his aforesaid messengers, several fellow labourers and ministers of the word of whom the first and principal were Mellitus, Justus, Paulinus, and Rufinianus, and by them all things in general that were necessary for the worship and service of the church, viz., sacred vessels and vestments for the altars, also ornaments for the churches, and vestments for the priests and clerks, as likewise relics of the holy apostles and martyrs; besides many books. He also sent letters, wherein he signified that he had transmitted the pall to him, and at the same time directed how he should constitute bishops in Britain. The letters were in these words—

"*To his most reverend and holy brother and fellow bishop, Augustine; Gregory, the servant of the servants of God.* Though it be certain, that the unspeakable rewards of the eternal kingdom are reserved for those who labour for Almighty God, yet it is requisite that we bestow on them the advantage of honours, to the end that they may by this recompence be enabled the more vigorously to apply themselves to the care of their spiritual work. And, in regard that the new church of the English is, through the goodness of the Lord, and your labours, brought to the grace of God, we grant you the use of the pall in the same, only for the performing of the solemn service of the mass; so that you in several places ordain twelve bishops, who shall be subject to your jurisdiction, so that the bishop of London shall, for the future, be always consecrated by his own synod, and that he receive the honour of the pall from this holy and apostolical see, which I, by the grace of God, now serve. But we will have you send to the city of York such a bishop as you shall think fit to ordain; yet so, that if that city, with the places adjoining, shall receive the word of God, that bishop shall also ordain twelve bishops, and enjoy the honour of a metropolitan; for we design, if we live, by the help of God, to bestow on him also the pall; and yet we will have him to be subservient to your authority; but after your decease, he shall so preside over the bishops he shall ordain, as to be in no way subject to the jurisdiction of the bishop of London. But for the future let this distinction be between the bishops of the cities of London and York, that he may have the precedence who shall be first ordained. But let them unanimously dispose, by common advice and uniform conduct, whatsoever is to be done for the zeal of Christ; let them judge rightly, and perform what they judge convenient in a uniform manner.

"But to you, my brother, shall, by the authority of our God, and Lord Jesus Christ, be subject not only those bishops you shall ordain, and those that shall be ordained by the bishop of York, but also all the priests in Britain; to the end that from the mouth and life of your holiness they may learn the rule of believing rightly, and living well, and fulfilling their office in faith and good manners, they may, when it shall please the Lord, attain the heavenly kingdom. God preserve you in safety, most reverend brother.

"Dated the 22nd of June, in the nineteenth year of the reign of our most pious lord and emperor, Mauritius Tiberius, the eighteenth year after the consulship of our said lord. The fourth indiction."

CHAPTER XXX

A COPY OF THE LETTER WHICH POPE GREGORY SENT TO THE
ABBOT MELLITUS, THEN GOING INTO BRITAIN. [A.D. 601.]

THE aforesaid messengers being departed, the holy father, Gregory,
sent after them letters worthy to be preserved in memory, wherein
he plainly shows what care he took of the salvation of our nation.
The letter was as follows—

"*To his most beloved son, the Abbot Mellitus; Gregory, the servant of the
servants of God.* We have been much concerned, since the departure
of our congregation that is with you, because we have received no
account of the success of your journey. When, therefore, Almighty
God shall bring you to the most reverend Bishop Augustine, our
brother, tell him what I have, upon mature deliberation on the
affair of the English, determined upon, viz., that the temples of the
idols in that nation ought not to be destroyed; but let the idols that
are in them be destroyed; let holy water be made and sprinkled in
the said temples, let altars be erected, and relics placed. For if
those temples are well built, it is requisite that they be converted
from the worship of devils to the service of the true God; that the
nation, seeing that their temples are not destroyed, may remove
error from their hearts, and knowing and adoring the true God,
may the more familiarly resort to the places to which they have
been accustomed. And because they have been used to slaughter
many oxen in the sacrifices to devils, some solemnity must be
exchanged for them on this account, as that on the day of the ded-
ication, or the nativities of the holy martyrs, whose relics are there
deposited, they may build themselves huts of the boughs of trees,
about those churches which have been turned to that use from
temples, and celebrate the solemnity with religious feasting, and
no more offer beasts to the Devil, but kill cattle to the praise of God
in their eating, and return thanks to the Giver of all things for their
sustenance; to the end that, whilst some gratifications are outwardly permitted them, they may the more easily consent to the

inward consolations of the grace of God. For there is no doubt that it is impossible to efface every thing at once from their obdurate minds; because he who endeavours to ascend to the highest place, rises by degrees or steps, and not by leaps. Thus the Lord made Himself known to the people of Israel in Egypt; and yet He allowed them the use of the sacrifices which they were wont to offer to the Devil, in his own worship; so as to command them in his sacrifice to kill beasts, to the end that, changing their hearts, they might lay aside one part of the sacrifice, whilst they retained another; that whilst they offered the same beasts which they were wont to offer, they should offer them to God, and not to idols; and thus they would no longer be the same sacrifices. This it behoves your affection to communicate to our aforesaid brother, that he, being there present, may consider how he is to order all things. God preserve you in safety, most beloved son.

"Given the 17th of June, in the nineteenth year of the reign of our lord, the most pious emperor, Mauritius Tiberius, the eighteenth year after the consulship of our said lord. The fourth indiction."

CHAPTER XXXI

POPE GREGORY, BY LETTER, EXHORTS AUGUSTINE NOT TO GLORY IN HIS MIRACLES. [A.D. 601.]

AT which time he also sent Augustine a letter concerning the miracles that he had heard had been wrought by him; wherein he admonishes him not to incur the danger of being puffed up by the number of them. The letter was in these words—

"I know, most loving brother, that Almighty God, by means of your affection, shows great miracles in the nation which He has chosen. Wherefore it is necessary that you rejoice with fear, and tremble whilst you rejoice, on account of the same heavenly gift; viz., that you may rejoice because the souls of the English are by outward miracles drawn to inward grace; but that you fear, lest, amidst the wonders that are wrought, the weak mind may be puffed up in its own presumption, and as it is externally raised to honour, it may thence inwardly fall by vainglory. For we must call to mind, that when the disciples returned with joy after preaching, and said to their heavenly Master, 'Lord, in thy name, even the devils are subject to us;' they were presently told, 'Do not rejoice on this account, but rather rejoice for that your names are written in heaven.' For they placed their thoughts on private and temporal joys, when they rejoiced in miracles; but they are recalled from the private to the public, and from the temporal to the eternal joy, when it is said to them, 'Rejoice for this, because your names are written in heaven.' For all the elect do not work miracles, and yet the names of all are written in heaven. For those who are disciples of the truth ought not to rejoice, save for that good thing which all men enjoy as well as they, and of which their enjoyment shall be without end.

"It remains, therefore, most dear brother, that amidst those things, which through the working of our Lord, you outwardly perform, you always inwardly strictly judge yourself, and clearly understand both what you are yourself, and how much grace is in that same nation, for the conversion of which you have also received the gift of working miracles. And if you remember that you have at any time offended our Creator, either by word or deed, that you always call it to mind, to the end that the remembrance of your guilt may crush the vanity which rises in your heart. And whatsoever you shall receive, or have received, in relation to working miracles, that you consider the same, not as conferred on you, but on those for whose salvation it has been given you."

CHAPTER XXXII

POPE GREGORY SENDS LETTERS AND PRESENTS TO KING ETHELBERT

THE same holy Pope Gregory, at the same time, sent a letter to King Ethelbert, with many presents of several sorts; being desirous to glorify the king with temporal honours, at the same time that he rejoiced that through his labour and zeal he had attained the knowledge of the heavenly glory. The copy of the said letter is as follows—

"To the most glorious Lord, and his most excellent son, Ethelbert, king of the English, Bishop Gregory. Almighty God advances all good men to the government of nations, that He may by their means bestow the gifts of his mercy on those over whom they are placed. This we know to have been done in the English nation, over whom your glory was therefore placed, that by means of the goods which are granted to you, heavenly benefits might also be conferred on the nation that is subject to you. Therefore, my illustrious son, do you carefully preserve the grace which you have received from the Divine goodness, and hasten to promote the Christian faith, which you have embraced, among the people under your subjection; multiply the zeal of your uprightness in their conversion; suppress the worship of idols; overthrow the structures of the temples; edify the manners of your subjects by much cleanness of life, exhorting, terrifying, soothing, correcting, and giving examples of good works, that you may find Him your rewarder in heaven, whose name and knowledge you shall spread abroad upon earth. For He also will render the fame of your honour more glorious to posterity, whose honour you seek and maintain among the nations.

"For even so Constantine, our most pious emperor, recovering the Roman commonwealth from the perverse worship of idols, subjected the same with himself to our Almighty God and Lord Jesus Christ, and was himself, with the people under his subjection, entirely converted to Him. Whence it followed, that his praises transcended the fame of former princes; and he as much excelled his predecessors in renown as he did in good works. Now, therefore, let your glory hasten to infuse into the kings and people that are subject to you, the knowledge of one God, Father, Son, and Holy Ghost; that you may both surpass the ancient kings of your nation in praise and merit, and become by so much the more secure against your own sins before the dreadful judgment of Almighty God, as you shall wipe away the sins of others in your subjects.

"Willingly hear, devoutly perform, and studiously retain in your memory, whatsoever you shall be advised by our most reverend brother, Bishop Augustine, who is instructed in the monastical rule, full of the knowledge of the holy Scripture, and, by the help of God, endued with good works; for if you give ear to him in what he speaks for Almighty God, the same Almighty God will the sooner hear him praying for you. But if (which God avert!) you slight his words, how shall Almighty God hear him in your behalf, when you neglect to hear him for God? Unite yourself, therefore, to him with all your mind, in the fervour of faith, and further his endeavours, through the assistance of that virtue which the Divinity affords you, that He may make you partaker of his kingdom, whose faith you cause to be received and maintained in your own.

"Besides, we would have your glory know, we find in the holy Scripture, from the words of the Almighty Lord, that the end of this present world, and the kingdom of the saints, is about to come, which will never terminate. But as the same end of the world approaches, many things are at hand which were not before, viz. changes of air, and terrors from heaven, and tempests out of the order of the seasons, wars, famines, plagues, earthquakes in several places; which things will not, nevertheless, happen in our days, but will all follow after our days. If you, therefore, find any of these things to happen in your country, let not your mind be in any way disturbed; for these signs of the end of the world are sent before, for this reason, that we may be solicitous for our souls, suspicious of the hour of death, and may be found prepared with good works to meet our Judge. Thus much, my illustrious son, I have said in few words, to the end that when the Christian faith shall increase in your kingdom, our discourse to you may also be more copious, and we may be pleased to say the more, in proportion as joy for the conversion of your nation is multiplied in our mind.

"I have sent you some small presents, which will not appear small, when received by you with the blessing of the holy apostle, Peter. May Almighty God, therefore, perfect in you his grace which He has begun, and prolong your life here through a course of many years, and after a time receive you into the congregation of the heavenly country. May heavenly grace preserve your excellency in safety.

"Given the 22nd day of June, in the nineteenth year of the reign of the most pious emperor, Mauritius Tiberius, in the eighteenth year after his consulship. Fourth indiction."

CHAPTER XXXIII

AUGUSTINE REPAIRS THE CHURCH OF OUR SAVIOUR, AND BUILDS THE MONASTERY OF ST. PETER THE APOSTLE; PETER THE FIRST ABBAT OF THE SAME. [A.D. 602.]

AUGUSTINE having his episcopal see granted him in the royal city, as has been said, and being supported by the king, recovered therein a church, which he was informed had been built by the ancient Roman Christians, and consecrated it in the name of our holy Saviour, God and Lord, Jesus Christ, and there established a residence for himself and his successors. He also built a monastery not far from the city to the eastward, in which, by his advice, Ethelbert erected from the foundation the church of the blessed apostles, Peter and Paul, and enriched it with several donations; wherein the bodies of the same Augustine, and of all the bishops of Canterbury, and of the kings of Kent, might be buried. However, Augustine himself did not consecrate that church, but Laurentius, his successor.

The first abbat of that monastery was the priest Peter, who, being sent ambassador into France, was drowned in a bay of the sea, which is called Amfleat, and privately buried by the inhabitants of the place; but Almighty God, to show how deserving a man he was, caused a light to be seen over his grave every night; till the neighbours who saw it, perceiving that he had been a holy man that was buried there, inquiring who, and from whence he was, carried away the body, and interred it in the church, in the city of Boulogne, with the honour due to so great a person.

CHAPTER XXXIV

ETHELFRID, KING OF THE NORTHUMBRIANS, HAVING
VANQUISHED THE NATIONS OF THE SCOTS, EXPELS THEM
FROM THE TERRITORIES OF THE ENGLISH. [A.D. 603.]

AT this time, Ethelfrid, a most worthy king, and ambitious of glory,
governed the kingdom of the Northumbrians, and ravaged the
Britons more than all the great men of the English, insomuch that
he might be compared to Saul, once king of the Israelites, excepting only this, that he was ignorant of the true religion. For he conquered more territories from the Britons, either making them
tributary, or driving the inhabitants clean out, and planting English
in their places, than any other king or tribune. To him might justly
be applied the saying of the patriarch blessing his son in the person
of Saul, "Benjamin shall ravin as a wolf; in the morning he shall
devour the prey, and at night he shall divide the spoil." Hereupon,
Ædan, king of the Scots that inhabit Britain, being concerned at
his success, came against him with an immense and mighty army,
but was beaten by an inferior force, and put to flight; for almost all
his army was slain at a famous place, called Degsastan, that is,
Degsastone. In which battle also Theodbald, brother to Ethelfrid,
was killed, with almost all the forces he commanded. This war
Ethelfrid put an end to in the year 603 after the incarnation of our
Lord, the eleventh of his own reign, which lasted twenty-four years,
and the first year of the reign of Phocas, who then governed the
Roman empire. From that time, no king of the Scots durst come
into Britain to make war on the English to this day.

BOOK II

CHAPTER I

ON THE DEATH OF THE BLESSED POPE GREGORY. [A.D. 605.]

AT this time, that is, in the year of our Lord 605, the blessed Pope Gregory, after having most gloriously governed the Roman apostolic see thirteen years, six months, and ten days, died, and was translated to the eternal see of the heavenly kingdom. Of whom, in regard that he by his zeal converted our nation, the English, from the power of Satan to the faith of Christ, it behoves us to discourse more at large in our Ecclesiastical History, for we may and ought rightly to call him our apostle; because, whereas he bore the pontifical power over all the world, and was placed over the churches already reduced to the faith of truth, he made our nation, till then given up to idols, the church of Christ, so that we may be allowed thus to attribute to him the character of an apostle; for though he is not an apostle to others, yet he is so to us; for we are the seal of his apostleship in our Lord.

He was by nation a Roman, son of Gordian, deducing his race from ancestors that were not only noble, but religious. And Felix, once bishop of the same apostolical see, a man of great honour in Christ and his church, was his great-grandfather. Nor did he exercise the nobility of religion with less virtue of devotion than his parents and kindred. But that worldly nobility which he seemed to have, by the help of the Divine Grace, he entirely used to gain the honour of eternal dignity; for soon quitting his secular habit, he repaired to a monastery, wherein he began to behave himself with so much grace of perfection that (as he was afterwards wont with tears to testify) his mind was above all transitory things; that he despised all that is subject to change; that he used to think of nothing but what was heavenly; that whilst detained by the body, he by contemplation broke through the bonds of flesh; and that he loved death, which is a terror to almost all men, as the entrance into life, and the reward of his labours. This he said of himself, not to boast of his progress in virtue, but rather to bewail the decay, which, as he was wont to declare, he imagined he sustained through the pastoral care. In short, when he was, one day, in private, discoursing with Peter, his deacon, after having enumerated the former virtues of his mind, he with grief added, "But now, on account of the pastoral care, it is entangled with the affairs of laymen, and, after so beautiful an appearance of repose, is defiled with the dust of earthly action. And after having wasted itself by condescending to many things that are without, when it desires the inward things, it returns to them less qualified to enjoy them. I therefore consider what I endure, I consider what I have lost, and when I behold that loss, what I bear appears the more grievous."

This the holy man said out of the excess of his humility. But it becomes us to believe that he lost nothing of his monastic perfection by his pastoral care, but rather that he improved the more through the labour of converting many, than by the former repose of his conversation, and chiefly because, whilst exercising the pontifical function, he provided to have his house made a monastery. And when first drawn from the monastery, ordained to the ministry of the altar, and sent as respondent to Constantinople from the apostolic see, though he now mixed with the people of the palace, yet he intermitted not his former heavenly life; for some of the brethren of his monastery, having out of brotherly charity followed him to the royal city, he kept them for the better following of regular observances, viz. that at all times, by their example, as he writes himself, he might be held fast to the calm shore of prayer, as it were with the cable of an anchor, whilst he should be tossed up and down by the continual waves of worldly affairs; and daily among them, by the intercourse of studious reading, strengthen his mind whilst it was shaken with temporal concerns. By their company he was not only guarded against earthly assaults, but more and more inflamed in the exercises of a heavenly life.

For they persuaded him to give a mystical exposition of the book of holy Job, which is involved in great obscurity; nor could he refuse to undertake that work, which brotherly affection imposed on him for the future benefit of many; but in a wonderful manner, in five and thirty books of exposition, taught how that same book is to be understood literally; how to be referred to the mysteries of Christ and the church; and in what sense it is to be adapted to every one of the faithful. This work he began when legate in the royal city, but finished it at Rome after being made pope. Whilst he was still in the royal city, he, by the assistance of the Divine grace of Catholic truth, crushed in its first rise a heresy newly started, concerning the state of our resurrection. For Eutychius, bishop of that city, taught, that our body, in that glory of resurrection, would be impalpable, and more subtile than the wind and air; which he hearing, proved by force of truth, and by the instance of the resurrection of our Lord, that this doctrine was every way opposite to the Christian faith. For the Catholic faith is that our body, sublimed by the glory of immortality, is rendered subtile by the effect of the spiritual power, but palpable by the reality of nature; according to the example of our Lord's body, of which, when risen from the dead, He Himself says to his disciples, "Touch me and see, for a spirit hath not flesh and bones, as ye see me have." In asserting which faith, the venerable Father Gregory so earnestly laboured against the rising heresy, and by the assistance of the most pious emperor, Tiberius Constantine, so fully suppressed it, that none has been since found to revive it.

He likewise composed another notable book, called "Liber Pastoralis," wherein he manifestly showed what sort of persons ought to be preferred to govern the church; how such rulers ought to live; with how much discretion to instruct every one of their hearers, and how seriously to reflect every day on their own frailty. He also wrote forty homilies on the Gospel, which he equally divided into two volumes; and composed four books of dialogues, into which, at the request of Peter, his deacon, he collected the miracles of the saints whom he either knew, or had heard to be most renowned in Italy, for an example to posterity to lead their lives; to the end that, as he taught in his books of Expositions, what virtues ought to be laboured for, so by describing the miracles of saints, he might make known the glory of those virtues. He further, in twenty-two homilies, discovered how much light there is concealed in the first and last parts of the prophet Ezekiel, which seemed the most obscure. Besides which, he wrote the "Book of Answers," to the questions of Augustine, the first bishop of the English nation, as we have shown above, inserting the same book entire in this history; besides the useful little "Synodical Books," which he composed with the bishops of Italy on the necessary affairs of the church; and also familiar letters to certain persons. And it is the more wonderful that he could write so many and such large volumes, in regard that almost all the time of his youth, to use his own words, he was often tormented with pains in his bowels, and a weakness of his stomach, whilst he was continually suffering from slow fever. But whereas at the same time he carefully reflected that, as the Scripture testifies, "Every son that is received is scourged," the more he laboured and was depressed under those present evils, the more he assured himself of his eternal salvation.

Thus much may be said of his immortal genius, which could not be restrained by such severe bodily pains; for other popes applied themselves to building, or adorning of churches with gold and silver, but Gregory was entirely intent upon gaining souls. Whatsoever money he had, he diligently took care to distribute and give to the poor, that his righteousness might endure for ever, and his horn be exalted with honour; so that what blessed Job said might be truly said of him, "When the ear heard me, then it blessed me; and when the eye saw me, it gave witness to me: because I delivered the poor that cried, and the fatherless, and him that had none to help him. The blessing of him that was ready to perish came upon me, and I caused the widow's heart to sing for joy. I put on righteousness, and it clothed me; my judgment was as a robe and diadem. I was the eye to the blind, and feet was I to the lame. I was father to the poor; and the cause which I knew not, I searched out. And I brake the jaws of the wicked, and plucked the spoil out of his teeth." And a little after: "If I have withheld," says he, "the poor from their desire; or have caused the eye of the widow to fail; or have eaten my morsel myself alone, and the fatherless hath not eaten thereof. For of my youth compassion grew up with me, and from my mother's womb it came forth with me."

To these works of piety and righteousness this also may be added, that he saved our nation, by the preachers he sent hither, from the teeth of the old enemy, and made it partaker of eternal liberty; in whose faith and salvation rejoicing, and worthily commending the same, he in his exposition on holy Job, says, "Behold, a tongue of Britain, which only knew how to utter barbarous language, has long since begun to resound the Hebrew Hallelujah! Behold, the once swelling ocean now serves prostrate at the feet of the saints; and its barbarous motions, which earthly princes could not subdue with the sword, are now, through the fear of God, bound by the mouths of priests with words only; and he that when an infidel stood not in awe of fighting troops, now a believer, fears the tongues of the humble! For by reason that the virtue of the Divine knowledge is infused into it by precepts, heavenly words, and conspicuous miracles, it is curbed by the dread of the same Divinity, so as to fear to act wickedly, and bends all its desires to arrive at eternal glory." In which words holy Gregory declares this also, that St. Augustine and his companions brought the English to receive the truth, not only by the preaching of words, but also by showing of heavenly signs. The holy Pope Gregory, among other things, caused masses to be celebrated in the churches of the apostles, Peter and Paul, over their bodies. And in the celebration of masses, he added three phrases full of great goodness and perfection: "And dispose our days in thy peace, and preserve us from eternal damnation, and rank us in the number of thy elect, through Christ our Lord."

He governed the church in the days of the Emperors Mauritius and Phocas, but passing out of this life in the second year of the same Phocas, he departed to the true life which is in heaven. His body was buried in the church of St. Peter the Apostle, before the sacristy, on the 4th day of March, to rise one day in the same body in glory with the rest of the holy pastors of the church. On his tomb was written this epitaph—

> Earth! take that body which at first you gave,
> Till God again shall raise it from the grave.
> His soul amidst the stars finds heavenly day;
> In vain the gates of darkness make essay
> On him whose death but leads to life the way.
> To the dark tomb, this prelate, though decreed,
> Lives in all places by his pious deed.
> Before his bounteous board pale Hunger fled;
> To warm the poor he fleecy garments spread;
> And to secure their souls from Satan's power.
> He taught by sacred precepts every hour.
> Nor only taught; but first th' example led,
> Lived o'er his rules, and acted what he said.
> To English Saxons Christian truth he taught,
> And a believing flock to heaven he brought.
> This was thy work and study, this thy care,
> Offerings to thy Redeemer to prepare.
> For these to heavenly honours raised on high,
> Where thy reward of labours ne'er shall die.

Nor is the account of St. Gregory, which has been handed down to us by the tradition of our ancestors, to be passed by in silence, in relation to his motives for taking such interest in the salvation of our nation. It is reported, that some merchants, having just arrived at Rome on a certain day, exposed many things for sale in the marketplace, and abundance of people resorted thither to buy: Gregory himself went with the rest, and, among other things, some boys were set to sale, their bodies white, their countenances beautiful, and their hair very fine. Having viewed them, he asked, as is said, from what country or nation they were brought? and was told, from the island of Britain, whose inhabitants were of such personal appearance. He again inquired whether those islanders were Christians, or still involved in the errors of paganism? and was informed that they were pagans. Then fetching a deep sigh from the bottom of his heart, "Alas! what pity," said he, "that the author of darkness is possessed of men of such fair countenances; and that being remarkable for such graceful aspects, their minds should be void of inward grace." He therefore again asked, what was the name of that nation? and was answered, that they were called Angles. "Right," said he, for they have an Angelic face, and it becomes such to be co-heirs with the Angels in heaven. What is the name," proceeded he, "of the province from which they are brought?" It was replied, that the natives of that province were called Deiri. "Truly are they *De ira*," said he, "withdrawn from wrath, and called to the mercy of Christ. How is the king of that province called?" They told him his name was Ælla: and he, alluding to the name, said, "Hallelujah, the praise of God the Creator must be sung in those parts."

Then repairing to the bishop of the Roman apostolical see (for he was not himself then made pope), he entreated him to send some ministers of the word into Britain to the nation of the English, by whom it might be converted to Christ; declaring himself ready to undertake that work, by the assistance of God, if the apostolic pope should think fit to have it so done. Which not being then able to perform, because, though the pope was willing to grant his request, yet the citizens of Rome could not be brought to consent that so noble, so renowned, and so learned a man should depart the city; as soon as he was himself made pope, he perfected the long-desired work, sending other preachers, but himself by his prayers and exhortations assisting the preaching, that it might be successful. This account, as we have received it from the ancients, we have thought fit to insert in our Ecclesiastical History.

CHAPTER II

AUGUSTINE ADMONISHED THE BISHOPS OF THE BRITONS TO CATHOLIC PEACE AND UNITY, AND TO THAT EFFECT WROUGHT A HEAVENLY MIRACLE IN THEIR PRESENCE; AND OF THE VENGEANCE THAT PURSUED THEM FOR THEIR CONTEMPT. [A.D. 603.]

IN the meantime, Augustine, with the assistance of King Ethelbert, drew together to a conference the bishops, or doctors, of the next province of the Britons, at a place which is to this day called Augustine's Ac, that is, Augustine's Oak, on the borders of the Wiccii and West Saxons; and began by brotherly admonitions to persuade them, that preserving Catholic unity with him, they should undertake the common labour of preaching the Gospel to the Gentiles. For they did not keep Easter Sunday at the proper time, but from the fourteenth to the twentieth moon; which computation is contained in a revolution of eighty-four years. Besides, they did several other things which were against the unity of the church. When, after a long disputation, they did not comply with the entreaties, exhortations, or rebukes of Augustine and his companions, but preferred their own traditions before all the churches in the world, which in Christ agree among themselves, the holy father, Augustine, put an end to this troublesome and tedious contention, saying, "Let us beg of God, who causes those who are of one mind to live in his Father's house, that He will vouchsafe, by his heavenly tokens, to declare to us, which tradition is to be followed; and by what means we are to find our way to his heavenly kingdom. Let some infirm person be brought, and let the faith and practice of those, by whose prayers he shall be healed, be looked upon as acceptable to God, and be adopted by all." The adverse party unwillingly consenting, a blind man of the English race was brought, who having been presented to the priests of the Britons, found no benefit or cure from their ministry; at length, Augustine, compelled by real necessity, bowed his knees to the Father of our Lord Jesus Christ, praying that the lost sight might be restored to the blind man, and by the corporeal enlightening of one man, the light of spiritual grace might be kindled in the hearts of many of the faithful. Immediately the blind man received sight, and Augustine was by all declared the preacher of the Divine truth. The Britons then confessed, that it was the true way of righteousness which Augustine taught; but that they could not depart from their ancient customs without the consent and leave of their people. They therefore desired that a second synod might be appointed, at which more of their number would be present.

This being decreed, there came (as is asserted) seven bishops of the Britons, and many most learned men, particularly from their most noble monastery, which, in the English tongue, is called Bancornburg, over which the Abbat Dinooth is said to have presided at that time. They that were to go to the aforesaid council, repaired first to a certain holy and discreet man, who was wont to lead an eremitical life among them, advising with him, whether they ought, at the preaching of Augustine, to forsake their traditions. He answered, "If he is a man of God, follow him."—"How shall we know that?" said they. He replied, "Our Lord saith, Take my yoke upon you, and learn of me, for I am meek and lowly in heart; if therefore, Augustine is meek and lowly of heart, it is to be believed that he has taken upon him the yoke of Christ, and offers the same to you to take upon you. But, if he is stern and haughty, it appears that he is not of God, nor are we to regard his words." They insisted again, "And how shall we discern even this?"—"Do you contrive," said the anchorite, "that he may first arrive with his company at the place where the synod is to be held; and if at your approach he shall rise up to you, hear him submissively, being assured that he is the servant of Christ; but if he shall despise you, and not rise up to you, whereas you are more in number, let him also be despised by you."

They did as he directed; and it happened that when they came, Augustine was sitting on a chair, which they observing, were in a passion, and charging him with pride, endeavoured to contradict all he said. He said to them, "You act in many particulars contrary to our custom, or rather the custom of the universal church, and yet, if you will comply with me in these three points, viz. to keep Easter at the due time; to administer baptism, by which we are again born to God, according to the custom of the holy Roman Apostolic Church; and jointly with us to preach the word of God to the English nation, we will readily tolerate all the other things you do, though contrary to our customs." They answered they would do none of those things, nor receive him as their archbishop; for they alleged among themselves, that "if he would not now rise up to us, how much more will he contemn us, as of no worth, if we shall begin to be under his subjection?" To whom the man of God, Augustine, is said, in a threatening manner, to have foretold, that in case they would not join in unity with their brethren, they should be warred upon by their enemies; and, if they would not preach the way of life to the English nation, they should at their hands undergo the vengeance of death. All which, through the dispensation of the Divine judgment, fell out exactly as he had predicted.

For afterwards the warlike king of the English, Ethelfrid, of whom we have already spoken, having raised a mighty army, made a very great slaughter of that perfidious nation, at the City of Legions, which by the English is called Legacestir, but by the Britons more rightly Carlegion. Being about to give battle, he observed their priests, who were come together to offer up their prayers to God for the soldiers, standing apart in a place of more safety; he inquired who they were? or what they came together to do in that place? Most of them were of the monastery of Bangor, in which, it is reported, there was so great a number of monks, that the monastery being divided into seven parts, with a ruler over each, none of those parts contained less than three hundred men, who all lived by the labour of their hands. Many of these, having observed a fast of three days, resorted among others to pray at the aforesaid battle, having one Brocmail appointed for their protector, to defend them whilst they were intent upon their prayers, against the swords of the barbarians. King Ethelfrid being informed of the occasion of their coming, said, "If then they cry to their God against us, in truth, though they do not bear arms, yet they fight against us, because they oppose us by their prayers." He, therefore, commanded them to be attacked first, and then destroyed the rest of the impious army, not without considerable loss of his own forces. About twelve hundred of those that came to pray are said to have been killed, and only fifty to have escaped by flight. Brocmail turning his back with his men, at the first approach of the enemy, left those whom he ought to have defended, unarmed and exposed to the swords of the enemies. Thus was fulfilled the prediction of the holy Bishop Augustine, though he himself had been long before taken up into the heavenly kingdom; that those perfidious men should feel the vengeance of temporal death also, because they had despised the offer of eternal salvation.

CHAPTER III

HOW ST. AUGUSTINE MADE MELLITUS AND JUSTUS BISHOPS; AND OF HIS DEATH. [A.D. 604.]

IN the year of our Lord 604, Augustine, archbishop of Britain, ordained two bishops, viz. Mellitus and Justus; Mellitus to preach to the province of the East-Saxons, who are divided from Kent by the river Thames, and border on the Eastern sea. Their metropolis is the city of London, which is situated on the banks of the aforesaid river, and is the mart of many nations resorting to it by sea and land. At that time, Sabert, nephew to Ethelbert by his sister Ricula, reigned over the nation, though he was under subjection to Ethelbert, who, as has been said above, had command over all the nations of the English as far as the river Humber. But when this province also received the word of truth, by the preaching of Mellitus, King Ethelbert built the church of St. Paul, in the city of London, where he and his successors should have their episcopal see. As for Justus, Augustine ordained him bishop in Kent, at the city which the English nation named Rhofescestir, from one that was formerly the chief man of it, called Rhof. It was almost twenty-four miles distant from the city of Canterbury to the westward, and contains a church dedicated to St. Andrew, the apostle. King Ethelbert, who built it, bestowed many gifts on the bishops of both those churches, as well as on that of Canterbury, adding lands and possessions for the use of those who were with the bishops.

After this, the beloved of God, Father Augustine, died, and his body was deposited without, close by the church of the apostles, Peter and Paul, above spoken of, by reason that the same was not yet finished, nor consecrated, but as soon as it was dedicated, the body was brought in, and decently buried in the north porch thereof; wherein also were interred the bodies of all the succeeding archbishops, except two only, Theodorus and Berthwald, whose bodies are within that church, because the aforesaid porch could contain no more. Almost in the midst of this church is an altar dedicated in honour of the blessed Pope Gregory, at which every Saturday their service is solemnly performed by the priest of that place. On the tomb of the said Augustine is written this epitaph—

"Here rests the Lord Augustine, first archbishop of Canterbury, who, being formerly sent hither by the blessed Gregory, bishop of the city of Rome, and by God's assistance supported with miracles, reduced King Ethelbert and his nation from the worship of idols to the faith of Christ, and having ended the days of his office in peace, died the 26th day of May, in the reign of the same king."

CHAPTER IV

LAURENTIUS AND HIS BISHOPS ADMONISH THE SCOTS
TO OBSERVE THE UNITY OF THE HOLY CHURCH, PARTIC-
ULARLY IN KEEPING OF EASTER; MELLITUS GOES TO
ROME. [A.D. 605.]

LAURENTIUS succeeded Augustine in the bishopric, having been
ordained thereto by the latter, in his lifetime, lest, upon his death,
the state of the church, as yet unsettled, might begin to falter, if it
should be destitute of a pastor, though but for one hour. Wherein
he also followed the example of the first pastor of the church, that
is, of the most blessed prince of the apostles, Peter, who, having
founded the church of Christ at Rome, is said to have consecrated
Clement his assistant in preaching the Gospel, and at the same
time his successor. Laurentius, being advanced to the degree of an
archbishop, laboured indefatigably, both by frequent exhortations
and examples of piety, to raise to perfection the foundations of the
church, which had been so nobly laid. In short, he not only took
care of the new church formed among the English, but endeavoured also to employ his pastoral solicitude among the ancient
inhabitants of Britain, as also the Scots, who inhabit the island of
Ireland, which is next to Britain. For when he understood that the
course of life and profession of the Scots in their aforesaid country,
as well as of the Britons in Britain, was not truly ecclesiastical, especially that they did not celebrate the solemnity of Easter at the due
time, but thought that the day of the resurrection of our Lord was,
as has been said above, to be celebrated between the 14th and 20th
of the moon; he wrote, jointly with his fellow bishops, an exhorta-
tory epistle, entreating and conjuring them to observe unity of
peace, and conformity with the church of Christ spread throughout the world. The beginning of which epistle is as follows—

*"To our most dear brothers, the lords bishops and abbats throughout
Scotland, Laurentius, Mellitus, and Justus, servants of the servants of
God.* When the apostolic see, according to the universal custom

which it has followed elsewhere, sent us to these western parts to preach to pagan nations, we came into this island, which is called Britain, without possessing any previous knowledge of its inhabitants. We held both the Britons and Scots in great esteem for sanctity, believing that they had proceeded according to the custom of the universal church; but coming acquainted with the errors of the Britons, we thought the Scots had been better; but we have been informed by Bishop Dagan, coming into this aforesaid island, and the Abbat Columbanus in France, that the Scots in no way differ from the Britons in their behaviour; for Bishop Dagan coming to us, not only refused to eat with us, but even to take his repast in the same house where we were entertained."

The same Laurentius and his fellow bishops wrote a letter to the priests of the Britons, suitable to his rank, by which he endeavoured to confirm them in Catholic unity; but what he gained by so doing the present times still declare.

About this time, Mellitus, bishop of London, went to Rome, to confer with Pope Boniface about the necessary affairs of the English church. And the same most reverend pope, assembling a synod of the bishops of Italy, to prescribe orders for the life and peace of the monks, Mellitus also sat among them, in the eighth year of the reign of the Emperor Phocas, the thirteenth indiction, on the 27th of February, to the end that he also by his authority might confirm such things as should be regularly decreed, and at his return into Britain might carry the same to the churches of the English, to be prescribed and observed; together with letters which the same pope sent to the beloved of God, Archbishop Laurentius, and to all the clergy; as likewise to King Ethelbert and the English nation. This pope was Boniface, who came fourth after Pope Gregory, and who obtained of the Emperor Phocas that the temple called by the ancients Pantheon, as representing all the gods, should be given to the Church of Christ; wherein he, having purified it from contamination, dedicated a church to the holy mother of God, and to all Christ's martyrs, to the end that, the devils being excluded, the blessed company of the saints might have therein a perpetual memorial.

CHAPTER V

HOW, AFTER THE DEATH OF THE KINGS ETHELBERT AND
SABERT, THEIR SUCCESSORS RESTORED IDOLATRY; FOR
WHICH REASON, BOTH MELLITUS AND JUSTUS DEPARTED
OUT OF BRITAIN. [A.D. 616.]

IN the year of our Lord's incarnation 616, which is the twenty-first year after Augustine and his companions were sent to preach to the English nation, Ethelbert, king of Kent, having most gloriously governed his temporal kingdom fifty-six years, entered into the eternal joys of the kingdom which is heavenly. He was the third of the English kings that had the sovereignty of all the southern provinces that are divided from the northern by the river Humber, and the borders contiguous to the same; but the first of the kings that ascended to the heavenly kingdom. The first who had the like sovereignty was Elli, king of the South-Saxons; the second, Celin, king of the West-Saxons, who, in their own language, is called Ceaulin; the third, as has been said, was Ethelbert, king of Kent; the fourth was Redwald, king of the East-Angles, who, whilst Ethelbert lived, had been subservient to him. The fifth was Edwin, king of the nation of the Northumbrians, that is, of those who live on the north side of the river Humber, who, with great power, commanded all the nations, as well of the English as of the Britons who inhabit Britain, except only the people of Kent, and he reduced also under the dominion of the English, the Mevanian Islands of the Britons, lying between Ireland and Britain; the sixth was Oswald, the most Christian king of the Northumbrians, who also had the same extent under his command; the seventh, Oswy, brother to the former, held the same dominions for some time, and for the most part subdued and made tributary the nations of the Picts and Scots, which possess the northern parts of Britain: but of these hereafter.

King Ethelbert died on the 24th day of the month of February, twenty-one years after he had received the faith, and was buried in St. Martin's porch within the church of the blessed apostles Peter and Paul, where also lies his queen, Bertha. Among other benefits which he conferred upon the nation, he also, by the advice of wise persons, introduced judicial decrees, after the Roman model; which, being written in English, are still kept and observed by them. Among which, he in the first place set down what satisfaction should be given by those who should steal anything belonging to the church, the bishop, or the other clergy, resolving to give protection to those whose doctrine he had embraced.

This Ethelbert was the son of Irminric, whose father was Octa, whose father was Orric, surnamed Oisc, from whom the kings of Kent are wont to be called Oiscings. His father was Hengist, who, being invited by Vortigern, first came into Britain, with his son Oisc, as has been said above.

But after the death of Ethelbert, the accession of his son Eadbald proved very prejudicial to the new church; for he not only refused to embrace the faith of Christ, but was also defiled with such a sort of fornication, as the apostle testifies, was not heard of, even among the Gentiles; for he kept his father's wife. By both which crimes he gave occasion to those to return to their former uncleanness, who, under his father, had, either for favour, or through fear of the king, submitted to the laws of faith and chastity. Nor did the perfidious king escape without Divine punishment and correction; for he was troubled with frequent fits of madness, and possessed by an evil spirit. This confusion was increased by the death of Sabert, king of the East-Saxons, who departing to the heavenly kingdom, left three sons, still pagans, to inherit his temporal crown. They immediately began to profess idolatry, which, during their father's reign, they had seemed a little to abandon, and they granted free liberty to the people under their government to serve idols. And when they saw the bishop, whilst celebrating mass in the church, give the eucharist to the people, they, puffed up with barbarous folly, were wont, as it is reported, to say to him, "Why do you not give us also that white bread, which you used to give to our father Saba (for so they used to call him), and which you still continue to give to the people in the church?" To whom he answered, "If you will be washed in that laver of salvation, in which your father was washed, you may also partake of the holy bread of which he partook; but if you despise the laver of life, you may not receive the bread of life." They replied, "We will not enter into that laver, because we do not know that we stand in need of it, and yet we will eat of that bread." And being often earnestly admonished by him, that the same could not be done, nor any one admitted to partake of the sacred oblation without the holy cleansing, at last, they said in anger, "If you will not comply with us in so small a matter as that is which we require, you shall not stay in our province." And accordingly they obliged him and his followers to depart from their kingdom. Being forced from thence, he came into Kent, to advise with his fellow bishops, Laurentius and Justus, what was to be done in that case; and it was unanimously agreed, that it was better for them all to return to their own country, where they might serve God in freedom, than to continue without any advantage among those barbarians, who had revolted from the faith. Mellitus and Justus accordingly went away first, and withdrew into France, designing there to await the event of things. But the kings, who had driven from them the preacher of the truth, did not continue long unpunished in their heathenish worship. For marching out to battle against the nation of the Gewissæ, they were all slain with their army. However, the people, having been once turned to wickedness, though the authors of it were destroyed, would not be corrected, nor return to the unity of faith and charity which is in Christ.

CHAPTER VI

LAURENTIUS, BEING REPROVED BY THE APOSTLE, CONVERTS KING EADBALD TO CHRIST; MELLITUS AND JUSTUS ARE RECALLED. [A.D. 616.]

LAURENTIUS, being about to follow Mellitus and Justus, and to quit Britain, ordered his bed to be laid the night before in the church of the blessed apostles, Peter and Paul, which has been often mentioned before; wherein having laid himself to take some rest, after he had poured out many prayers and tears to God for the state of the church, he fell asleep; in the dead of night, the blessed prince of the apostles appeared to him, and scourging him a long time with apostolical severity, asked of him, "Why he would forsake the flock which he had committed to him? or to what shepherds he would commit Christ's sheep that were in the midst of wolves? Have you," said he, "forgotten my example, who, for the sake of those little ones, whom Christ recommended to me in token of his affection, underwent at the hands of infidels and enemies of Christ, bonds, stripes, imprisonment, afflictions, and lastly, the death of the cross, that I might at last be crowned with him?" Laurentius, the servant of Christ, being excited by these words and stripes, the very next morning repaired to the king, and taking off his garment, showed the scars of the stripes which he had received. The king, astonished, asked, "Who had presumed to give such stripes to so great a man?" And was much frightened when he heard that the bishop had suffered so much at the hands of he apostle of Christ for his salvation. Then abjuring the worship of idols, and renouncing his unlawful marriage, he embraced the faith of Christ, and being baptized, promoted the affairs of the church to the utmost of his power.

He also sent over into France, and recalled Mellitus and Justus, and commanded them freely to return to govern their churches, which they accordingly did, one year after their departure. Justus, indeed, returned to the city of Rochester, where he had before presided; but the Londoners would not receive Bishop Mellitus, choosing rather to be under their idolatrous high priests; for King Eadbald had not so much authority in the kingdom as his father, nor was he able to restore the bishop to his church against the will and consent of the pagans. But he and his nation, after his conversion to our Lord, diligently followed the Divine precepts. Lastly, he built the church of the holy Mother of God, in the monastery of the most blessed prince of the apostles, which was afterwards consecrated by Archbishop Mellitus.

CHAPTER VII

BISHOP MELLITUS BY PRAYER QUENCHES A FIRE IN HIS
CITY. [A.D. 619.]

IN this king's reign, the holy Archbishop Laurentius was taken
up to the heavenly kingdom: he was buried in the church and
monastery of the holy Apostle Peter, close by his predecessor
Augustine, on the 2nd day of the month of February. Mellitus,
who was bishop of London, was the third archbishop of
Canterbury from Augustine; Justus, who was still living, governed
the church of Rochester. These ruled the church of the English
with much industry and labour, and received letters of exhortation from Boniface, bishop of the Roman apostolic see, who
presided over the church after Deusdedit, in the year of our
Lord 619. Mellitus laboured under an infirmity of body, that is,
the gout; but his mind was sound, cheerfully passing over all
earthly things, and always aspiring to love, seek, and attain to
those which are celestial. He was noble by birth, but much
nobler in mind.

In short, that I may give one testimony of his virtue, by
which the rest may be guessed at, it happened once that the
city of Canterbury, being by carelessness set on fire, was in danger of being consumed by the spreading conflagration; water
was thrown over the fire in vain; a considerable part of the city
was already destroyed, and the fierce flame advancing towards
the bishop, when he, confiding in the Divine assistance, where
human failed, ordered himself to be carried towards the raging
fire, that was spreading on every side. The church of the four
crowned Martyrs was in the place where the fire raged most.
The bishop being carried thither by his servants, the sick man
averted the danger by prayer, which a number of strong men
had not been able to perform by much labour. Immediately,
the wind, which blowing from the south had spread the conflagration throughout the city, turning to the north, prevented

the destruction of those places that had lain in its way, and then ceasing entirely, the flames were immediately extinguished. And thus the man of God, whose mind was inflamed with the fire of Divine charity, and who was wont to drive away the powers of the air by his frequent prayers, from doing harm to himself, or his people, was deservedly allowed to prevail over the worldly winds and flames, and to obtain that they should not injure him or his.

This archbishop also, having ruled the church five years, departed to heaven in the reign of King Eadbald, and was buried with his predecessors in the monastery and church, which we have so often mentioned, of the most blessed prince of the apostles, in the year of our Lord's incarnation 624, on the 24th day of April.

CHAPTER VIII

POPE BONIFACE SENDS THE PALL AND AN EPISTLE TO JUSTUS, SUCCESSOR TO MELLITUS. [A.D. 624.]

JUSTUS, bishop of Rochester, immediately succeeded Mellitus in the archbishopric. He consecrated Romanus bishop of that see in his own stead, having obtained leave of ordaining bishops from Pope Boniface, whom we mentioned above to have been successor to Deusdedit: of which licence this is the form—

"Boniface, to his most beloved brother Justus. Not only the contents of your letter, but the perfection which your work has obtained, has informed us how devoutly and diligently you have laboured, my brother, for the Gospel of Christ; for Almighty God has not forsaken either the mystery of his name, or the fruit of your labours, having Himself faithfully promised to the preachers of the Gospel, 'Lo! I am with you alway, even unto the end of the world;' which promise his mercy has particularly manifested in this ministry of yours, opening the hearts of nations to receive the mystery of your preaching. For He has enlightened the acceptable course of your endeavours, by the approbation of his

grace; granting a plentiful increase to your faithful management of the talents committed to you, and which you may secure for many generations. This is by that reward conferred on you, who, constantly adhering to the ministry enjoined you, with laudable patience await the redemption of that nation, whose salvation is set on foot that they may profit by your merits, our Lord Himself saying, 'He that perseveres to the end shall be saved.' You are, therefore, saved by the hope of patience, and the virtue of endurance, to the end that the hearts of infidels, being cleansed from their natural and superstitious disease, might obtain the mercy of their Redeemer: for having received the letters of our son Ethelwald, we perceive with how much knowledge of the sacred word your mind, my brother, has brought over his mind to the belief in real conversion and the true faith. Therefore, firmly confiding in the long-suffering of the Divine clemency, we believe there will, through the ministry of your preaching, ensue most full salvation not only of the nations subject to him, but also of those that neighbour round about; to the end, that as it is written, the reward of a perfect work may be conferred on you by our Lord, the giver of all good things: and that the universal confession of all nations, having received the mystery of the Christian faith, may declare, that their 'Sound went into all the earth, and their words unto the ends of the world.'

"We have also, my brother, encouraged by zeal for what is good, sent you by the bearer of these, the pall, which we have only given leave to use in the celebration of the sacred mysteries; granting you likewise to ordain bishops when there shall be occasion, through the mercy of our Lord; that so the Gospel of Christ, by the preaching of many, may be spread abroad in all the nations that are not yet converted. You must, therefore, endeavour, my brother, to preserve with unblemished sincerity of mind that which you have received through the favour of the Apostolic See, as an emblem whereof you have obtained so principal an ornament to be borne on your shoulders. And make it your business, imploring the Divine goodness, so to behave yourself, that you may present before the tribunal of the Supreme Judge that is to come, the rewards of the favour granted you, not with guiltiness, but with the benefit of souls.

"God preserve you in safety, most dear brother!"

CHAPTER IX

THE REIGN OF KING EDWIN, AND HOW PAULINUS, COMING TO PREACH THE GOSPEL, FIRST CONVERTED HIS DAUGHTER AND OTHERS TO THE FAITH OF CHRIST. [A.D. 625.]

AT this time the nation of the Northumbrians, that is, the nation of the Angles that live on the north side of the river Humber, with their king, Edwin, received the faith through the preaching of Paulinus, above mentioned. This Edwin, as a reward of his receiving the faith, and as an earnest of his share in the heavenly kingdom, received an increase of that which he enjoyed on earth, for he reduced under his dominion all the borders of Britain that were provinces either of the aforesaid nation, or of the Britons, a thing which no British king had ever done before; and he in like manner subjected to the English the Mevanian islands, as has been said above. The first whereof, which is to the southward, is the largest in extent, and most fruitful, containing nine hundred and sixty families, according to the English computation; the other above three hundred.

The occasion of this nation's embracing the faith was, their aforesaid king, being allied to the kings of Kent, having taken to wife Ethelberga, otherwise called Tate, daughter to King Ethelbert. He having by his ambassadors asked her in marriage of her brother Eadbald, who then reigned in Kent, was answered, "That it was not lawful to marry a Christian virgin to a pagan husband, lest the faith and the mysteries of the heavenly King should be profaned by her cohabiting with a king that was altogether a stranger to the worship of the true God." This answer being brought to Edwin by his messengers, he promised in no manner to act in opposition to the Christian faith, which the virgin professed; but would give leave to her, and all that went with her, men or women, priests or ministers, to follow their faith and worship after the custom of the Christians. Nor did he deny, but that he would embrace the same religion, if, being examined by wise persons, it should be found more holy and more worthy of God.

Hereupon the virgin was promised, and sent to Edwin, and pursuant to what had been agreed on, Paulinus, a man beloved of God, was ordained bishop, to go with her, and by daily exhortations, and celebrating the heavenly mysteries, to confirm her and her company, lest they should be corrupted by the company of the pagans. Paulinus was ordained bishop by the Archbishop Justus, on the 21st day of July, in the year of our Lord 625, and so he came to King Edwin with the aforesaid virgin as a companion of their union in the flesh. But his mind was wholly bent upon reducing the nation to which he was sent to the knowledge of truth; according to the words of the apostle, "To espouse her to one husband, that he might present her as a chaste virgin to Christ." Being come into that province, he laboured much, not only to retain those that went with him, by the help of God, that they should not revolt from the faith, but, if he could, to convert some of the pagans to a state of grace by his preaching. But, as the apostle says, though he laboured long in the word, "The god of this world blinded the minds of them that believed not, lest the light of the glorious Gospel of Christ should shine unto them."

The next year there came into the province a certain assassin, called Eumer, sent by the king of the West-Saxons, whose name was Cuichelm, in hopes at once to deprive King Edwin of his kingdom and his life. He had a two-edged dagger, dipped in poison, to the end, that if the wound were not sufficient to kill the king, it might be performed by the venom. He came to the king on the first day of Easter, at the river Derwent, where then stood the regal city, and being admitted as if to deliver a message from his master, whilst he was in an artful manner delivering his pretended embassy, he started on a sudden, and drawing the dagger from under his garment, assaulted the king; which Lilla, the king's beloved minister, observing, having no buckler at hand to secure the king from death, interposed his own body to receive the stroke; but the wretch struck so home, that he wounded the king through the knight's body. Being then attacked on all sides with swords, he in that confusion also slew another soldier, whose name was Forthhere.

On that same holy night of Easter Sunday, the queen had brought forth to the king a daughter, called Eanfled. The king, in the presence of Bishop Paulinus, gave thanks to his gods for the birth of his daughter; and the bishop, on the other hand, returned thanks to Christ, and endeavoured to persuade the king, that by his prayers to Him he had obtained that the queen should bring forth the child in safety, and without much pain. The king, delighted with his words, promised, that in case God would grant him life and victory over the king by whom the assassin had been sent, he would cast off his idols, and serve Christ; and as a pledge that he would perform his promise, he delivered up that same daughter to Paulinus, to be consecrated to Christ. She was the first baptized of the nation of the Northumbrians, on Whitsunday, with twelve others of her family. At that time, the king, being recovered of the wound which he had received, marched with his army against the nation of the West-Saxons; and having begun the war, either slew or subdued all those that he had been informed had conspired to murder him. Returning thus victorious unto his own country, he would not immediately and unadvisedly embrace the mysteries of the Christian faith, though he no longer worshipped idols, ever since he made the promise that he would serve Christ; but thought fit first at leisure to be instructed, by the venerable Paulinus, in the knowledge of faith, and to confer with such as he knew to be the wisest of his prime men, to advise what they thought was fittest to be done in that case. And being a man of extraordinary sagacity, he often sat alone by himself a long time, silent as to his tongue, but deliberating in his heart how he should proceed, and which religion he should adhere to.

CHAPTER X

POPE BONIFACE, BY LETTER, EXHORTS THE SAME KING
TO EMBRACE THE FAITH. [A.D. 625.]

AT this time he received letters from Pope Boniface [IV.] exhorting him to embrace the faith, which were as follows—

COPY OF THE LETTER OF THE HOLY AND APOSTOLIC POPE OF
THE CHURCH OF ROME, BONIFACE, TO THE GLORIOUS EDWIN,
KING OF THE ENGLISH.

"To the illustrious Edwin, king of the English, Bishop Boniface, the servant of the servants of God. Although the power of the Supreme Deity cannot be expressed by human speech, as consisting in its own greatness, and in invisible and unsearchable eternity, so that no sharpness of wit can comprehend or express it; yet in regard that the goodness of God, to give some notion of itself, having opened the doors of the heart, has mercifully, by secret inspiration, infused into the minds of men such things as He is willing shall be declared concerning Himself, we have thought fit to extend our priestly care to make known to you the fulness of the Christian faith; to the end that, informing you of the Gospel of Christ, which our Saviour commanded should be preached to all nations, they might offer to you the cup of life and salvation.

"Thus the goodness of the Supreme Majesty, which, by the word of his command, made and created all things, the heaven, the earth, the sea, and all that is in them, disposing the order by which they should subsist, hath, with the counsel of his co-eternal Word, and the unity of the Holy Spirit, formed man after his own likeness, out of the slime of the earth; and granted him such super-eminent prerogative, as to place him above all others; so that, observing the command which was given him, his continuance should be to eternity. This God,—Father, Son, and Holy Ghost, which is an undivided Trinity,—mankind, from the east unto the west, by confession of faith to the saving of their souls, do worship and adore, as the Creator of all things, and their own Maker; to whom also the heights of empire, and the powers of the world, are subject, because the bestowal of all kingdoms is granted by his disposition. It hath pleased Him, therefore, of his great mercy, and for the greater benefit of all his creatures, by his Holy Spirit wonderfully to kindle the cold hearts also of the nations seated at the extremities of the earth in the knowledge of Himself.

"For we suppose your excellency has, from the country lying so near, fully understood what the clemency of our Redeemer has effected in the enlightening of our glorious son, King Eadbald, and the nations under his subjection; we therefore trust, with assured confidence of celestial hope, that his wonderful gift will be also conferred on you; since we understand that your illustrious consort, which is known to be a part of your body, is illuminated with the reward of eternity, through the regeneration of holy baptism. We have, therefore, taken care by these presents, with all possible affection, to exhort your illustrious selves, that, abhorring idols and their worship, and contemning the follies of temples, and the deceitful flatteries of auguries, you believe in God the Father Almighty, and his Son Jesus Christ, and the Holy Ghost, to the end that, being discharged from the bonds of captivity to the Devil, by believing you may, through the co-operating power of the holy and undivided Trinity, be partaker of the eternal life.

"How great guilt they lie under, who adhere to the pernicious superstitions and worship of idolatry, appears by the examples of the perdition of those whom they worship. Wherefore it is said of them by the Psalmist, 'All the gods of the Gentiles are devils, but the Lord made the heavens.' And again, 'they have eyes and do apt see, they have ears and do not hear, they have noses and do not smell, they have hands and do not feel, they have feet and do not walk. Therefore they are like those that confide in them.' For how can they have any power to yield assistance, that are made for you out of corruptible matter, by the hands of your inferiors and subjects, to wit, on whom you have by human art bestowed an inanimate similitude of members? Who, unless they be moved by you, will not be able to walk; but, like a stone fixed in one place, being so formed, and having no understanding, but absorbed in insensibility, have no power of doing harm or good. We cannot, therefore, upon mature deliberation, find out how you come to be so deceived as to follow and worship those gods, to whom you yourselves have given the likeness of a body.

"It behoves you, therefore, by taking upon you the sign of the holy cross, by which the human race is redeemed, to root out of your hearts all those arts and cunning of the Devil, who is ever jealous of the works of the Divine goodness, and to lay hold and break in pieces those which you have hitherto made your material gods. For the very destruction and abolition of these, which could never receive life or sense from their makers, may plainly demonstrate to you how worthless they were which you till then had worshipped, when you yourselves, who have received life from the Lord, are certainly better than they, as Almighty God has appointed you to be descended, after many ages and through many generations, from the first man whom He formed. Draw near, then, to the knowledge of Him who created you, who breathed the breath of life into you, who sent his only-begotten Son for your redemption, to cleanse you from original sin, that being delivered from the power of the Devil's wickedness, He might bestow on you a heavenly reward.

"Hear the words of the preachers, and the Gospel of God, which they declare to you, to the end that, believing, as has been said, in God the Father Almighty, and in Jesus Christ his Son, and the Holy Ghost, and the indivisible Trinity, having put to flight the sensualities of devils, and driven from you the suggestions of the venomous and deceitful enemy, and being born again by water and the Holy Ghost, you may, through his assistance and bounty, dwell in the brightness of eternal glory with Him in whom you shall believe. We have, moreover, sent you the blessing of your protector, the blessed Peter, prince of the apostles, that is, a shirt, with one gold ornament, and one garment of Ancyra, which we pray your highness to accept with the same goodwill as it is friendly intended by us."

CHAPTER XI

POPE BONIFACE ADVISES QUEEN ETHELBERGA TO USE HER BEST ENDEAVOURS FOR THE SALVATION OF HER CONSORT, KING EDWIN. [A.D. 625.]

THE same pope also wrote to King Edwin's consort, Ethelberga, to this effect—

THE COPY OF THE LETTER OF THE MOST BLESSED AND APOSTOLIC BONIFACE, POPE OF THE CITY OF ROME, TO ETHELBERGA, KING EDWIN'S QUEEN.

"*To the illustrious lady his daughter, Queen Ethelberga, Boniface, bishop, servant of the servants of God:* The goodness of our Redeemer has with much providence offered the means of salvation to the human race, which He rescued, by the shedding of his precious blood, from the bonds of captivity to the Devil; so that making his name known in divers ways to the Gentiles, they might acknowledge their Creator by embracing the mystery of the Christian faith, which thing, the mystical purification of your regeneration plainly shows to have been bestowed upon the mind of your highness by God's bounty. Our mind, therefore, has been much rejoiced in the benefit of our Lord's goodness, for that He has vouchsafed, in your conversion, to kindle a spark of the orthodox religion, by which He might the more easily inflame in his love the understanding, not only of your glorious consort, but also of all the nation that is subject to you.

"For we have been informed by those, who came to acquaint us with the laudable conversion of our illustrious son, King Eadbald, that your highness, also, having received the wonderful sacrament of the Christian faith, continually excels in the performance of works pious and acceptable to God. That you like-wise carefully refrain from the worship of idols, and the deceits of temples and auguries, and having changed your devotion, are so wholly taken up with the love of your Redeemer, as never to cease lending your assistance for the propagation of the Christian faith. And our fatherly charity having earnestly inquired concerning your illustrious husband, we were given to understand that he still served abominable idols, and would not yield obedience or give ear to the voice of the preachers. This occasioned us no small grief, for that part of your body still remained a stranger to the knowledge of the supreme and undivided Trinity. Whereupon we, in our fatherly care, did not delay to admonish your Christian highness, exhorting you, that, with the help of the Divine inspira-tion, you will not defer to do that which, both in season and out of season, is required of us; that with the co-operating power of our Lord and Saviour Jesus Christ, your husband also may be added to the number of Christians; to the end that you may thereby enjoy the rights of marriage in the bond of a holy and unblemished union. For it is written, 'They two shall be in one flesh.' How can it be said, that there is unity between you, if he continues a stranger to the brightness of your faith, by the inter-position of dark and detestable error?

"Wherefore, applying yourself continually to prayer, do not cease to beg of the Divine Mercy the benefit of his illumination; to the end, that those whom the union of carnal affection has made in a manner but one body, may, after death, continue in perpetual union, by the bond of faith. Persist, therefore, illustrious daughter, and to the utmost of your power endeavour to soften the hardness of his heart by insinuating the Divine precepts; making him sensi-ble how noble the mystery is which you have received by believing, and how wonderful is the reward which, by the new birth, you have merited to obtain. Inflame the coldness of his heart by the knowledge of the Holy Ghost, that by the abolition of the cold and pernicious worship of paganism, the heat of Divine faith may enlighten his understanding through your frequent exhortations;

that the testimony of the holy Scripture may appear the more conspicuous, fulfilled by you, 'The unbelieving husband shall be saved
by the believing wife.' For to this effect you have obtained the
mercy of our Lord's goodness, that you may return with increase
the fruit of faith, and the benefits entrusted in your hands; for
through the assistance of his mercy we do not cease with frequent
prayers to beg that you may be able to perform the same.

"Having premised thus much, in pursuance of the duty of our
fatherly affection, we exhort you, that when the opportunity of a
bearer shall offer, you will as soon as possible acquaint us with the
success which the Divine Power shall grant by your means in the
conversion of your consort, and of the nation subject to you; to
the end, that our solicitude, which earnestly expects what apper-
tains to the salvation of you and yours, may, by hearing from you,
be set at rest; and that we, discerning more fully the brightness of
the Divine propitiation diffused in you, may with a joyful confession abundantly return due thanks to God, the Giver of all good
things, and to St. Peter, the prince of apostles. We have, moreover,
sent you the blessing of your protector, St. Peter, the prince of the
apostles, that is, a silver looking-glass, and a gilt ivory comb, which
we entreat your glory will receive with the same kind affection as it
is known to be sent by us."

CHAPTER XII

KING EDWIN IS PERSUADED TO BELIEVE BY A VISION WHICH
HE HAD SEEN WHEN HE WAS IN EXILE. [BEFORE A.D. 625.]

THUS the aforesaid Pope Boniface wrote for the salvation of King
Edwin and his nation. But a heavenly vision, which the Divine
Mercy was pleased once to reveal to this king, when he was in banishment at the court of Redwald, king of the Angles, was of no little use in urging him to embrace and understand the doctrines of
salvation. Paulinus, therefore, perceiving that it was a very difficult
task to incline the king's lofty mind to the humility of the way of

salvation, and to embrace the mystery of the cross of life, and at the same time using both exhortation with men, and prayer to God, for his and his subjects' salvation; at length, as we may suppose, it was shown him in spirit what was the vision that had been formerly revealed to the king. Nor did he lose any time, but immediately admonished the king to perform the vow which he made, when he received the oracle, promising to put the same in execution, if he was delivered from the trouble he was at that time under, and should be advanced to the throne.

The vision was this. When Ethelfrid, his predecessor, was persecuting him, he for many years wandered in a private manner through several places and kingdoms, and at last came to Redwald, beseeching him to give him protection against the snares of his powerful persecutor. Redwald willingly admitted him, and promised to perform what he requested. But when Ethelfrid understood that he had appeared in that province, and that he and his companions were hospitably entertained by Redwald, he sent messengers to offer that king a great sum of money to murder him, but without effect. He sent a second and a third time, bidding more and more each time, and threatening to make war on him if he refused. Redwald, either terrified by his threats, or gained by his gifts, complied with his request, and promised either to kill Edwin, or to deliver him up to the ambassadors. This being observed by a trusty friend of his, he went into his chamber, where he was going to bed, for it was the first hour of the night; and calling him out, discovered what the king had promised to do with him, adding, "If, therefore, you think fit, I will this very hour conduct you out of this province, and lead you to a place where neither Redwald nor Ethelfrid shall ever find you." He answered, "I thank you for your good will, yet I cannot do what you propose, or be guilty of breaking the compact I have made with so great a king, when he has done me no harm, nor offered me any injury; but, on the contrary, if I must die, let it rather be by his hand than by that of any meaner person. For whither shall I now fly, when I have for so many years been a vagabond through all the provinces of Britain, to escape the hands of my enemies?" His friend being gone, Edwin remained alone without, and sitting with a heavy heart before the palace, began to be overwhelmed with many thoughts, not knowing what to do, or which way to turn himself.

When he had remained a long time in silence, brooding over his misfortunes in anguish of mind, he, on a sudden, in the dead of night, saw approaching a person, whose face and habit were equally strange, at which unexpected sight he was not a little frightened. The stranger coming close up, saluted him, and asked him, "Why he sat there alone and melancholy on a stone at that time, when all others were taking their rest, and were fast asleep?" Edwin, in his turn, asked, "What it was to him, whether he spent the night within doors or abroad?" The stranger, in reply, said, "Do not think that I am ignorant of the cause of your grief, your watching, and sitting alone without. For I know who you are, and why you grieve, and the evils which you fear will fall upon you. But tell me, what reward you will give the man that shall deliver you out of this anguish, and persuade Redwald neither to do you any harm himself, nor to deliver you up to be murdered by your enemies." Edwin replied, "That he would give that person all that he was able for so singular a favour." The other further added, "What if I also assure you, that you shall overcome your enemies, and surpass in power, not only all your own progenitors, but even all that have reigned before you over the English nation?" Edwin, encouraged by these questions, did not hesitate to promise that he would make a suitable return to him who should so highly oblige him. Then said the other, "But if he who foretells so much good as is to befall you, can also give you better advice for your life and salvation than any of your progenitors or kindred ever heard of, do you consent to submit to him, and to follow his wholesome counsel?" Edwin did not hesitate to promise that he would in all things follow the directions of that man who should deliver him from so many calamities, and raise him to a throne.

Having received this answer, the person that talked to him laid his hand on his head saying, "When this sign shall be given you, remember this present discourse that has passed between us, and do not delay the performance of what you now promise." Having uttered these words, he is said to have immediately vanished, that the king might understand it was not a man, but a spirit, that had appeared to him.

Whilst the royal youth still sat there alone, glad of the comfort he had received, but seriously considering who he was, or whence he came, that had so talked to him, his above-mentioned friend came to him, and saluting him with a pleasant countenance, "Rise," said he, "go in and compose yourself to sleep without fear; for the king's resolution is altered, and he designs to do you no harm, but rather to perform the promise which he made you; for when he had privately acquainted the queen with his intention of doing what I told you before, she dissuaded him from it, declaring it was unworthy of so great a king to sell his good friend in such distress for gold, and to sacrifice his honour, which is more valuable than all other ornaments, for the lucre of money." In short, the king did as he was advised, and not only refused to deliver up the banished man to his enemy's messengers, but assisted him to recover his kingdom. For as soon as the ambassadors were returned home, he raised a mighty army to make war on Ethelfrid; who, meeting him with much inferior forces (for Redwald had not given him time to gather all his power), was slain on the borders of the kingdom of Mercia, on the east side of the river that is called Idle. In this battle, Redwald's son, called Regnhere, was killed; and thus Edwin, pursuant to the oracle he had received, not only escaped the danger from the king his enemy, but, by his death, succeeded him in the throne.

King Edwin, therefore, delaying to receive the word of God at the preaching of Paulinus, and using for some time, as has been said, to sit several hours alone, and seriously to ponder with himself what he was to do, and what religion he was to follow, the man of God came to him, laid his right hand on his head, and asked, "Whether he knew that sign?" The king in a trembling condition, was ready to fall down at his feet, but he raised him up, and in a familiar manner said to him, "Behold, by the help of God you have escaped the hands of the enemies whom you feared. Behold you have of his gift obtained the kingdom which you desired. Take heed not to delay that which you promised to perform; embrace the faith, and keep the precepts of Him who, delivering you from temporal adversity, has raised you to the honour of a temporal kingdom; and if, from this time forward, you shall be obedient to his will, which through me He signifies to you, He will not only deliver you from the everlasting torments of the wicked, but also make you partaker with Him of his eternal kingdom in heaven."

CHAPTER XIII

OF THE COUNCIL HE HELD WITH HIS CHIEF MEN ABOUT EMBRACING THE FAITH OF CHRIST, AND HOW THE HIGH PRIEST PROFANED HIS OWN ALTARS. [A.D. 627.]

THE king, hearing these words, answered, that he was both willing and bound to receive the faith which he taught; but that he would confer about it with his principal friends and counsellers, to the end that if they also were of his opinion, they might all together be cleansed in Christ the Fountain of Life. Paulinus consenting, the king did as he said; for, holding a council with the wise men, he asked of every one in particular what he thought of the new doctrine, and the new worship that was preached? To which the chief of his own priests, Coifi, immediately answered, "O king, consider what this is which is now preached to us; for I verily declare to you, that the religion which we have hitherto professed has, as far as I can learn, no virtue in it. For none of your people has applied himself more diligently to the worship of our gods than I; and yet there are many who receive greater favours from you, and are more preferred than I, and are more prosperous in all their undertakings. Now if the gods were good for any thing, they would rather forward me, who have been more careful to serve them. It remains, therefore, that if upon examination you find those new doctrines, which are now preached to us, better and more efficacious, we immediately receive them without any delay."

Another of the king's chief men, approving of his words and exhortations, presently added: "The present life of man, O king, seems to me, in comparison of that time which is unknown to us, like to the swift flight of a sparrow through the room wherein you sit at supper in winter, with your commanders and ministers, and a good fire in the midst, whilst the storms of rain and snow prevail abroad; the sparrow, I say, flying in at one door, and immediately out at another, whilst he is within, is safe from the wintry storm; but after a short space of fair weather, he immediately vanishes out of your sight, into the dark winter from which he had emerged. So this life of man appears for a short space, but of what went before, or what is to follow, we are utterly ignorant. If, therefore, this new doctrine contains something more certain, it seems justly to deserve to be followed." The other elders and king's councillors, by Divine inspiration, spoke to the same effect.

But Coifi added, that he wished more attentively to hear Paulinus discourse concerning the God whom he preached; which he having by the king's command performed, Coifi, hearing his words, cried out, "I have long since been sensible that there was nothing in that which we worshipped; because the more diligently I sought after truth in that worship, the less I found it. But now I freely confess, that such truth evidently appears in this preaching as can confer on us the gifts of life, of salvation, and of eternal happiness. For which reason I advise, O king, that we instantly abjure and set fire to those temples and altars which we have consecrated without reaping any benefit from them." In short, the king publicly gave his licence to Paulinus to preach the Gospel, and renouncing idolatry, declared that he received the faith of Christ: and when he inquired of the high priest who should first profane the altars and temples of their idols, with the enclosures that were about them, he answered, "I; for who can more properly than myself destroy those things which I worshipped through ignorance, for an example to all others, through the wisdom which has been given me by the true God?" Then immediately, in contempt of his former superstitions, he desired the king to furnish him with arms and a stallion; and mounting the same, he set out to destroy the idols; for it was not lawful before for the high priest either to carry arms, or to ride on any but a mare. Having, therefore, girt a sword about him, with a spear in his hand, he mounted the king's stallion and proceeded to the idols. The multitude, beholding it, concluded he was distracted; but he lost no time, for as soon as he drew near the temple he profaned the same, casting into it the spear which he held; and rejoicing in the knowledge of the worship of the true God, he commanded his companions to destroy the temple, with all its enclosures, by fire. This place where the idols were is still shown, not far from York, to the eastward, beyond the river Derwent, and is now called Godmundingham, where the high priest, by the inspiration of the true God, profaned and destroyed the altars which he had himself consecrated.

CHAPTER XIV

KING EDWIN AND HIS NATION BECOME CHRISTIANS; PAULINUS BAPTIZES THEM. [A.D. 627.]

KING Edwin, therefore, with all the nobility of the nation, and a large number of the common sort, received the faith, and the washing of regeneration, in the eleventh year of his reign, which is the year of the incarnation of our Lord 627, and about one hundred and eighty after the coming of the English into Britain. He was baptized at York, on the holy day of Easter, being the 12th of April, in the church of St. Peter the Apostle, which he himself had built of timber, whilst he was catechising and instructing in order to receive baptism. In that city also he appointed the see of the bishopric of his instructor and bishop, Paulinus. But as soon as he was baptized, he took care, by the direction of the same Paulinus, to build in the same place a larger and nobler church of stone, in the midst whereof that same oratory which he had first erected should be enclosed. Having therefore laid the foundation, he began to build the church square, encompassing the former oratory. But before the whole was raised to the proper height, the wicked assassination of the king left that work to be finished by Oswald his sucessor. Paulinus, for the space of six years from that time, that is, till the end of the reign of that king, by his consent and favour, preached the word of God in that country, and all that were preordained to eternal life believed and were baptized. Among whom were Osfrid and Eadfrid, King Edwin's sons, who were both born to him, whilst he was in banishment, of Quenberga, the daughter of Cearl, king of the Mercians.

Afterwards other children of his by Queen Ethelberga were baptized, viz. Ethelhun and his daughter Etheldrith, and another, Wuscfrea, a son; the first two of which were snatched out of this life whilst they were still in their white garments, and buried in the church at York. Iffi, the son of Osfrid, was also baptized, and many more noble and illustrious persons. So great was then the fervour of the faith, as is reported, and the desire of the washing of salvation among the nation of the Northumbrians, that Paulinus at a certain time coming with the king and queen to the royal country-seat, which is called Adgefrin, stayed there with them thirty-six days, fully occupied in catechising and baptizing; during which days, from morning till night, he did nothing else but instruct the people resorting from all villages and places, in Christ's saving word; and when instructed, he washed them with the water of absolution in the river Glen, which is close by. This town, under the following kings, was abandoned, and another was built instead of it, at the place called Melmin.

These things happened in the province of the Bernicians; but in that of the Deiri also, where he was wont often to be with the king, he baptized in the river Swale, which runs by the village of Cataract; for as yet oratories, or fonts, could not be made in the early infancy of the church in those parts. But he built a church in Campodonum, which afterwards the pagans, by whom King Edwin was slain, burnt, together with all the town. In the place of which the later kings built themselves a country-seat in the country called Loidis. But the altar, being of stone, escaped the fire and is still preserved in the monastery of the most reverend abbat and priest, Thridwulf, which is in Elmete wood.

CHAPTER XV

THE PROVINCE OF THE EAST ANGLES RECEIVES THE FAITH OF CHRIST. [A.D. 627.]

EDWIN was so zealous for the worship of truth, that he likewise persuaded Eorpwald, king of the East Saxons, and son of Redwald, to abandon his idolatrous superstitions, and with his whole province to receive the faith and sacraments of Christ. And indeed his father Redwald had long before been admitted to the sacrament of the Christian faith in Kent, but in vain; for on his return home, he was seduced by his wife and certain perverse teachers, and turned back from the sincerity of the faith; and thus his latter state was worse than the former; so that, like the ancient Samaritans, he seemed at the same time to serve Christ and the gods whom he had served before; and in the same temple he had an altar to sacrifice to Christ, and another small one to offer victims to devils; which temple, Aldwulf, king of that same province, who lived in our time, testifies had stood until his time, and that he had seen it when he was a boy. The aforesaid King Redwald was noble by birth, though ignoble in his actions, being the son of Tytilus, whose father was Uuffa, from whom the kings of the East Angles are called Uuffings.

Eorpwald was, not long after he had embraced the Christian faith, slain by one Richbert, a pagan; and from that time the province was under error for three years, till the crown came into the possession of Sigebert, brother to the same Eorpwald, a most Christian and learned man, who was banished, and went to live in France during his brother's life, and was there admitted to the sacraments of the faith, whereof he made it his business to cause all his province to partake as soon as he came to the throne. His exertions were much promoted by the Bishop Felix, who, coming to Honorius, the archbishop, from Burgundy, where he had been born and ordained, and having told him what he desired, he sent him to preach the word of life to the aforesaid nation of the Angles. Nor were his good wishes in vain; for the pious husband-man reaped therein a large harvest of believers, delivering all that province (according to the signification of his name, Felix) from long iniquity and infelicity, and bringing it to the faith and works of righteousness, and the gifts of everlasting happiness. He had the see of his bishopric appointed him in the city Dommoc, and having presided over the same province with pontifical authority seventeen years, he ended his days there in peace.

CHAPTER XVI

HOW PAULINUS PREACHED IN THE PROVINCE OF LINDSEY; AND OF THE REIGN OF EDWIN. [A.D. 628.]

PAULINUS also preached the word to the province of Lindsey, which is the first on the south side of the river Humber, stretching out as far as the sea; and he first converted the governor of the city of Lincoln, whose name was Blecca, with his whole family. He like-wise built, in that city, a stone church of beautiful workmanship; the roof of which having either fallen through age, or been thrown down by enemies, the walls are still to be seen standing, and every year some miraculous cures are wrought in that place, for the ben-efit of those who have faith to seek the same. In that church, Justus having departed to Christ, Paulinus consecrated Honorius bishop in his stead, as will be hereafter mentioned in its proper place. A certain abbat and priest of the monastery of Peartaneu, a man of singular veracity, whose name was Deda, in relation to the faith of this province told me that one of the oldest persons had informed him, that he himself had been baptized at noon-day, by the Bishop

Paulinus, in the presence of King Edwin, with a great number of the people, in the river Trent, near the city, which in the English tongue is called Tiovulfingacestir; and he was also wont to describe the person of the same Paulinus, that he was tall of stature, a little stooping, his hair black, his visage meagre, his nose slender and aquiline, his aspect both venerable and majestic. He had also with him in the ministry, James, the deacon, a man of zeal and great fame in Christ's church, who lived even to our days.

It is reported that there was then such perfect peace in Britain, wheresoever the dominion of King Edwin extended, that, as is still proverbially said, a woman with her new-born babe might walk throughout the island, from sea to sea, without receiving any harm. That king took such care for the good of his nation, that in several places where he had seen clear springs near the highways, he caused stakes to be fixed, with brass dishes hanging at them, for the conveniency of travellers; nor durst any man touch them for any other purpose than that for which they were designed, either through the dread they had of the king, or for the affection which they bore him. His dignity was so great throughout his dominions, that his banners were not only borne before him in battle, but even in time of peace, when he rode about his cities, towns, or provinces, with his officers, the standard-bearer was wont to go before him. Also, when he walked along the streets, that sort of banner which the Romans call Tufa, and the English, Tuuf, was in like manner borne before him.

CHAPTER XVII

EDWIN RECEIVES LETTERS OF EXHORTATION FROM POPE HONORIUS, WHO ALSO SENDS PAULINUS THE PALL. [A.D. 634.]

AT that time Honorius, successor to Boniface, was prelate of the apostolic see, who, when he understood that the nation of the Northumbrians, with their king, had been, by the preaching of

Paulinus, converted to the faith and confession of Christ, sent the pall to the said Paulinus, and with it letters of exhortation to King Edwin, exciting him, with fatherly charity, that his people should persist in the faith of truth, which they had received. The contents of which letter were as follow—

"*To his most noble son, and excellent lord, Edwin king of the Angles, Bishop Honorius, servant of the servants of God, greeting:* The integrity of your Christian character, in the worship of your Creator, is so much inflamed with the fire of faith, that it shines out far and near, and, being reported throughout the world, brings forth plentiful fruits of your labours. For your conduct as a king is based upon the knowledge which by orthodox preaching you have obtained of your God and Creator, whereby you believe and worship Him, and as far as man is able, pay Him the sincere devotion of your mind. For what else are we able to offer to our God, but in endeavouring to worship, and to pay Him our vows, persisting in good actions, and confessing Him the Creator of mankind? And, therefore, most excellent son, we exhort you with such fatherly charity as is requisite, that you with careful mind, and constant prayers, every way labour to preserve this gift, that the Divine Mercy has vouchsafed to call you to his grace; to the end, that He, who has been pleased to deliver you from all errors, and bring you to the knowledge of his name, may likewise prepare you mansions in the heavenly country. Employing yourselves, therefore, in reading the works of my Lord Gregory, your preacher, of apostolical memory, represent before yourself the tenderness of his doctrine, which he zealously employed for the sake of your souls; that his prayers may increase your kingdom and people, and present you blameless before Almighty God. We are preparing with a willing mind immediately to grant those things which you hoped would be by us ordained for your priests, which we do on account of the sincerity of your faith, which has been often made known to us in terms of praise by the bearers of these presents. We have sent two palls to the two metropolitans, Honorius and Paulinus; to the intent, that when either of them shall be called out of this world to his Creator, the other may, by this authority of ours, substitute another bishop in his place; which privilege we are induced to grant, as well in regard to your charitable affection, as of the large and extensive provinces which lie between us and you; that we may in all things afford our concurrence to your devotion, according to your desires. May God's grace preserve your excellency in safety!"

CHAPTER XVIII

HONORIUS, WHO SUCCEEDED JUSTUS IN THE BISHOPRIC OF CANTERBURY, RECEIVES THE PALL AND LETTERS FROM POPE HONORIUS. [A.D. 634.]

In the meantime, Archbishop Justus was taken up to the heavenly kingdom, on the 10th of November, and Honorius, who was elected to the see in his stead, came to Paulinus to be ordained, and meeting him at Lincoln was there consecrated the fifth prelate of the Church of Canterbury from Augustine. To him also the aforesaid Pope Honorius sent the pall, and a letter, wherein he ordains the same that he had before established in his epistle to King Edwin, viz. that when either of the bishops of Canterbury or of York shall depart this life, the survivor of the same degree shall have power to ordain a priest in the room of him that is departed; that it might not be necessary always to travel to Rome, at so great a distance by sea and land, to ordain an archbishop. Which letter we have also thought fit to insert in this our history—

"*Honorius to his most beloved brother Honorius:* Among the many good gifts which the mercy of our Redeemer is pleased to bestow on his servants, the munificent bounty of love is never more conspicuous than when He permits us by brotherly intercourse, as it were face to face, to exhibit our mutual love. For which gift we continually return thanks to his majesty; and we humbly beseech Him, that He will ever confirm your piety in preaching the Gospel, and bringing forth fruit, and following the rule of your master and head, his holy servant, St. Gregory; and that, for the advancement of his church, He may by your means add further increase; to the end, that the souls already won by you and your predecessors, beginning with our Lord Gregory, may grow strong and be further extended by faith and works in the fear of God and charity; that so the promises of the word of God may hereafter be brought to pass in you; and that this voice may call you away to the everlasting happiness. 'Come unto me all ye that labour and are heavy laden, and I will give you rest.' And again, 'Well done, thou good and faithful servant; thou hast been faithful over a few things, I will make thee ruler over many things; enter thou into the joy of thy Lord.' And we, most beloved brothers, offering you these words of exhortation, out of our abundant charity, do not hesitate further to grant those things which we perceive may be suitable for the privileges of your churches.

"Wherefore, pursuant to your request, and to that of the kings our sons, we do by these presents, in the name of St. Peter, prince of the apostles, grant you authority, that when the Divine Grace shall call either of you to Himself, the survivor shall ordain a bishop in the room of him that is deceased. To which effect also we have sent a pall to each of you, for celebrating the said ordination; that by the authority of our precept, you may make an ordination acceptable to God; because the long distance of sea and land that lies between us and you, has obliged us to grant you this, that no loss may happen to your church in any way, on account of any pretence whatever, but that the devotion of the people committed to you may be more fully extended. God preserve you in safety, most dear brother! Given the 11th day of June, in the twenty-fourth year of the reign of our most pious emperor, Heraclius, and the twenty-third after his consulship; and in the twenty-third of his son Constantine, and the third after his consulship; and in the third year of the most illustrious Cæsar, his son Heraclius, the seventh indiction; that is, in the year of the incarnation of our Lord, 634."

CHAPTER XIX

HOW THE AFORESAID HONORIUS FIRST, AND AFTER-
WARDS JOHN, WROTE LETTERS TO THE NATION OF THE
SCOTS, CONCERNING THE OBSERVANCE OF EASTER, AND
THE PELAGIAN HERESY. [A.D. 634.]

THE same Pope Honorius also wrote to the Scots [Irish], whom he
had found to err in the observance of Easter, as has been shown
above, earnestly exhorting them not to think their small number,
placed in the utmost borders of the earth, wiser than all the
ancient and modern churches of Christ, throughout the world;
and not to celebrate a different Easter, contrary to the Paschal calculation, and the synodical decrees of all the bishops upon earth.
Likewise John, who succeeded Severinus, successor to the same
Honorius, being yet but pope elect, sent to them letters of great
authority and erudition for correcting the same error; evidently
showing, that Easter Sunday is to be found between the fifteenth
moon and the twenty-first, as was proved in the Council of Nice.
He also in the same epistle admonished them to be careful to
crush the Pelagian heresy, which he had been informed was reviv-
ing among them. The beginning of the epistle was as follows—

"*To our most beloved and most holy Tomianus, Columbanus,
Cromanus, Dimanus, and Baithanus, bishops; to Cromanus, Hernianus,
Laistranus, Scellanus, and Segenus, priests; to Saranus and the rest of the
Scottish doctors, or abbats, health from Hilarius, the arch-priest, and keeper
of the place of the holy Apostolic See; John, the deacon, and elect in the
name of God; from John, the chief secretary and keeper of the place of the
holy Apostolic See, and from John, the servant of God, and counsellor of the
same Apostolic See.* The writings which were brought by the bearers
to Pope Severinus, of holy memory, were left, at his death, without
an answer to the things contained in them. Lest such intricate
questions should remain unresolved, we opened the same, and
found that some of your province, endeavouring to revive a new
heresy out of an old one, contrary to the orthodox faith, do

through ignorance reject our Easter, when Christ was sacrificed; and contend that the same should be kept on the fourteenth moon with the Hebrews."

By this beginning of the epistle it evidently appears that this heresy sprang up among them of very late times, and that not all their nation, but only some of them, had fallen into the same.

After having laid down the manner of keeping Easter, they add this concerning the Pelagians in the same epistle.

"And we have also understood that the poison of the Pelagian heresy again springs up among you; we, therefore, exhort you, that you put away from your thoughts all such venomous and superstitious wickedness. For you cannot be ignorant how that execrable heresy has been condemned; for it has not only been abolished these two hundred years, but it is also daily anathematised for ever by us; and we exhort you, now that the weapons of their controversy have been burnt; not to rake up the ashes. For who will not detest that insolent and impious proposition, 'That man can live without sin of his own free will, and not through God's grace?' And in the first place, it is the folly of blasphemy to say that man is without sin, which none can be, but only the Mediator of God and man, the man Christ Jesus, who was conceived and born without sin; for all other men, being born in original sin, are known to bear the mark of Adam's prevarication, even whilst they are without actual sin, according to the saying of the prophet, 'For behold, I was shapen in iniquity; and in sin did my mother conceive me.'"

CHAPTER XX

EDWIN BEING SLAIN, PAULINUS RETURNS INTO KENT, AND HAS THE BISHOPRIC OF ROCHESTER CONFERRED UPON HIM. [A.D. 633.]

EDWIN reigned most gloriously seventeen years over the nations of the English and the Britons, six whereof, as has been said, he also was a servant in the kingdom of Christ. Cadwalla, king of the

Britons, rebelled against him, being supported by Penda, a most warlike man of the royal race of the Mercians, and who from that time governed that nation twenty-two years with various success. A great battle being fought in the plain that is called Heathfield, Edwin was killed on the 12th of October, in the year of our Lord 633, being then forty-seven years of age, and all his army was either slain or dispersed. In the same war also, before him, fell Osfrid, one of his sons, a warlike youth; Eanfrid, another of them, compelled by necessity, went over to King Penda, and was by him afterwards, in the reign of Oswald, slain, contrary to his oath. At this time a great slaughter was made in the church or nation of the Northumbrians; and the more so because one of the commanders, by whom it was made, was a pagan, and the other a barbarian, more cruel than a pagan; for Penda, with all the nation of the Mercians, was an idolater, and a stranger to the name of Christ; but Cadwalla, though he bore the name and professed himself a Christian, was so barbarous in his disposition and behaviour, that he neither spared the female sex, nor the innocent age of children, but with savage cruelty put them to tormenting deaths, ravaging all their country for a long time, and resolving to cut off all the race of the English within the borders of Britain. Nor did he pay any respect to the Christian religion which had newly taken root among them; it being to this day the custom of the Britons not to pay any respect to the faith and religion of the English, nor to correspond with them any more than with pagans. King Edwin's head was brought to York, and afterwards into the church of St. Peter the Apostle, which he had begun, but which his successor Oswald finished, as has been said before. It was deposited in the porch of St. Gregory, Pope, from whose disciples he had received the word of life.

The affairs of the Northumbrians being in confusion, by reason of this disaster, without any prospect of safety except in flight, Paulinus, taking with him Queen Ethelberga, whom he had before brought thither, returned into Kent by sea, and was honourably received by the Archbishop Honorius and King Eadbald. He came thither under the conduct of Bassus, a most valiant soldier of King Edwin, having with him Eanfleda, the daughter, and Wuscfrea, the son of Edwin, as also Iffi, the son of Osfrid, his son, whom afterwards the mother, for fear of Eadbald and Oswald, sent over into France to be bred up by King Dagobert, who was her friend; and there they both died in infancy, and were buried in the church with the honour due to royal children and to innocents of Christ. He also brought with him many rich goods of King Edwin, among which were a large gold cross, and a golden chalice, dedicated to the use of the altar, which are still preserved, and shown in the church of Canterbury.

At that time the church of Rochester had no bishop, for Romanus, the prelate thereof, being sent to Pope Honorius, by Archbishop Justus, as his legate, was drowned in the Italian Sea; and thereupon Paulinus, at the request of Archbishop Honorius, and King Eadbald, took upon him the charge of the same, and held it until he departed to heaven, with the glorious fruits of his labours; and, dying in that church, he left there the pall which he had received from the pope of Rome. He had left behind him in his church at York, James, the deacon, a holy ecclesiastic, who continuing long after in that church, by teaching and baptizing, rescued much prey from the power of the old enemy of mankind; from whom the village, where he mostly resided, near Cataract, has its name to this day. He was extraordinarily skilful in singing, and when the province was afterwards restored to peace, and the number of the faithful increased, he began to teach many of the church to sing, according to the custom of the Romans, or of the Cantuarians. And being old and full of days, as the Scripture says, he went the way of his forefathers.

BOOK III

CHAPTER I

HOW KING EDWIN'S NEXT SUCCESSORS LOST BOTH
THE FAITH OF THEIR NATION AND THE KINGDOM;
BUT THE MOST CHRISTIAN KING OSWALD RETRIEVED
BOTH. [A.D. 633.]

EDWIN being slain in battle, the kingdom of the Deira, to which
province his family belonged, and where he first began to reign,
devolved on Osric, the son of his uncle Elfric, who, through the
preaching of Paulinus, had also received the faith. But the kingdom of the Bernicians—for into these two provinces the nation of
the Northumbrians was formerly divided—was possessed by
Eanfrid, the son of Ethelfrid, who derived his origin from the
royal family of that province. For all the time that Edwin reigned,
the sons of the aforesaid Ethelfrid, who had reigned before him,
with many of the nobility, lived in banishment among the Scots or
Picts, and were there instructed according to the doctrine of the
Scots, and received the grace of baptism. Upon the death of the
king, their enemy, they returned home, and Eanfrid, as the eldest
of them, mentioned above, became king of the Bernicians. Both
those kings, as soon as they obtained the government of their
earthly kingdoms, renounced and lost the faith of the heavenly
kingdom, and again delivered themselves up to be defiled by the
abominations of their former idols.

But soon after, the king of the Britons, Cadwalla, slew them both, through the rightful vengeance of Heaven, though the act was base in him. He first slew Osric, the next summer; for, being besieged by him in a strong town, he sallied out on a sudden with all his forces, by surprise, and destroyed him and all his army. After this, for the space of a year, he reigned over the provinces of the Northumbrians, not like a victorious king, but like a rapacious and bloody tyrant, and at length brought to the same end Eanfrid, who unadvisedly came to him with only twelve chosen soldiers, to sue for peace. To this day, that year is looked upon as unhappy, and hateful to all good men; as well on account of the apostasy of the English kings, who had renounced the faith, as of the outrageous tyranny of the British king. Hence it has been agreed by all who have written about the reigns of the kings, to abolish the memory of those perfidious monarchs, and to assign that year to the reign of the following king, Oswald, a man beloved by God. This last king, after the death of his brother Eanfrid, advanced with an army, small, indeed, in number, but strengthened with the faith of Christ; and the impious commander of the Britons was slain, though he had most numerous forces, which he boasted nothing could withstand, at a place in the English tongue called Denises-burn, that is, Denis's-brook.

CHAPTER II

HOW, AMONG INNUMERABLE OTHER MIRACULOUS CURES WROUGHT BY THE CROSS, WHICH KING OSWALD, BEING READY TO ENGAGE AGAINST THE BARBARIANS, ERECTED, A CERTAIN YOUTH HAD HIS LAME ARM HEALED. [A.D. 635.]

THE place is shown to this day, and held in much veneration, where Oswald, being about to engage, erected the sign of the holy cross, and on his knees prayed to God that he would assist his worshippers in their great distress. It is further reported, that the cross being made in haste, and the hole dug in which it was to be fixed, the king himself, full of faith, laid hold of it and held it with both his hands, till it was set fast by throwing in the earth; and this done, raising his voice, he cried to his army, "Let us all kneel, and jointly beseech the true and living God Almighty, in his mercy, to defend us from the haughty and fierce enemy; for He knows that we have undertaken a just war for the safety of our nation." All did as he had commanded, and accordingly advancing towards the enemy with the first dawn of day, they obtained the victory, as their faith deserved. In that place of prayer very many miraculous cures are known to have been performed, as a token and memorial of the king's faith; for even to this day, many are wont to cut off small chips from the wood of the holy cross, which being put into water, men or cattle drinking thereof, or sprinkled with that water, are immediately restored to health.

The place in the English tongue is called Heavenfield, or the Heavenly Field, which name it formerly received as a presage of what was afterwards to happen, denoting, that there the heavenly trophy would be erected, the heavenly victory begun, and heavenly miracles be wrought to this day. The same place is near the wall with which the Romans formerly enclosed the island from sea to sea, to restrain the fury of the barbarous nations, as has been said before. Hither also the brothers of the church of Hagulstad, which is not far from thence, repair yearly on the day before that on which King Oswald was afterwards slain, to watch there for the health of his soul, and having sung many psalms, to offer for him in the morning the sacrifice of the holy oblation. And since that good custom has spread, they have lately built and consecrated a church there, which has attached additional sanctity and honour to that place: and this with good reason; for it appears that there was no sign of the Christian faith, no church, no altar erected throughout all the nations of the Bernicians, before that new commander of the army, prompted by the devotion of his faith, set up the cross as he was going to give battle to his barbarous enemy.

Nor is it foreign to our purpose to relate one of the many miracles that have been wrought at this cross. One of the brothers of the same church of Hagulstad, whose name is Bothelm, and who is still living, a few years since, walking carelessly on the ice at night, suddenly fell and broke his arm; a most raging pain commenced in the broken part, so that he could not lift his arm to his mouth for the violence of the anguish. Hearing one morning that one of the brothers designed to go to the place of the holy cross, he desired him, at his return, to bring him a bit of that venerable wood, saying, he believed that with the help of God he might thereby be healed. The brother did as he was desired; and returning in the evening, when the brothers were sitting at table, gave him some of the old moss which grew on the surface of the wood. As he sat at table, having no place to lay up that which was brought him, he put the same into his bosom; and forgetting when he went to bed to put it by, left it in his bosom. Awaking in the middle of the night, he felt something cold lying by his side, and putting his hand to feel what it was, he found his arm and hand as sound as if he had never felt any such pain.

CHAPTER III

THE SAME KING OSWALD, ASKING A BISHOP OF THE SCOTTISH NATION, HAD AIDAN SENT HIM, AND GRANTED HIM AN EPISCOPAL SEE IN THE ISLE OF LINDISFARNE. [A.D. 635.]

THE same Oswald, as soon as he ascended the throne, being desirous that all his nation should receive the Christian faith, whereof he had found happy experience in vanquishing the barbarians, sent to the elders of the Scots, among whom himself and his followers, when in banishment, had received the sacrament of baptism, desiring they would send him, a bishop, by whose instruction and ministry the English nation, which he governed, might be taught the advantages, and receive the sacraments of the Christian faith. Nor were they slow in granting his request; but sent him Bishop Aidan, a man of singular meekness, piety, and moderation; zealous in the cause of God, though not altogether according to knowledge; for he was wont to keep Easter Sunday according to the custom of his country, which we have before so often mentioned, from the fourteenth to the twentieth moon; the northern province of the Scots, and all the nation of the Picts, celebrating Easter then after that manner, and believing that they therein followed the writings of the holy and praiseworthy Father Anatolius; the truth of which every skilful person can discern. But the Scots which dwelt in the South of Ireland had long since, by the admonition of the bishop of the Apostolic See, learned to observe Easter according to the canonical custom.

On the arrival of the bishop, the king appointed him his episcopal see in the isle of Lindisfarne, as he desired. Which place, as the tide flows and ebbs twice a day, is enclosed by the waves of the sea like an island; and again, twice in the day, when the shore is left dry, becomes contiguous to the land. The king also humbly and willingly in all cases giving ear to his admonitions, industriously applied himself to build and extend the church of Christ in his kingdom; wherein, when the bishop, who was not skilful in the English tongue, preached the gospel, it was most delightful to see the king himself interpreting the word of God to his commanders and ministers, for he had perfectly learned the language of the Scots during his long banishment. From that time many of the Scots came daily into Britain, and with great devotion preached the word to those provinces of the English, over which King Oswald reigned, and those among them that had received priest's orders, administered to them the grace of baptism. Churches were built in several places; the people joyfully flocked together to hear the word; money and lands were given of the king's bounty to build monasteries; the English, great and small, were, by their Scottish masters, instructed in the rules and observance of regular discipline; for most of them that came to preach were monks. Bishop Aidan was himself a monk of the island called Hii, whose monastery was for a long time the chief of almost all those of the northern Scots, and all those of the Picts, and had the direction of their people. That island belongs to Britain, being divided from it by a small arm of the sea, but had been long since given by the Picts, who inhabit those parts of Britain, to the Scottish monks, because they had received the faith of Christ through their preaching.

CHAPTER IV

WHEN THE NATION OF THE PICTS RECEIVED THE FAITH. [A.D. 565.]

In the year of our Lord 565, when Justin, the younger, the successor of Justinian, had the government of the Roman empire, there came into Britain a famous priest and abbat, a monk by habit and life, whose name was Columba, to preach the word of God to the provinces of the northern Picts, who are separated from the southern parts by steep and rugged mountains; for the southern Picts, who dwell on this side of those mountains, had long before, as is reported, forsaken the errors of idolatry, and embraced the truth, by the preaching of Ninias, a most reverend bishop and holy man of the British nation, who had been regularly instructed at Rome, in the faith and mysteries of the truth; whose episcopal see, named after St. Martin the bishop, and famous for a stately church (wherein he and many other saints rest in the body), is still in existence among the English nation. The place belongs to the province of the Bernicians, and is generally called the White House, because he there built a church of stone, which was not usual among the Britons.

Columba came into Britain in the ninth year of the reign of Bridius, who was the son of Meilochon, and the powerful king of the Pictish nation, and he converted that nation to the faith of Christ, by his preaching and example, whereupon he also received of them the aforesaid island for a monastery, for it is not very large, but contains about five families, according to the English computation. His successors hold the island to this day; he was also buried therein, having died at the age of seventy-seven, about thirty-two years after he came into Britain to preach. Before he passed over into Britain, he had built a noble monastery in Ireland, which, from the great number of oaks, is in the Scottish tongue called Dearmach—The Field of Oaks. From both which monasteries, many others had their beginning through his disciples, both in Britain and Ireland; but the monastery in the island where his body lies, is the principal of them all.

That island has for its ruler an abbat, who is a priest, to whose direction all the province, and even the bishops, contrary to the usual method, are subject, according to the example of their first teacher, who was not a bishop, but a priest and monk; of whose life and discourses some writings are said to be preserved by his disciples. But whatsoever he was himself, this we know for certain, that he left successors renowned for their continency, their love of God, and observance of monastic rules. It is true they followed uncertain rules in their observance of the great festival, as having none to bring them the synodal decrees for the observance of Easter, by reason of their being so far away from the rest of the world; wherefore they only practised such works of piety and chastity as they could learn from the prophetical, evangelical, and apostolical writings. This manner of keeping Easter continued among them for the space of 150 years, till the year of our Lord's incarnation 715.

But then the most reverend and holy father and priest, Egbert, of the English nation, who had long lived in banishment in Ireland for the sake of Christ, and was most learned in the Scriptures, and renowned for long perfection of life, came among them, corrected their error, and reduced them to the true and canonical day of Easter; the which they nevertheless did not always keep on the fourteenth moon with the Jews, as some imagined, but on Sunday, although not in the proper week. For, as Christians, they knew that the resurrection of our Lord, which happened on the first day after the Sabbath, was always to be celebrated on the first day after the Sabbath; but being rude and barbarous, they had not learned when that same first day after the Sabbath, which is now called the Lord's day, should come. But because they had not laid aside the fervent grace of charity, they were worthy to be informed in the true knowledge of this particular, according to the promise of the apostle, saying, "And if in any thing ye be otherwise minded, God shall reveal even this unto you." Of which we shall speak more fully in its proper place.

CHAPTER V

OF THE LIFE OF BISHOP AIDAN. [A.D. 635.]

FROM the aforesaid island, and college of monks, was Aidan sent to instruct the English nation in Christ, having received the dignity of a bishop at the time when Segenius, abbat and priest, presided over that monastery; whence, among other instructions for life, he left the clergy a most salutary example of abstinence or continence; it was the highest commendation of his doctrine, with all men, that he taught no otherwise than he and his followers had lived; for he neither sought nor loved any thing of this world, but delighted in distributing immediately among the poor whatsoever was given him by the kings or rich men of the world. He was wont to traverse both town and country on foot, never on horseback, unless compelled by some urgent necessity; and wherever in his way he saw any, either rich or poor, he invited them, if infidels, to embrace the mystery of the faith; or if they were believers, to strengthen them in the faith, and to stir them up by words and actions to alms and good works.

His course of life was so different from the slothfulness of our times, that all those who bore him company, whether they were shorn monks or laymen, were employed in meditation, that is, either in reading the Scriptures, or learning psalms. This was the daily employment of himself and all that were with him, wheresoever they went; and if it happened, which was but seldom, that he was invited to eat with the king, he went with one or two clerks, and having taken a small repast, made haste to be gone with them, either to read or write. At that time, many religious men and women, stirred up by his example, adopted the custom of fasting on Wednesdays and Fridays, till the ninth hour, throughout the year, except during the fifty days after Easter. He never gave money to the powerful men of the world, but only meat, if he happened to entertain them; and, on the contrary, whatsoever gifts of money he received from the rich, he either distributed them, as has been said, to the use of the poor, or bestowed them in ransoming such as had been wrongfully sold for slaves. Moreover, he afterwards made many of those he had ransomed his disciples, and after having taught and instructed them, advanced them to the order of priesthood.

It is reported, that when King Oswald had asked a bishop of the Scots to administer the word of faith to him and his nation, there was first sent to him another man of more austere disposition, who, meeting with no success, and being unregarded by the English people, returned home, and in an assembly of the elders reported, that he had not been able to do any good to the nation he had been sent to preach to, because they were uncivilized men, and of a stubborn and barbarous disposition. They, as is testified, in a great council seriously debated what was to be done, being desirous that the nation should receive the salvation it demanded, and grieving that they had not received the preacher sent to them. Then said Aidan, who was also present in the council, to the priest then spoken of, "I am of opinion, brother, that you were more severe to your unlearned hearers than you ought to have been, and did not at first, conformably to the apostolic rule, give them the milk of more easy doctrine, till being by degrees nourished with the word of God, they should be capable of greater perfection, and be able to practise God's sublimer precepts." Having heard these words, all present began diligently to weigh what he had said, and presently concluded, that he deserved to be made a bishop, and ought to be sent to instruct the incredulous and unlearned; since he was found to be endued with singular discretion, which is the mother of other virtues, and accordingly being ordained, they sent him to their friend, King Oswald, to preach; and he, as time proved, afterwards appeared to possess all other virtues, as well as the discretion for which he was before remarkable.

CHAPTER VI

OF KING OSWALD'S WONDERFUL PIETY. [A.D. 635.]

KING Oswald, with the nation of the English which he governed being instructed by the teaching of this most reverend prelate, not only learned to hope for a heavenly kingdom unknown to his progenitors, but also obtained of the same one Almighty God, who made heaven and earth, larger earthly kingdoms than any of his ancestors. In short, he brought under his dominion all the nations and provinces of Britain, which are divided into four languages, viz. the Britons, the Picts, the Scots, and the English. When raised to that height of dominion, wonderful to relate, he always continued humble, affable, and generous to the poor and strangers.

In short, it is reported, that when he was once sitting at dinner, on the holy day of Easter, with the aforesaid bishop, and a silver dish full of dainties before him, and they were just ready to bless the bread, the servant, whom he had appointed to relieve the poor, came in on a sudden, and told the king, that a great multitude of needy persons from all parts were sitting in the streets begging some alms of the king; he immediately ordered the meat set before him to be carried to the poor, and the dish to be cut in pieces and divided among them. At which sight, the bishop who sat by him, much taken with such an act of piety, laid hold of his right hand, and said, "May this hand never perish." Which fell out according to his prayer, for his arm and hand, being cut off from his body, when he was slain in battle, remain entire and uncorrupted to this day, and are kept in a silver case, as revered relics, in St. Peter's church in the royal city, which has taken its name from Bebba, one of its former queens. Through this king's management the provinces of the Deiri and the Bernicians, which till then had been at variance, were peacefully united and moulded into one people. He was nephew to King Edwin by his sister Acha; and it was fit that so great a predecessor should have in his own family so great a person to succeed him in his religion and sovereignty.

CHAPTER VII

HOW THE WEST SAXONS RECEIVED THE WORD OF GOD BY THE PREACHING OF BIRINUS; AND OF HIS SUCCESSORS, AGILBERT AND ELEUTHERIUS. [A.D. 635.]

AT that time, the West Saxons, formerly called Gewissæ, in the reign of Cynegils, embraced the faith of Christ, at the preaching of Bishop Birinus, who came into Britain by the advice of Pope Honorius; having promised in his presence that he would sow the seed of the holy faith in the inner parts beyond the dominions of the English, where no other teacher had been before him. Hereupon he received episcopal consecration from Asterius, bishop of Genoa; but on his arrival in Britain, he first entered the nation of the Gewissæ, and finding all there most confirmed pagans, he thought it better to preach the word of God there, than to proceed further to seek for others to preach to.

Now, as he preached in the aforesaid province, it happened that the king himself, having been catechised, was baptized together with his people, and Oswald, the most holy and victorious king of the Northumbrians, being present, received him as he came forth from baptism, and by an alliance most pleasing and acceptable to God, first adopted him, thus regenerated, for his son, and then took his daughter in marriage. The two kings gave to the bishop the city called Dorcic, there to settle his episcopal see; where having built and consecrated churches, and by his labour called many to the Lord, he departed this life, and was buried in the same city; but many years after, when Hedda was bishop, he was translated thence to the city of Winchester, and laid in the church of the blessed apostles, Peter and Paul.

The king also dying, his son Coinwalch succeeded him in the throne, but refused to embrace the mysteries of the faith, and of the heavenly kingdom; and not long after also he lost the dominion of his earthly kingdom; for he put away the sister of Penda, king of the Mercians, whom he had married, and took another wife; whereupon a war ensuing, he was by him expelled his kingdom, and withdrew to Anna, king of the East Saxons, where living three years in banishment, he found and received the true faith, and was baptized; for the king, with whom he lived in his banishment, was a good man, and happy in a good and pious offspring, as we shall show hereafter.

But when Coinwalch was restored to his kingdom, there came into that province out of Ireland, a certain bishop called Agilbert, by nation a Frenchman, but who had then lived a long time in Ireland, for the purpose of reading the Scriptures. This bishop came of his own accord to serve this king, and preach to him the word of life. The king, observing his erudition and industry, desired him to accept an episcopal see, and stay there as his bishop. Agilbert complied with the prince's request, and presided over those people many years. At length the king, who understood none but the language of the Saxons, grown weary of that bishop's barbarous tongue, brought into the province another bishop of his own nation, whose name was Wini, who had been ordained in France; and dividing his province into two dioceses, appointed this last his episcopal see in the city of Winchester, by the Saxons called Wintancestir. Agilbert, being highly offended, that the king should do this without his advice, returned into France, and being made bishop of the city of Paris, died there, aged and full of days. Not many years after his departure out of Britain, Wini was also expelled from his bishopric, and took refuge with Wulfhere, king of the Mercians, of whom he purchased for money the see of the city of London, and remained bishop thereof till his death. Thus the province of the West Saxons continued no small time without a bishop.

During which time, the king of that nation, sustaining very great losses in his kingdom from his enemies, at length bethought himself, that as he had been before expelled from the throne for his infidelity, and had been restored when he received the faith of Christ, his kingdom, being destitute of a bishop, was justly deprived of the Divine protection. He, therefore, sent messengers into France to Agilbert, humbly entreating him to return to the bishopric of his nation. But he excused himself, and affirmed that he could not go, because he was bound to the bishopric of his own city; however, that he might not seem to refuse him assistance, he sent in his stead thither the priest Eleutherius, his nephew, who, if he thought fit, might be ordained his bishop, saying, "He thought him worthy of a bishopric." The king and the people received him honourably, and entreated Theodore, then archbishop of Canterbury, to consecrate him their bishop. He was accordingly consecrated in the same city, and many years zealously governed the whole bishopric of the West Saxons by synodical authority.

CHAPTER VIII

HOW EARCONBERT, KING OF KENT, ORDERED THE IDOLS TO BE DESTROYED; AND OF HIS DAUGHTER EARCON-GOTA, AND HIS KINSWOMAN ETHELBERGA, VIRGINS, CONSECRATED TO GOD. [A.D. 640.]

IN the year of our Lord 640, Eadbald, king of Kent, departed this life, and left his kingdom to his son Earconbert, which he most nobly governed twenty-four years and some months. He was the first of the English kings that of his supreme authority commanded the idols, throughout his whole kingdom, to be forsaken and destroyed, and the fast of forty days before Easter to be observed; and that the same might not be neglected, he appointed proper and condign punishments for the offenders. His daughter Earcongota, as became the offspring of such a parent, was a most virtuous virgin, always serving God in a monastery in France, built by a most noble abbess, called Fara, at a place called Brie; for at that time but few monasteries being built in the country of the Angles, many were wont, for the sake of monastic conversation, to repair to the monasteries of the Franks or Gauls; and they also sent their daughters there to be instructed, and delivered to their heavenly bridegroom, especially in the monasteries of Brie, of Chelles, and Andelys. Among whom was also Sethrid, daughter of the wife of Anna, king of the East Angles, above mentioned; and Ethelberga, natural daughter of the same king; both of whom, though strangers, were for their virtue made abbesses of the monastery of Brie. Sexberga, that king's eldest daughter, wife to Earconbert, king of Kent, had a daughter called Earcongota, of whom we are about to speak.

Many wonderful works and miracles of this virgin, dedicated to God, are to this day related by the inhabitants of that place; but it shall suffice us to say something briefly of her passage out of this world to the heavenly kingdom. The day of her departure drawing near, she visited the cells of the infirm servants of Christ, and particularly those that were of a great age, or most noted for probity of life, and humbly recommending herself to their prayers, let them know that her death was at hand, as she knew by revelation, which she said she had received in this manner. She had seen a number of men, all in white, come into the monastery, and being asked by her, "What they wanted, and what they did there?" they answered, "They had been sent thither to carry away with them the gold medal that had been brought thither from Kent." That same night, at the dawn of morning, leaving the darkness of this world, she departed to the light of heaven. Many of the brethren of that monastery that were in other houses, declared they had then plainly heard concerts of angels singing, and the noise as it were of a multitude entering the monastery. Whereupon going out immediately to see what it might be, they saw an extraordinary great light coming down from heaven, which conducted that holy soul, set loose from the bonds of the flesh, to the eternal joys of the celestial country. They add other miracles that were wrought the same night in the same monastery; but as we must proceed to other matters, we leave them to be related by those to whom such things belong. The body of this venerable virgin and bride of Christ was buried in the church of the blessed protomartyr, Stephen. It was thought fit, three days after, to take up the stone that covered the grave, and to raise it higher in the same place, and while they did this, so great a fragrancy of perfume rose from below, that it seemed to all the brothers and sisters there present, as if a store of the richest balsams had been opened.

Her aunt also, Ethelberga above mentioned, preserved the glory so pleasing to God, of perpetual virginity, in great continency of body, but the extent of her virtue became more conspicuous after her death. Whilst she was abbess, she began to build in her monastery a church, in honour of all the apostles, wherein she desired her body might be buried; but when that work was advanced half way, she was prevented by death from finishing it, and buried in the very place of the church where she had desired. After her death, the brothers occupied themselves with other things, and this structure was intermitted for seven years, at the expiration whereof they resolved, by reason of the greatness of the work, wholly to lay aside the building of the church, but to remove the abbess's bones from thence to some other church that was finished and consecrated; but, on opening her tomb, they found the body as free from decay as it had been from the corruption of carnal concupiscence, and having washed it again and put on it other clothes, they removed the same to the church of St. Stephen, Martyr, whose nativity (or commemoration-day) is celebrated with much magnificence on the 7th of July.

CHAPTER IX

HOW MIRACULOUS CURES HAVE BEEN FREQUENTLY
DONE IN THE PLACE WHERE KING OSWALD WAS KILLED;
AND HOW, FIRST, A TRAVELLER'S HORSE WAS RESTORED
AND AFTERWARDS A YOUNG GIRL CURED OF THE
PALSY. [A.D. 642.]

OSWALD, the most Christian king of the Northumbrians, reigned nine years, including that year which is to be held accursed for the brutal impiety of the king of the Britons, and the apostasy of the English kings; for, as was said above, it is agreed by the unanimous consent of all, that the names of the apostates should be erased from the catalogue of the Christian kings, and no date ascribed to their reign. After which period, Oswald was killed in a great battle, by the same pagan nation and pagan king of the Mercians, who had slain his predecessor Edwin, at a place called in the English tongue Maserfield, in the thirty-eighth year of his age, on the fifth day of the month of August.

How great his faith was towards God, and how remarkable his devotion, has been made evident by miracles since his death; for, in the place where he was killed by the pagans, fighting for his country, infirm men and cattle are healed to this day. Whereupon many took up the very dust of the place where his body fell, and putting it into water, did much good with it to their friends who were sick. This custom came so much into use, that the earth being carried away by degrees, there remained a hole as deep as the height of a man. Nor is it to be wondered that the sick should be healed in the place where he died; for, whilst he lived, he never ceased to provide for the poor and infirm, and to bestow alms on them, and assist them. Many miracles are said to have been wrought in that place, or with the earth carried from thence; but we have thought it sufficient to mention two, which we heard from our ancestors.

It happened, not long after his death, that a man was travelling near that place, when his horse on a sudden began to tire, to stand stock still, hang down his head, and foam at the mouth, and, at length, as his pain increased, he fell to the ground; the rider dismounted, and throwing some straw under him, waited to see whether the beast would recover or die. At length, after much rolling about in extreme anguish, the horse happened to come to the very place where the aforesaid king died. Immediately the pain ceased, the beast gave over his struggles, and, as is usual with tired cattle, turned gently from side to side, and then starting up, perfectly recovered, began to graze on the green herbage; which the man observing, being an ingenious person, he concluded there must be some wonderful sanctity in the place where the horse had been healed, and left a mark there, that he might know the spot again. After which he again mounted his horse, and repaired to the inn where he intended to stop. On his arrival he found a girl, niece to the landlord, who had long languished under the palsy; and when the friends of the family, in his presence, lamented the girl's calamity, he gave them an account of the place where his horse had been cured. In short, she was put into a cart and carried and laid down at the place. At first she slept awhile, and when she awaked found herself healed of her infirmity. Upon which she called for water, washed her face, put up her hair, and dressed her head, and returned home on foot, in good health, with those who had brought her.

CHAPTER X

THE POWER OF THE EARTH OF THAT PLACE AGAINST FIRE. [A.D. 642.]

ABOUT the same time, another person of the British nation, as is reported, happened to travel by the same place, where the aforesaid battle was fought, and observing one particular spot of ground greener and more beautiful than any other part of the field, he judiciously concluded with himself that there could be no other cause for that unusual greenness, but that some person of more holiness than any other in the army had been killed there. He therefore took along with him some of that earth, tying it up in a linen cloth, supposing it would some time or other be of use for curing sick people, and proceeding on his journey, came at night to a certain village, and entered a house where the neighbours were feasting at supper; being received by the owners of the house, he sat down with them at the entertainment, hanging the cloth, in which he had brought the earth, on a post against the wall. They sat long at supper and drank hard, with a great fire in the middle of the room; it happened that the sparks flew up and caught the top of the house, which being made of wattles and thatch, was presently in a flame; the guests ran out in a fright, without being able to put a stop to the fire. The house was consequently burnt down, only that post on which the earth hung remained entire and untouched. On observing this, they were all amazed, and inquiring into it diligently, understood that the earth had been taken from the place where the blood of King Oswald had been shed. These miracles being made known and reported abroad, many began daily to frequent that place, and received health to themselves and theirs.

CHAPTER XI

OF THE HEAVENLY LIGHT THAT APPEARED ALL THE
NIGHT OVER THE BONES OF KING OSWALD, AND HOW
PERSONS POSSESSED WITH DEVILS WERE DELIVERED BY
HIS BONES. [A.D. 697.]

AMONG the rest, I think we ought not to pass over, in silence, the heavenly favours and miracles that were shown when King Oswald's bones were found, and translated into the church where they are now preserved. This was done by the zealous care of Osthrida, queen of the Mercians, the daughter of his brother Oswy, who reigned after him, as shall be said hereafter.

There is a noble monastery in the province of Lindsey, called Beardeneu, which that queen and her husband Ethelred much loved, and conferred upon it many honours and ornaments. It was here that she was desirous to lay the venerable bones of her uncle. When the wagon in which those bones were carried arrived towards evening at the aforesaid monastery, they that were in it refused to admit them, because, though they knew him to be a holy man, yet, as he was originally of another province, and had reigned over them as a foreign king, they retained their ancient aversion to him, even after death. Thus it came to pass that the relics were left in the open air all that night, with only a large tent spread over them; but the appearance of a heavenly miracle showed with how much reverence they ought to be received by all the faithful; for during that whole night, a pillar of light, reaching from the wagon up to heaven, was seen by almost all the inhabitants of the province of Lindsey. Hereupon, in the morning, the brethren who had refused it the day before, began themselves earnestly to pray that those holy relics, so beloved by God, might be deposited among them. Accordingly, the bones, being washed, were put into a shrine which they had made for that purpose, and placed in the church, with due honour; and that there might be a perpetual memorial of the royal person of this holy man, they hung up over the monument his banner made of gold and purple; and poured out the water in which they had washed the bones, in a corner of the sacred place. From that time, the very earth which received that holy water, had the virtue of expelling devils from the bodies of persons possessed.

Lastly, when the aforesaid queen afterwards made some stay in that monastery, there came to visit her a certain venerable abbess, who is still living, called Ethelhilda, the sister of the holy men, Ethelwin and Aldwin, the first of whom was bishop in the province of Lindsey, the other abbat of the monastery of Peartaneu; not far from which was the monastery of Ethelhilda. When this lady was come, in a conversation between her and the queen, the discourse, among other things, turning upon Oswald, she said, that she also had that night seen a light reaching from the relics up to heaven. The queen thereupon added, that the very dust of the pavement on which the water that washed the bones had been spilt, had already healed many sick persons. The abbess thereupon desired that some of the said dust might be given her, which she tied up in a cloth, and, putting it into a casket, returned home. Some time after, when she was in her monastery, there came to it a guest, who was wont often in the night to be on a sudden grievously tormented with an evil spirit; he being hospitably entertained, and gone to bed after supper, was on a sudden seized by the Devil, and began to cry out, to gnash his teeth, to foam at the mouth, and to distort his limbs in a most strange manner. None being able to hold or bind him, the servant ran, and knocking at the door, acquainted the abbess. She, opening the monastery door, went out herself with one of the nuns to the men's apartment, and calling a priest, desired he would go with her to the sufferer. Being come thither, and seeing many more present, who had not been able, though they endeavoured it, to hold the tormented person and prevent his convulsive motions, the priest used exorcisms, and did all he could to assuage the madness of the unfortunate man, but, though he took much pains, could not prevail. When no hopes appeared of easing him, the abbess bethought herself of the dust, and immediately ordered her servant to go and fetch her the casket in which it was. As soon as she came with what she had been sent for into the porch of the house, in the inner part whereof the possessed person was tormented, he was presently silent, and laid down his head, as if he had been falling asleep, stretching out all his limbs to rest. All present were silent, and stood attentive to see the end of the affair. After some time, the man that had been tormented sat up, and fetching a deep sigh, said, "Now I am like a sound man, for I am restored to my senses." They earnestly inquired how that came to pass, and he answered, "As soon as that virgin drew near the porch of this house, with the casket she brought, all the evil spirits that vexed me departed, and were no more to be seen." Then the abbess gave him a little of that dust, and the priest having prayed, he had a very quiet night; nor did he, from that time forward, receive the least disturbance from his old enemy.

CHAPTER XII

OF A BOY CURED OF AN AGUE AT ST. OSWALD'S TOMB. [A.D. 642.]

SOME time after, there was a certain little boy in the said monastery, who had been long troubled with an ague; he was one day anxiously expecting the hour that his fit was to come on, when one of the brothers, coming in to him, said, "Shall I tell you, child, how you may be cured of this distemper? Rise, go into the church, and get close to St. Oswald's tomb; stay there quiet, and do not leave it; do not come away, or stir from the place, till the time that your fit is to go off: then I will go in and fetch you away." The boy did as he was advised, and the disease durst not affect him as he sat by the saint's tomb; but fled so absolutely, that he felt it no more, either the second or third day, or ever after. The brother that came from thence, and told me this, added, that at the time when he was talking with me, the young man was then still living in the monastery, on whom, when a boy, that miraculous cure had been wrought. Nor is it to be wondered that the prayers of that king who was then reigning with our Lord, should be very efficacious with him, since he, whilst yet governing his temporal kingdom, was also wont to pray and take more pains for that which is eternal. In short, it is reported, that he often continued in prayer from the hour of morning thanksgiving till it was day; and that by reason of his constant custom of praying or giving thanks to God, he was wont always, wherever he sat, to hold his hands turned up on his knees. It is also given out, and become a proverb, "That he ended his life in prayer;" for when he was beset with weapons and enemies, he perceived he must immediately be killed, and prayed to God for the souls of his army. Whence it is proverbially said, "Lord, have mercy on their souls, said Oswald, as he fell to the ground." His bones, therefore, were translated to the monastery which we have mentioned, and buried therein: but the king that slew him commanded his head, hands, and arms to be cut off from the body, and set upon stakes. But his successor in the throne, Oswy, coming thither the next year with his army, took them down, and buried his head in the church of Lindisfarne, and the hands and arms in his royal city.

CHAPTER XIII

OF A CERTAIN PERSON IN IRELAND THAT WAS RECOVERED, WHEN AT THE POINT OF DEATH, BY THE BONES OF KING OSWALD. [A.D. 642.]

NOR was the fame of the renowned Oswald confined to Britain, but, spreading the rays of his healing brightness even beyond the sea, reached also to Germany and Ireland. In short, the most reverend prelate, Acca, is wont to relate, that when, in his journey to Rome, he and his bishop Wilfrid stayed some time with Wilbrord, now the holy bishop of the Fresons, he had often heard him talk of the wonders that had been wrought in that province at the relics of that most reverend king. And that in Ireland, when, being yet only a priest, he led a pilgrim's life therein for love of the eternal country, the fame of that king's sanctity was already spread far and near. One of the miracles, among the rest, which he related, we have thought fit to insert in our history.

"At the time," said he, "of the mortality which made such great havoc in Britain and Ireland, among others, the infection reached a certain scholar of the Scottish race, a man indeed learned in worldly literature, but in no way solicitous or studious of his eternal salvation; who, seeing his death near at hand, began to fear, lest, as soon as he was dead he should be hurried away to hell for his sins. He sent for me, who was in that neighbourhood, and whilst he was trembling and sighing, with a mournful voice made his complaint to me, in this manner: 'You see that my distemper increases, and that I am now reduced to the point of death. Nor do I question but that after the death of my body, I shall be immediately snatched away to the perpetual death of my soul, and cast into the torments of hell, since for a long time, amidst all my reading of divine books, I have rather addicted myself to vice, than to keep the commandments of God. But it is my resolution, if the Divine Mercy shall grant me a new term of life, to correct my vicious habits, and totally to reform my mind and course of life in obedience to the Divine will. But I am sensible, that I have no merits of my own to obtain a prolongation of life, nor can I confide in it, unless it shall please God to forgive me, through the assistance of those who have faithfully served Him. We have heard, and the report is universal, that there was in your nation a king, of wonderful sanctity, called Oswald, the excellency of whose faith and virtue is become renowned even after his death by the working of miracles. I beseech you, if you have any relics of his in your custody, that you will bring the same to me; in case the Lord shall be pleased, through his merits, to have mercy on me.' I answered, 'I have indeed some of the stake on which his head was set up by the pagans, when he was killed, and if you believe, with a sincere heart, the Divine Goodness may, through the merit of so great a man, both grant you a longer term of life here, and render you worthy of admittance into eternal life.' He answered immediately, 'That he had entire faith therein.' Then I blessed some water, and put into it a chip of the aforesaid oak, and gave it the sick man to drink. He presently found ease, and, recovering of his sickness, lived a long time after; and, being entirely converted to God in heart and actions, wherever he came, he spoke of the goodness of his merciful Creator, and the honour of His faithful servant."

CHAPTER XIV

ON THE DEATH OF PAULINUS, ITHAMAR WAS MADE
BISHOP OF ROCHESTER IN HIS STEAD. OF THE WONDER-
FUL HUMILITY OF KING OSWIN, WHO WAS CRUELLY
SLAIN BY OSWY. [A.D. 642.]

OSWALD being translated to the heavenly kingdom, his brother
Oswy, a young man of about thirty years of age, succeeded him on
the throne of his earthly kingdom, and held it twenty-eight years
with much trouble, being harassed by the pagan king, Penda, and
by the pagan nation of the Mercians, that had slain his brother, as
also by his son Alfred, and by his cousin-german Ethelwald, the
son of his brother who reigned before him. In his second year,
that is, in the year of our Lord 644, the most reverend Father
Paulinus, formerly bishop of York, but then of the city of
Rochester, departed to our Lord, on the 10th day of October, having held the bishopric nineteen years, two months, and twenty-
one days; and was buried in the sacristy of the blessed Apostle
Andrew, which King Ethelbert had built from the foundation, in
the same city of Rochester. In his place, Archbishop Honorius
ordained Ithamar, of the Kentish nation, but not inferior to his
predecessors for learning and conduct of life.

Oswy, during the first part of his reign, had a partner in the royal
dignity called Oswin, of the race of King Edwin, and son to Osric, of
whom we have spoken above, a man of wonderful piety and devotion, who governed the province of the Deiri seven years in very
great prosperity, and was himself beloved by all men. But Oswy, who
governed all the other northern part of the nation beyond the
Humber, that is, the province of the Bernicians, could not live at
peace with him; but on the contrary, the causes of their disagree-
ment being heightened, he murdered him most cruelly. For when
they had raised armies against one another, Oswin perceived that
he could not maintain a war against one who had more auxiliaries
than himself, and he thought it better at that time to lay aside all

thoughts of engaging, and to preserve himself for better times. He therefore dismissed the army which he had assembled, and ordered all his men to return to their own homes, from the place that is called Wilfaresdun, that is, Wilfar's Hill, which is almost ten miles distant from the village called Cataract, towards the north-west. He himself, with only one trusty soldier, whose name was Tondhere, withdrew and lay concealed in the house of Earl Hunwald, whom he imagined to be his most assured friend. But, alas! it was otherwise; for the earl betrayed him, and Oswy, in a detestable manner, by the hands of his commander, Ethilwin, slew him and the soldier aforesaid. This happened on the 20th of August, in the ninth year of his reign, at a place called Ingethlingum, where afterwards, to atone for his crime, a monastery was built, wherein prayers were to be daily offered up to God for the souls of both kings, that is, of him that was murdered, and of him that commanded him to be killed.

King Oswin was of a graceful aspect, and tall of stature, affable in discourse, and courteous in behaviour; and most bountiful, as well to the ignoble as the noble; so that he was beloved by all men for his qualities of body and mind, and persons of the first rank came from almost all provinces to serve him. Among other virtues and rare endowments, if I may so express it, humility is said to have been the greatest, which it will suffice to prove by one example.

He had given an extraordinarily fine horse to Bishop Aidan, which he might either use in crossing rivers, or in performing a journey upon any urgent necessity, though he was wont to travel ordinarily on foot. Some short time after, a poor man meeting him, and asking alms, he immediately dismounted, and ordered the horse, with all his royal furniture, to be given to the beggar; for he was very compassionate, a great friend to the poor, and, as it were, the father of the wretched. This being told to the king, when they were going in to dinner, he said to the bishop, "Why would you, my lord bishop, give the poor man that royal horse, which was necessary for your use? Had not we many other horses of less value, and of other sorts, which would have been good enough to give to the poor, and not to give that horse, which I had particularly chosen for yourself?" To whom the bishop instantly answered, "What is it you say, O king? Is that foal of a mare more dear to you than the Son of God?" Upon this they went in to dinner, and the bishop sat in his place; but the king, who was come from hunting, stood warming himself, with his attendants, at the fire. Then, on a sudden, whilst he was warming himself, calling to mind what the bishop had said to him, he ungirt his sword, and gave it to a servant, and in a hasty manner fell down at the bishop's feet, beseeching him to forgive him; "For from this time forward," said he, "I will never speak any more of this, nor will I judge of what, or how much of our money you shall give to the sons of God." The bishop was much moved at this sight, and starting up, raised him, saying, "He was entirely reconciled to him, if he would sit down to his meat, and lay aside all sorrow." The king, at the bishop's command and request, beginning to be merry, the bishop, on the other hand, grew so melancholy as to shed tears. His priest then asking him, in the language of his country, which the king and his servants did not understand, why he wept, "I know," said he, "that the king will not live long; for I never before saw so humble a king; whence I conclude that he will soon be snatched out of this life, because this nation is not worthy of such a ruler." Not long after, the bishop's prediction was fulfilled by the king's death, as has been said above. But Bishop Aidan himself was also taken out of this world, twelve days after the king he loved, on the 31st of August, to receive the eternal reward of his labours from our Lord.

CHAPTER XV

HOW BISHOP AIDAN FORETOLD TO CERTAIN SEAMEN A STORM THAT WOULD HAPPEN, AND GAVE THEM SOME HOLY OIL TO LAY IT. [A.D. 651.]

How great the merits of Aidan were, was made manifest by the all-seeing Judge, with the testimony of miracles, whereof it will suffice to mention three as a memorial. A certain priest, whose name was

Utta, a man of great gravity and sincerity, and on that account honoured by all men, even the princes of the world, being ordered to Kent, to bring from thence, as wife for King Oswy, Eanfleda, the daughter of King Edwin, who had been carried thither when her father was killed; and intending to go thither by land, but to return with the virgin by sea, repaired to Bishop Aidan, entreating him to offer up his prayers to our Lord for him and his company, who were then to set out on their journey. He, blessing and recommending them to our Lord, at the same time gave them some holy oil, saying, "I know that when you go abroad, you will meet with a storm and contrary wind; but do you remember to cast this oil I give you into the sea, and the wind shall cease immediately; you will have pleasant calm weather, and return home safe."

All which fell out as the bishop had predicted. For in the first place, the winds raging, the sailors endeavoured to ride it out at anchor, but all to no purpose; for the sea breaking in on all sides, and the ship beginning to be filled with water, they all concluded that certain death was at hand; the priest at last, remembering the bishop's words, laid hold of the phial and cast some of the oil into the sea, which, as had been foretold, became presently calm. Thus it came to pass that the man of God, by the spirit of prophecy, foretold the storm that was to happen, and by virtue of the same spirit, though absent, appeased the same. Which miracle was not told me by a person of little credit, but by Cynemund, a most faithful priest of our church, who declared that it was related to him by Utta, the priest, on and by whom the same was wrought.

CHAPTER XVI

HOW THE SAME AIDAN, BY HIS PRAYERS, SAVED THE ROYAL CITY WHEN FIRED BY THE ENEMY. [A.D. 651.]

ANOTHER notable miracle of the same father is related by many such as were likely to have knowledge thereof; for during the time that he was bishop, the hostile army of the Mercians, under the command of Penda, cruelly ravaged the country of the Northumbrians far and near, even to the royal city; which has its name from Bebba, formerly its queen. Not being able to enter it by force, or by a long siege, he endeavoured to burn it; and having destroyed all the villages in the neighbourhood of the city, he brought to it an immense quantity of planks, beams, wattles and thatch, wherewith he encompassed the place to a great height on the land side, and when the wind set upon it, he fired the mass, designing to burn the town.

At that time, the most reverend Bishop Aidan resided in the isle of Farne, which is nearly two miles from the city; for thither he was wont often to retire to pray in private, that he might be undisturbed. Indeed, this solitary residence of his is to this day shown in that island. When he saw the flames of fire and the smoke carried by the boisterous wind above the city walls, he is reported, with eyes and hands lifted up to heaven, to have said, "Behold, Lord, how great mischief Penda does!" Which words were hardly uttered, when the wind immediately turning from the city, drove back the flames upon those who had kindled them, so that some being hurt, and all frightened, they forbore any further attempts against the city, which they perceived was protected by the hand of God.

CHAPTER XVII

HOW THE POST OF THE CHURCH ON WHICH BISHOP AIDAN WAS LEANING WHEN HE DIED, COULD NOT BE BURNT WHEN THE REST OF THE CHURCH WAS CONSUMED BY FIRE; AND OF HIS INWARD LIFE. [A.D. 651.]

AIDAN was in the king's country-house, not far from the city of which we have spoken above, at the time when death separated him from his body, after he had been bishop sixteen years; for having a church and a chamber there, he was wont often to go and stay there, and to make excursions to preach in the country round about, which he likewise did at other of the king's country-seats, having nothing of his own besides his church and a few fields about it. When he was sick they set up a tent for him close to the wall at the west end of the church, by which means it happened that he gave up the ghost, leaning against a post that was on the outside to strengthen the wall. He died in the seventeenth year of his episcopacy, the last day of the month of August. His body was thence translated to the isle of Lindisfarne, and buried in the churchyard belonging to the brethren. Some time after, when a larger church was built there and dedicated in honour of the blessed prince of the apostles, his bones were translated thither, and deposited on the right hand of the altar, with the respect due to so great a prelate.

Finan, who had likewise come from the same monastery of Hii in the Scottish island, succeeded him, and continued a considerable time in the bishopric. It happened some years after, that Penda, king of the Mercians, coming into these parts with a hostile army, destroyed all he could with fire and sword, and burned down the village and church above mentioned, where the bishop died; but it fell out in a wonderful manner that the post, which he had leaned upon when he died, could not be consumed by the fire which consumed all about it. This miracle being taken notice of, the church was soon rebuilt in the same place, and that very post was set up on the outside, as it had been before, to strengthen the wall. It happened again, some time after, that the same village and church were burned down the second time, and even then the fire could not touch that post; and when in a most miraculous manner the fire broke through the very holes in it wherewith it was fixed to the building, and destroyed the church, yet it could do no hurt to the said post. The church being therefore built there the third time, they did not, as before, place that post on the outside as a support, but within, as a memorial of the miracle; and the people coming in were wont to kneel there, and implore the Divine mercy. And it is manifest that since then many have been healed in that same place, as also that chips being cut off from that post, and put into water, have healed many from their distempers.

I have written thus much concerning the person and works of the aforesaid Aidan, in no way commending or approving what he imperfectly understood in relation to the observance of Easter; nay, very much detesting the same, as I have most manifestly proved in the book I have written, "De Temporibus"; but, like an impartial historian, relating what was done by or with him, and commending such things as are praiseworthy in his actions, and preserving the memory thereof for the benefit of the readers; viz. his love of peace and charity; his continence and humility; his mind superior to anger and avarice, and despising pride and vainglory; his industry in keeping and teaching the heavenly commandments; his diligence in reading and watching; his authority becoming a priest in reproving the haughty and powerful, and at the same time his tenderness in comforting the afflicted, and relieving or defending the poor. To say all in a few words, as near as I could be informed by those that knew him, he took care to omit none of those things which he found in the apostolical or prophetical writings, but to the utmost of his power endeavoured to perform them all.

These things I much love and admire in the aforesaid bishop; because I do not doubt that they were pleasing to God; but I do not praise or approve his not observing Easter at the proper time, either through ignorance of the canonical time appointed, or, if he knew it, being prevailed on by the authority of his nation, not to follow the same. Yet this I approve in him, that in the celebration of his Easter, the object which he had in view in all he said, did, or preached, was the same as ours, that is, the redemption of mankind, through the passion, resurrection and ascension into heaven of the man Jesus Christ, who is mediator betwixt God and man. And therefore he always celebrated the same, not, as some falsely imagine, on the fourteenth moon, like the Jews, whatsoever the day was, but on the Lord's day, from the fourteenth to the twentieth moon; and this he did from his belief of the resurrection of our Lord happening on the day after the Sabbath, and for the hope of our resurrection, which also he, with the holy Church, believed would happen on the same day after the Sabbath, now called the Lord's day.

CHAPTER XVIII

OF THE LIFE AND DEATH OF THE RELIGIOUS KING SIGE-BERT. [A.D. 635.]

AT this time, the kingdom of the East Angles, after the death of Earpwald, the successor of Redwald, was subject to his brother Sigebert, a good and religious man, who long before had been baptized in France, whilst he lived in banishment, flying from the enmity of Redwald; and returning home, as soon as he ascended the throne, being desirous to imitate the good institutions which he had seen in France, he set up a school for youth to be instructed in literature, and was assisted therein by Bishop Felix, who came to him from Kent, and who furnished him with masters and teachers after the manner of that country.

This king became so great a lover of the heavenly kingdom, that quitting the affairs of his crown, and committing the same to his kinsman, Ecgric, who before held a part of that kingdom, he went himself into a monastery, which he had built, and having received the tonsure, applied himself rather to gain a heavenly throne. Some time after this, it happened that the nation of the Mercians, under King Penda, made war on the East Angles; who, finding themselves inferior in martial affairs to their enemy, entreated Sigebert to go with them to battle, to encourage the soldiers. He refused, upon which they drew him against his will out of the monastery, and carried him to the army, hoping that the soldiers would be less disposed to flee in the presence of him, who had once been a notable and a brave commander. But he, still keeping in mind his profession, whilst in the midst of a royal army, would carry nothing in his hand but a wand, and was killed with King Ecgric; and the pagans pressing on, all their army was either slaughtered or dispersed.

Anna, the son of Eni, of the blood royal, a good man, and father of an excellent family of children, succeeded them in the kingdom. Of whom we shall speak hereafter; he being also slain by the same pagan commander as his predecessor had been.

CHAPTER XIX

HOW FURSEY BUILT A MONASTERY AMONG THE EAST
ANGLES, AND OF HIS VISIONS AND SANCTITY, OF WHICH,
HIS FLESH REMAINING UNCORRUPTED AFTER DEATH
BORE TESTIMONY. [A.D. 633.]

WHILST Sigebert still governed the kingdom, there came out of
Ireland a holy man called Fursey renowned both for his words and
actions, and remarkable for singular virtues, being desirous to live
a stranger for our Lord, wherever an opportunity should offer. On
coming into the province of the East Saxons, he was honourably
received by the aforesaid king, and performing his usual employment of preaching the Gospel, by the example of his virtue and
the efficacy of his discourse, converted many unbelievers to Christ,
and confirmed in his faith and love those that already believed.

Here he fell into some infirmity of body, and was thought worthy
to see a vision from God; in which he was admonished diligently to
proceed in the ministry of the word which he had undertaken, and
indefatigably to continue his usual watching and prayers; inasmuch
as his end was certain, but the hour of it would be uncertain,
according to the saying of our Lord, "Watch ye therefore, because
ye know not the day nor the hour." Being confirmed by this vision,
he applied himself with all speed to build a monastery on the
ground which had been given him by King Sigebert, and to establish regular discipline therein. This monastery was pleasantly situated in the woods, and with the sea not far off; it was built within
the area of a castle, which in the English language is called
Cnobheresburg, that is, Cnobher's Town; afterwards, Anna, king of
that province, and the nobility, embellished it with more stately
buildings and donations. This man was of noble Scottish blood, but
much more noble in mind than in birth. From his boyish years, he
had particularly applied himself to reading sacred books, and following monastic discipline, and, as is most becoming to holy men,
he carefully practised all that he learned was to be done.

In short, he built himself the monastery, wherein he might with more freedom indulge his heavenly studies. There, falling sick, as the book about his life informs us, he fell into a trance, and quitting his body from the evening till the cock crew, he was found worthy to behold the choirs of angels, and to hear the praises which are sung in heaven. He was wont to declare, that among other things he distinctly heard this: "The saints shall advance from one virtue to another." And again, "The God of gods shall be seen in Sion." Being restored to his body at that time, and again taken from it three days after, he not only saw the greater joys of the blessed, but also extraordinary combats of evil spirits, who by frequent accusations wickedly endeavoured to obstruct his journey to heaven; but the angels protecting him, all their endeavours were in vain. Concerning which particulars, if any one desires to be more fully informed, that is, with what subtle fraud the devils represented both his actions and superfluous words, and even his thoughts, as if they had been written down in a book; and what pleasing or disagreeable things he was informed of by the angels and saints, or just men who appeared to him among the angels; let him read the little book of his life which I have mentioned, and I believe he will thereby reap much spiritual profit.

But there is one thing among the rest, which we have thought may be beneficial to many if inserted in this history. When he had been lifted up on high, he was ordered by the angels that conducted him to look back upon the world. Upon which, casting his eyes downward, he saw, as it were, a dark and obscure valley underneath him. He also saw four fires in the air, not far distant from each other. Then asking the angels, what fires those were? he was told, they were the fires which would kindle and consume the world. One of them was of falsehood, when we do not fulfil that which we promised in baptism, to renounce the Devil and all his works. The next of covetousness, when we prefer the riches of the world to the love of heavenly things. The third of discord, when we make no difficulty to offend the minds of our neighbours even in needless things. The fourth of iniquity, when we look upon it as no crime to rob and to defraud the weak. These fires, increasing by degrees, extended so as to meet one another, and being joined, became an immense flame. When it drew near, fearing for himself, he said to the angel, "Lord, behold the fire draws near me." The angel answered, "That which you did not kindle shall not burn you; for though this appears to be a terrible and great fire, yet it tries every man according to the merits of his works; for every man's concupiscence shall burn in the fire; for as every one burns in the body through unlawful pleasure, so when discharged of the body, he shall burn in the punishment which he has deserved."

Then he saw one of the three angels, who had been his conductors throughout both visions, go before and divide the flame of fire, whilst the other two, flying about on both sides, defended him from the danger of that fire. He also saw devils flying through the fire, raising conflagrations of wars against the just. Then followed accusations of the wicked spirits against him, the defence of the good angels in his favour, and a more extended view of the heavenly troops; as also of holy men of his own nation, who, as he had long since been informed, had been deservedly advanced to the degree of priesthood, from whom he heard many things that might be very salutary to himself, or to all others that would listen to them. When they had ended their discourse, and returned to heaven with the angelic spirits, the three angels remained with the blessed Fursey, of whom we have spoken before, and who were to bring him back to his body. And when they approached the aforesaid immense fire, the angel divided the flame, as he had done before; but when the man of God came to the passage so opened amidst the flames, the unclean spirits, laying hold of one of those whom they tormented in the fire, threw him at him, and, touching his shoulder and jaw, burned them. He knew the man, and called to mind that he had received his garment when he died; and the angel, immediately laying hold, threw him back into the fire, and the malignant enemy said, "Do not reject him whom you before received; for as you accepted the goods of him who was a sinner, so you must partake of his punishment." The angel replying, said,

"He did not receive the same through avarice, but in order to save his soul." The fire ceased, and the angel, turning to him, added, "That which you kindled burned in you; for had you not received the money of this person that died in his sins, his punishment would not burn in you." And proceeding in his discourse, he gave him wholesome advice for what ought to be done towards the salvation of such as repented.

Being afterwards restored to his body, throughout the whole course of his life he bore the mark of the fire which he had felt in his soul, visible to all men on his shoulder and jaw; and the flesh publicly showed, in a wonderful manner, what the soul had suffered in private. He always took care, as he had done before, to persuade all men to the practice of virtue, as well by his example, as by preaching. But as for the matter of his visions, he would only relate them to those who, from holy zeal and desire of reformation, wished to learn the same. An ancient brother of our monastery is still living, who is wont to declare that a very sincere and religious man told him, that he had seen Fursey himself in the province of the East Angles, and heard those visions from his mouth; adding, that though it was in most sharp winter weather, and a hard frost, and the man was sitting in a thin garment when he related it, yet he sweated as if it had been in the greatest heat of summer, either through excessive fear, or spiritual consolation.

To return to what we were saying before, when, after preaching the word of God many years in Scotland [Ireland], he could no longer bear the crowds that resorted to him, leaving all that he seemed to possess, he departed from his native island, and came with a few brothers through the Britons into the province of the English, and preaching the word of God there, as has been said, built a noble monastery. These things being rightly performed, he became desirous to rid himself of all business of this world, and even of the monastery itself, and forthwith left the same, and the care of souls, to his brother Fullan, and the priests Gobban and Dicull, and being himself free from all that was worldly, resolved to end his life as a hermit. He had another brother called Ultan, who, after a long monastical probation, had also adopted the life of an anchorite. Repairing all alone to him, he lived a whole year with him in continence and prayer, and laboured daily with his hands.

Afterwards seeing the province in confusion by the irruptions of the pagans, and presaging that the monasteries would be also in danger, he left all things in order, and sailed over into France, and being there honourably entertained by Clovis, king of the Franks, or by the patrician Erconwald, he built a monastery in the place called Latiniacum, and falling sick not long after, departed this life. The same Erconwald took his body, and deposited it in the porch of a church he was building in his town of Perrone, till the church itself should be dedicated. This happened twenty-seven days after, and the body being taken from the porch, to be re-buried near the altar, was found as entire as if he had just then died. And again, four years after, a more decent tabernacle or chapel being built for the same body to the eastward of the altar, it was still found free from corruption, and translated thither with due honour; where it is well known that his merits, through the divine operation, have been declared by many miracles. These things and the incorruption of his body we have taken notice of, that the sublimeness of this man may be the better known to the readers. All which, whosoever will read it, will find more fully described, as also about his fellow-labourers, in the book of his life before mentioned.

CHAPTER XX

HONORIUS DYING, DEUSDEDIT IS CHOSEN ARCHBISHOP OF CANTERBURY, OF THOSE WHO WERE AT THAT TIME BISHOPS OF THE EAST ANGLES, AND OF THE CHURCH OF ROCHESTER. [A.D. 653.]

IN the meantime, Felix, bishop of the East Angles, dying, when he had held that see seventeen years, Honorius ordained Thomas his deacon, of the province of the Girvii, in his place; and he departing this life when he had been bishop five years, Bertgils, surnamed Boniface, of the province of Kent, was appointed in his stead.

Honorius himself also, having run his course, departed this life in the year of our Lord 653, on the 30th of September; and when the see had been vacant a year and six months, Deusdedit, of the nation of the South Saxons, was chosen the sixth archbishop of Canterbury. To ordain whom, Ithamar, bishop of Rochester, came thither. His ordination was on the 26th of March, and he ruled nine years, four months, and two days; when he also died. Ithamar consecrated in his place Damian, who was of the race of the South Saxons.

CHAPTER XXI

HOW THE PROVINCE OF THE MIDLAND ANGLES BECAME CHRISTIAN UNDER KING PEADA. [A.D. 653.]

AT this time, the Middle Angles, under their Prince Peada, the son of King Penda, received the faith and sacraments of the truth. Being an excellent youth, and most worthy of the title and person of a king, he was by his father elevated to the throne of that nation, and came to Oswy, king of the Northumbrians, requesting to have his daughter Elfleda given him to wife; but could not obtain his desires unless he would embrace the faith of Christ, and be baptized, with the nation which he governed. When he heard the preaching of truth, the promise of the heavenly kingdom, and the hope of resurrection and future immortality, he declared that he would willingly become a Christian, even though he should be refused the virgin; being chiefly prevailed on to receive the faith by King Oswy's son Alfrid, who was his relation and friend, and had married his sister Cyneberga, the daughter of King Penda.

Accordingly he was baptized by Bishop Finan, with all his earls and soldiers, and their servants, that came along with him, at a noted village belonging to the king, called At the Wall. And having received four priests, who for their erudition and good life were deemed proper to instruct and baptize his nation, he returned home with much joy. These priests were Cedd and Adda, and Betti and Diuma; the last of whom was by nation a Scot, the others English. Adda was brother to Utta, whom we have mentioned before, a renowned priest, and abbat of the monastery of Gateshead. The aforesaid priests, arriving in the province with the prince, preached the word, and were willingly listened to; and many, as well of the nobility as the common sort, renouncing the abominations of idolatry, were baptized daily.

Nor did King Penda obstruct the preaching of the word among his people, the Mercians, if any were willing to hear it; but, on the contrary, he hated and despised those whom he perceived not to perform the works of faith, when they had once received the faith, saying, "They were contemptible and wretched who did not obey their God, in whom they believed." This was begun two years before the death of King Penda.

But when he was slain, and Oswy, the most Christian king, succeeded him in the throne, Diuma, one of the aforesaid four priests, was made bishop of the Midland Angles, as also of the Mercians, being ordained by Bishop Finan; for the scarcity of priests was the occasion that one prelate was set over two nations. Having in a short time gained many people to our Lord, he died among the Midland Angles, in the country called Feppingum; and Ceollach, of the Scottish nation, succeeded him in the bishopric. This prelate, not long after, left his bishopric, and returned to the island of Hii, which, among the Scots, was the chief and head of many monasteries. His successor in the bishopric was Trumhere, a religious man, and educated in the monastic life of the English nation, but ordained bishop by the Scots, which happened in the days of King Wulfhere, of whom we shall speak hereafter.

CHAPTER XXII

HOW THE EAST SAXONS AGAIN RECEIVED THE FAITH, WHICH THEY HAD BEFORE CAST OFF UNDER KING SIGEBERT, THROUGH THE PREACHING OF CEDD. [A.D. 653.]

AT that time, also, the East Saxons, at the instance of King Oswy, again received the faith, which they had formerly cast off when they expelled Mellitus, their bishop. For Sigebert, who reigned next to Sigebert surnamed The Little, was then king of that nation, and a friend to King Oswy, who, when he often came to him into the province of the Northumbrians, used to endeavour to persuade him that those could not be gods that had been made by the hands of men; that a stock or a stone could not be proper matter to form a god, the remains whereof were either burned in the fire, or framed into any vessels for the use of men, or else were cast out as refuse, trampled on and bruised to dust. That God is rather to be understood as of incomprehensible majesty and invisible to human eyes, almighty, eternal, the Creator of heaven and earth, and of mankind; who governs and will judge the world in righteousness; whose everlasting seat is in heaven, and not in vile and fading matter; and that it ought in reason to be concluded, that all those who have learned and obeyed the will of Him by whom they were created, will receive from Him eternal rewards. King Oswy having often, in a friendly and brotherly manner, said this and much more to the like effect, at length, with the consent of his friends, he believed, and after consulting with those about him, and exhorting them, they all agreed and gave their approbation, and were baptized with him by Bishop Finan, in the king's village above spoken of, which is called At the Wall, because it is close by the wall with which the Romans formerly divided the island of Britain, at the distance of twelve miles from the eastern sea.

King Sigebert, being now become a citizen of the eternal kingdom, returned to the seat of his temporal kingdom, requesting of Oswy that he would give him some teachers, who might convert his nation to the faith of Christ, and baptize them. Oswy, accordingly, sending into the province of the Midland Angles, invited to him the man of God, Cedd, and, giving him another priest for his companion, sent them to preach to the East Saxons. When these two, travelling to all parts of that country, had gathered a numerous church to our Lord, it happened that Cedd returned home, and came to the church of Lindisfarne to confer with Bishop Finan; who, finding how successful he had been in the work of the Gospel, made him bishop of the church of the East Saxons, calling

147

to him two other bishops to assist at the ordination. Cedd, having received the episcopal dignity, returned to his province, and pursuing the work he had begun with more ample authority, built churches in several places, ordaining priests and deacons to assist him in the work of faith, and the ministry of baptizing, especially in the city which, in the language of the Saxons, is called Ithancestir, as also in that which is named Tilaburg; the first of which places is on the bank of the Pante, the other on the bank of the Thames, where, gathering a flock of servants of Christ, he taught them to observe the discipline of regular life, as far as those rude people were then capable.

Whilst the doctrine of everlasting life was thus, for a considerable time, making progress, to the joy of the king and of all the people, it happened that the king, at the instigation of the enemy of all good men, was murdered by his own kindred. They were two brothers who did this wicked deed; and being asked what had moved them to it, had nothing else to answer, but that they had been incensed against the king, and hated him, because he was too apt to spare his enemies, and easily to forgive the wrongs they had done him, upon their entreaty. Such was the crime for which the king was killed, because he observed the precepts of the Gospel with a devout heart; in which innocent death, however, his real offence was also punished, according to the prediction of the man of God. For one of those earls that murdered him was unlawfully married, which the bishop not being able to prevent or correct, he excommunicated him, and commanded all that would give ear to him not to enter within his house, nor to eat of his meat. The king made slight of this inhibition, and being invited by the earl, went to an entertainment at his house, and when he was going thence, the bishop met him. The king, beholding him, immediately dismounted from his horse, trembling, and fell down at his feet, begging pardon for his offence; for the bishop, who was likewise on horseback, had also alighted. Being much incensed, he touched the king, lying in that humble posture, with the rod he held in his hand, and using his pontifical authority, spoke thus: "I say to you, forasmuch as you would not refrain from the house of that wicked and condemned person, you shall die in that very house." Yet it is to be believed, that such a death of a religious man not only blotted out his offence, but also added to his merit; because it happened on account of his pious observance of the commands of Christ.

Sigebert was succeeded in the kingdom by Suidhelm, the son of Sexbald, who was baptized by the same Cedd, in the province of the East Angles, at the king's country-seat, called Rendelsham, that is, Rendil's Mansion; and Ethelwald, king of the East Angles, brother to Anna, king of the same people, was his godfather.

CHAPTER XXIII

BISHOP CEDD, HAVING A PLACE GIVEN HIM BY KING ETHELWALD, CONSECRATES THE SAME TO OUR LORD WITH PRAYER AND FASTING. OF HIS DEATH. [A.D. 659.]

THE same man of God, whilst he was bishop among the East Saxons, was also wont several times to visit his own country, Northumberland, to make exhortations. Ethelwald, the son of King Oswald, who reigned among the Deiri, finding him a holy, wise, and good man, desired him to accept some land to build a monastery, to which the king himself might frequently resort, to offer his prayers and hear the word, and be buried in it when he died; for he believed that he should receive much benefit by the prayers of those who were to serve God in that place. The king had before with him a brother of the same bishop, called Celin, a man no less devoted to God, who, being a priest, was wont to administer to him the word and the sacraments of the faith; by whose means he chiefly came to know and love the bishop. That prelate, therefore, complying with the king's desires, chose himself a place to build a monastery among craggy and distant mountains, which looked more like lurking-places for robbers and retreats for wild beasts, than habitations for men; to the end that, according to the prophecy of Isaiah, "In the habitations where before dragons dwelt, might be grass with reeds and rushes;" that is, that the fruits of good work should spring up, where before beasts were wont to dwell, or men to live after the manner of beasts.

The man of God, desiring first to cleanse the place for the monastery from former crimes, by prayer and fasting, that it might become acceptable to our Lord, and so to lay the foundations, requested of the king that he would give him leave to reside there all the approaching time of Lent to pray. All which days, except Sundays, he fasted till the evening, according to custom, and then took no other sustenance than a little bread, one hen's egg, and a little milk mixed with water. This, he said, was the custom of those of whom he had learned the rule of regular discipline; first, to consecrate to our Lord, by prayer and fasting, the places which they had newly received for building a monastery or a church. When there were ten days of Lent still remaining, there came a messenger to call him to the king; and he, that the religious work might not be intermitted, on account of the king's affairs, entreated his priest Cynebil, who was also his own brother, to complete that which had been so piously begun. Cynebil readily complied, and when the time of fasting and prayer was over, he there built the monastery, which is now called Lestingau, and established therein the religious customs of Lindisfarne, where they had been educated.

Cedd for many years having charge of the bishopric in the aforesaid province, and of this monastery, over which he had placed superiors, it happened that he came thither at a time when there was a mortality, and fell sick and died. He was first buried in the open air; but in the process of time a church was built of stone in the monastery, in honour of the Mother of God, and his body interred in the same, on the right hand of the altar.

The bishop left the monastery to be govened after him by his brother Chad, who was afterwards made bishop, as shall be said in its place. For the four brothers we have mentioned, Cedd and Cynebil, Celin and Ceadda [Chad], which is a rare thing to be met with, were all celebrated priests of our Lord, and two of them also came to be bishops. When the brethren who were in his monastery, in the province of the East Saxons, heard that the bishop was dead in the province of the Northumbrians, about thirty men of that monastery came thither, being desirous either to live near the body of their father, if it should please God, or to die there and be buried. Being lovingly received by their brethren and fellow soldiers in Christ, all of them died there by the afore-said pestilence, except one little boy, who was delivered from death by his father's prayers. For when he had lived there a long time after, and applied himself to the reading of sacred writ, he was informed that he had not been regenerated by the water of baptism, and being then washed in the laver of salvation, he was afterwards promoted to the order of priesthood, and proved very useful to many in the church. I do not doubt that he was delivered at the point of death, as I have said, by the intercession of his father, whilst he was embracing his beloved corpse, that so he might himself avoid eternal death, and by teaching, exhibit the ministry of life and salvation to others of the brethren.

CHAPTER XXIV

KING PENDA BEING SLAIN, THE MERCIANS RECEIVED THE FAITH OF CHRIST, AND OSWY GAVE POSSESSIONS AND TERRITORIES TO GOD, FOR BUILDING MONAS-TERIES, IN ACKNOWLEDGMENT FOR THE VICTORY OBTAINED. [A.D. 655.]

AT this time, King Oswy was exposed to the fierce and intolerable irruptions of Penda, king of the Mercians, whom we have so often mentioned, and who had slain his brother; at length, necessity compelling him, he promised to give him greater gifts than can be imagined, to purchase peace; provided that the king would return home, and cease to destroy the provinces of his kingdom. That perfidious king refused to grant his request, and resolved to extir-pate all his nation, from the highest to the lowest; whereupon he had recourse to the protection of the Divine goodness for deliverance from his barbarous and impious foes, and binding himself by a vow, said, "If the pagan will not accept of our gifts, let us offer them to Him that will, the Lord our God." He then vowed, that if he should come off victorious, he would dedicate his daughter to our Lord in holy virginity, and give twelve farms to build monasteries. After this he gave battle with a very small army against superior forces: indeed, it is reported that the pagans had three times the number of men; for they had thirty legions, led on by most noted commanders. King Oswy and his son Alfrid met them with a very small army, as has been said, but confiding in the conduct of Christ; his other son, Egfrid, was then kept an hostage at the court of Queen Cynwise, in the province of the Mercians. King Oswald's son Ethelwald, who ought to have assisted them, was on the enemy's side, and led them on to fight against his country and uncle; though, during the battle, he withdrew, and awaited the event in a place of safety. The engagement beginning, the pagans were defeated, the thirty commanders, and those who had come to his assistance were put to flight, and almost all of them slain; among whom was Ethelhere, brother and successor to Anna, king of the East Angles, who had been the occasion of the war, and who was now killed, with all his soldiers. The battle was fought near the river Vinwed, which then, with the great rains, had not only filled its channel, but overflowed its banks, so that many more were drowned in the flight than destroyed by the sword.

Then King Oswy, pursuant to the vow he had made to our Lord, returned thanks to God for the victory, and gave his daughter Elfleda, who was scarce a year old, to be consecrated to Him in perpetual virginity; delivering also twelve small portions of land, wherein earthly warfare should cease, and in which there should be a perpetual residence and subsistence for monks to follow the warfare which is spiritual, and pray diligently for the peace of his nation. Of those possessions six were in the province of the Deiri, and the other six in that of the Bernicians. Each of the said possessions contained ten families, that is, a hundred and twenty in all.

The aforesaid daughter of King Oswy, thus dedicated to God, was put into the monastery, called Heruteu, or, "The island of the Hart," where, at that time, the Abbess Hilda presided, and, two years after, having acquired a possession of ten families, at the place called Streaneshalch, she built a monastery there, in which the aforesaid king's daughter was first a learner, and afterwards a teacher of the monastic life; till, being sixty years of age, the blessed virgin departed to the nuptials and embraces of her heavenly bridegroom. In that same monastery, she and her father, Oswy, her mother, Eanfleda, her mother's father, Edwin, and many other noble persons, are buried in the church of the holy Apostle Peter. King Oswy concluded the aforesaid war in the country of Loidis, in the thirteenth year of his reign, on the 15th of November, to the great benefit of both nations; for he both delivered his own people from the hostile depredations of the pagans, and, having cut off the wicked king's head, converted the Mercians and the adjacent provinces to the grace of the Christian faith.

Diuma was made the first bishop of the Mercians, as also of Lindisfarne and the Midland Angles, as has been said above, and he died and was buried among the Midland Angles. The second was Ceollach, who, quitting the episcopal office whilst still alive, returned into Scotland, to which nation he belonged as well as Bishop Diuma. The third was Trumhere, an Englishman, but taught and ordained by the Scots, being abbat in the monastery that is called Ingethlingum, and is the place where King Oswin was killed, as has been said above; for Queen Eanfleda, his kinswoman, in satisfaction for his unjust death, begged of King Oswy that he would give the aforesaid servant of God a place there to build a monastery, because he also was kinsman to the slaughtered king; in which monastery continual prayers should be offered up for the eternal health of the kings, both of him that had been slain, and of him that caused it to be done. The same King Oswy governed the Mercians, as also the people of the other southern provinces, three years after he had slain King Penda; and he likewise subdued the greater part of the Picts to the dominion of the English.

At which time he gave to the above-mentioned Peada, son to King Penda, who was his kinsman, the kingdom of the Southern Mercians, consisting, as is reported, of 5000 families, divided by the river Trent from the Northern Mercians, whose land contained 7000 families; but that Peada was the next spring very wickedly killed, by the treachery, as is said, of his wife, during the very time of celebrating Easter. Three years after the death of King Penda, Immin, and Eafa, and Eadbert, generals of the Mercians, rebelled against King Oswy, setting up for their king, Wulfhere, son to the said Penda, a youth, whom they had kept concealed; and expelling the officers of the foreign king, they at once recovered their liberty and their lands; and being thus free, together with their king, they rejoiced to serve Christ the true King, that they might obtain the everlasting kingdom which is in heaven. This king governed the Mercians seventeen years, and had for his first bishop Trumhere, above spoken of; the second Jaruman; the third Chad; the fourth Winfrid. All these, succeeding each other regularly under King Wulfhere, discharged the episcopal duties to the Mercian nation.

CHAPTER XXV

HOW THE CONTROVERSY AROSE ABOUT THE DUE TIME OF KEEPING EASTER, WITH THOSE THAT CAME OUT OF SCOTLAND. [A.D. 652.]

IN the meantime, Bishop Aidan being dead, Finan, who was ordained and sent by the Scots, succeeded him in the bishopric, and built a church in the Isle of Lindisfarne, the episcopal see; nevertheless, after the manner of the Scots, he made it, not of stone, but of hewn oak, and covered it with reeds; and the same was afterwards dedicated in honour of St. Peter the Apostle, by the reverend Archbishop Theodore. Eadbert, also bishop of that place, took off the thatch, and covered it, both roof and walls, with plates of lead.

At this time, a great and frequent controversy happened about the observance of Easter; those that came from Kent or France affirming, that the Scots kept Easter Sunday contrary to the custom of the universal church. Among them was a most zealous defender of the true Easter, whose name was Ronan, a Scot by nation, but instructed in ecclesiastical truth, either in France or Italy, who, disputing with Finan, convinced many, or at least induced them to make a more strict inquiry after the truth; yet he could not prevail upon Finan, but, on the contrary, made him the more inveterate by reproof, and a professed opposer of the truth, being of a hot and violent temper. James, formerly the deacon of the venerable Archbishop Paulinus, as has been said above, kept the true and Catholic Easter, with all those that he could persuade to adopt the right way. Queen Eanfleda and her followers also observed the same as she had seen practised in Kent, having with her a Kentish priest that followed the Catholic mode, whose name was Romanus. Thus it is said to have happened in those times that Easter was twice kept in one year; and that when the king having ended the time of fasting, kept his Easter, the queen and her followers were still fasting, and celebrating Palm Sunday. This difference about the observance of Easter, whilst Aidan lived, was patiently tolerated by all men, as being sensible, that though he could not keep Easter contrary to the custom of those who had sent him, yet he industriously laboured to practise all works of faith, piety, and love, according to the custom of all holy men; for which reason he was deservedly beloved by all; even by those who differed in opinion concerning Easter, and was held in veneration, not only by indifferent persons, but even by the bishops, Honorius of Canterbury, and Felix of the East Angles.

But after the death of Finan, who succeeded him, when Colman, who was also sent out of Scotland, came to be bishop, a greater controversy arose about the observance of Easter, and the rules of ecclesiastical life. Whereupon this dispute began naturally to influence the thoughts and hearts of many, who feared, lest having received the name of Christians, they might happen to run, or to have run, in vain. This reached the ears of King Oswy and his son

Alfrid; for Oswy, having been instructed and baptized by the Scots, and being very perfectly skilled in their language, thought nothing better than what they taught. But Alfrid, having been instructed in Christianity by Wilfrid, a most learned man, who had first gone to Rome to learn the ecclesiastical doctrine, and spent much time at Lyons with Dalfin, archbishop of France, from whom also he had received the ecclesiastical tonsure, rightly thought this man's doctrine ought to be preferred before all the traditions of the Scots. For this reason he had also given him a monastery of forty families, at a place called Rhypum; which place, not long before, he had given to those that followed the system of the Scots for a monastery; but forasmuch as they afterwards, being left to their choice, prepared to quit the place rather than alter their opinion, he gave the place to him, whose life and doctrine were worthy of it.

Agilbert, bishop of the West Saxons, above-mentioned, a friend to King Alfrid and to Abbat Wilfrid, had at that time come into the province of the Northumbrians, and was making some stay among them; at the request of Alfrid, made Wilfrid a priest in his monastery. He had in his company a priest, whose name was Agatho. The controversy being there started, concerning Easter, or the tonsure, or other ecclesiastical affairs, it was agreed, that a synod should be held in the monastery of Streaneshalch, which signifies the Bay of the Lighthouse, where the Abbess Hilda, a woman devoted to God, then presided; and that there this controversy should be decided. The kings, both father and son, came thither, Bishop Colman with his Scottish clerks, and Agilbert with the priests Agatho and Wilfrid, James and Romanus were on their side; but the Abbess Hilda and her followers were for the Scots, as was also the venerable Bishop Cedd, long before ordained by the Scots, as has been said above, and he was in that council a most careful interpreter for both parties.

King Oswy first observed, that it behoved those who served one God to observe the same rule of life; and as they all expected the same kingdom in heaven, so they ought not to differ in the celebration of the Divine mysteries; but rather to inquire which was the truest tradition, that the same might be followed by all; he then commanded his bishop, Colman, first to declare what the custom was which he observed, and whence it derived its origin. Then Colman said, "The Easter which I keep, I received from my elders, who sent me bishop hither; all our forefathers, men beloved of God, are known to have kept it after the same manner; and that the same may not seem to any contemptible or worthy to be rejected, it is the same which St. John the Evangelist, the disciple beloved of our Lord, with all the churches over which he presided, is recorded to have observed." Having said thus much, and more to the like effect, the king commanded Agilbert to show whence his custom of keeping Easter was derived, or on what authority it was grounded. Agilbert answered, "I desire that my disciple, the priest Wilfrid, may speak in my stead; because we both concur with the other followers of the ecclesiastical tradition that are here present, and he can better explain our opinion in the English language, than I can by an interpreter."

Then Wilfrid, being ordered by the king to speak, delivered himself thus:—"The Easter which we observe, we saw celebrated by all at Rome, where the blessed apostles, Peter and Paul, lived, taught, suffered, and were buried; we saw the same done in Italy and in France, when we travelled through those countries for pilgrimage and prayer. We found the same practised in Africa, Asia, Egypt, Greece, and all the world, wherever the church of Christ is spread abroad, through several nations and tongues, at one and the same time; except only these and their accomplices in obstinacy, I mean the Picts and the Britons, who foolishly, in these two remote islands of the world, and only in part even of them, oppose all the rest of the universe." When he had so said, Colman answered, "It is strange that you will call our labours foolish, wherein we follow the example of so great an apostle, who was thought worthy to lay his head on our Lord's bosom, when all the world knows him to have lived most wisely." Wilfrid replied, "Far be it from us to charge John with folly, for he literally observed the precepts of the Jewish law, whilst the church still Judaized in many points, and the apostles were not able at once to cast off all the observances of the law which had been instituted by God. In which way it is necessary that all who come to the faith should forsake the idols which were invented by devils, that they might not give scandal to the Jews that were among the Gentiles. For this reason it was, that Paul circumcised Timothy, that he offered sacrifice in the temple, that he shaved his head with Aquila and Priscilla at Corinth; for no other advantage than to avoid giving scandal to the Jews. Hence it was, that James said, to the same Paul, 'You see, brother, how many thousands of the Jews have believed; and they are all zealous for the law. And yet, at this time, the Gospel spreading throughout the world, it is needless, nay, it is not lawful, for the faithful either to be circumcised, or to offer up to God sacrifices of flesh.' So John, pursuant to the custom of the law, began the celebration of the feast of Easter, on the fourteenth day of the first month, in the evening, not regarding whether the same happened on a Saturday, or any other day. But when Peter preached at Rome, being mindful that our Lord arose from the dead, and gave the world the hopes of resurrection, on the first day after the Sabbath, he understood that Easter ought to be observed, so as always to stay till the rising of the moon on the fourteenth day of the first moon, in the evening, according to the custom and precepts of the law, even as John did. And when that came, if the Lord's day, then called the first day after the Sabbath, was the next day, he began that very evening to keep Easter, as we all do at this day. But if the Lord's day did not fall the next morning after the fourteenth moon, but on the sixteenth, or the seventeenth, or any other moon till the twenty-first, he waited for that, and on the Saturday before, in the evening, began to observe the holy solemnity of Easter. Thus it came to pass, that Easter Sunday was only kept from the fifteenth moon to the twenty-first. Nor does this evangelical and apostolic tradition abolish the law, but rather fulfil it; the command being to keep the passover from the fourteenth moon of the first month in the evening to the twenty-first moon of the same month in the evening; which observance all the succes-sors of St. John in Asia, since his death, and all the church through-out the world, have since followed; and that this is the true Easter, and the only one to be kept by the faithful, was not newly decreed by the council of Nice, but only confirmed afresh; as the Church History informs us.

"Thus it appears, that you, Colman, neither follow the example of John, as you imagine, nor that of Peter, whose traditions you knowingly contradict; and that you neither agree with the law nor the Gospel in the keeping of your Easter. For John, keeping the Paschal time according to the decree of the Mosaic law, had no regard to the first day after the Sabbath, which you do not practise, who celebrate Easter only on the first day after the Sabbath. Peter kept Easter Sunday between the fifteenth and the twenty-first moon, which you do not, but keep Easter Sunday from the fourteenth to the twentieth moon; so that you often begin Easter on the thir-teenth moon in the evening, whereof neither the law made any mention, nor did our Lord, the Author and Giver of the Gospel, on that day, but on the fourteenth, either eat the old passover in the evening, or deliver the sacraments of the New Testament, to be cel-ebrated by the church, in memory of his passion. Besides, in your celebration of Easter, you utterly exclude the twenty-first moon, which the law ordered to be principally observed. Thus, as I said before, you agree neither with John nor Peter, nor with the law, nor the Gospel, in the celebration of the greatest festival."

To this Colman rejoined: "Did Anatolius, a holy man, and much commended in church history, act contrary to the law and the Gospel, when he wrote, that Easter was to be celebrated from the fourteenth to the twentieth? Is it to be believed that our most reverend Father Columba and his successors, men beloved by God, who kept Easter after the same manner, thought or acted contrary to the Divine writings? Whereas there were many among them, whose sanctity is testified by heavenly signs and the working of miracles, whose life, customs, and discipline I never cease to follow, not questioning their being saints in heaven."

"It is evident," said Wilfrid, "that Anatolius was a most holy, learned, and commendable man; but what have you to do with him, since you do not observe his decrees? For he, following the rule of truth in his Easter, appointed a revolution of nineteen years, which either you are ignorant of, or if you know it, though it is kept by the whole church of Christ, yet you despise it. He so computed the fourteenth moon in the Easter of our Lord, that according to the custom of the Egyptians, he acknowledged it to be the fifteenth moon in the evening; so in like manner he assigned the twentieth to Easter-Sunday, as believing that to be the twenty-first moon, when the sun had set, which rule and distinction of his it appears you are ignorant of, in that you sometimes keep Easter before the full of the moon, that is, on the thirteenth day. Concerning your Father Columba and his followers, whose sanctity you say you imitate, and whose rules and precepts you observe, which have been confirmed by signs from heaven, I may answer, that when many, on the day of judgment, shall say to our Lord, 'That in his name they prophesied, and cast out devils, and wrought many wonders,' our Lord will reply, 'That He never knew them.' But far be it from me, that I say so of your fathers, because it is much more just to believe what is good, than what is evil, of persons whom one does not know. Wherefore I do not deny those to have been God's servants, and beloved by Him, who with rustic simplicity, but pious intentions, have themselves loved Him. Nor do I think that such keeping of Easter was very prejudicial to them, as long as none came to show them a more perfect rule; and yet I do believe that they, if any catholic adviser had come among them, would have as readily followed his admonitions, as they are known to have kept those commandments of God, which they had learned and knew.

"But as for you and your companions, you certainly sin, if, having heard the decrees of the Apostolic See, and of the universal church, and that the same is confirmed by holy writ, you refuse to follow them; for, though your fathers were holy, do you think that their small number, in a corner of the remotest island, is to be preferred before the universal church of Christ throughout the world? And if that Columba of yours (and, I may say, ours also, if he was Christ's servant), was a holy man and powerful in miracles, yet could he be preferred before the most blessed prince of the apostles, to whom our Lord said, 'Thou art Peter, and upon this rock I will build my church, and the gates of hell shall not prevail against it, and to thee I will give the keys of the kingdom of heaven?'"

When Wilfred had spoken thus, the king said, "Is it true, Colman, that these words were spoken to Peter by our Lord?" He answered, "It is true, O king!" Then says he, "Can you show any such power given to your Columba?" Colman answered, "None." Then added the king, "Do you both agree that these words were principally directed to Peter, and that the keys of heaven were given to him by our Lord?" They both answered, "We do." Then the king concluded, "And I also say unto you, that he is the door-keeper, whom I will not contradict, but will, as far as I know and am able, in all things obey his decrees, lest, when I come to the gates of the kingdom of heaven, there should be none to open them, he being my adversary who is proved to have the keys." The king having said this, all present, both great and small, gave their assent, and renouncing the more imperfect institution, resolved to conform to that which they found to be better.

CHAPTER XXVI

COLMAN, BEING WORSTED, RETURNED HOME; TUDA SUCCEEDED HIM IN THE BISHOPRIC; THE STATE OF THE CHURCH UNDER THOSE TEACHERS. [A.D. 664.]

THE disputation being ended, and the company broken up, Agilbert returned home. Colman, perceiving that his doctrine was rejected, and his sect despised, took with him such as would not comply with the Catholic Easter and the tonsure (for there was much controversy about that also), and went back into Scotland, to consult with his people what was to be done in this case. Cedd, forsaking the practices of the Scots, returned to his bishopric, having submitted to the Catholic observance of Easter. This disputation happened in the year of our Lord's incarnation 664, which was the twenty-second year of the reign of King Oswy, and the thirtieth of the episcopacy of the Scots among the English; for Aidan was bishop seventeen years, Finan ten, and Colman three.

When Colman was gone back into his own country, God's servant, Tuda, was made bishop of the Northumbrians in his place, having been instructed and ordained bishop among the Southern Scots, having also the ecclesiastical tonsure of his crown, according to the custom of that province, and observing the Catholic time of Easter. He was a good and religious man, but governed his church a very short time; he came out of Scotland whilst Colman was yet bishop, and, both by word and example, diligently taught all persons those things that appertain to the faith and truth. But Eata, who was abbat of the monastery of Melrose, a most reverend and meek man, was appointed abbat over the brethren that stayed in the church of Lindisfarne, when the Scots went away; they say, Colman, upon his departure, requested and obtained this of King Oswy, because Eata was one of Aidan's twelve boys of the English nation, whom he received when first made bishop there, to be instructed in Christ; for the king much loved Bishop Colman on account of his singular discretion. This is the same Eata, who, not long after, was made bishop of the same church of Lindisfarne. Colman carried home with him part of the bones of the most reverend Father Aidan, and left part of them in the church where he had presided, ordering them to be interred in the sacristy.

The place which he governed shows how frugal he and his predecessors were, for there were very few houses besides the church found at their departure; indeed, no more than were barely sufficient for their daily residence; they had also no money, but cattle; for if they received any money from rich persons, they immediately gave it to the poor; there being no need to gather money, or provide houses for the entertainment of the great men of the world; for such never resorted to the church, except to pray and hear the word of God. The king himself, when opportunity offered, came only with five or six servants, and having performed his devotions in the church, departed. But if they happened to take a repast there, they were satisfied with only the plain and daily food of the brethren, and required no more; for the whole care of those teachers was to serve God, not the world—to feed the soul, and not the belly.

For this reason the religious habit was at that time in great veneration; so that wheresoever any clergyman or monk happened to come, he was joyfully received by all persons, as God's servant; and if they chanced to meet him upon the way, they ran to him, and bowing, were glad to be signed with his hand, or blessed with his mouth. Great attention was also paid to their exhortations; and on Sundays they flocked eagerly to the church, or the monasteries, not to feed their bodies, but to hear the word of God; and if any priest happened to come into a village, the inhabitants flocked together to hear from him the word of life; for the priests and clergymen went into the village on no other account than to preach, baptize, visit the sick, and, in few words, to take care of souls; and they were so free from worldly avarice that none of them received lands and possessions for building monasteries, unless they were compelled to do so by the temporal authorities; which custom was for some time after observed in all the churches of the Northumbrians. But enough has now been said on this subject.

CHAPTER XXVII

EGBERT, A HOLY MAN OF THE ENGLISH NATION, LED A MONASTIC LIFE IN IRELAND. [A.D. 664.]

IN the same year of our Lord's incarnation, 664, there happened an eclipse of the sun, on the third of May, about ten o'clock in the morning. In the same year, a sudden pestilence also depopulated the southern coasts of Britain, and afterwards extending into the province of the Northumbrians, ravaged the country far and near, and destroyed a great multitude of men. To which plague the aforesaid priest Tuda fell a victim, and was honourably buried in the monastery of Pegnaleth. This pestilence did no less harm in the island of Ireland. Many of the nobility, and of the lower ranks of the English nation, were there at that time, who, in the days of the Bishops Finan and Colman, forsaking their native island, retired thither, either for the sake of Divine studies, or of a more continent life; and some of them presently devoted themselves to a monastical life, others chose rather to apply themselves to study, going about from one master's cell to another. The Scots willingly received them all, and took care to supply them with food, as also to furnish them with books to read, and their teaching, gratis.

Among these were Ethelhun and Egbert, two youths of great capacity, of the English nobility. The former of whom was brother to Ethelwin, a man no less beloved by God, who also afterwards went over into Ireland to study, and having been well instructed, returned into his own country, and being made bishop in the province of Lindsey, long governed that church worthily and creditably. These two being in the monastery which in the language of the Scots is called Rathmelsigi, and having lost all their companions, who were either cut off by the mortality, or dispersed into other places, fell both desperately sick of the same distemper, and were grievously afflicted. Of these, Egbert (as I was informed by a priest venerable for his age, and of great veracity, who declared he had heard those things from his own mouth), concluding that he was at the point of death, went out of his chamber, where the sick lay, in the morning, and sitting alone in a convenient place, began seriously to reflect upon his past actions, and, being full of compunction at the remembrance of his sins, bedewed his face with tears, and prayed fervently to God that he might not die yet, before he could make amends for the offences which he had committed in his infancy and younger years, or might further exercise himself in good works. He also made a vow that he would, for the sake of God, live in a strange place, so as never to return into the island of Britain, where he was born; that besides the canonical times of singing psalms, he would, unless prevented by corporeal infirmity, say the whole Psalter daily to the praise of God; and that he would every week fast one whole day and a night. Returning home, after his tears, prayers, and vows, he found his companion asleep, and going to bed himself, began to compose himself to rest. When he had lain quiet awhile, his comrade awaking, looked on him, and said, "Alas, Brother Egbert, what have you done? I was in hopes that we should have entered together into life everlasting; but know that what you prayed for is granted." For he had learned in a vision what the other had requested, and that his prayer was granted.

In short, Ethelhun died the next night; but Egbert, shaking off his distemper, recovered and lived a long time after to grace the priestly office, which he had received, by his worthy behaviour; and after much increase of virtue, according to his desire, he at length, in the year of our Lord's incarnation 729, being ninety years of age, departed to the heavenly kingdom. He led his life in great perfection of humility, meekness, continence, simplicity, and justice. Thus he was a great benefactor, both to his own nation, and to those of the Scots and Picts among whom he lived a stranger, by his example of life, his industry in teaching, his authority in reproving, and his piety in giving away much of what he received from the bounty of the rich. He also added this to his vow above-mentioned; during Lent, he would eat but one meal a day, allowing himself nothing but bread and thin milk, and even that by measure. That milk, new the day before, he kept in a vessel, and the next day skimming off the cream, drank the rest, as has been said, with a little bread. Which sort of abstinence he likewise always observed forty days before the nativity of our Lord, and as many after the solemnity of Pentecost, that is, of the Quinquagesima.

CHAPTER XXVIII

TUDA BEING DEAD, WILFRID WAS ORDAINED, IN FRANCE,
AND CHAD, IN THE PROVINCE OF THE WEST SAXONS, TO
BE BISHOPS OF THE NORTHUMBRIANS. [A.D. 665.]

IN the meantime, King Alfrid sent the priest, Wilfrid, to the king
of France, to be consecrated bishop over him and his people. That
prince sent him to be ordained by Agilbert, who, as was said above,
having left Britain, was made bishop of the city of Paris, and by
him Wilfrid was honourably consecrated, several bishops meeting
together for that purpose in a village belonging to the king, called
Compiegne. He made some stay in the parts beyond the sea, after
his consecration, and Oswy, following the example of the king his
son, sent a holy man, of modest behaviour, well read in the
Scripture, and diligently practising those things which he had
learned therein, to be ordained bishop of the church of York. This
was a priest called Ceadda [Chad], brother to the reverend prelate
Cedd, of whom mention has been often made, and abbat of the
monastery of Lestingau. With him the king also sent his priest
Eadhed, who was afterwards, in the reign of Egfrid, made bishop
of the church of Ripon. On arriving in Kent, they found that
Archbishop Deusdedit was departed this life, and no other prelate
as yet appointed in his place; whereupon they proceeded to the
province of the West Saxons, where Wini was bishop, and by him
the person above-mentioned was consecrated bishop; two bishops
of the British nation, who kept Easter Sunday according to the
canonical manner, from the fourteenth to the twentieth day of the
moon, as has been said, being taken to assist at the ordination; for
at that time there was no other bishop in all Britain canonically
ordained, besides that Wini.

Chad, being thus consecrated bishop, began immediately to
devote himself to ecclesiastical truth and to chastity; to apply himself to humility, continence, and study; to travel about, not on
horseback, but after the manner of the apostles, on foot, to preach

the Gospel in towns, the open country, cottages, villages, and castles; for he was one of the disciples of Aidan, and endeavoured to
instruct his people, by the same actions and behaviour, according
to his and his brother Cedd's example. Wilfrid also being made a
bishop, came into Britain, and in like manner by his doctrine
brought into the English Church many rules of Catholic observance. Whence it followed, that the Catholic institutions daily
gained strength, and all the Scots that dwelt in England either
conformed to these, or returned into their own country.

CHAPTER XXIX

HOW THE PRIEST WIGHARD WAS SENT FROM BRITAIN TO ROME, TO BE CONSECRATED ARCHBISHOP, OF HIS DEATH THERE, AND OF THE LETTERS OF THE APOSTOLIC POPE GIVING AN ACCOUNT THEREOF. [A.D. 665.]

AT this time the most noble King Oswy, of the province of the
Northumbrians, and Egbert of Kent, having consulted together
about the state of the English Church (for Oswy, though educated
by the Scots, perfectly understood that the Roman was the
Catholic and Apostolic Church), with the consent of the holy
church of the English nation, accepted of a good man, and fit
priest, to be made a bishop, called Wighard, one of Bishop
Deusdedit's clergy, and sent him to Rome to be ordained bishop,
to the end that he, having received the degree of an archbishop,
might ordain Catholic prelates for the churches of the English
nation throughout all Britain. But Wighard, arriving at Rome, was
cut off by death, before he could be consecrated bishop, and the
following letter was sent back into Britain to King Oswy—

*"To the most excellent Lord, our son, Oswy, king of the Saxons,
Vitalian, bishop, servant of the servants of God.* We have received your
excellency's pleasing letters; by reading whereof we understand
your most pious devotion and fervent love to obtain everlasting
life; and that by the protecting hand of God you have been con-

verted to the true and apostolic faith, hoping that as you reign in your nation, so you will hereafter reign in Christ. Blessed be the nation, therefore, that has been found worthy to have such a wise king and worshipper of God; forasmuch as he is not himself alone a worshipper of God, but also studies day and night the conversion of all his subjects to the Catholic and apostolic faith, to the redemption of his own soul. Who will not rejoice at hearing such pleasant things? Who will not be delighted at such good works? Because your nation has believed in Christ the Almighty God, according to the words of the Divine prophets, as it is written in Isaiah, 'In that day there shall be a root of Jesse, which shall stand for an ensign of the people; to him shall the Gentiles seek.' And again, 'Listen, O isles, unto me, and hearken ye people from afar.' And a little after, 'It is a light thing that thou shouldst be my servant to raise up the tribes of Jacob, and to restore the preserved of Israel. I will also give thee for a light to the Gentiles, that thou mayest be my salvation to the ends of the earth.' And again, 'Kings shall see, princes also shall arise and worship.' And presently after, 'I have given thee for a covenant of the people, to establish the earth, and possess the desolate heritages; that thou mayest say to the prisoners, Go forth; to them that are in darkness, Show yourselves.' And again, 'I the Lord have called thee in righteousness, and will hold thine hand, and will keep thee, and give thee for a light of the Gentiles, and for a covenant of the people; to open the blind eyes, to bring out the prisoner from the prison, and them that sit in darkness from the prison-house.'

"Behold, most excellent son, how plain it is, not only of you, but also of all the nations of the prophets, that they shall believe in Christ, the Creator of all things. Wherefore it behoves your highness, as being a member of Christ, in all things, continually to follow the pious rule of the prince of the apostles, in celebrating Easter, and in all things delivered by the blessed apostles, Peter and Paul, whose doctrine daily enlightens the hearts of believers, even as the two heavenly lights, the sun and moon, daily illumine all the earth."

And after some lines, wherein he speaks of celebrating Easter uniformly throughout all the world, he adds,—

"We have not been able now to find, considering the length of the journey, a man, docile, and qualified in all respects to be a bishop, according to the tenor of your letters. But as soon as such a proper person shall be found, we will send him well instructed to your country, that he may, by word of mouth, and through the Divine oracles, with the assistance of God, root out all the enemy's tares throughout your island. We have received the presents sent by your highness to the blessed prince of the apostles, for an eternal memorial, and return you thanks, and always pray for your safety with the clergy of Christ. But he that brought these presents has been removed out of this world, and is buried at the church of the apostles, for whom we have been much concerned, because he died here. However, we have ordered the blessed gifts of the holy martyrs, that is, the relics of the blessed apostles, Peter and Paul, and of the holy martyrs, Laurentius, John, and Paul, and Gregory, and Pancratius, to be delivered to the bearers of these our letters, to be by them delivered to you. And to your consort also, our spiritual daughter, we have by the aforesaid bearers sent a cross, with a gold key to it, made out of the most holy chains of the apostles, Peter and Paul; at whose pious endeavours all the Apostolic See rejoices with us, as much as her pious works shine and blossom before God.

"We therefore desire your highness will hasten, according to our wish, to dedicate all your island to Christ our God; for you certainly have for your protector, the Redeemer of mankind, our Lord Jesus Christ, who will prosper you in all things, that you may bring together a new people of Christ; establishing there the Catholic and apostolic faith. For it is written, 'Seek first the kingdom of God and his righteousness, and all these things shall be added to you.' Truly your highness seeks, and shall no doubt obtain, that all your islands shall be made subject to you, as is our wish and desire. Saluting your excellency with fatherly affection, we always pray to the Divine Goodness, that it will vouchsafe to assist you and yours in all good works, that you may reign with Christ in the world to come. May the Heavenly Grace preserve your excellency in safety!"

In the next book we shall have a more suitable occasion to show you who was found out and consecrated in Wighard's place.

CHAPTER XXX

THE EAST SAXONS, DURING A PESTILENCE, RETURNING TO IDOLATRY, ARE IMMEDIATELY BROUGHT BACK FROM THEIR ERROR BY THE BISHOP JARUMAN. [A.D. 665.]

AT the same time, the Kings Sighere and Sebbi, though subject to Wulfhere, king of the Mercians, governed the province of the East Saxons after Suidhelm, of whom we have spoken above. That province labouring under the aforesaid mortality, Sighere, with that part of the people, that was under his dominion, forsook the mysteries of the Christian faith, and turned apostate. For the king himself, and many of the commons and great men, being fond of this life, and not seeking after another, or rather not believing that there was any other, began to restore the temples that had been abandoned, and to adore idols, as if they might by those means be protected against the mortality. But Sebbi, his companion and co-heir in the kingdom, with his people, very devoutly preserved the faith which he had embraced, and, as we shall show hereafter, ended his faithful life with much felicity.

King Wulfhere, understanding that the faith of the province was partly profaned, sent Bishop Jaruman, who was successor to Trumhere, to correct that error, and restore the province to the truth. He proceeded with much discretion (as I was informed by a priest who bore him company in that journey, and had been his fellow labourer in the word), for he was a religious and good man, and travelling through all the country, far and near, reduced both the aforesaid king and people to the way of righteousness, so that, either forsaking or destroying the temples and altars which they had erected, they opened the churches, and rejoiced in confessing the name of Christ, which they had opposed, being more desirous to die in Him with the faith of the resurrection, than to live in the filth of apostasy among their idols. These things being performed, the priests and teachers returned home with joy.

BOOK IV

CHAPTER I

DEUSDEDIT, ARCHBISHOP OF CANTERBURY, DYING, WIGHARD WAS SENT TO ROME TO SUCCEED HIM IN THAT DIGNITY; BUT HE DYING THERE, THEODORE WAS ORDAINED ARCHBISHOP, AND SENT INTO BRITAIN WITH THE ABBAT HADRIAN. [A.D. 664.]

IN the above-mentioned year of the aforesaid eclipse, which was presently followed by the pestilence, in which also Bishop Colman, being overcome by the unanimous consent of the Catholics, returned home, Deusdedit, the sixth bishop of the church of Canterbury, died on the 14th of July. Erconbert, also, king of Kent, departed this life the same month and day; leaving his kingdom to his son Egbert, which he held nine years. The see then became vacant for some considerable time, until the priest Wighard, a man skilled in ecclesiastical discipline, of the English race, was sent to Rome by the said King Egbert, and Oswy, king of the Northumbrians, as was briefly mentioned in the foregoing book, with a request that he might be ordained bishop of the church of England; sending at the same time presents to the apostolic pope, and many vessels of gold and silver. Arriving at Rome, where Vitalian presided at that time over the Apostolic See, and having made known to the aforesaid pope the occasion of his journey, he was not long after snatched away, with almost all his companions that went with him, by a pestilence which happened at that time.

But the apostolic pope having consulted about that affair, made diligent inquiry for some one to send to be archbishop of the English churches. There was then in the Niridian monastery, which is not far from the city of Naples in Campania, an abbat, called Hadrian, by nation an African, well versed in holy writ, experienced in monastical and ecclesiastical discipline, and excellently skilled both in the Greek and Latin tongues. The pope, sending for him, commanded him to accept of the bishopric, and repair into Britain; he answered, that he was unworthy of so great a dignity, but said he could name another, whose learning and age were fitter for the episcopal office. And having proposed to the pope a certain monk, belonging to a neighbouring monastery of virgins, whose name was Andrew, he was by all that knew him judged worthy of a bishopric; but bodily infirmity prevented his being advanced to the episcopal station. Then again Hadrian was pressed to accept of the bishopric; but he desired a respite for a time, to see whether he could find another fit to be ordained bishop.

There was at that time in Rome, a monk, called Theodore, well known to Hadrian, born at Tarsus in Cilicia, a man well instructed in worldly and Divine literature, as also in Greek and Latin; of known probity of life, and venerable for age, being sixty-six years old. Hadrian offered him to the pope to be ordained bishop, and prevailed; but upon these conditions, that he should conduct him into Britain, because he had already travelled through France twice upon several occasions, and was, therefore, better acquainted with the way, and was, moreover, sufficiently provided with men of his own; as also that being his fellow labourer in doctrine, he might take special care that Theodore should not, according to the custom of the Greeks, introduce anything contrary to the true faith into the church where he presided. Hadrian, being ordained sub-deacon, waited four months for his hair to grow, that it might be shorn into the shape of a crown; for he had before the tonsure of St. Paul, the apostle, after the manner of the eastern people. He was ordained by Pope Vitalian, in the year of our Lord 668, on Sunday, the 26th of March, and on the 27th of May was sent with Hadrian into Britain.

They proceeded by sea to Marseilles, and thence by land to Arles, and having there delivered to John, archbishop of that city, Pope Vitalian's letters of recommendation, were by him detained till Ebrin, the king's mayor of the palace, sent them a pass to go where they pleased. Having received the same, Theodore repaired to Agilbert, bishop of Paris, of whom we have spoken above, and was by him kindly received, and long entertained. But Hadrian went first to Emme, and then to Faro, bishops of Sens and Meaux, and lived with them a considerable time; for the hard winter had obliged them to rest wherever they could. King Egbert, being informed by messengers that the bishop they had asked of the Roman prelate was in the kingdom of France, sent thither his præfect, Redfrid, to conduct him; who, being arrived there, with Ebrin's leave, conveyed him to the port of Quentavic; where, being indisposed, he made some stay, and as soon as he began to recover, sailed over into Britain. But Ebrin detained Hadrian, suspecting that he went on some message from the emperor to the kings of Britain, to the prejudice of his kingdom, of which he at that time took especial care; however, when he found that he really had no such commission, he discharged him, and permitted him to follow Theodore. As soon as he came, he received from him the monastery of St. Peter the apostle, where the archbishops of Canterbury are usually buried, as I have said before; for at his departure, the apostolic lord had ordered that he should provide for him in his diocese, and give him a suitable place to live in with his followers.

CHAPTER II

THEODORE VISITS ALL PLACES; THE CHURCHES OF THE
ENGLISH BEGIN TO BE INSTRUCTED IN HOLY LITERA-
TURE, AND IN THE CATHOLIC TRUTH; PUTTA IS MADE
BISHOP OF THE CHURCH OF ROCHESTER IN THE ROOM
OF DAMIANUS. [A.D. 669.]

THEODORE arrived at his church the second year after his consecration, on Sunday, the 27th of May, and held the same twenty-one
years, three months, and twenty-six days. Soon after, he visited all
the island, wherever the tribes of the Angles inhabited, for he was
willingly entertained and heard by all persons; and everywhere
attended and assisted by Hadrian, he taught the right rule of life,
and the canonical custom of celebrating Easter. This was the first
archbishop whom all the English church obeyed. And forasmuch
as both of them were, as has been said before, well read both in
sacred and in secular literature, they gathered a crowd of disciples, and there daily flowed from them rivers of knowledge to
water the hearts of their hearers; and, together with the books of
holy writ, they also taught them the arts of ecclesiastical poetry,
astronomy, and arithmetic. A testimony of which is, that there are
still living at this day some of their scholars, who are as well versed
in the Greek and Latin tongues as in their own, in which they were
born. Nor were there ever happier times since the English came
into Britain; for their kings, being brave men and good Christians,
they were a terror to all barbarous nations, and the minds of all
men were bent upon the joys of the heavenly kingdom of which
they had just heard; and all who desired to be instructed in sacred
reading had masters at hand to teach them.

From that time also they began in all the churches of the
English to learn sacred music, which till then had been only
known in Kent. And, excepting James above-mentioned, the first
singing-master in the churches of the Northumbrians was Eddi,

surnamed Stephen, invited from Kent by the most reverend Wilfrid, who was the first of the bishops of the English nation that taught the churches of the English the Catholic mode of life.

Theodore, visiting all parts, ordained bishops in proper places, and with their assistance corrected such things as he found faulty. Among the rest, when he upbraided Bishop Chad that he had not been duly consecrated, he, with great humility, answered, "If you know I have not duly received episcopal ordination, I willingly resign the office, for I never thought myself worthy of it; but, though unworthy, in obedience submitted to undertake it." Theodore, hearing his humble answer, said that he should not resign the bishopric, and he himself completed his ordination after the Catholic manner. But at the time when Deusdedit died, and a bishop for the church of Canterbury was by request ordained and sent, Wilfrid was also sent out of Britain into France to be ordained; and because he returned before Theodore, he ordained priests and deacons in Kent till the archbishop should come to his see. Being arrived in the city of Rochester, where the see had been long vacant by the death of Damianus, he ordained a person better skilled in ecclesiastical discipline, and more addicted to simplicity of life than active in worldly affairs. His name was Putta, and he was extraordinarily skilful in the Roman style of church music, which he had learned from the disciples of the holy Pope Gregory.

CHAPTER III

HOW CHAD, ABOVE-MENTIONED, WAS MADE BISHOP OF THE MERCIANS. OF HIS LIFE, DEATH, AND BURIAL. [A.D. 669.]

AT that time, the Mercians were governed by King Wulfhere, who, on the death of Jaruman, desired of Theodore to supply him and his people with a bishop; but Theodore would not obtain a new one for them, but requested of King Oswy that Chad might be their bishop. He then lived retired at his monastery, which is at

Lestingau, Wilfrid filling the bishopric of York, and of all the Northumbrians, and likewise of the Picts, as far as the dominions of King Oswy extended. And, seeing that it was the custom of that most reverend prelate to go about the work of the Gospel to several places rather on foot than on horseback, Theodore commanded him to ride whenever he had a long journey to undertake; and finding him very unwilling to omit his former pious labour, he himself, with his hands, lifted him on the horse; for he thought him a holy man, and therefore obliged him to ride wherever he had need to go. Chad having received the bishopric of the Mercians and Lindisfarne, took care to administer the same with great rectitude of life, according to the example of the ancients. King Wulfhere also gave him land of fifty families, to build a monastery, at the place called Ad Barve, or "At the Wood," in the province of Lindsey, wherein marks of the regular life instituted by him continue to this day.

He had his episcopal see in the place called Lichfield, in which he also died, and was buried, and where the see of the succeeding bishops of that province still continues. He had built himself a habitation not far from the church, wherein he was wont to pray and read with seven or eight of the brethren, as often as he had any spare time from the labour and ministry of the word. When he had most gloriously governed the church in that province two years and a half, the Divine Providence so ordaining, there came round a season like that of which Ecclesiastes says, "That there is a time to cast stones, and a time to gather them;" for there happened a mortality sent from heaven, which, by means of the death of the flesh, translated the stones of the church from their earthly places to the heavenly building. And when, after many of the church of that most reverend prelate had been taken out of the flesh, his hour also drew near wherein he was to pass out of this world to our Lord, it happened one day that he was in the aforesaid dwelling, with only one brother, called Owini, his other companions being upon some reasonable occasion returned to the church. Now Owini was a monk of great merit, having forsaken the world with the pure intention of obtaining the heavenly reward; worthy in all respects to have the secrets of our Lord revealed to him, and worthy to have credit given by his hearers to what he said, for he came with Queen Etheldrid from the province of the East Angles, and was her prime minister, and governor of her family. As the fervour of his faith increased, resolving to renounce the world, he did not go about it slothfully, but so fully forsook the things of this world, that, quitting all he had, clad in a plain garment, and carrying an axe and hatchet in his hand, he came to the monastery of that most reverend prelate, called Lestingau; denoting, that he did not go to the monastery to live idle, as some do, but to labour, which he also confirmed by practice; for as he was less capable of meditating on the Holy Scriptures, he the more earnestly applied himself to the labour of his hands. In short, he was received by the bishop into the house aforesaid, and there entertained with the brethren, and whilst they were engaged within in reading, he was without, doing such things as were necessary.

One day when he was thus employed abroad, and his companions were gone to the church, as I began to state, the bishop was alone reading or praying in the oratory of that place, when on a sudden, as he afterwards said, he heard the voice of persons singing most sweetly and rejoicing, and appearing to descend from heaven. Which voice he said he first heard coming from the southeast, and that afterwards it drew near him, till it came to the roof of the oratory where the bishop was, and entering therein, filled the same and all about it. He listened attentively to what he heard, and after about half an hour, perceived the same song of joy to ascend from the roof of the said oratory, and to return to heaven the same way it came, with inexpressible sweetness. When he had stood some time astonished, and seriously revolving in his mind what it might be, the bishop opened the window of the oratory, and making a noise with his hand, as he was often wont to do, ordered him to come in to him. He accordingly went hastily in, and the bishop said to him, "Make haste to the church, and cause the seven brothers to come hither, and do you come with them." When they were come, he first admonished them to preserve the virtue of peace among themselves, and towards all others; and indefatigably to practise the rules of regular discipline, which they had either been taught by him, or seen him observe or had noticed in the words or actions of the former fathers. Then he added, that the day of his death was at hand; for, said he, "that amiable guest, who was wont to visit our brethren, has vouchsafed also to come to me this day, and to call me out of this world. Return, therefore, to the church, and speak to the brethren, that they in their prayers recommend my passage to our Lord, and that they be careful to provide for their own, the hour whereof is uncertain, by watching, prayer, and good works."

When he had spoken thus much and more, and they, having received his blessing, had gone away in sorrow, he who had heard the heavenly song returned alone, and prostrating himself on the ground, said, "I beseech you, father, may I be permitted to ask a question?"—"Ask what you will," answered the bishop. Then he added, "I entreat you to tell me what song of joy was that which I heard coming upon this oratory, and after some time returning to heaven?" The bishop answered, "If you heard the singing, and know of the coming of the heavenly company, I command you, in the name of our Lord, that you do not tell the same to any before my death. They were angelic spirits, who came to call me to my heavenly reward, which I have always longed after, and they promised they would return seven days hence, and take me away with them." Which was accordingly fulfilled, as had been said to him; for being presently seized with a languishing distemper, and the same daily increasing, on the seventh day, as had been promised to him, when he had prepared for death by receiving the body and blood of our Lord, his soul being delivered from the prison of the body, the angels, as may justly be believed, attending him, he departed to the joys of heaven.

It is no wonder that he joyfully beheld the day of his death, or rather the day of our Lord, which he had always carefully expected till it came; for notwithstanding his many merits of continence, humility, teaching, prayer, voluntary poverty, and other virtues, he was so full of the fear of God, so mindful of his last end in all his actions, that, as I was informed by one of the brothers who instructed me in Divinity, and who had been bred in his monastery, and under his direction, whose name was Trumhere, if it happened that there blew a strong gust of wind when he was reading or doing any other thing, he immediately called upon God for mercy, and begged it might be extended to all mankind. If the wind grew stronger, he closed his book, and prostrating himself on the ground, prayed still more earnestly. But, if it proved a violent storm of wind or rain, or else that the earth and air were filled with thunder and lightning, he would repair to the church, and devote himself to prayers and repeating of psalms till the weather became calm. Being asked by his followers why he did so, he answered, "Have not you read—'The Lord also thundered in the heavens, and the Highest gave forth his voice. Yea, he sent out his arrows and scattered them; and he shot out lightnings, and discomfited them.' For the Lord moves the air, raises the winds, darts lightning, and thunders from heaven, to excite the inhabitants of the earth to fear Him; to put them in mind of the future judgment; to dispel their pride, and vanquish their boldness, by bringing into their thoughts that dreadful time, when the heavens and the earth being in a flame, He will come in the clouds, with great power and majesty, to judge the quick and the dead. Wherefore," said he, "it behoves us to answer his heavenly admonition with due fear and love; that, as often as He lifts his hand through the trembling sky, as it were to strike, but does not yet let it fall, we may immediately implore his mercy; and searching the recesses of our hearts, and cleansing the filth of our vices, we may carefully behave ourselves so as never to be struck."

With this revelation and account of the aforesaid brother, concerning the death of this prelate, agrees the discourse of the most reverend Father Egbert, above spoken of, who long led a monastic life with the same Chad, when both were youths, in Ireland, praying, observing continency, and meditating on the Holy Scriptures. But when he afterwards returned into his own country, the other continued in a strange country for our Lord's sake till the end of his life. A long time after, Hygbald, a most holy and continent man, who was an abbat in the province of Lindsey, came out of Britain to visit him, and whilst these holy men were discoursing of the life of the former fathers, and rejoicing to imitate the same, mention was made of the most reverend prelate, Chad, whereupon Egbert said, "I know a man in this island, still in the flesh, who, when that prelate passed out of this world, saw the soul of his brother Cedd, with a company of angels, descending from heaven, who, having taken his soul along with them, returned thither again." Whether he said this of himself, or some other, we do not certainly know; but the same being said by so great a man, there can be no doubt of the truth thereof.

Chad died on the 2nd of March, and was first buried by St. Mary's Church, but afterwards, when the church of the most holy prince of the apostles, Peter, was built, his bones were translated into it. In both which places, as a testimony of his virtue, frequent miraculous cures are wont to be wrought. And of late, a certain distracted person, who had been wandering about everywhere, arrived there in the evening, unknown or unregarded by the keepers of the place, and having rested there all the night, went out in his perfect senses the next morning, to the surprise and delight of all; thus showing that a cure had been performed on him through the goodness of God. The place of the sepulchre is a wooden monument, made like a little house, covered, having a hole in the wall, through which those that go thither for devotion usually put in their hand and take out some of the dust, which they put into water and give to sick cattle or men to drink, upon which they are presently eased of their infirmity, and restored to health. In his place, Theodore ordained Winfrid, a good and modest man, to preside, as his predecessors had done, over the bishoprics of the Mercians, the Midland Angles, and the Lindisfarnes, of all which, Wulfhere, who was still living, was king. Winfrid was one of the clergy of the prelate he had succeeded, and had for a considerable time filled the office of deacon under him.

CHAPTER IV

BISHOP COLMAN, HAVING LEFT BRITAIN, BUILT TWO
MONASTERIES IN SCOTLAND; THE ONE FOR THE SCOTS,
THE OTHER FOR THE ENGLISH HE HAD TAKEN ALONG
WITH HIM. [A.D. 667.]

IN the meantime, Colman, the Scottish bishop, departing from
Britain, took along with him all the Scots he had assembled in the
isle of Lindisfarne, and also about thirty of the English nation,
who had been all instructed in the monastic life; and leaving some
brothers in his church, he repaired first to the isle of Hii (Iona),
whence he had been sent to preach the word of God to the
English nation. Afterwards he retired to a small island, which is to
the west of Ireland, and at some distance from its coast, called in
the language of the Scots, Inisbofinde, the Island of the White
Heifer. Arriving there, he built a monastery, and placed in it the
monks he had brought of both nations; who not agreeing among
themselves, by reason that the Scots, in the summer season, when
the harvest was to be brought in, leaving the monastery, wandered
about through places with which they were acquainted; but
returned again the next winter, and would have what the English
had provided to be in common; Colman sought to put an end to
this dissension, and travelling about far and near, he found a place
in the island of Ireland fit to build a monastery, which, in the language of the Scots, is called Mageo, and brought a small part of it
of the earl to whom it belonged, to build his monastery thereon;
upon condition, that the monks residing there should pray to our
Lord for him who had let them have the place. Then building a
monastery, with the assistance of the earl and all the neighbours,
he placed the English there, leaving the Scots in the aforesaid
island. This monastery is to this day possessed by English inhabitants; being the same that, grown up from a small beginning to be
very large, is generally called Mageo; and as all things have long
since been brought under a better method, it contains an exem-

plary society of monks, who are gathered there from the province of the English, and live by the labour of their hands, after the example of the venerable fathers, under a rule and a canonical abbat, in much continency and singleness of life.

CHAPTER V

OF THE DEATH OF THE KINGS OSWY AND EGBERT, AND OF THE SYNOD HELD AT HERTFORD, IN WHICH ARCH-BISHOP THEODORE PRESIDED. [A.D. 670.]

IN the year of the incarnation of our Lord 670, being the second year after Theodore arrived in England, Oswy, king of the Northumbrians, fell sick, and died, in the fifty-eighth year of his age. He at that time bore so great affection to the Roman apostolical institution, that had he recovered of his sickness, he had designed to go to Rome, and there to end his days at the Holy Places, having entreated Bishop Wilfrid, by the promise of a considerable donation in money, to conduct him on his journey. He died on the 15th of February, leaving his son Egfrid his successor in the kingdom. In the third year of his reign, Theodore assembled a synod of bishops, and many other teachers of the church, who loved and were acquainted with the canonical statutes of the fathers. When they were met together, he began, as became a prelate, to enjoin the observance of such things as were agreeable to the unity and the peace of the church. The purport of which synodical proceedings is as follows—

"In the name of our Lord God and Saviour Jesus Christ, who reigns for ever and for ever, and governs his church, it was thought meet that we should assemble, according to the custom of the venerable canons, to treat about the necessary affairs of the church. We met on the 24th day of September, the first indiction, at a place called Hertford, myself, Theodore, the unworthy bishop of the see of Canterbury, appointed by the Apostolic See, our fellow priest and most reverend brother, Bisi, bishop of the East Angles; also by his proxies, our brother and fellow priest, Wilfrid bishop of the nation of the Northumbrians, as also our brothers and fellow priests, Putta, bishop of the Kentish castle, called Rochester; Eleutherius, bishop of the West Saxons, and Winfrid, bishop of the province of the Mercians. When we were all met together, and were sat down in order, I said, 'I beseech you, most dear brothers, for the love and fear of our Redeemer, that we may all treat in common for our faith; to the end that whatsoever has been decreed and defined by the holy and reverend fathers, may be inviolably observed by all.' This and much more I spoke tending to the preservation of the charity and unity of the church; and when I had ended my discourse, I asked every one of them in order, whether they consented to observe the things that had been formerly canonically decreed by the fathers? To which all our fellow priests answered, 'It so pleases us, and we will all most willingly observe with a cheerful mind whatever is laid down in the canons of the holy fathers.' I then produced the said book of canons, and publicly showed them ten chapters in the same, which I had marked in several places, because I knew them to be of the most importance to us, and entreated that they might be most particularly received by them all.

"Chapter I. That we all in common keep the holy day of Easter on the Sunday after the fourteenth moon of the first month.

"II. That no bishop intrude into the diocese of another, but be satisfied with the government of the people committed to him.

"III. That it shall not be lawful for any bishop to trouble monasteries dedicated to God, nor to take anything forcibly from them.

"IV. That monks do not remove from one place to another, that is, from monsatery to monastery, unless with the consent of their own abbat; but that they continue in the obedience which they promised at the time of their conversion.

"V. That no clergyman, forsaking his own bishop, shall wander about, or be anywhere entertained without letters of recommendation from his own prelate. But if he shall be once received, and will not return when invited, both the receiver, and the person received, be under excommunication.

"VI. That bishops and clergymen, when travelling, shall be content with the hospitality that is afforded them; and that it be not lawful for them to exercise any priestly function without leave of the bishop in whose diocese they are.

"VII. That a synod be assembled twice a year; but in regard that several causes obstruct the same, it was approved by all, that we should meet on the 1st of August once a year, at the place called Clofeshoch.

"VIII. That no bishop, through ambition, shall set himself before another; but that they shall all observe the time and order of their consecration.

"IX. It was generally set forth, that more bishops should be made, as the number of believers increased; but this matter for the present was passed over.

"X. Of marriages; that nothing be allowed but lawful wedlock; that none commit incest; no man quit his true wife, unless, as the gospel teaches, on account of fornication. And if any man shall put away his own wife, lawfully joined to him in matrimony, that he take no other, if he wishes to be a good Christian, but continue as he is, or else be reconciled to his own wife.

"These chapters being thus treated of and defined by all, to the end, that for the future, no scandal of contention might arise from any of us, or that things be falsely set forth, it was thought fit that every one of us should, by subscribing his hand, confirm all the particulars so laid down. Which definitive judgment of ours, I dictated to be written by Titillus our notary. Done in the month and indiction aforesaid. Whosoever, therefore, shall presume in any way to oppose or infringe this decision, confirmed by our consent, and by the subscription of our hands, according to the decree of the canons, must take notice, that he is excluded from all sacerdotal functions, and from our society. May the Divine Grace preserve us in safety, living in the unity of his holy church."

This synod was held in the year from the incarnation of our Lord 673. In which year, Egbert, king of Kent, died in the month of July; his brother Lothere succeeded him on the throne, which he had held eleven years and seven months. Bisi, the bishop of the East Angles, who is said to have been in the aforesaid synod, was successor to Boniface, before spoken of, a man of much sanctity and religion; for when Boniface died, after having been bishop seventeen years, he was by Theodore substituted in his place. Whilst he was still alive, but hindered by much sickness from administering his episcopal functions, two bishops, Ecci and Badwin, were elected and consecrated in his place; from which time to the present, that province has had two bishops.

CHAPTER VI

WINFRID BEING DEPOSED, SEXWULF WAS PUT INTO HIS SEE, AND EARCONWALD MADE BISHOP OF THE EAST SAXONS. [A.D. 674.]

NOT long after, Theodore, the archbishop, taking offence at some disobedience of Winfrid, bishop of the Mercians, deposed him from his bishopric when he had been possessed of it but a few years, and in his place made Sexwulf bishop, who was founder and abbat of the monastery of Medeshamstead, in the country of the Girvii. Winfrid, thus deposed, returned to his monastery of Ad Barve, and there ended his life in holy conversation.

He then also appointed Earconwald bishop of the East Saxons, in the city of London, over whom at that time presided Sebbi and Sighere, of whom mention has been made above. This Earconwald's life and conversation, as well when he was bishop as before his advancement to that dignity, is reported to have been most holy, as is even at this time testified by heavenly miracles; for to this day, his horse-litter, in which he was wont to be carried when sick, is kept by his disciples, and continues to cure many of agues and other distempers; and not only sick persons who are laid in that litter, or close by it, are cured; but the very chips of it, when carried to the sick, are wont immediately to restore them to health.

This man, before he was made bishop, had built two famous monasteries, the one for himself, and the other for his sister Ethelberga, and established them both in regular discipline of the best kind. That for himself was in the county of Surrey, by the river Thames, at a place called Ceortesei, that is, the Island of Ceorot; that for his sister in the province of the East Saxons, at the place called Bercingum, wherein she might be a mother and nurse of devout women. Being put into the government of that monastery, she behaved herself in all respects as became the sister of such a brother, living herself regularly, and piously, and orderly, providing for those under her, as was also manifested by heavenly miracles.

CHAPTER VII

HOW IT WAS INDICATED BY A HEAVENLY LIGHT WHERE THE BODIES OF THE NUNS SHOULD BE BURIED IN THE MONASTERY OF BARKING. [A.D. 676.]

IN this monastery many miracles were wrought, which have been committed to writing by many, from those who knew them, that their memory might be preserved, and following generations edified; some whereof we have also taken care to insert in our Ecclesiastical History. When the mortality, which we have already so often mentioned, ravaging all around, had also seized on that part of this monastery where the men resided, and they were daily hurried away to meet their God, the careful mother of the society began often to inquire in the convent, of the sisters, where they would have their bodies buried, and where a church-yard should be made when the same pestilence should fall upon that part of the monastery in which God's female servants were divided from the men, and they should be snatched away out of this world by the same destruction. Receiving no certain answer, though she often put the question to the sisters, she and all of them received a most certain answer from heaven. For one night, when the morning psalm was ended, and those servants of

Christ were gone out of their oratory to the tombs of the brothers who had departed this life before them, and were singing the usual praises to our Lord, on a sudden a light from heaven, like a great sheet, came down upon them all, and struck them with so much terror, that they, in consternation, left off singing. But that resplendent light, which seemed to exceed the sun at noonday, soon after rising from that place, removed to the south side of the monastery, that is, to the westward of the oratory, and having continued there some time, and covered those parts in the sight of them all, withdrew itself up again to heaven, leaving conviction in the minds of all, that the same light, which was to lead or to receive the souls of those servants of God into heaven, was intended to show the place in which their bodies were to rest, and await the day of the resurrection. This light was so great, that one of the eldest of the brothers, who at the same time was in their oratory with another younger than himself, related in the morning, that the rays of light which came in at the crannies of the doors and windows, seemed to exceed the utmost brightness of daylight itself.

CHAPTER VIII

A LITTLE BOY, DYING IN THE SAME MONASTERY, CALLED UPON A VIRGIN THAT WAS TO FOLLOW HIM; ANOTHER AT THE POINT OF LEAVING HER BODY, SAW SOME SMALL PART OF THE FUTURE GLORY. [A.D. 676.]

THERE was, in the same monastery, a boy, not above three years old, called Esica; who, by reason of his infant age, was bred up among the virgins dedicated to God, and there to pursue his studies. This child being seized by the aforesaid pestilence, when he was at the last gasp, called three times upon one of the virgins consecrated to God, directing his words to her by her own name, as if she had been present, Eadgith! Eadgith! Eadgith! and thus ending his temporal life, entered into that which is eternal. The virgin, whom he called, was immediately seized, where she was, with the same distemper, and departing this life the same day on which she had been called, followed him that called her into the heavenly country.

Likewise, one of those same servants of God, being ill of the same disease, and reduced to extremity, began on a sudden, about midnight, to cry out to them that attended her, desiring they would put out the candle that was lighted there; which, when she had often repeated, and yet no one did it, at last she said, "I know you think I speak this in a raving fit, but let me inform you it is not so; for I tell you, that I see this house filled with so much light, that your candle there seems to me to be dark." And when still no one regarded what she said, or returned any answer, she added, "Let that candle burn as long as you will; but take notice, that it is not my light, for my light will come to me at the dawn of the day." Then she began to tell, that a certain man of God, who had died that same year, had appeared to her, telling her that at the break of day she should depart to the heavenly light. The truth of which vision was made out by the virgin's dying as soon as the day appeared.

CHAPTER IX

OF THE SIGNS WHICH WERE SHOWN FROM HEAVEN WHEN THE MOTHER OF THAT CONGREGATION DEPARTED THIS LIFE. [A.D. 676.]

WHEN Ethelberga, the pious mother of that holy congregation, was about to be taken out of this world, a wonderful vision appeared to one of the sisters, called Tortgith; who, having lived many years in that monastery, always endeavoured, in all humility and sincerity, to serve God, and took care to assist the same mother in keeping up regular discipline, by instructing; and reproving the younger ones. Now, in order that her virtue might be perfected in affliction, according to the apostle, she was suddenly seized with a most grievous distemper, under which, through the good providence of our Redeemer, she suffered very much for the space of nine years; to the end, that whatever stain of vice remained amidst her virtues, either through ignorance or neglect, might all be eradicated by the fire of long tribulation. This person, going out of her chamber one night, just at the first dawn of the day, plainly saw as it were a human body, which was brighter than the sun, wrapped up in a sheet, and lifted up on high, being taken out of the house in which the sisters used to reside. Then looking earnestly to see what it was that drew up the glorious body which she beheld, she perceived it was drawn up as it were by cords brighter than gold, until, entering into the open heavens, it could no longer be seen by her. Reflecting on this vision, she made no doubt that some one of the society would soon die, and her soul be lifted up to heaven by her good works as it were by golden cords, which accordingly happened; for a few days after, the beloved of God, Ethelberga, mother of that society, was delivered out of the prison of the flesh; and her life is known to have been such that no person who knew her ought to question but that the heavenly kingdom was open to her, when she departed from this world.

There was also, in the same monastery, a certain nun, of noble worldly origin, and much nobler in the love of the world to come; who had, for many years, been so disabled in all her body, that she could not move a single limb. Being informed that the venerable abbess's body was carried into the church, till it could be buried, she desired to be carried thither, and to be bowed down towards it, after the manner of one praying; which being done, she spoke to her as if she had been living, and entreated her that she would obtain of the mercy of our compassionate Creator, that she might be delivered from such great and lasting pains; nor was it long before her prayer was heard: for being taken out of the flesh twelve days after, she exchanged her temporal afflictions for an eternal reward. Three years after the death of this lady, the above-mentioned servant of Christ, Tortgith, was so far spent with the distemper before mentioned, that her bones would scarcely hang together; and, at last, when the time of her dissolution was at hand, she not only lost the use of her other limbs, but also of her tongue; which having continued three days and as many nights, she was, on a sudden, relieved by a spiritual vision, opened her mouth and eyes, and looking up to heaven, began thus to direct her discourse to the vision which she saw: "Your coming is very acceptable to me, and you are welcome!" Having so said, she was silent awhile, as it were, waiting for the answer of the person she saw and spoke to; then, as if displeased, she said, "I am not pleased with this;" then pausing awhile, she said again, "If it cannot be to-day, I beg the delay may not be long;" and again holding her peace for a short while, she concluded thus: "If it is positively so decreed, and the resolution cannot be altered, I beg that it may be no longer deferred than this next night." Having so said, and being asked by those about her to whom she talked, she said, "With my most dear mother, Ethelberga;" by which they understood, that she was come to acquaint her that the time of her departure was at hand; for, as she had desired, after one day and night, she was delivered from the bonds and infirmity of the flesh, and entered the joys of eternal salvation.

CHAPTER X

A BLIND WOMAN, PRAYING IN THE BURIAL-PLACE OF THAT MONASTERY, WAS RESTORED TO HER SIGHT. [A.D. 676.]

HILDELITH, a devout servant of God, succeeded Ethelberga in the office of abbess, and presided over that monastery many years, till she was of an extreme old age, with exemplary conduct, in the observance of regular discipline, and in the care of providing all things for the public use. The narrowness of the place where the monastery is built, led her to think that the bones of the male and female servants of Christ, which had been there buried, should be taken up, and translated into the church of the blessed mother of God, and interred in one place; whoever wishes to read it, may find in the book from which we have gathered these things, how often a brightness of heavenly light was seen there, and a fragrancy of wonderful odour smelled, and what other miracles were wrought.

However, I think it by no means fit to pass over the miraculous cure, which the same book informs us was wrought in the churchyard of the said religious house. There lived in that neighbourhood a certain earl, whose wife was seized with a dimness in her eyes, which at length became so bad, that she could not see the least glimpse of light: having continued some time in total darkness, on a sudden she bethought herself that she might recover her lost sight, if she were carried to the monastery of the nuns, and there pray for the same, at the relics of the saints. Nor did she lose any time in performing what she had thought of: for being conducted by her maids to the monastery, which was very near, and professing that she had perfect faith that she should be there healed, she was led into the burial-place, and having long prayed there on her knees, she did not fail to be heard, for as she rose from prayer, before she went out of the place, she received the gift of sight which she had desired; and whereas she had been led thither by her servants, she now returned home joyfully without help: as if she had lost her sight to no other end than that she might make it appear how great light the saints enjoyed in heaven, and how great was the power of their virtue.

CHAPTER XI

SEBBI, KING OF THE SAME PROVINCE, ENDS HIS LIFE IN A MONASTERY. [A.D. 694.]

AT that time, as the same little book informs us, Sebbi, a devout man, of whom mention has been made above, governed the kingdom of the East Saxons. He was much addicted to religious actions, almsgiving, and frequent prayer; preferring a private and monastic life to all the wealth and honours of his kingdom, which sort of life he would also long before have undertaken, had not his wife positively refused to be divorced from him; for which reason many were of opinion, and often said so, that a person of such a disposition ought rather to have been a bishop than a king. When he had been thirty years a king, and a soldier of the heavenly kingdom, he fell into a violent sickness, of which he died, and admonished his wife, that they should then at least jointly devote themselves to the service of God, since they could no longer enjoy, or rather serve, the world. Having with much difficulty obtained this of her, he repaired to Waldhere, bishop of London, who had succeeded Earconwald, and with his blessing received the religious habit, which he had long desired. He also carried to him a considerable sum of money, to be given to the poor, reserving nothing to himself, but rather coveting to remain poor in spirit for the sake of the kingdom of heaven.

When the aforesaid distemper increased upon him, and he perceived the day of his death to be drawing near, being a man of a royal disposition, he began to apprehend lest, when under pain, and at the approach of death, he might be guilty of anything unworthy of his person, either in words, or any motion of his limbs. Wherefore, calling to him the aforesaid bishop of London, in which city he then was, he entreated him that none might be present at his death, besides the bishop himself, and two of his attendants. The bishop having promised that he would most willingly perform the same, not long after the man of God composed himself to sleep, and saw a comforting vision, which took from him all anxiety for the aforesaid uneasiness; and, moreover, showed him on what day he was to depart this life. For, as he afterwards related, he saw three men in bright garments come to him; one of whom sat down before his bed, whilst his companions stood and inquired about the state of the sick man they came to see: he who was sitting in front of the bed said, that his soul should depart his body without any pain, and with a great splendour of light; and declared that he should die the third day after; both which particulars happened, as he had been informed by the vision; for on the third day after, he suddenly fell, as it were, into a slumber, and breathed out his soul without any sense or pain.

A stone coffin having been provided for burying his body, when they came to lay it in the same, they found his body a span longer than the coffin. Hereupon they hewed away the stone, and made the coffin about two fingers longer; but neither would it then contain the body. Under this difficulty of entombing him, they had thoughts either to get another coffin, or else to shorten the body, by bending it at the knees, if they could. But a wonderful event, caused by Providence, prevented the execution of either of those designs; for on a sudden, in the presence of the bishop, and Sighard, the son of the king who had turned monk, and who reigned after him jointly with his brother Suefred, and of a considerable number of men, that same coffin was found to answer the length of the body, insomuch that a pillow might also be put in at the head; and at the feet the coffin was four fingers longer than the body. He was buried in the church of the blessed Apostle of the Gentiles, by whose instructions he had learned to hope for heavenly things.

CHAPTER XII

HEDDA SUCCEEDS ELEUTHERIUS IN THE BISHOPRIC OF THE WEST SAXONS; CUICHELM SUCCEEDS PUTTA IN THAT OF ROCHESTER, AND IS HIMSELF SUCCEEDED BY GEBMUND; AND WHO WERE THEN BISHOPS OF THE NORTHUMBRIANS. [A.D. 673.]

ELEUTHERIUS was the fourth bishop of the West Saxons; for Birinus was the first, Agilbert the second, and Wini the third. When Kenwalk, in whose reign the said Eleutherius was made bishop, died, his under-rulers took upon them the kingdom of the people, and dividing it among themselves, held it ten years; and during their rule he died, and Hedda succeeded him in the bishopric, having been consecrated by Theodore, in the city of London; during whose prelacy, Cadwalla, having subdued and removed those rulers, took upon him the government. When he had reigned two years, and whilst the same bishop still governed the church, he quitted his sovereignty for the love of the heavenly kingdom, and, going away to Rome, ended his days there, as shall be said more fully hereafter.

In the year of our Lord's incarnation 676, when Ethelred, king of the Mercians, ravaged Kent with a powerful army, and profaned churches and monasteries, without regard to religion, or the fear of God, he among the rest destroyed the city of Rochester; Putta, who was bishop, was absent at that time, but when he understood that his church was ravaged, and all things taken away, he went to Sexwulf, bishop of the Mercians, and having received of him a certain church, and a small spot of land, ended his days there in peace; in no way endeavouring to restore his bishopric, because (as has been said above) he was more industrious in spiritual than in worldly affairs; serving God only in that church, and going wherever he was desired, to teach church music. Theodore consecrated Cuichelm bishop of Rochester in his stead; but he, not long after, departing from his bishopric for want of necessaries, and withdrawing to other parts, Gebmund was substituted in his place.

In the year of our Lord's incarnation, 678, which is the eighth of the reign of Egfrid, in the month of August, appeared a star, called a comet, which continued for three months, rising in the morning, and darting out, as it were, a pillar of radiant flame. The same year a dissension broke out between King Egfrid and the most reverend prelate, Wilfrid, who was driven from his see, and two bishops substituted in his stead, to preside over the nation of the Northumbrians, namely, Bosa, to preside over the nation of the Deiri; and Eata over that of the Bernicians; the former having his see in the city of York, the latter in the church of Hagulstad, or else Lindisfarne; both of them promoted to the episcopal dignity from a society of monks. With them also was Edhed ordained bishop in the province of Lindsey, which King Egfrid had but newly subdued, having overcome and vanquished Wulfhere; and this was the first bishop of its own which that province had; the second was Ethelwin; the third Edgar; the fourth Cynebert, who is there at present. Before Edhed, Sexwulf was bishop as well of that province as of the Mercians and Midland Angles; so that, when expelled from Lindsey, he continued in the government of those provinces. Edhed, Bosa, and Eata, were ordained at York by Archbishop Theodore; who also, three years after the departure of Wilfrid, added two bishops to their number; Tumbert, in the church of Hagulstad, Eata still continuing in that of Lindisfarne; and Trumwine in the province of the Picts, which at that time was subject to the English. Edhed returning from Lindsey, because Ethelred had recovered that province, was placed by him over the church of Ripon.

CHAPTER XIII

BISHOP WILFRID CONVERTS THE PROVINCE OF THE SOUTH SAXONS TO CHRIST. [A.D. 681.]

BEING expelled from his bishopric, and having travelled in several parts, Wilfrid went to Rome. He afterwards returned to Britain; and though he could not, by reason of the enmity of the aforesaid king, be received into his own country or diocese, yet he could not be restrained from preaching the Gospel; for, taking his way into the province of the South Saxons, which extends from Kent on the west and south, as far as the West Saxons, and contains land of 7000 families, who at that time were still pagans, he administered to them the word of faith, and the baptism of salvation. Ethelwalch, king of that nation, had been, not long before, baptized in the province of the Mercians, by the persuasion of King Wulfhere, who was present, and was also his godfather, and as such gave him two provinces, viz., the Isle of Wight, and the province of Meanwara, in the nation of the West Saxons. The bishop, therefore, with the king's consent, or rather to his great satisfaction, baptized the principal generals and soldiers of that country; and the priests, Eappa, and Padda, and Burghelm, and Eadda, either then, or afterwards, baptized the rest of the people. The queen, whose name was Ebba, had been christened in her own island, the province of the Wiccii. She was the daughter of Eanfrid, the brother of Eanher, who were both Christians, as were their people; but all the province of the South Saxons were strangers to the name and faith of God. There was among them a certain monk of the Scottish nation, whose name was Dicul, who had a very small monastery, at the place called Bosanham, encompassed with the sea and woods, and in it five or six brothers, who served our Lord in poverty and humility; but none of the natives cared either to follow their course of life, or hear their preaching.

But Bishop Wilfrid, by preaching to them, not only delivered them from the misery of perpetual damnation, but also from an inexhaustible calamity of temporal death, for no rain had fallen in that province in three years before his arrival, whereupon a dreadful famine ensued, which cruelly destroyed the people. In short, it is reported, that very often, forty or fifty men, being spent with want, would go together to some precipice, or to the sea-shore, and there, hand in hand, perish by the fall, or be swallowed up by the waves. But on the very day on which the nation received the baptism of faith, there fell a soft but plentiful rain; the earth revived again, and the verdure being restored to the fields, the season was pleasant and fruitful. Thus the former superstition being rejected, and idolatry exploded, the hearts and flesh of all rejoiced in the living God, and became convinced that He who is the true God had, through his heavenly grace, enriched them with wealth, both temporal and spiritual. For the bishop, when he came into the province, and found so great misery from famine, taught them to get their food by fishing; for their sea and rivers abounded in fish, but the people had no skill to take them, except eels alone. The bishop's men having gathered eel-nets everywhere, cast them into the sea, and by the blessing of God took three hundred fishes of several sorts, which, being divided into three parts, they gave a hundred to the poor, a hundred to those of whom they had the nets, and kept a hundred for their own use. By this benefit the bishop gained the affections of them all, and they began more readily at his preaching to hope for heavenly goods, seeing that by his help they had received those which are temporal.

At this time, King Ethelwalch gave to the most reverend prelate, Wilfrid, land of eighty-seven families, to maintain his company who were in banishment, which place is called Selsey, that is, the Island of the Sea-Calf. That place is encompassed by the sea on all sides, except the west, where is an entrance about the cast of a sling in width; which sort of place is by the Latins called a peninsula, by the Greeks, a chersonesus. Bishop Wilfrid, having this place given him, founded therein a monastery, which his successors possess to this day, and established a regular course of life, chiefly of the brethren he had brought with him; for he both in word and action performed the duties of a bishop in those parts during the space of five years, until the death of King Egfrid. And forasmuch as the aforesaid king, together with the said place, gave him all the goods that were therein, with the lands and men, he instructed them in the faith of Christ, and baptized them all. Among whom were two hundred and fifty men and women slaves, all of whom he, by baptism, not only rescued from the servitude of the Devil, but gave them their bodily liberty also, and exempted them from the yoke of human servitude.

CHAPTER XIV

HOW A PESTILENTIAL MORTALITY CEASED THROUGH THE INTERCESSION OF KING OSWALD. [A.D. 681.]

IN this monastery, at that time, certain manifestations of the heavenly grace arc said to have been shown forth; for the tyranny of the Devil having been recently exploded, the faith of Christ began to prevail therein. Of which number I have thought it proper to perpetuate the memory of one which the most reverend Bishop Acca was wont to relate to me, affirming it had been told him by most creditable brothers of the same monastery. About the same time that this province of the South Saxons embraced the faith of Christ, a grievous mortality ran through many provinces of Britain; which, also, by the Divine dispensation, reached to the aforesaid monastery, then governed by the most reverend and religious priest of Christ, Eappa; and many, as well of those that had come thither with the bishop, as of those that had been called to the faith of the same province of the South Saxons, were snatched away out of this world. The brethren, in consequence, thought fit to keep a fast of three days, and to implore the Divine goodness, that it would vouchsafe to extend mercy to them, either by delivering those that were in danger by the distemper from death, or by delivering those who departed this life from eternal damnation.

There was at that time in the monastery, a little boy, of the Saxon nation, lately called to the faith, who had been seized with the same distemper, and had long kept his bed. On the second day of the fasting and praying, it happened that the said boy was, about the second hour of the day, left alone in the place where he lay sick, and through the Divine disposition, the most blessed princes of the apostle vouchsafed to appear to him; for he was a lad of an extraordinarily mild and innocent disposition, and with sincere devotion observed the mysteries of the faith which he had received. The apostles therefore, saluting him in a most affectionate manner, said, "My child, do not fear death, about which you are so uneasy; for we will this day conduct you to the heavenly kingdom; but you are first to stay till the masses are said, that having received the body and blood of our Lord, to support you on your journey, and being so discharged through sickness and death, you may be carried up to the everlasting joys in heaven.

"Call therefore to you the priest, Eappa, and tell him, that the Lord has heard your prayers and devotion, and has favourably accepted of your fast, and not one more shall die of this plague, either in the monastery or its adjacent possessions; but all your people who anywhere labour under this distemper, shall be eased of their pain, and restored to their former health, except you alone, who are this day to be delivered by death, and to be carried into heaven, to behold our Lord Christ, whom you have faithfully served: this favour the Divine mercy has vouchsafed to grant you, through the intercession of the godly and dear servant of God, King Oswald, who formerly ruled over the nation of the Northumbrians, with the authority of a temporal king, and such devotion of Christian piety as leads to the heavenly kingdom; for this very day that king was killed in war by the infidels, and taken up to the everlasting joys of souls in heaven, and associated among the number of the elect. Let them look in their books, wherein the departure of the dead is set down, and they will find that he was, this day, as we have said, taken out of this world. Let them, therefore, celebrate masses in all the oratories of this monastery, either in thanksgiving for their prayers being heard, or else in memory of the aforesaid King Oswald, who once governed their nation; and therefore he humbly offered up his prayers to our Lord for them, as for strangers of his nation; and let all the brethren, assembling in the church, communicate in the heavenly sacrifices, and so let them cease to fast, and refresh themselves with food."

The boy called the priest, and repeated all these words to him; the priest particularly inquired after the habit and form of the men that had appeared to him. He answered, "Their habit was noble, and their countenances most pleasant and beautiful, such as I had never seen before, nor did I think there could be any men so graceful and comely. One of them indeed was shorn like a clerk, the other had a long beard; and they said that one of them was called Peter, the other Paul; and both of them the servants of our Lord and Saviour Jesus Christ, sent by Him from heaven to protect our monastery." The priest believed what the boy said, and going thence immediately, looked in his chronicle, and found that King Oswald had been killed on that very day. He then called the brethren, ordered dinner to be provided, masses to be said, and all of them to communicate as usual; causing also part of the Lord's oblation of the same sacrifice to be carried to the sick boy.

Soon after this, the boy died, on that same day; and by his death proved that what he had heard from the apostles of God was true. A further testimony of the truth of his words was, that no person besides himself, belonging to the same monastery, died at that time. By which vision, many that heard of it were wonderfully excited to implore the Divine mercy in adversity, and to adopt the wholesome remedy of fasting. From that time, the day of the nativity of that king and soldier of Christ began to be yearly honoured with the celebration of masses, not only in that monastery, but in many other places.

CHAPTER XV

KING CÆDWALLA, HAVING SLAIN ETHELWALCH, KING OF THE WEST SAXONS, WASTED THAT PROVINCE WITH RAPINE AND SLAUGHTER. [A.D. 685.]

IN the meantime, Cædwalla, a daring young man, of the royal race of the Gewissæ, who had been banished his country, came with an army, slew Ethelwalch, and wasted that country with much slaughter and plundering; but he was soon expelled by Berthun and Andhun, the king's commanders, who afterwards held the government of that province. The first of them was afterwards killed by the same Cædwalla, when he was king of the Gewissæ, and the province was more entirely subdued: Ina, likewise, who reigned after Cædwalla, kept that country under the like servitude for several years; for which reason, during all that time, they had no bishop of their own; but their first bishop, Wilfrid, having been recalled home, they were subject to the bishop of the Gewissæ, *i. e.* the West Saxons, in the city of Winchester.

CHAPTER XVI

HOW THE ISLE OF WIGHT RECEIVED CHRISTIAN INHABI-
TANTS, AND TWO ROYAL YOUTHS OF THAT ISLAND WERE
KILLED IMMEDIATELY AFTER BAPTISM. [A.D. 686.]

AFTER Cædwalla had possessed himself of the kingdom of the
Gewissæ, he also took the Isle of Wight, which till then was
entirely given over to idolatry, and by cruel slaughter endeavoured to destroy all the inhabitants thereof, and to place in their
stead people from his own province; having bound himself by a
vow, though he was not yet, as is reported, regenerated in Christ,
to give the fourth part of the land, and of the booty, to our Lord,
if he took the island, which he performed by giving the same for
our Lord to the use of Bishop Wilfrid, who happened at the time
to have accidentally come thither out of his own nation. The
measure of that island, according to the computation of the
English, is of twelve hundred families, and accordingly the bishop
had given him land of three hundred families. The part which he
received, he committed to one of his clerks called Bernwin, who
was his sister's son, assigning him a priest, whose name was
Hiddila, who might administer the word and baptism of salvation
to all that would be saved.

Here I think it ought not to be omitted that the first fruits of
the natives of that island who, by believing, secured their salvation, were two royal youths, brothers to Atwald, king of the
island, who were honoured by the particular grace of God. For
when the enemy approached, they made their escape out of the
island, and passed over into the neighbouring province of the
Jutes; where, being conducted to the place called At the Stone,
as they thought to be concealed from the victorious king, they
were betrayed and ordered to be killed. This being made known
to a certain abbat and priest, whose name was Cynebert, who
had a monastery not far from thence, at a place called
Reodford, that is, the Ford of Reeds, he came to the king, who

then lay privately in those parts, to be cured of the wounds which he had received whilst he was fighting in the Isle of Wight, and begged of him that if the lads must inevitably be killed, he might be allowed first to instruct them in the mysteries of the faith. The king consented, and the bishop having taught them the word of truth, and cleansed their souls by baptism, made the entrance into the kingdom of heaven sure to them. Then the executioner being at hand, they joyfully underwent the temporal death, through which they did not doubt they were to pass to the life of the soul, which is everlasting. Thus, after all the provinces of the island of Britain had embraced the faith of Christ, the Isle of Wight also received the same; yet being under the affliction of foreign subjection, no man there received the ministry, or rank of a bishop, before Daniel, who is now bishop of the West Saxons.

The island is situated opposite the division between the South Saxons and the Gewissæ, being separated from it by a sea, three miles over, which is called Solente. In this narrow sea, the two tides of the ocean, which flow round Britain from the immense northern ocean, daily meet and oppose one another beyond the mouth of the river Homelea, which runs into that narrow sea, from the lands of the Jutes, which belong to the country of the Gewissæ; after this meeting and struggling together of the two seas, they return into the ocean from whence they come.

CHAPTER XVII

OF THE SYNOD HELD IN THE PLAIN OF HEATHFIELD, WHERE ARCHBISHOP THEODORE PRESIDED. [A.D. 680.]

ABOUT this time, Theodore being informed that the faith of the church at Constantinople was much perplexed by the heresy of Eutyches, and desiring to preserve the churches of the English, over which he presided, from that infection, an assembly of many venerable priests and doctors was convened, at which he diligently inquired into their doctrines, and found they all unanimously agreed in the Catholic faith. This he took care to have committed to writing by the authority of the synod, as a memorial, and for the instruction of succeeding generations; the beginning of which instrument is as follows—

"In the name of our Lord and Saviour Jesus Christ, in the tenth year of the reign of our most pious lord, Egfrid, king of the Northumbrians, the seventeenth of October, the eighth indiction; and in the sixth year of the reign of Ethelfrid, king of the Mercians, in the seventeenth year of the reign of Aldhulf, of the East Angles, in the seventh year of the reign of Lothair, king of Kent; Theodore, by the grace of God, archbishop of the island of Britain, and of the city of Canterbury, being president, and the other venerable bishops of the island of Britain sitting with him, the holy Gospels being laid before them, at the place which, in the Saxon tongue, is called Heathfield, we conferred together, and expounded the true and orthodox faith, as our Lord Jesus in the flesh delivered the same to his disciples, who saw Him present, and heard his words, and as it is delivered in the creed of the holy fathers, and by all holy and universal synods in general, and by the consent of all approved doctors of the Catholic church; we, therefore, following them jointly and orthodoxly, and professing accordance to their divinely inspired doctrine, do believe, and do, according to the holy fathers, firmly confess, properly and truly, the Father, and Son, and Holy Ghost, a trinity consubstantial in unity, and unity in trinity, that is, one God subsisting in three consubstantial persons, of equal honour and glory."

And after much more of this sort, appertaining to the confession of the true faith, this holy synod added to its instrument, "We have received the five holy and general councils of the blessed fathers acceptable to God; that is, of 318 bishops, who were assembled at Nice, against the most impious Arius and his tenets; and at Constantinople, of 150, against the madness of Macedonius and Eudoxius, and their tenets; and at Ephesus, first of 200, against the most wicked Nestorius, and his tenets; and at Chalcedon, of 360, against Eutyches and Nestorius, and their tenets; and again, at Constantinople, in a fifth council, in the reign of Justinian the younger, against Theodorus and Theodoret, and the epistles of Iba, and their tenets, against Cyril;" and again a little lower, "the synod held in the city of Rome, in the time of the blessed Pope Martin, in the eighth indiction, and in the ninth year of the most pious Emperor Constantine, we receive: and we glorify our Lord Jesus Christ, as they glorified Him, neither adding nor diminishing anything; anathematizing those with our hearts and mouths whom they anathematized, and receiving those whom they received, glorifying God the Father, who is without beginning, and his only-begotten Son generated from eternity, and the Holy Ghost proceeding from the Father and the Son in an ineffable manner, as those holy apostles, prophets, and doctors, whom we have above-mentioned, did declare. And all we, who, with Archbishop Theodore, have thus expounded the Catholic faith, have also subscribed thereto."

CHAPTER XVIII

OF JOHN, THE SINGER OF THE APOSTOLIC SEE, WHO CAME INTO BRITAIN TO TEACH. [A.D. 680.]

AMONG those who were present at this synod, was the venerable John, archchanter of the church of the holy Apostle Peter, and abbat of the monastery of St. Martin, who came lately from Rome, by order of Pope Agatho, together with the most reverend Abbat Biscop, surnamed Benedict, of whom mention has been made above, and this John, with the rest, signed the declaration of the Catholic faith. For the said Benedict, having built a monastery in Britain, in honour of the most blessed prince of the apostles, at the mouth of the river Were, went to Rome with Ceolfrid, his companion and fellow-labourer in that work, who was after him abbat of the same monastery; he had been several times before at Rome, and was now honourably received by Pope Agatho of blessed memory; from whom he also obtained the confirmation of the immunities of this monastery, being a bull of privilege signed by apostolical authority, pursuant to what he knew to be the will and grant of King Egfrid, by whose consent and gift of land he had built that monastery.

He then received the aforesaid Abbat John to be conducted into Britain, that he might teach in his monastery the method of singing throughout the year, as it was practised at St. Peter's at Rome. The Abbat John did as he had been commanded by the pope, teaching the singers of the said monastery the order and manner of singing and reading aloud, and committing to writing all that was requisite throughout the whole course of the year for the celebration of festivals; all which are still observed in that monastery, and have been copied by many others elsewhere. The said John not only taught the brothers of that monastery; but such as had skill in singing resorted from almost all the monasteries of the same province to hear him; and many invited him to teach in other places.

Besides singing and reading, he had also been directed by the pope carefully to inform himself concerning the faith of the English church, and to give an account thereof at his return to Rome. For he also brought with him the decision of the synod of the blessed Pope Martin and 105 bishops, held not long before at Rome, principally against those who taught but one will and operation in Christ, and gave it to be transcribed in the aforesaid monastery of the most religious Abbat Benedict. The men who followed such opinion, much perplexed the faith of the church of Constantinople at that time; but by the help of God they were then discovered and subdued. Wherefore, Pope Agatho, being desirous to be informed concerning the state of the church in Britain, as well as in other provinces, and to what extent it was clear from the contagion of heretics, gave this affair in charge to the most reverend Abbat John, then appointed to go to Britain. The synod we have spoken of having been called for this purpose in Britain, the Catholic faith was found untainted in them all, and a copy of the same given him to carry to Rome.

But in his return to his own country, soon after crossing the sea, he fell sick and died; and his body, for the sake of St. Martin, in whose monastery he presided, was by his friends carried to Tours, and honourably buried; for he had been kindly entertained there when he went into Britain, and earnestly entreated by the brethren, that in his return to Rome he would take that road, and give them a visit. In short, he was there supplied with some to conduct him on his way, and assist him in the work enjoined him. Though he died by the way, yet the testimony of the faith of the English nation was carried to Rome, and most agreeably received by the apostolic pope, and all those that heard or read it.

CHAPTER XIX

HOW QUEEN ETHELDRIDA ALWAYS PRESERVED HER VIRGINITY, AND HER BODY SUFFERED NO CORRUPTION IN THE GRAVE. [A.D. 660.]

KING Egfrid took to wife, Etheldrida, the daughter of Anna, king of the East Angles, of whom mention has been often made; a man very religious, and in all respects renowned for his inward disposition and actions. She had before been given in marriage to another, viz. to Tonbert, chief of the Southern Girvii; but he died soon after he had received her, and she was given to the aforesaid king. Though she lived with him twelve years, yet she preserved the glory of perfect virginity, as I was informed by Bishop Wilfrid, of blessed memory, of whom I inquired, because some questioned the truth thereof; and he told me that he was an undoubted witness of her virginity, forasmuch as Egfrid promised he would give many lands and much money, if he could persuade the queen to consent to pay the marriage duty, for he knew the queen loved no man so much as himself; and it is not to be doubted that the same might in one instance take place in our age, which true histories tell us happened several times in former ages, through the assistance of the same Lord who has promised to continue with us unto the end of the world; for the miraculous circumstance that her flesh, being buried, could not suffer corruption, is a token that she had not been defiled by familiarity with man.

She had long requested the king that he would permit her to lay aside worldly cares, and to serve only the true King, Christ, in a monastery; and having at length with difficulty prevailed, she went as a nun into the monastery of the Abbess Ebba, who was aunt to King Egfrid, at the place called the city Coludi, having taken the veil from the hands of the aforesaid Bishop Wilfrid; but a year after she was herself made abbess in the country called Ely, where, having built a monastery, she began, by works and examples of a heavenly life, to be the virgin mother of very many virgins dedicated to God. It is reported of her, that from the time of her entering into the monastery, she never wore any linen but only woollen garments, and would rarely wash in a hot bath, unless just before any of the great festivals, as Easter, Whitsuntide, and the Epiphany, and then she did it last of all, after having, with the assistance of those about her, first washed the other servants of God there present; besides, she seldom did eat above once a day, excepting on the great solemnities, or some other urgent occasion, unless some considerable distemper obliged her. From the time of matins she continued in the church at prayer till it was day; some also say, that by the spirit of prophecy, she, in the presence of all, not only foretold the pestilence of which she was to die, but also the number of those that should be then snatched away out of her monastery. She was taken to our Lord, in the midst of her flock, seven years after she had been made abbess; and, as she had ordered, was buried among them, in such a manner as she had died, in a wooden coffin.

She was succeeded in the office of abbess by her sister Sexberga, who had been wife to Erconbert, king of Kent; who, when her sister had been buried sixteen years, thought fit to take up her bones, and, putting them into a new coffin, to translate them into the church. Accordingly she ordered some of the brothers to provide a stone to make a coffin of; they accordingly went on board ship, because the country of Ely is on every side encompassed with the sea or marshes, and has no large stones, and came to a small abandoned city, not far from thence, which, in the language of the English, is called Grantchester, and presently, near the city walls, they found a white marble coffin, most beautifully wrought, and neatly covered with a lid of the same sort of stone. Concluding therefore that God had prospered their journey, they returned thanks to Him, and carried it to the monastery.

The body of the holy virgin and spouse of Christ, when her grave was opened, being brought into sight, was found as free from corruption as if she had died and been buried on that very day; as the aforesaid Bishop Wilfrid, and many others that know it, can testify. But the physician, Cynefrid, who was present at her death, and when she was taken up out of the grave, was wont of more certain knowledge to relate, that in her sickness she had a very great swelling under her jaw. "And I was ordered," said he, "to lay open that swelling, to let out the noxious matter in it, which I did, and she seemed to be somewhat more easy for two days, so that many thought she might recover from her distemper; but the third day the former pains returning, she was soon snatched out of the world, and exchanged all pain and death for everlasting life and health. And when so many years after her bones were to be taken out of the grave, a pavilion being spread over it, all the congregation of brothers were on the one side, and of sisters on the other, standing about it singing, and the abbess, with a few, being gone to take up and wash the bones, on a sudden we heard the abbess within loudly cry out, 'Glory be to the name of the Lord.' Not long after they called me in, opening the door of the pavilion, where I found the body of the holy virgin taken out of the grave and laid on a bed, as if it had been asleep; then taking off the veil from the face, they also showed the incision which I had made, healed up; so that, to my great astonishment, instead of the open gaping wound with which she had been buried, there then appeared only an extraordinarily slender scar.

"Besides, all the linen cloths in which the body had been buried, appeared entire and as fresh as if they had been that very day wrapped about her chaste limbs." It is reported, that when she was much troubled with the aforesaid swelling and pain in her jaw, she was much pleased with that sort of distemper, and wont to say, "I know that I deservedly bear the weight of my sickness on my neck, for I remember, when I was very young, I bore there the needless weight of jewels; and therefore I believe the Divine goodness would have me endure the pain in my neck, that I may be absolved from the guilt of my needless levity, having now, instead of gold and precious stones, a red swelling and burning on my neck." It happened also that by the touch of that linen, devils were expelled from bodies possessed, and other distempers were sometimes cured; and the coffin she was first buried in is reported to have cured some of distempers in the eyes, who, praying with their heads touching that coffin, presently were delivered from the pain or dimness in their eyes. They washed the virgin's body, and having clothed it in new garments, brought it into the church, and laid it in the coffin that had been brought, where it is held in great veneration to this day. The coffin was found in a wonderful manner, as fit for the virgin's body as if it had been made purposely for her, and the place for the head particularly cut, exactly fit for her head, and shaped to a nicety.

Ely is in the province of the East Angles, a country of about six hundred families, in the nature of an island, enclosed, as has been said, either with marshes or waters, and therefore it has its name from the great plenty of eels taken in those marshes; there the aforesaid servant of Christ desired to have a monastery, because, as we have before observed, she was descended from that same province of the East Angles.

CHAPTER XX

A HYMN ON THE AFORESAID HOLY VIRGIN. [A.D. 660.]

I think it proper to insert in this history a hymn of virginity, which I composed in elegiac verse several years ago, in praise and honour of the same queen and spouse of Christ; and therefore truly a queen, because the spouse of Christ; and to imitate the method of the Holy Scripture, in whose history many poetical pieces are inserted which are known to be composed in metre.

Hail, Triune Power, who rulest every age,
Assist the numbers which my pen engage.
Let Maro wars in loftier numbers sing,
I sound the praises of our heavenly King.
Chaste is my verse, nor Helen's rape I write;
Light tales like these, but prove the mind as light.
See! from on high the God descends, confined
In Mary's womb, to rescue lost mankind.
Behold! a spotless maid a God brings forth,
A God is born, who gave e'en nature birth!
The virgin-choir the mother-maid resound,
And chaste themselves, her praises shout around.
Her bright example numerous vot'ries raise,
Tread spotless paths, and imitate her ways.
The blessed Agatha and Eulalia trust
Sooner to flames, than far more dangerous lust.
Tecula and chaste Euphemia overcame
The fear of beasts to save a virgin name.
Agnes and sweet Cecilia, joyful maids,
Smile while the pointed sword their breasts invades.
Triumphing joy attends the peaceful soul,
Where heat, nor rain, nor wishes mean control.
Thus Etheldrida, pure from sensual crime,
Bright shining star! arose to bless our time.
Born of a regal race, her sire a king,

211

More noble honour to her lord shall bring.
A queen her name, her hand a sceptre rears,
But greater glories wait above the spheres.
What man wouldst thou desire? See Christ is made
Her spouse, her blessed Redeemer weds the maid.
While you attend the heavenly Mother's train,
Thou shalt be mother of a heavenly reign.
The holy maid who twelve years sat a queen,
A cloister'd nun devote to God was seen.
Noted for pious deeds, her spotless soul
Left the vile world, and soar'd above the pole.
Sixteen Novembers since was the blest maid
Entomb'd, whose flesh no putrid damps invade.
Thy grace, O Christ! for in the coffin's found
No tainted vest wrapping the corpse around.
The swelling dropsy, and dire atrophy,
A pale disease from the blest vestments fly.
Rage fires the fiend, who whilom Eve betray'd.
While shouting angels hail the glorious maid.
See! wedded to her God, what joy remains,
In earth, or heaven, see! with her God she reigns!
Behold! the spouse, the festal torches shine,
He comes! behold! what joyful gifts are thine!
Thou a new song on the sweet harp shalt sing,
A hymn of praise to thy celestial King.
None from the flock of the throned Lamb shall move,
Whom grateful passion bind, and heavenly love

CHAPTER XXI

BISHOP THEODORE MADE PEACE BETWEEN THE KINGS EGFRID AND ETHELRED. [A.D. 679.]

IN the ninth year of the reign of King Egfrid, a great battle was fought between him and Ethelred, king of the Mercians, near the river Trent, and Elfwin, brother to King Egfrid, was slain, a youth about eighteen years of age, and much beloved by both provinces, for King Ethelred had married his sister Osthritha. There was now reason to expect a more bloody war, and more lasting enmity between those kings and their fierce nations; but Theodore the bishop, beloved of God, relying on the Divine assistance, by his wholesome admonitions extinguished the dangerous fire that was breaking out; so that the kings and their people on both sides being appeased, no man was put to death, but only the usual mulct paid to the king for his brother that had been killed; and this peace continued long after between those kings and their kingdoms.

CHAPTER XXII

HOW A CERTAIN CAPTIVE'S CHAINS FELL OFF WHEN MASSES WERE SUNG FOR HIM. [A.D. 679.]

IN the aforesaid battle, wherein Elfwin, the king's brother, was killed, a memorable fact is known to have happened, which I think ought not to be passed by in silence; for the relation of the same will conduce to the salvation of many. In that battle, one Imma, a youth belonging to the king, was left as dead, and having lain so all that day and the next night among the dead bodies, at length he came to himself, and sitting, bound up his wounds in the best way he could. Then having rested awhile, he stood up, and began to go off to seek some friends that might take care of him; but in so doing he was discovered and taken by some of the enemy's army, and carried before their lord, who was an earl belonging to King Ethelred. Being asked by him who he was, and fearing to own himself a soldier, he answered, "He was a peasant, poor and married, and that he came to the army with others to bring provisions to the soldiers." The earl entertained him, and ordered his wounds to be dressed; and when he began to recover, to prevent his escaping, he ordered him to be bound; but that could not be performed, for as soon as they that bound him were gone, his bonds were all loosened.

He had a brother called Tunna, who was a priest and abbat of a monastery in the city which from him is still called Tunnacester. Hearing that his brother had been killed in the fight, he went to see whether he could find his body; and finding another very like him in all respects, concluding it to be his, he carried the same to his monastery, and buried it honourably, and took care often to say masses for the absolution of his soul; the celebration whereof occasioned what I have said, that none could bind him but he was presently loosed again. In the meantime, the earl that kept him was amazed, and began to inquire why he could not be bound; whether he had any spells about him, as are spoken of in fabulous stories. He answered, "He knew nothing of those contrivances; but I have," said he, "a brother who is a priest in my country, and I know that he, supposing me to be killed, causes masses to be said for me; and if I were now in the other life, my soul there, through his intercession, would be delivered from pain."

Having continued with the earl some time, those who attentively observed him, by his countenance, mien, and discourse, took notice, that he was not of the meaner sort, as he had said, but of some quality. The earl then privately sending for him, pressed to know who he was, promising to do him no harm, if he would ingenuously confess his quality. Which when he had done, declaring that he had been the king's servant, the earl answered, "I perceived by your answers that you were no peasant. And now you deserve to die, because all my brothers and relations were killed in that fight; yet I will not put you to death, because it will be a breach of my promise."

As soon, therefore, as he was recovered, he sold him at London, to a Freson, but he could not be bound by him the whole way as he was led along; but though his enemies put several sorts of bonds on him, they were all loosed. The buyer, perceiving that he could in no way be bound, gave him leave to ransom himself if he could; now it was at the third hour (nine in the morning) when the masses were wont to be said, that his bonds were generally loosed. He, having taken an oath that he would either return, or send him the money for his ransom, went into Kent to King Lothaire, who was son to the sister of Queen Etheldrida, above spoken of, for he had once been her servant. From him he obtained the price of his ransom, and as he had promised, sent it to his master.

Returning afterwards into his own country, and coming to his brother, he gave him an exact account of all his fortunes, good and bad; and by his relation he understood, that his bonds had been generally loosed at those times when masses had been celebrated for him; and that other advantages which had accrued to him in his time of danger, had been conferred on him from Heaven, through the intercession of his brother, and the oblation of his saving sacrifice. Many persons, on hearing this account from the aforesaid man, were stirred up in the faith and devotion of piety either to prayer, or to almsgiving, or to offer up to our Lord the sacrifice of the holy oblation, for the deliverance of their friends who had departed this world; for they understood and knew that such saving sacrifice was available for the eternal redemption both of body and soul. This story was also told me by some of those who had heard it related by the person himself to whom it happened; therefore, I have thought fit to insert it in my Ecclesiastical History as I had it related to me.

CHAPTER XXIII

OF THE LIFE AND DEATH OF THE ABBESS HILDA. [A.D. 680.]

IN the year of the incarnation of our Lord 680, the most religious servant of Christ, Hilda, abbess of the monastery that is called Streaneshalch, as above-mentioned, after having performed many heavenly works on earth, passed from thence to receive the rewards of the heavenly life, on the 17th of November, at the age of sixty-six years; the first thirty-three of which she spent living most nobly in the secular habit; and more nobly dedicated the remaining half to our Lord in a monastic life. For she was nobly born, being the daughter of Hereric, nephew to King Edwin, with which king she also embraced the faith and mysteries of Christ, at the preaching of Paulinus, the first bishop of the Northumbrians, of blessed memory, and preserved the same undefiled till she attained to the sight of him in heaven.

Resolving to quit the secular habit, and to serve him alone, she withdrew into the province of the East Angles, for she was allied to the king; being desirous to pass over from thence into France, to forsake her native country and all she had, and so live a stranger for our Lord in the monastery of Cale, that she might with more ease attain to the eternal kingdom in heaven; because her sister Heresuid, mother to Aldwulf, king of the East Angles, at that time living in the same monastery, under regular discipline, was waiting for her eternal reward. Being led by her example, she continued a whole year in the aforesaid province, with the design of going abroad; afterwards, Bishop Aidan being recalled home, he gave her the land of one family on the north side of the river Wear; where for a year she also led a monastic life, with very few companions.

After this she was made abbess in the monastery called Heruteu, which monastery had been founded, not long before, by the religious servant of Christ, Heiu, who is said to have been the first woman that in the province of the Northumbrians took upon her the habit and life of a nun, being consecrated by Bishop Aidan; but she, soon after she had founded that monastery, went away to the city of Calcacestir, and there fixed her dwelling. Hilda, the servant of Christ, being set over that monastery, began immediately to reduce all things to a regular system, according as she had been instructed by learned men; for Bishop Aidan, and other religious men that knew her and loved her, frequently visited and diligently instructed her, because of her innate wisdom and inclination to the service of God.

When she had for some years governed this monastery, wholly intent upon establishing a regular life, it happened that she also undertook either to build or to arrange a monastery in the place called Streaneshalch [Whitby], which work she industriously performed; for she put this monastery under the same regular discipline as she had done the former; and taught there the strict observance of justice, piety, chastity, and other virtues, and particularly of peace and charity; so that, after the example of the primitive church, no person was there rich, and none poor, all being in common to all, and none having any property. Her prudence was so great, that not only indifferent persons, but even kings and princes, as occasion offered, asked and received her advice; she obliged these who were under her direction to attend so much to reading of the Holy Scriptures, and to exercise themselves so much in works of justice, that many might be there found fit for ecclesiastical duties, and to serve at the altar.

In short, we afterwards saw five bishops taken out of that monastery, and all of them men of singular merit and sanctity, whose names were Bosa, Hedda, Oftfor, John, and Wilfrid. We have above taken notice, that the first of them was consecrated bishop at York; of the second, it is to be observed that he was appointed bishop of Dorchester. Of the two last we shall speak hereafter, as they were consecrated: the first was bishop of Hagulstad, the second of the church of York; of the third, we will here take notice that, having applied himself to the reading and observation of the Scriptures in both the monasteries of Hilda, at length, being desirous to attain to greater perfection, he went into Kent, to Archbishop Theodore, of blessed memory; where having spent some more time in sacred studies, he also resolved to go to Rome, which, in those days, was reckoned of great moment: returning thence into Britain, he took his way into the province of the Wiccii, where King Osric then ruled, and continued there a long time, preaching the word of faith, and making himself an example of good life to all that saw and heard him. At that time, Bosel, the bishop of that province, laboured under such weakness of body, that he could not perform the episcopal functions; for which reason, this Oftfor was, by universal consent, chosen bishop in his stead, and by order of King Ethelred, consecrated by Bishop

Wilfrid, of blessed memory, who was then bishop of the Midland Angles, because Archbishop Theodore was dead, and no other bishop ordained in his place. Before the aforesaid man of God, Bosel, Tatfrid, a most learned and industrious man, and of excellent ability, had been chosen bishop there, from the same abbess's monastery, but had been snatched away by an untimely death, before he could be ordained.

Thus this servant of Christ, Abbess Hilda, whom all that knew her called Mother, for her singular piety and grace, was not only an example of good life, to those that lived in her monastery, but afforded occasion of amendment and salvation to many who lived at a distance, to whom the fame was brought of her industry and virtue; for it was necessary that the dream which her mother, Bregusuit, had, during her infancy, should be fulfilled. At the time that her husband, Hereric, lived in banishment, under Cerdic, king of the Britons, where he was also poisoned, she fancied, in a dream, that she was seeking for him most carefully, and could find no sign of him anywhere; but, after having used all her industry to seek him, she found a most precious jewel under her garment, which, whilst she was looking on it very attentively, cast such a light as spread itself throughout all Britain; which dream was brought to pass in her daughter that we speak of, whose life was a bright example, not only to herself, but to all who desired to live well.

When she had governed this monastery many years, it pleased Him who has made such merciful provision for our salvation, to give her holy soul the trial of a long sickness, to the end that, according to the apostle's example, her virtue might be perfected in infirmity. Falling into a fever, she fell into a violent heat, and was afflicted with the same for six years continually; during all which time she never failed either to return thanks to her Maker, or publicly and privately to instruct the flock committed to her charge; for by her own example she admonished all persons to serve God dutifully in perfect health, and always to return thanks to Him in adversity, or bodily infirmity. In the seventh year of her sickness, the distemper turning inwards, she approached her last day, and about cockcrowing, having received the holy communion to further her on her way, and called together the servants of Christ that were within the same monastery, she admonished them to preserve evangelical peace among themselves, and with all others; and as she was making her speech, she joyfully saw death approaching, or if I may speak in the words of our Lord, passed from death to life.

That same night it pleased Almighty God, by a manifest vision, to make known her death in another monastery, at a distance from hers, which she had built that same year, and is called Hackness. There was in that monastery, a certain nun called Begu, who, having dedicated her virginity to God, had served Him upwards of thirty years in monastical conversation. This nun, being then in the dormitory of the sisters, on a sudden heard the well-known sound of a bell in the air, which used to awake and call them to prayers, when any one of them was taken out of this world, and opening her eyes, as she thought, she saw the top of the house open, and a strong light pour in from above; looking earnestly upon that light, she saw the soul of the aforesaid servant of God in that same light, attended and conducted to heaven by angels. Then awaking, and seeing the other sisters lying round about her, she perceived that what she had seen was either in a dream or a vision; and rising immediately in a great fright, she ran to the virgin who then presided in the monastery instead of the abbess, and whose name was Frigyth, and, with many tears and sighs, told her that the Abbess Hilda, mother of them all, had departed this life, and had in her sight ascended to eternal bliss, and to the company of the inhabitants of heaven, with a great light, and with angels conducting her. Frigyth having heard it, awoke all the sisters, and calling them to the church, admonished them to pray and sing psalms for her soul; which they did during the remainder of the night; and at break of day, the brothers came with news of her death, from the place where she had died. They answered that they knew it before, and then related how and when they had heard it, by which it appeared that her death had been revealed to them in a vision the very same hour that the others said she had died. Thus it was by Heaven happily ordained, that when some saw her departure out of this world, the others should be acquainted with her admittance into the spiritual life which is eternal. These monasteries are about thirteen miles distant from each other.

It is also reported, that her death was, in a vision, made known the same night to one of the holy virgins who loved her most passionately, in the same monastery where the said servant of God died. This nun saw her soul ascend to heaven in the company of angels; and this she declared, the very same hour that it happened, to those servants of Christ that were with her; and awakened them to pray for her soul, even before the rest of the congregation had heard of her death. The truth of which was known to the whole monastery in the morning. This same nun was at that time with some other servants of Christ, in the remotest part of the monastery, where the women newly converted were wont to be upon trial, till they were regularly instructed, and taken into the society of the congregation.

CHAPTER XXIV

THERE WAS IN THE SAME MONASTERY A BROTHER, ON WHOM THE GIFT OF WRITING VERSES WAS BESTOWED BY HEAVEN. [A.D. 680.]

THERE was in this abbess's monastery a certain brother, particularly remarkable for the grace of God, who was wont to make pious and religious verses, so that whatever was interpreted to him out of Scripture, he soon after put the same into poetical expressions of much sweetness and humility, in English, which was his native language. By his verses the minds of many were often excited to despise the world, and to aspire to heaven. Others after him attempted, in the English nation, to compose religious, poems, but none could ever compare with him, for he did not learn the art of poetry from men, but from God; for which reason he never could compose any trivial or vain poem, but only those which relate to religion suited his religious tongue; for having lived in a secular habit till he was well advanced in years, he had never learned anything of versifying; for which reason being sometimes at entertainments, when it was agreed for the sake of mirth that all present should sing in their turns, when he saw the instrument come towards him, he rose up from table and returned home.

Having done so at a certain time, and gone out of the house where the entertainment was, to the stable, where he had to take care of the horses that night, he there composed himself to rest at the proper time; a person appeared to him in his sleep, and saluting him by his name, said, "Cædmon, sing some song to me." He answered, "I cannot sing; for that was the reason why I left the enter-tainment, and retired to this place because I could not sing." The other who talked to him, replied, "However, you shall sing."—"What shall I sing?" rejoined he. "Sing the beginning of created beings," said the other. Hereupon he presently began to sing verses to the praise of God, which he had never heard, the purport whereof was thus:—We are now to praise the Maker of the heavenly kingdom, the power of the Creator and his counsel, the deeds of the Father of glory. How He, being the eternal God, became the author of all mir-acles, who first, as almighty preserver of the human race, created heaven for the sons of men as the roof of the house, and next the earth. This is the sense, but not the words in order as he sang them in his sleep: for verses, though never so well composed, cannot be literally translated out of one language into another, without losing much of their beauty and loftiness. Awaking from his sleep, he remembered all that he had sung in his dream, and soon added much more to the same effect in verse worthy of the Deity.

In the morning he came to the steward, his superior, and having acquainted him with the gift he had received, was conducted to the abbess, by whom he was ordered, in the presence of many learned men, to tell his dream, and repeat the verses, that they might all give their judgment what it was, and whence his verse proceeded. They all concluded, that heavenly grace had been conferred on him by our Lord. They expounded to him a passage in holy writ, either historical, or doctrinal, ordering him, if he could, to put the same into verse. Having undertaken it, he went away, and returning the next morning, gave it to them composed in most excellent verse; whereupon the abbess, embracing the grace of God in the man, instructed him to quit the secular habit, and take upon him the monastic life; which being accordingly done, she associated him to the rest of the brethren in her monastery, and ordered that he should be taught the whole series of sacred history. Thus Cædmon, keeping in mind all he heard, and as it were chewing the cud, converted the same into most harmonious verse; and sweetly repeating the same, made his masters in their turn his hearers. He sang the creation of the world, the origin of man, and all the history of Genesis: and made many verses on the departure of the children of Israel out of Egypt, and their entering into the land of promise, with many other histories from holy writ; the incarnation, passion, resurrection of our Lord, and his ascension into heaven; the coming of the Holy Ghost, and the preaching of the apostles; also the terror of future judgment, the horror of the pains of hell, and the delights of heaven; besides many more about the Divine benefits and judgments, by which he endeavoured to turn away all men from the love of vice, and to excite in them the love of, and application to, good actions; for he was a very religious man, humbly submissive to regular discipline, but full of zeal against those who behaved themselves otherwise; for which reason he ended his life happily.

For when the time of his departure drew near, he laboured for the space of fourteen days under a bodily infirmity which seemed to prepare the way, yet so moderate that he could talk and walk the whole time. In his neighbourhood was the house to which those that were sick, and like shortly to die, were carried. He desired the person that attended him, in the evening, as the night came on in which he was to depart this life, to make ready a place there for him to take his rest. This person, wondering why he should desire it, because there was as yet no sign of his dying soon, did what he had ordered. He accordingly went there, and conversing pleasantly in a joyful manner with the rest that were in the house before, when it was past midnight, he asked them, whether they had the Eucharist there? They answered, "What need of the Eucharist? for you are not likely to die, since you talk so merrily with us, as if you were in perfect health."—"However," said he, "bring me the Eucharist." Having received the same into his hand, he asked, whether they were all in charity with him, and without any enmity or rancour? They answered, that they were all in perfect charity, and free from anger; and in their turn asked him, whether he was in the same mind towards them? He answered, "I am in charity, my children, with all the servants of God." Then strengthening himself with the heavenly viaticum, he prepared for the entrance into another life, and asked, how near the time was when the brothers were to be awakened to sing the nocturnal praises of our Lord? They answered, "It is not far off." Then he said, "Well, let us wait that hour;" and signing himself with the sign of the cross, he laid his head on the pillow, and falling into a slumber, ended his life so in silence.

Thus it came to pass, that as he had served God with a simple and pure mind, and undisturbed devotion, so he now departed to his presence, leaving the world by a quiet death; and that tongue, which had composed so many holy words in praise of the Creator, uttered its last words whilst he was in the act of signing himself with the cross, and recommending himself into his hands, and by what has been here said, he seems to have had foreknowledge of his death.

CHAPTER XXV

OF THE VISION THAT APPEARED TO A CERTAIN MAN OF GOD BEFORE THE MONASTERY OF THE CITY COLUDI WAS BURNED DOWN. [A.D. 679.]

AT this time, the monastery of virgins, called the city of Coludi, above-mentioned, was burned down, through carelessness; and yet all that knew the same, might observe that it happened through the malice of those who dwelt in it, and chiefly of those who seemed to be the greatest. But there wanted not a warning of the approaching punishment from the Divine goodness, by which they might have stood corrected, and by fasting, prayers, and tears, like the Ninevites, have averted the anger of the just Judge.

There was in that monastery a man of the Scottish race, called Adamnan, leading a life entirely devoted to God in continence and prayer, insomuch that he never took any food or drink, except only on Sundays and Thursdays; but often spent whole nights in prayer. This austerity of life he had first adopted from necessity to correct his evil propensities; but in process of time the necessity became a custom.

For in his youth he had been guilty of some wicked action, for which, when he came to himself, he conceived extraordinary horror, and dreaded lest he should be punished for the same by the upright Judge. Repairing, therefore, to a priest, who he hoped might show him the way of salvation, he confessed his guilt, and desired to be advised how he might avoid the future wrath of God. The priest having heard his offence, said, "A great sore requires much attention in the cure; and, therefore, give yourself up as far as you are able to fasting, reading of psalms, and prayer, to the end, that thus preventing the wrath of our Lord, in confession, you may find Him merciful." Being highly affected with the grief of a guilty conscience, and desiring, as soon as possible, to be loosed from the inward fetters of sin, which lay heavy upon him, he answered, "I am young in years, and strong of body, and shall, therefore, easily bear whatever you shall enjoin me to do, so that I may be saved in the day of our Lord; though you should command me to spend the whole night in prayer standing, and to pass the whole week in abstinence." The priest replied, "It is too much for you to hold out the whole week without bodily sustenance; but it is sufficient to fast two or three days; do this till I come again to you in a short time, when I will more fully show you what you are to do, and how long to continue your penance." Having so said, and prescribed the measure of his penance, the priest went away, and upon some sudden occasion passed over into Ireland, whence he derived his origin, and returned no more to him, as he had appointed. Remembering this injunction and his own promise, he totally addicted himself to tears, penance, holy watching, and continence; so that he only fed on Thursdays and Sundays, as has been said; and ate nothing all the other days of the week. When he heard that his priest was gone to Ireland, and had died there, he ever after observed that same abstinence, according to his direction; and as he had begun that course through the fear of God, in penitence for his guilt, so he still continued the same unremittingly for the Divine love, and in hope of his reward.

Having practised this carefully for a long time, it happened that he had gone on a certain day to a distance from the monastery, accompanied by one of the brothers; and as they were returning from this journey, when they drew near to the monastery, and beheld its lofty buildings, the man of God burst out into tears, and his countenance discovered the trouble of his heart. His companion, perceiving it, asked what was the reason, to which he answered: "The time is at hand, when a devouring fire shall consume all the structures which you here behold, both public and private." The other, hearing these words, as soon as they came into the monastery, told them to Ebba, the mother of the congregation. She, with good cause, being much concerned at that prediction, called the man to her, and narrowly inquired of him how he came to know it. He answered, "Being busy one night lately in watching and singing psalms, I on a sudden saw a person unknown standing by me, and being startled at his presence, he bade me not to fear, and speaking to me in a familiar manner, 'You do well,' said he, 'in that you spend this night-time of rest, not in giving yourself up to sleep, but in watching and prayer.' I answered, 'I know I have great need of wholesome watching, and earnest praying to our Lord to pardon my transgressions.' He replied, 'You are in the right, for you and many more do need to redeem their sins by good works, and when they cease from labouring about temporal affairs, then to labour the more eagerly for the desire of heavenly goods; but this very few do; for I, having now visited all this monastery regularly, have looked into every one's chambers and beds, and found none of them except yourself busy about the care of his soul; but all of them, both men and women, either indulge themselves in slothful sleep, or are awake in order to commit sin; for even the cells that were built for praying or reading, are now converted into places of feasting, drinking, talking, and other delights; the very virgins dedicated to God, laying aside the respect due to their profession, whensoever they are at leisure, apply themselves to weaving fine garments, either to use in adorning themselves like brides, to the danger of their condition, or to gain the friendship of strange men; for which reason, a heavy judgment from heaven is deservedly ready to fall on this place and its inhabitants by devouring fire.'" The abbess said, "Why did you not sooner acquaint me with what you knew?" He answered, "I was afraid to do it, out of respect to you, lest you should be too much afflicted; yet you may have this comfort, that the calamity will not happen in your days." This vision being divulged abroad, the inhabitants of that place were for a few days in some little fear, and leaving off their sins, began to punish themselves; but after the abbess's death they returned to their former wickedness, nay, they became more wicked; and when they thought themselves in peace and security, they soon felt the effects of the aforesaid judgment.

That all this fell out thus, was told me by my most reverend fellow-priest, Edgils, who then lived in that monastery. Afterwards, when many of the inhabitants had departed thence, on account of the destruction, he lived a long time in our monastery, and died there. We have thought fit to insert this in our History, to admonish the reader of the works of our Lord, how terrible He is in his counsels on the sons of men, lest we should at some time or other indulge in the pleasures of flesh, and dreading the judgment of God too little, fall under his sudden wrath, and either be severely afflicted with temporal losses, or else being more severely tried, be snatched away to eternal perdition.

CHAPTER XXVI

OF THE DEATH OF THE KINGS EGFRID AND LOTHERE.
[A.D. 684.]

In the year of our Lord's incarnation 684, Egfrid, king of the Northumbrians, sending Beort, his general, with an army, into Ireland, miserably wasted that harmless nation, which had always been most friendly to the English; insomuch that in their hostile rage they spared not even the churches or monasteries. Those islanders, to the utmost of their power, repelled force with force, and imploring the assistance of the Divine mercy, prayed long and fervently for vengeance; and though such as curse cannot possess the kingdom of God, it is believed, that those who were justly cursed on account of their impiety, did soon suffer the penalty of their guilt from the avenging hand of God; for the very next year, that same king, rashly leading his army to ravage the province of the Picts, much against the advice of his friends, and particularly of Cuthbert, of blessed memory, who had been lately ordained bishop, the enemy made show as if they fled, and the king was drawn into the straits of inaccessible mountains, and slain, with the greatest part of his forces, on the 20th of May, in the fortieth year of his age, and the fifteenth of his reign. His friends, as has been said, advised him not to engage in this war; but he having the year before refused to listen to the most reverend father, Egbert, advising him not to attack the Scots, who did him no harm, it was laid upon him as a punishment for his sin, that he should not now regard those who would have prevented his death.

From that time the hopes and strength of the English crown "began to waver and retrograde;" for the Picts recovered their own lands, which had been held by the English and the Scots that were in Britain, and some of the Britons their liberty, which they have now enjoyed for about forty-six years. Among the many English that then either fell by the sword, or were made slaves, or escaped by flight out of the country of the Picts, the most reverend man of God, Trumwine, who had been made bishop over them, withdrew with his people that were in the monastery of Abercurnig, seated in the country of the English, but close by the arm of the sea which parts the lands of the English and the Scots. Having recommended his followers, wheresoever he could, to his friends in the monasteries, he chose his own place of residence in the monastery, which we have so often mentioned, of men and women servants of God, at Streaneshalch; and there he, for several years, led a life in all monastical austerity, not only to his own, but to the benefit of many, with a few of his own people; and dying there, he was buried in the church of St. Peter the Apostle, with the honour due to his life and rank. The royal virgin, Elfled, with her mother, Eanfled, whom we have mentioned before, then presided over that monastery; but when the bishop came thither, this devout woman found in him extraordinary assistance in governing, and comfort to herself. Alfrid succeeded Egfrid in the throne, being a man most learned in Scripture, said to be brother to the other, and son to King Oswy: he nobly retrieved the ruined state of the kingdom, though within narrower bounds.

The same year, being the 685th from the incarnation of our Lord, Lothere, king of Kent, died on the sixth of February, when he had reigned twelve years after his brother Egbert, who had reigned nine years: he was wounded in battle with the South Saxons, whom Edric, the son of Egbert, had raised against him, and died whilst his wound was being dressed. After him, the same Edric reigned a year and a half. On his death, kings of doubtful title, or foreigners, for some time wasted the kingdom, till the lawful king, Wictred, the son of Egbert, being settled in the throne, by his piety and zeal delivered his nation from foreign invasion.

CHAPTER XXVII

CUTHBERT, A MAN OF GOD, IS MADE BISHOP; AND HOW
HE LIVED AND TAUGHT WHILST STILL IN A MONASTIC
LIFE. [A.D. 685.]

THE same year that King Egfrid departed this life, he (as has been said) promoted to the bishopric of the church of Lindisfarne the holy and venerable Cuthbert, who had for many years led a solitary life, in great continence of body and mind, in a very small island, called Farne, distant almost nine miles from that same church, in the ocean. From his very childhood he had always been inflamed with the desire of a religious life; but he took upon him the habit and name of a monk when he was a young man: he first entered into the monastery of Melrose, which is on the bank of the river Tweed, and was then governed by the Abbat Eata, a meek and simple man, who was afterwards made bishop of the church of Hagulstad or Lindisfarne, as has been said above, over which monastery at that time was placed Boisil, a priest of great virtue and of a prophetic spirit. Cuthbert, humbly submitting himself to this man's direction, from him received both the knowledge of the Holy Scriptures, and example of good works.

After he had departed to our Lord, Cuthbert was placed over that monastery, where he instructed many in regular life, both by the authority of a master, and the example of his own behaviour. Nor did he afford admonitions and an example of a regular life to his monastery alone, but endeavoured to convert the people round about far and near from the life of foolish custom, to the love of heavenly joys; for many profaned the faith which they had received by their wicked actions; and some also, in the time of a mortality, neglecting the sacraments of faith which they had received, had recourse to the false remedies of idolatry, as if they could have put a stop to the plague sent from God, by enchantments, spells, or other secrets of the hellish art. In order to correct the error of both sorts, he often went out of the monastery, sometimes on horseback, but oftener on foot, and repaired to the neighbouring towns, where he preached the way of truth to such as were gone astray; which had been also done by Boisil in his time. It was then the custom of the English people, that when a clerk or priest came into the town, they all, at his command, flocked together to hear the word; willingly heard what was said, and more willingly practised those things that they could hear or understand. But Cuthbert was so skilful an orator, so fond was he of enforcing his subject, and such a brightness appeared in his angelic face, that no man present presumed to conceal from him the most hidden secrets of his heart, but all openly confessed what they had done; because they thought the same guilt could not be concealed from him, and wiped off the guilt of what they had so confessed with worthy fruits of penance, as he commanded. He was wont chiefly to resort to those places, and preach in such villages, as being seated high up amid craggy uncouth mountains, were frightful to others to behold, and whose poverty and barbarity rendered them inaccessible to other teachers; which nevertheless he, having entirely devoted himself to that pious labour, did so industriously apply himself to polish with his doctrine, that when he departed out of his monastery, he would often stay a week, sometimes two or three, and sometimes a whole month, before he returned home, continuing among the mountains to allure that rustic people by his preaching and example to heavenly employments.

This venerable servant of our Lord, having thus spent many years in the monastery of Melrose, and there become conspicuous by many miracles, his most reverend abbat, Eata, removed him to the isle of Lindisfarne, that he might there also, by the authority of a superior and his own example, instruct the brethren in the observance of regular discipline; for the same reverend father then governed that place also as abbat; for, from ancient times, the bishop was wont to reside there with his clergy, and the abbat with his monks, who were likewise under the care of the bishop; because Aidan, who was the first bishop of the place, being himself a monk, brought monks thither, and settled the monastic institution there; as the blessed Father Augustine is known to have done before in Kent, the most reverend Pope Gregory writing to him, as has been said above, to this effect:—"But since, my brother, having been instructed in monastic rules, you must not live apart from your clergy in the church of the English, which has been lately, through the help of God, converted to the faith; you must, therefore, establish that course of life, which was among our ancestors in the primitive church, among whom, none called anything that he possessed his own; but all things were in common to them."

CHAPTER XXVIII

THE SAME ST. CUTHBERT, BEING AN ANCHORITE, BY HIS PRAYERS OBTAINED A SPRING IN A DRY SOIL, AND HAD A CROP FROM SEED SOWN BY HIMSELF OUT OF SEASON. [A.D. 664.]

AFTER this, Cuthbert, advancing in his meritorious and devout intentions, proceeded even to the adoption of a hermit's life of solitude, as we have mentioned. But forasmuch as we several years ago wrote enough of his life and virtues, both in heroic verse and prose, it may suffice at present only to mention this, that when he was about to repair to the island, he made this protestation to the brothers, saying, "If it shall please the Divine goodness to grant me, that I may live in that place by the labour of my hands, I will willingly reside there; but if not, I will, by God's permission, very soon return to you." The place was quite destitute of water, corn, and trees; and being infested by evil spirits, very ill suited for human habitation; but it became in all respects habitable, at the desire of the man of God; for upon his arrival the wicked spirits withdrew. When he had there, after expelling the enemies, with the assistance of the brethren, built himself a small dwelling, with a trench about it, and the necessary cells and an oratory, he ordered the brothers to dig a pit in the floor of the dwelling, although the ground was hard and stony, and no hopes appeared of any spring.

Having done this upon the faith and at the request of the servant of God, the next day it appeared full of water, and to this day affords plenty of its heavenly bounty to all that resort thither. He also desired that all instruments for husbandry might be brought him, and some wheat; and having sown the same at the proper season, neither stalk, nor so much as a leaf, sprouted from it by the next summer. Hereupon the brethren visiting him according to custom, he ordered barley to be brought him, in case it were either the nature of the soil, or the Divine will, that such grain should rather grow there. He sowed it in the same field just as it was brought him, after the proper time of sowing, and consequently without any likelihood of its coming to good; but a plentiful crop immediately came up, and afforded the man of God the means which he had so ardently desired of supporting himself by his own labour.

When he had here served God in solitude many years, the mound which encompassed his habitation being so high, that he could from thence see nothing but heaven, to which he so ardently aspired, it happened that a great synod was assembled in the presence of King Egfrid, near the river Alne, at a place called Twyford, which signifies "the two fords," in which Archbishop Theodore, of blessed memory, presided, Cuthbert was, by the unanimous consent of all, chosen bishop of the church of Lindisfarne. They could not, however, persuade him to leave his monastery, though many messengers and letters were sent to him; at last the aforesaid king himself, with the most holy Bishop Trumwine, and other religious and great men, passed over into the island; many also of the brothers of the same isle of Lindisfarne assembled together for the same purpose: they all knelt, conjured him by our Lord, and with tears and entreaties, till they drew him, also in tears, from his retreat, and forced him to the synod. Being arrived there, after much opposition, he was overcome by the unanimous resolution of all present, and submitted to take upon himself the episcopal dignity; being chiefly prevailed upon by the mention that Boisil, the servant of God, when he had prophetically foretold all things that were to befall him, had also predicted that he should be a bishop. However, the consecration was not appointed immediately; but after the winter, which was then at hand, it was performed at Easter, in the city of York, and in the presence of the aforesaid King Egfrid; seven bishops meeting on the occasion, among whom, Theodore, of blessed memory, was primate. He was first elected bishop of the church of Hagulstad, in the place of Tumbert, who had been deposed from the episcopal dignity; but in regard that he chose rather to be placed over the church of Lindisfarne, in which he had lived, it was thought fit that Eata should return to the see of the church of Hagulstad, to which he had been first ordained, and that Cuthbert should take upon him the government of the church of Lindisfarne.

Following the example of the apostles, he became an ornament to the episcopal dignity, by his virtuous actions; for he both protected the people committed to his charge, by constant prayer, and excited them, by most wholesome admonitions, to heavenly practices; and, which is the greatest help in teachers, he first showed in his behaviour what he taught was to be performed by others; for he was much inflamed with the fire of Divine charity, modest in the virtue of patience, most diligently intent on devout prayers, and affable to all that came to him for comfort. He thought it equivalent to praying, to afford the infirm brethren the help of his exhortations, well knowing that he who said "Thou shalt love the Lord thy God," said likewise, "Thou shalt love thy neighbour as thyself." He was also remarkable for penitential abstinence, and always intent upon heavenly things, through the grace of humility: lastly, when he offered up to God the sacrifice of the saving victim, he commended his prayer to God, not with a loud voice, but with tears drawn from the bottom of his heart.

Having spent two years in his bishopric, he returned to his island and monastery, being advertised by a Divine oracle, that the day of his death, or rather of his life, was drawing near; as he, at that time, with his usual simplicity, signified to some persons, though in terms which were somewhat obscure, but which were nevertheless afterwards plainly understood; while to others he declared the same openly.

233

CHAPTER XXIX

ST. CUTHBERT FORETOLD TO THE ANCHORITE, HERE-BERT, THAT HIS DEATH WAS AT HAND. [A.D. 687.]

THERE was a certain priest, venerable for the probity of his life and manners, called Herebert, who had long been united with the man of God, Cuthbert, in the bonds of spiritual friendship. This man leading a solitary life in the island of that great lake from which the river Derwent flows, was wont to visit him every year, and to receive from him spiritual advice. Hearing that Bishop Cuthbert was come to the city of Lugubalia, he repaired thither to him, according to custom, being desirous to be still more and more inflamed in heavenly desires through his wholesome admonitions. Whilst they alternately entertained one another with the delights of the celestial life, the bishop, among other things, said, "Brother Herebert, remember at this time to ask me all the questions you wish to have resolved, and say all you design; for we shall see one another no more in this world. For I am sure that the time of my dissolution is at hand, and I shall speedily put off this tabernacle of the flesh." Hearing these words, he fell down at his feet, and shedding tears, with a sigh, said, "I beseech you, by our Lord, not to forsake me; but that you remember your most faithful companion, and entreat the Supreme Goodness that, as we served Him together upon earth, we may depart together to see his bliss in heaven. For you know that I have always endeavoured to live according to your directions, and whatsoever faults I have committed, either through ignorance or frailty, I have instantly submitted to correction according to your will." The bishop applied himself to prayer, and having presently had intimation in the spirit that he had obtained what he asked of the Lord, he said, "Rise, brother, and do not weep, but rejoice, because the Heavenly Goodness has granted what we desired."

The event proved the truth of this promise and prophecy, for after their parting at that time, they no more saw one another in the flesh; but their souls quitting their bodies on the very same day, that is, on the 20th of March, they were immediately again united in spirit, and translated to the heavenly kingdom by the ministry of angels. But Herebert was first prepared by a tedious sickness, through the dispensation of the Divine Goodness, as may be believed, to the end that if he was anything inferior in merit to the blessed Cuthbert, the same might be made up by the chastising pain of a long sickness, that being thus made equal in grace to his intercessor, as he departed out of the body at the very same time with him, so he might be received into the same seat of eternal bliss.

The most reverend father died in the isle of Farne, earnestly entreating the brothers that he might also be buried in that same place, where he had served God a considerable time. However, at length yielding to their entreaties, he consented to be carried back to the isle of Lindisfarne, and there buried in the church. This being done accordingly, the venerable Bishop Wilfrid held the episcopal see of that church one year, till such time as one was chosen to be ordained in the room of Cuthbert. Afterwards Edbert was consecrated, a man renowned for his knowledge in the Divine writings, as also for keeping the Divine precepts, and chiefly for almsgiving, so that, according to the law, he every year gave the tenth part, not only of four-footed beasts, but also of all corn and fruit, as also of garments, to the poor.

CHAPTER XXX

ST. CUTHBERT'S BODY WAS FOUND ALTOGETHER UNCORRUPTED AFTER IT HAD BEEN BURIED ELEVEN YEARS; HIS SUCCESSOR IN THE BISHOPRIC DEPARTED THIS WORLD NOT LONG AFTER. [A.D. 698.]

IN order to show with how much glory the man of God, Cuthbert, lived after death, his holy life having been before his death signalised by frequent miracles; when he had been buried eleven years, Divine Providence put it into the minds of the brethren to take up his bones, expecting, as is usual with dead bodies, to find all the flesh consumed and reduced to ashes, and the rest dried up, and intending to put the same into a new coffin, and to lay them in the same place, but above the pavement, for the honour due to him. They acquainted Bishop Edbert with their design, and he consented to it, and ordered that the same should be done on the anniversary of his burial. They did so, and opening the grave, found all the body whole, as if it had been alive, and the joints pliable, more like one asleep than a dead person; besides, all the vestments the body had on were not only found, but wonderful for their freshness and gloss. The brothers seeing this, with much amazement hastened to tell the bishop what they had found; he being then alone in a place remote from the church, and encompassed by the sea. There he always used to spend the time of Lent, and was wont to continue there with great devotion, forty days before the birth of our Lord, in abstinence, prayer, and tears. There also his venerable predecessor, Cuthbert, had some time served God in private, before he went to the isle of Farne.

They brought him also some part of the garments that had covered his holy body; which presents he thankfully accepted, and attentively listening to the miracles, he with wonderful affection kissed those garments, as if they had been still upon his father's body, and said, "Let the body be put into new garments in lieu of these you have brought, and so lay it into the coffin you have provided; for I am certain that the place will not long remain empty, having been sanctified with so many miracles of heavenly grace; and how happy is he to whom our Lord, the author and giver of all bliss, shall grant the privilege of lying in the same." The bishop having said this and much more, with many tears and great humility, the brothers did as he had commanded them, and when they had dressed the body in new garments, and laid it in a new coffin, they placed it on the pavement of the sanctuary. Soon after, God's beloved bishop, Edbert, fell grievously sick, and his distemper daily increasing, in a short time, that is, on the 6th of May, he also departed to our Lord, and they laid his body in the grave of the holy father Cuthbert, placing over it the coffin, with the uncorrupted remains of that father. The miracles sometimes wrought in that place testify the merits of them both; some of which we before preserved the memory of in the book of his life, and have thought fit to add some more in this History, which have lately come to our knowledge.

CHAPTER XXXI

OF ONE THAT WAS CURED OF A PALSY AT THE TOMB OF ST. CUTHBERT. [A.D. 698.]

THERE was in that same monastery a brother whose name was Bethwegen, who had for a considerable time waited upon the guests of the house, and is still living, having the testimony of all the brothers and strangers resorting thither, of being a man of much piety and religion, and serving the office put upon him only for the sake of the heavenly reward. This man, having on a certain day washed the mantles or garments which he used in the hospital, in the sea, was returning home, when on a sudden, about half way, he was seized with a sudden distemper in his body, insomuch that he fell down, and having lain some time, he could scarcely rise again. When at last he got up, he felt one half of his body, from the head to the foot, struck with palsy, and with much difficulty got home by the help of a staff. The distemper increased by degrees, and as night approached, became still worse, so that when day returned, he could scarcely rise or go alone. In this weak condition, a good thought came into his mind, which was to go to the church, the best way he could, to the tomb of the reverend father Cuthbert, and there, on his knees, to beg of the Divine Goodness either to be delivered from that disease, if it were for his good, or if the Divine Providence had ordained him longer to lie under the same for his punishment, that he might bear the pain with patience and a composed mind.

He did accordingly, and supporting his weak limbs with a staff, entered the church, and prostrating himself before the body of the man of God, he, with pious earnestness, prayed that, through his intercession, our Lord might be propitious to him. In the midst of his prayers, he fell as it were into a stupor, and, as he was afterwards wont to relate, felt a large and broad hand touch his head, where the pain lay, and by that touch, all the part of his body which had been affected with the distemper, was delivered from the weakness, and restored to health down to his feet. He then awoke, and rose up in perfect health, and returning thanks to God for his recovery, told the brothers what had happened to him; and to the joy of them all, returned the more zealously, as if chastened by his affliction, to the service which he was wont before so carefully to perform. The very garments which had been on Cuthbert's body, dedicated to God, either whilst living, or after he was dead, were not exempt from the virtue of performing cures, as may be seen in the book of his life and miracles, by such as shall read it.

CHAPTER XXXII

OF ONE WHO WAS CURED OF A DISTEMPER IN HIS EYE AT THE RELICS OF ST. CUTHBERT. [A.D. 698.]

NOR is that cure to be passed over in silence, which was performed by his relics three years ago, and was told me by the brother himself, on whom it was wrought. It happened in the monastery, which, being built near the river Dacore, has taken its name from the same, over which, at that time, the religious Suidbert presided as abbat. In that monastery was a youth whose eyelid had a great swelling on it, which growing daily, threatened the loss of the eye. The surgeons applied their medicines to ripen it, but in vain. Some said it ought to be cut off; others opposed it, for fear of worse consequences. The brother having long laboured under this malady, and seeing no human means likely to save his eye, but that, on the contrary, it grew daily worse, was cured on a sudden, through the Divine Goodness, by the relics of the holy father, Cuthbert; for the brethren, finding his body uncorrupted, after having been many years buried, took some part of the hair, which they might, at the request of friends, give or show, in testimony of the miracle.

One of the priests of the monastery, named Thridred, who is now abbat there, had a small part of these relics by him at that time. One day in the church he opened the box of relics, to give some part to a friend that begged it, and it happened that the youth who had the distempered eye was then in the church; the priest, having given his friend as much as he thought fit, delivered the rest to the youth to put it into its place. Having received the hairs of the holy head, by some fortunate impulse, he clapped them to the sore eyelid, and endeavoured for some time, by the application of them, to soften and abate the swelling. Having done this, he again laid the relics into the box, as he had been ordered, believing that his eye would soon be cured by the hairs of the man of God, which had touched it; nor did his faith disappoint him. It was then, as he is wont to relate it, about the second hour of the day; but he, being busy about other things that belonged to that day, about the sixth hour of the same, touching his eye on a sudden, found it as sound with the lid, as if there never had been any swelling or deformity on it.

BOOK V

CHAPTER I

HOW ETHELWALD, SUCCESSOR TO CUTHBERT, LEADING
AN EREMITICAL LIFE, CALMED A TEMPEST WHEN THE
BRETHREN WERE IN DANGER AT SEA. [A.D. 687.]

THE venerable Ethelwald, who had received the priesthood in
the monastery of Inhrypum, and had, by actions worthy of the
same, sanctified his holy office, succeeded the man of God,
Cuthbert, in the exercise of a solitary life, having practised the
same before he was bishop, in the isle of Farne. For the more certain demonstration of the life which he led, and his merit, I will
relate one miracle of his, which was told me by one of these
brothers for and on whom the same was wrought: viz. Guthfrid,
the venerable servant and priest of Christ, who, afterwards, as
abbat, presided over the brethren of the same church of
Lindisfarne, in which he had been educated.

"I came," says he, "to the island of Farne, with two others of the
brethren, to speak with the most reverend father, Ethelwald. Having
been refreshed with his discourse, and taken his blessing, as we were
returning home, on a sudden, when we were in the midst of the sea,
the fair weather which was wafting us over was checked, and there
ensued so great and dismal a tempest, that neither the sails nor oars
were of any use to us, nor had we anything to expect but death. After
long struggling with the wind and waves to no effect, we looked
behind us to see whether it was practicable at least to recover the

island from whence we came, but we found ourselves on all sides so enveloped in the storm, that there was no hope of escaping. But looking out as far as we could see, we observed, on the island of Farne, Father Ethelwald, beloved of God, come out of his cavern to watch our course; for, hearing the noise of the storm and raging sea, he was come out to see what would become of us. When he beheld us in distress and despair, he bowed his knees to the Father of our Lord Jesus Christ, in prayer for our life and safety; upon which, the swelling sea was calmed, so that the storm ceased on all sides, and a fair wind attended us to the very shore. When we had landed, and had dragged upon the shore the small vessel that brought us, the storm, which had ceased a short time for our sake, immediately returned, and raged continually during the whole day; so that it plainly appeared that the brief cessation of the storm had been granted from Heaven at the request of the man of God, in order that we might escape."

The man of God remained in the isle of Farne twelve years, and died there; but was buried in the church of St. Peter and Paul, in the isle of Lindisfarne, beside the bodies of the aforesaid bishops. These things happened in the days of King Alfred, who ruled the nation of the Northumbrians eighteen years after his brother Egfrid.

CHAPTER II

HOW BISHOP JOHN CURED A DUMB MAN BY BLESSING HIM. [A.D. 685.]

IN the beginning of the aforesaid reign, Bishop Eata died, and was succeeded in the prelacy of the church of Hagulstad by John, a holy man, of whom those that familiarly knew him are wont to tell many miracles; and more particularly, the reverend Berthun, a man of undoubted veracity, and once his deacon, now abbat of the monastery called Inderawood, that is, in the wood of the Deiri: some of which miracles we have thought fit to transmit to posterity. There is a certain building in a retired situation, and enclosed by a narrow wood and a trench, about a mile and a half from the church of Hagulstad, and separated from it by the river Tyne, having a burying-place dedicated to St. Michael the Archangel, where the man of God used frequently, as occasion offered, and particularly in Lent, to reside with a few companions. Being come thither once at the beginning of Lent, to stay, he commanded his followers to find out some poor person labouring under any grievous infirmity, or want, whom he might keep with him during those days, by way of alms, for so he was always used to do.

There was in a village not far off, a certain dumb youth, known to the bishop, for he often used to come into his presence to receive alms, and had never been able to speak one word. Besides, he had so much scurf and scabs on his head, that no hair ever grew on the top of it, but only some scattered hairs in a circle round about. The bishop caused this young man to be brought, and a little cottage to be made for him within the enclosure of the dwelling, in which he might reside, and receive a daily allowance from him. When one week of Lent was over, the next Sunday he caused the poor man to come in to him, and ordered him to put his tongue out of his mouth and show it him; then laying hold of his chin, he made the sign of the cross on his tongue, directing him to draw it back into his mouth and to speak. "Pronounce some word," said he; "say yea," which, in the language of the Angles, is the word of affirming and consenting, that is, yes. The youth's tongue was immediately loosed, and he said what he was ordered. The bishop, then pronouncing the names of the letters, directed him to say A; he did so, and afterwards B, which he also did. When he had named all the letters after the bishop, the latter proceeded to put syllables and words to him, which being also repeated by him, he commanded him to utter whole sentences, and he did it. Nor did he cease all that day and the next night, as long as he could keep awake, as those who were present relate, to talk something, and to express his private thoughts and will to others, which he could never do before; after the manner of the cripple, who, being healed by the Apostles Peter and John, stood up leaping, and walked, and went with them into the temple, walking, and skipping, and praising the Lord, rejoicing to have the use of his feet, which he had so long wanted. The bishop, rejoicing at his recovery of speech, ordered the physician to take in hand the cure of his scurfed head. He did so, and with the help of the bishop's blessing and prayers, a good head of hair grew as the flesh was healed. Thus the youth obtained a good aspect, a ready utterance, and a beautiful head of hair, whereas before he had been deformed, poor, and dumb. Thus rejoicing at his recovery, the bishop offered to keep him in his family, but he rather chose to return home.

CHAPTER III

THE SAME BISHOP, JOHN, BY HIS PRAYERS, HEALED A SICK MAIDEN. [A.D. 686.]

THE same Berthun told another miracle of the bishop's. When the reverend Wilfrid, after a long banishment, was admitted to the bishopric of the church of Hagulstad, and the aforesaid John, upon the death of Bosa, a man of great sanctity and humility, was, in his place, appointed bishop of York, he came, once upon a time, to the monastery of Virgins, at the place called Wetadun, where the Abbess Hereberga then presided. "When we were come thither," said he, "and had been received with great and universal joy, the abbess told us, that one of the virgins, who was her daughter in the flesh, laboured under a grievous distemper, having been lately bled in the arm, and whilst she was engaged in study, was seized with a sudden violent pain, which increased so that the wounded arm became worse, and so much swelled, that it could not be grasped with both hands; and thus being confined to her bed, through excess of pain, she was expected to die very soon. The abbess entreated the bishop that he would vouchsafe to go in and give her his blessing; for that she believed she would be the better for his blessing or touching her. He asked when the maiden had been bled? and being told that it was on the fourth day of the moon, said, 'You did very indiscreetly and unskilfully to bleed her on the fourth day of the moon; for I remember that Archbishop Theodore, of blessed memory, said, that bleeding at that time was very dangerous, when the light of the moon and the tide of the ocean is increasing; and what can I do to the girl if she is like to die?'

"The abbess still earnestly entreated for her daughter, whom she dearly loved, and designed to make abbess in her stead, and at last prevailed with him to go in to her. He accordingly went in, taking me with him to the virgin, who lay, as I said, in great anguish, and her arm swelled so fast that there was no bending of the elbow; the bishop stood and said a prayer over her, and having given his blessing, went out. Afterwards, as we were sitting at table, some one came in and called me out, saying, 'Coenberg' (that was the virgin's name) 'desires you will immediately go back to her.' I did so, and entering the house, perceived her countenance more cheerful, and like one in perfect health. Having seated myself down by her, she said, 'Would you like me to call for something to drink?'— 'Yes,' said I, 'and am very glad if you can.' When the cup was brought, and we had both drunk, she said, 'As soon as the bishop had said the prayer, given me his blessing, and gone out, I immediately began to mend; and though I have not yet recovered my former strength, yet all the pain is quite gone from my arm, where it was most intense, and from all my body, as if the bishop had carried it away with him; though the swelling of the arm still seems to remain.' When we departed from thence, the cure of the pain in her limbs was followed by the assuaging of the swelling; and the virgin being thus delivered from torture and death, returned praise to our Lord and Saviour, with his other servants who were there."

CHAPTER IV

THE SAME BISHOP HEALED AN EARL'S WIFE THAT WAS SICK, WITH HOLY WATER. [A.D. 686.]

THE same abbat related another miracle, similar to the former, of the aforesaid bishop. "Not very far from our monastery, that is, about two miles off, was the country-house of one Puch, an earl, whose wife had languished near forty days under a very acute disease, insomuch that for three weeks she could not be carried out of the room where she lay. It happened that the man of God was, at that time, invited thither by the earl to consecrate a church; and when that was done, the earl desired him to dine at his house. The bishop declined, saying, 'He must return to the monastery, which was very near.' The earl, pressing him more earnestly, vowed he would also give alms to the poor, if the bishop would break his fast that day in his house. I joined my entreaties to his, promising in like manner to give alms for the relief of the poor, if he would go and dine at the earl's house, and give his blessing. Having at length, with much difficulty, prevailed, we went in to dine. The bishop had sent to the woman that lay sick some of the holy water, which he had blessed for the consecration of the church, by one of the brothers that went along with me, ordering him to give her some to drink, and wash the place where her greatest pain was, with some of the same. This being done, the woman immediately got up in health, and perceiving that she had not only been delivered from her tedious distemper, but at the same time recovered the strength which she had lost, she presented the cup to the bishop and to us, and continued serving us with drink as she had begun till dinner was over; following the example of Peter's mother-in-law, who, having been sick of a fever, arose at the touch of our Lord, and having at once received health and strength, ministered to them."

CHAPTER V

THE SAME BISHOP RECOVERED ONE OF THE EARL'S SERVANTS FROM DEATH. [A.D. 686.]

AT another time also, being called to consecrate Earl Addi's church, when he had performed that duty, he was entreated by the earl to go in to one of his servants, who lay dangerously ill, and having lost the use of all his limbs, seemed to be just at death's door; and indeed the coffin had been provided to bury him in.

The earl urged his entreaties with tears, earnestly praying that he would go in and pray for him, because his life was of great consequence to him; and he believed that if the bishop would lay his hand upon him and give him his blessing, he would soon mend. The bishop went in, and saw him in a dying condition, and the coffin by his side, whilst all that were present were in tears. He said a prayer, blessed him, and on going out, as is the usual expression of comforters, said, "May you soon recover." Afterwards, when they were sitting at table, the lad sent to his lord, to desire he would let him have a cup of wine, because he was thirsty. The earl, rejoicing that he could drink, sent him a cup of wine, blessed by the bishop; which, as soon as he had drunk, he immediately got up, and, shaking off his late infirmity, dressed himself, and going in to the bishop, saluted him and the other guests, saying, "He would also eat and be merry with them." They ordered him to sit down with them at the entertainment, rejoicing at his recovery. He sat down, ate and drank merrily, and behaved himself like the rest of the company; and living many years after, continued in the same state of health. The aforesaid abbat says this miracle was not wrought in his presence, but that he had it from those who were there.

CHAPTER VI

THE SAME BISHOP, BY HIS PRAYERS AND BLESSING, DELIVERED FROM DEATH ONE OF HIS CLERKS, WHO HAD BRUISED HIMSELF BY A FALL. [A.D. 686.]

NOR do I think that this further miracle, which Herebald, the servant of Christ, says was wrought upon himself, is to be passed over in silence. He was then one of that bishop's clergy, but now presides as abbat in the monastery at the mouth of the river Tyne. "Being present," said he, "and very well acquainted with his course of life, I found it to be most worthy of a bishop, as far as it is lawful for men to judge; but I have known by the experience of others, and more particularly by my own, how great his merit was before

Him who is the judge of the heart; having been by his prayer and blessing brought back from the gates of death to the way of life. For, when in the prime of my youth, I lived among his clergy, applying myself to reading and singing, but not having yet altogether withdrawn my heart from youthful pleasures, it happened one day that as we were travelling with him, we came into a plain and open road, well adapted for galloping our horses. The young men that were with him, and particularly those of the laity, began to entreat the bishop to give them leave to gallop, and make trial of the goodness of their horses. He at first refused, saying, 'it was an idle request;' but at last, being prevailed on by the unanimous desire of so many, 'Do so,' said he, 'if you will, but let Herebald have no part in the trial.' I earnestly prayed that I might have leave to ride with the rest, for I relied on an excellent horse, which he had given me, but I could not obtain my request.

"When they had several times galloped backwards and forwards, the bishop and I looking on, my wanton humour prevailed, and I could no longer refrain, but though he forbade me, I struck in among them, and began to ride at full speed; at which I heard him call after me, 'Alas! how much you grieve me by riding after that manner.' Though I heard him, I went on against his command; but immediately the fiery horse taking a great leap over a hollow place, I fell, and lost both sense and motion, as if I had been dead; for there was in that place a stone, level with the ground, covered with only a small turf, and no other stone to be found in all that plain; and it happened, as a punishment for my disobedience, either by chance, or by Divine Providence so ordering it, that my head and hand, which in falling I had clapped to my head, hit upon that stone, so that my thumb was broken and my skull cracked, and I lay, as I said, like one dead.

"And because I could not move, they stretched a canopy for me to lie in. It was about the seventh hour of the day, and having lain still, and as it were dead from that time till the evening, I then revived a little, and was carried home by my companions, but lay speechless all the night, vomiting blood, because something was broken within me by the fall. The bishop was very much grieved at my misfortune, and expected my death, for he bore me extraordinary affection. Nor would he stay that night, as he was wont, among his clergy; but spent it all in watching and prayer alone, imploring the Divine goodness, as I imagine, for my health. Coming to me in the morning early, and having said a prayer over me, he called me by my name, and as it were waking me out of a heavy sleep, asked, 'Whether I knew who it was that spoke to me?' I opened my eyes and said, 'I do; you are my beloved bishop.'— 'Can you live?' said he. I answered, 'I may, through your prayers, if it shall please our Lord.'

"He then laid his hand on my head, with the words of blessing, and returned to prayer; when he came again to see me, in a short time, he found me sitting and able to talk; and, being induced by Divine instinct, as it soon appeared, began to ask me, 'Whether I knew for certain that I had been baptized?' I answered, 'I knew beyond all doubt that I had been washed in the laver of salvation, to the remission of my sins, and I named the priest by whom I knew myself to have been baptized.' He replied. 'If you were baptized by that priest, your baptism is not perfect; for I know him, and that having been ordained priest, he could not, by reason of the dulness of his understanding, learn the ministry of catechising and baptizing; for which reason I commanded him altogether to desist from his presumptuous exercising of the ministry, which he could not duly perform.' This said, he took care to catechise me at that very time; and it happened that he blew upon my face, on which I presently found myself better. He called the surgeon, and ordered him to close and bind up my skull where it was cracked; and having then received his blessing, I was so much better that I mounted on horseback the next day, and travelled with him to another place; and being soon after perfectly recovered, I received the baptism of life."

He continued in his see thirty-three years, and then ascending to the heavenly kingdom, was buried in St. Peter's Porch, in his own monastery, called Inderawood, in the year of our Lord's incarnation 721. For having, by his great age, become unable to govern his bishopric, he ordained Wilfrid, his priest, bishop of the church of York, and retired to the aforesaid monastery, and there ended his days in holy conversation.

CHAPTER VII

CÆDWALLA, KING OF THE WEST SAXONS, WENT TO ROME TO BE BAPTIZED; HIS SUCCESSOR INA ALSO DEVOUTLY REPAIRED TO THE SAME CHURCH OF THE HOLY APOS-TLES. [A.D. 688.]

IN the third year of the reign of Alfrid, Cædwalla, king of the West Saxons, having most honourably governed his nation two years, quitted his crown for the sake of our Lord and his everlasting kingdom, and went to Rome, being desirous to obtain the peculiar honour of being baptized in the church of the blessed apostles, for he had learned that in baptism alone, the entrance into heaven is opened to mankind; and he hoped at the same time, that laying down the flesh, as soon as baptized, he should immediately pass to the eternal joys of heaven; both which things, by the blessing of our Lord, came to pass according as he had conceived in his mind. For coming to Rome, at the time that Sergius was pope, he was baptized on the holy Saturday before Easter Day, in the year of our Lord 689, and being still in his white garments, he fell sick, and departed this life on the 20th of April, and was associated with the blessed in heaven. At his baptism, the aforesaid pope had given him the name of Peter, to the end that he might be also united in name to the most blessed prince of the apostles, to whose most holy body his pious love had brought him from the utmost bounds of the earth. He was likewise buried in his church, and by the pope's command an epitaph written on his tomb, wherein the memory of his devotion might be preserved for ever, and the readers or hearers might be inflamed with religious desire by the example of what he had done.

The epitaph was this—

> High state and place, kindred, a wealthy crown,
> Triumphs, and spoils in glorious battles won,
> Nobles, and cities walled, to guard his state,
> High palaces, and his familiar seat,
> Whatever honours his own virtue won,
> Or those his great forefathers handed down,
> Cædwal armipotent, from heaven inspir'd,
> For love of heaven hath left, and here retir'd;
> Peter to see, and Peter's sacred chair,
> The royal pilgrim travelled from afar,
> Here to imbibe pure draughts from his clear stream,
> And share the influence of his heavenly beam;
> Here for the glories of a future claim,
> Converted, chang'd his first and barbarous name.
> And following Peter's rule, he from his Lord
> Assumed the name at Father Sergius' word,
> At the pure font, and by Christ's grace made clean,
> In heaven is free from former taints of sin.
> Great was his faith, but greater God's decree,
> Whose secret counsels mortal cannot see:
> Safe came he, e'en from Britain's isle, o'er seas,
> And lands, and countries, and through dangerous ways,
> Rome to behold, her glorious temple see,
> And mystic presents offer'd on his knee.
> Now in the grave his fleshly members lie,
> His soul, amid Christ's flock, ascends the sky.
> Sure wise was he to lay his sceptre down,
> And gain in heaven above a lasting crown.

Here was deposited Cædwalla, called also Peter, king of the Saxons, on the twelfth day of the kalends of May, the second indiction. He lived about thirty years, in the reign of the most pious emperor, Justinian, in the fourth year of his consulship, in the second year of our apostolic lord, Pope Sergius.

When Cædwalla went to Rome, Ina succeeded him on the throne, being of the blood royal; and having reigned thirty-seven years over that nation, he gave up the kingdom in like manner to younger persons, and went away to Rome, to visit the blessed apostles, at the time when Gregory was pope, being desirous to spend some time of his pilgrimage upon earth in the neighbourhood of the holy place, that he might be more easily received by the saints into heaven. The same thing, about the same time, was done through the zeal of many of the English nation, noble and ignoble, laity and clergy, men and women.

CHAPTER VIII

ARCHBISHOP THEODORE DIES, BERTHWALD SUCCEEDS HIM AS ARCHBISHOP, AND, AMONG MANY OTHERS WHOM HE ORDAINED, HE MADE TOBIAS, A MOST LEARNED MAN, BISHOP OF THE CHURCH OF ROCHESTER. [A.D. 690.]

THE year after that in which Cædwalla died at Rome, that is, 690 after the incarnation of our Lord, Archbishop Theodore, of blessed memory, departed this life, old and full of days, for he was eighty-eight years of age; which number of years he had been wont long before to foretell to his friends that he should live, the same having been revealed to him in a dream. He held the bishopric twenty-two years, and was buried in St. Peter's church, where all the bodies of the bishops of Canterbury are buried. Of whom, as well as of his companions, of the same degree, it may rightly and truly be said, that their bodies are interred in peace, and their names shall live from generation to generation. For to say all in few words, the English churches received more advantage during the time of his pontificate than ever they had done before. His person, life, age, and death, are plainly described to all that resort thither, by the epitaph on his tomb, consisting of thirty-four heroic verses. The first whereof are these—

Here rests fam'd Theodore, a Grecian name,
Who had o'er England an archbishop's claim;
Happy and blessed, industriously he wrought,
And wholesome precepts to his scholars taught.

The four last are as follow—

And now it was September's nineteenth day,
When, bursting from its ligaments of clay,
His spirit rose to its eternal rest,
And joined in heaven the chorus of the blest.

Berthwald succeeded Theodore in the archbishopric, being abbat of the monastery of Raculph, which lies on the north side of the mouth of the river Genlade. He was a man learned in the Scriptures, and well instructed in ecclesiastical and monastic discipline, yet not to be compared to his predecessor. He was chosen bishop in the year of our Lord's incarnation 692, on the first day of July, Withred and Suebhard being kings in Kent; but he was consecrated the next year, on Sunday the 29th of June, by Godwin, metropolitan bishop of France, and was enthroned on Sunday the 31st of August. Among the many bishops whom he ordained was Tobias, a man learned in the Latin, Greek, and Saxon tongues, otherwise also possessing much erudition, whom he consecrated in the stead of Gebmund, bishop of that see, deceased.

CHAPTER IX

EGBERT, A HOLY MAN, WOULD HAVE GONE INTO GER-
MANY TO PREACH, BUT COULD NOT; WICTBERT WENT,
BUT MEETING WITH NO SUCCESS, RETURNED INTO IRE-
LAND, FROM WHENCE HE CAME. [A.D. 689.]

AT that time the venerable servant of Christ, and priest, Egbert, whom I cannot name but with the greatest respect, and who, as was said before, lived a stranger in Ireland to obtain hereafter a residence in heaven, proposed to himself to do good to many, by taking upon him the apostolical work, and preaching the word of God to some of those nations that had not yet heard it; many of which nations he knew there were in Germany, from whom the Angles or Saxons, who now inhabit Britain, are known to have derived their origin; for which reason they are still corruptly called Garmans by the neighbouring nation of the Britons. Such are the Prisons, the Rugins, the Danes, the Huns, the Ancient Saxons, and the Boructuars (or Bructers). There are also in the same parts many other nations still following pagan rites, to whom the aforesaid soldier of Christ designed to repair, sailing round Britain, and to try whether he could deliver any of them from Satan, and bring them over to Christ; or if this could not be done, to go to Rome, to see and adore the hallowed thresholds of the holy apostles and martyrs of Christ.

But the Divine oracles and certain events proceeding from heaven obstructed his performing either of those designs; for when he had made choice of some most courageous companions, fit to preach the word of God, as being renowned for their learning and virtue; when all things were provided for the voyage, there came to him on a certain day in the morning one of the brethren, formerly disciple and minister in Britain to the beloved priest of God, Boisil, when the said Boisil was superior of the monastery of Melrose, under the Abbat Eata, as has been said above. This brother told him the vision which he had seen that night. "When after the morning hymns," said he, "I had laid me down in my bed, and was fallen into a slumber, my former master and loving tutor, Boisil, appeared to me, and asked, 'Whether I knew him?' I said, 'I do; you are Boisil.' He answered, 'I am come to bring Egbert a message from our Lord and Saviour, which nevertheless must be delivered to him by you. Tell him, therefore, that he cannot perform the journey he has undertaken; for it is the will of God that he should rather go to instruct the monasteries of Columba.'" Now Columba was the first teacher of Christianity to the Picts beyond the mountains northward, and the founder of the monastery in the island Hii, which was for a long time much honoured by many tribes of the Scots and Picts; wherefore he is now by some called Columbkill, the name being compounded from Columb and Cell. Egbert, having heard the vision, ordered the brother that had told it him, not to mention it to any other, lest it should happen to be an illusion. However, when he considered of it with himself, he apprehended that it was real; yet would not desist from preparing for his voyage to instruct those nations.

A few days after the aforesaid brother came again to him, saying, "That Boisil had that night again appeared to him after matins, and said, 'Why did you tell Egbert that which I enjoined you in so light and cold a manner? However, go now and tell him, that whether he will or no, he shall go to Columb's monastery, because their ploughs do not go straight; and he is to bring them into the right way.'" Hearing this, Egbert again commanded the brother not to reveal the same to any person. Though now assured of the vision, he nevertheless attempted to undertake his intended voyage with the brethren. When they had put aboard all that was requisite for so long a voyage, and had waited some days for a fair wind, there arose one night on a sudden so violent a storm, that the ship was run aground, and part of what had been put aboard spoiled. However, all that belonged to Egbert and his companions was saved. Then he, saying, like the prophet, "This tempest has happened upon my account," laid aside the undertaking and stayed at home.

However, Wictbert, one of his companions, being famous for his contempt of the world and for his knowledge, for he had lived many years a stranger in Ireland, leading an eremitical life in great purity, went abroad, and arriving in Frisland, preached the word of salvation for the space of two years successively to that nation and to its king, Rathbed; but reaped no fruit of all his great labour among his barbarous auditors. Returning then to the beloved place of his peregrination, he gave himself up to our Lord in his wonted repose, and since he could not be profitable to strangers by teaching them the faith, he took care to be the more useful to his own people by the example of his virtue.

CHAPTER X

WILBRORD, PREACHING IN FRISLAND, CONVERTED MANY
TO CHRIST; HIS TWO COMPANIONS, THE HEWALDS, SUF-
FERED MARTYRDOM. [A.D. 690.]

WHEN the man of God, Egbert, perceived that neither he himself
was permitted to preach to the Gentiles, being withheld, on
account of some other advantage to the church, which had been
foretold him by the Divine oracle; nor that Wictbert, when he
went into those parts, had met with any success; he nevertheless
still attempted to send some holy and industrious men to the work
of the word, among whom was Wilbrord, a man eminent for his
merit and rank in the priesthood. They arrived there, twelve in
number, and turning aside to Pepin, duke of the Franks, were graciously received by him; and as he had lately subdued the Hither
Frisland, and expelled King Rathbed, he sent them thither to
preach, supporting them at the same time with his authority, that
none might molest them in their preaching, and bestowing many
favours on those who consented to embrace the faith. Thus it
came to pass, that with the assistance of the Divine grace, they in a
short time converted many from idolatry to the faith of Christ.

Two other priests of the English nation, who had long lived
strangers in Ireland, for the sake of the eternal kingdom, following the example of the former, went into the province of the
Ancient Saxons, to try whether they could there gain any to Christ
by preaching. They both bore the same name, as they were the
same in devotion, Hewald being the name of both, with this distinction, that, on account of the difference of their hair, the one
was called Black Hewald and the other White Hewald. They were
both piously religious, but Black Hewald was the more learned of
the two in Scripture. On entering that province, these men took
up their lodging in a certain steward's house, and requested that
he would conduct them to his lord, for that they had a message,
and something to his advantage, to communicate to him; for those

Ancient Saxons have no king, but several lords that rule their nation; and when any war happens, they cast lots indifferently, and on whomsoever the lot falls, him they follow and obey during the war; but as soon as the war is ended, all those lords are again equal in power. The steward received and entertained them in his house some days, promising to send them to his lord, as they desired.

But the barbarians finding them to be of another religion, by their continual prayer and singing of psalms and hymns, and by their daily offering the sacrifice of the saving oblation,—for they had with them sacred vessels and a consecrated table for an altar,—they began to grow jealous of them, lest if they should come into the presence of their chief, and converse with him, they should turn his heart from their gods, and convert him to the new religion of the Christian faith; and thus by degrees all their province should change its old worship for a new. Hereupon they, on a sudden, laid hold of them and put them to death; the White Hewald they slew immediately with the sword; but the Black they put to tedious torture and tore limb from limb, throwing them into the Rhine. The chief, whom they had desired to see, hearing of it, was highly incensed, that the strangers who desired to come to him had not been allowed; and therefore he sent and put to death all those peasants and burnt their village. The aforesaid priests and servants of Christ suffered on the 3rd of October.

Nor did their martyrdom want the honour of miracles; for their dead bodies having been cast into the river by the pagans, as has been said, were carried against the stream for the space of almost forty miles, to the place where their companions were. Moreover, a long ray of light, reaching up to heaven, shined every night over the place where they arrived, in the sight of the very pagans that had slain them. Moreover, one of them appeared in a vision by night to one of his companions, whose name was Tilmon, a man of illustrious and of noble birth, who from a soldier was become a monk, acquainting him that he might find their bodies in that place, where he should see rays of light reaching from heaven to the earth; which turned out accordingly; and their bodies being found, were interred with the honour due to martyrs; and the day of their passion or of their bodies being found, is celebrated in those parts with proper veneration. At length, Pepin, the most glorious general of the Franks, understanding these things, caused the bodies to be brought to him, and buried them with much honour in the church of the city of Cologne, on the Rhine. It is reported, that a spring gushed out in the place where they were killed, which to this day affords a plentiful stream.

CHAPTER XI

HOW THE VENERABLE SWIDBERT IN BRITAIN, AND WILBRORD AT ROME, WERE ORDAINED BISHOPS FOR FRISLAND. [A.D. 692.]

AT their first coming into Frisland, as soon as Wilbrord found he had leave given him by the prince to preach, he made haste to Rome, where Pope Sergius then presided over the apostolical see, that he might undertake the desired work of preaching the Gospel to the Gentiles, with his licence and blessing; and hoping to receive of him some relics of the blessed apostles and martyrs of Christ; to the end, that when he destroyed the idols, and erected churches in the nation to which he preached, he might have the relics of saints at hand to put into them, and having deposited them there, might accordingly dedicate those places to the honour of each of the saints whose relics they were. He was also desirous there to learn or to receive from thence many other things which so great a work required. Having obtained all that he wanted, he returned to preach.

At which time, the brothers who were in Frisland, attending the ministry of the word, chose out of their own number a man, modest of behaviour, and meek of heart, called Swidbert, to be ordained bishop for them. He, being sent into Britain, was consecrated by the most reverend Bishop Wilfrid, who, happening to be then driven out of his country, lived in banishment among the

Mercians; for Kent had no bishop at that time, Theodore being dead, and Berthwald, his successor, who was gone beyond the sea, to be ordained, not having returned.

The said Swidbert, being made bishop, returned from Britain not long after, and went among the Boructuarians; and by his preaching brought many of them into the way of truth; but the Boructuarians being not long after subdued by the Ancient Saxons, those who had received the word were dispersed abroad; and the bishop himself repaired to Pepin, who, at the request of his wife, Blithryda, gave him a place of residence in a certain island on the Rhine, which, in their tongue, is called Inlitore; where he built a monastery, which his heirs still possess, and for a time led a most continent life, and there ended his days.

When they who went over had spent some years teaching in Frisland, Pepin, with the consent of them all, sent the venerable Wilbrord to Rome, where Sergius was still pope, desiring that he might be consecrated archbishop over the nation of the Frisons; which was accordingly done, in the year of our Lord's incarnation 696. He was consecrated in the church of the Holy Martyr Cecilia, on her feast-day; the pope gave him the name of Clement, and sent him back to his bishopric, fourteen days after his arrival at Rome.

Pepin gave him a place for his episcopal see, in his famous castle, which in the ancient language of those people is called Wiltaburg, that is, the town of the Wilts; but, in the French tongue, Utrecht. The most reverend prelate having built a church there, and preaching the word of faith far and near, drew many from their errors, and erected several churches and monasteries. For not long after he constituted other bishops in those parts, from among the brethren that either came with him or after him to preach there; some of which are now departed in our Lord; but Wilbrord himself, surnamed Clement, is still living, venerable for old age, having been thirty-six years a bishop, and sighing after the rewards of the heavenly life, after the many spiritual conflicts which he has waged.

CHAPTER XII

OF ONE AMONG THE NORTHUMBRIANS, WHO ROSE FROM
THE DEAD, AND RELATED THE THINGS WHICH HE HAD
SEEN, SOME EXCITING TERROR AND OTHERS DELIGHT.
[A.D. 696.]

AT this time a memorable miracle, and like to those of former
days, was wrought in Britain; for, to the end that the living might be
saved from the death of the soul, a certain person, who had been
some time dead, rose again to life, and related many remarkable
things he had seen; some of which I have thought fit here briefly to
take notice of. There was a master of a family in that district of the
Northumbrians which is called Cuningham, who led a religious
life, as did also all that belonged to him. This man fell sick, and his
distemper daily increasing, being brought to extremity, he died in
the beginning of the night; but in the morning early, he suddenly
came to life again, and sat up, upon which all those that sat about
the body weeping, fled away in a great fright, only his wife, who
loved him best, though in a great consternation and trembling,
remained with him. He, comforting her, said, "Fear not, for I am
now truly risen from death, and permitted again to live among
men; however, I am not to live hereafter as I was wont, but from
henceforward after a very different manner." Then rising immediately, he repaired to the oratory of the little town, and continuing
in prayer till day, immediately divided all his substance into three
parts; one whereof he gave to his wife, another to his children, and
the third, belonging to himself, he instantly distributed among the
poor. Not long after, he repaired to the monastery of Melrose,
which is almost enclosed by the winding of the river Tweed, and
having been shaven, went into a private dwelling, which the abbat
had provided, where he continued till the day of his death, in such
extraordinary contrition of mind and body, that though his tongue
had been silent, his life declared that he had seen many things
either to be dreaded or coveted, which others knew nothing of.

Thus he related what he had seen. "He that led me had a shining countenance and a bright garment, and we went on silently, as I thought, towards the north-east. Walking on, we came to a vale of great breadth and depth, but of infinite length; on the left it appeared full of dreadful flames, the other side was no less horrid for violent hail and cold snow flying in all directions; both places were full of men's souls, which seemed by turns to be tossed from one side to the other, as it were by a violent storm; for when the wretches could no longer endure the excess of heat, they leaped into the middle of the cutting cold; and finding no rest there, they leaped back again into the middle of the unquenchable flames. Now whereas an innumerable multitude of deformed spirits were thus alternately tormented far and near, as far as could be seen, without any intermission, I began to think that this perhaps might be hell, of whose intolerable flames I had often heard talk. My guide, who went before me, answered to my thought, saying, 'Do not believe so, for this is not the hell you imagine.'

"When he had conducted me, much frightened with that horrid spectacle, by degrees, to the farther end, on a sudden I saw the place begin to grow dusk and filled with darkness. When I came into it, the darkness, by degrees, grew so thick, that I could see nothing besides it and the shape and garment of him that led me. As we went on through the shades of night, on a sudden there appeared before us frequent globes of black flames, rising as it were out of a great pit, and falling back again into the same. When I had been conducted thither, my leader suddenly vanished, and left me alone in the midst of darkness and this horrid vision, whilst those same globes of fire, without intermission, at one time flew up and at another fell back into the bottom of the abyss; and I observed that all the flames, as they ascended, were full of human souls, which, like sparks flying up with smoke, were sometimes thrown on high, and again, when the vapour of the fire ceased, dropped down into the depth below. Moreover, an insufferable stench came forth with the vapours, and filled all those dark places.

"Having stood there a long time in much dread, not knowing what to do, which way to turn, or what end I might expect, on a sudden I heard behind me the noise of a most hideous and wretched lamentation, and at the same time a loud laughing, as of a rude multitude insulting captured enemies. When that noise, growing plainer, came up to me, I observed a gang of evil spirits dragging the howling and lamenting souls of men into the midst of the darkness, whilst they themselves laughed and rejoiced. Among those men, as I could discern, there was one shorn like a clergyman, a layman, and a woman. The evil spirits that dragged them went down into the midst of the burning pit; and as they went down deeper, I could no longer distinguish between the lamentation of the men and the laughing of the devils, yet I still had a confused sound in my ears. In the meantime, some of the dark spirits ascended from that flaming abyss, and running forward, beset me on all sides, and much perplexed me with their glaring eyes and the stinking fire which proceeded from their mouths and nostrils; and threatened to lay hold on me with burning tongs, which they had in their hands, yet they durst not touch me, though they frightened me. Being thus on all sides enclosed with enemies and darkness, and looking about on every side for assistance, there appeared behind me, on the way that I came, as it were, the brightness of a star shining amidst the darkness; which increased by degrees, and came rapidly towards me: when it drew near, all those evil spirits, that sought to carry me away with their tongs, dispersed and fled.

"He, whose approach put them to flight, was the same that led me before; who, then turning towards the right, began to lead me, as it were, towards the south-east, and having soon brought me out of the darkness, conducted me into an atmosphere of clear light. While he thus led me in open light, I saw a vast wall before us, the length and height of which, in every direction, seemed to be altogether boundless. I began to wonder why we went up to the wall, seeing no door, window, or path through it. When we came to the wall, we were presently, I know not by what means, on the top of it, and within it was a vast and delightful field, so full of fragrant flowers that the odour of its delightful sweetness immediately dispelled the stink of the dark furnace, which had pierced me through and through. So great was the light in this place, that it seemed to exceed the brightness of the day, or the sun in its meridian height. In this field were innumerable assemblies of men in white, and many companies seated together rejoicing. As he led me through the midst of those happy inhabitants, I began to think that this might, perhaps, be the kingdom of heaven, of which I had often heard so much. He answered to my thought, saying, 'This is not the kingdom of heaven, as you imagine.'

"When we had passed those mansions of blessed souls and gone farther on, I discovered before me a much more beautiful light, and therein heard sweet voices of persons singing, and so wonderful a fragrancy proceeded from the place, that the other which I had before thought most delicious, then seemed to me but very indifferent; even as that extraordinary brightness of the flowery field, compared with this, appeared mean and inconsiderable. When I began to hope we should enter that delightful place, my guide on a sudden stood still; and then turning back, led me back by the way we came.

"When we returned to those joyful mansions of the souls in white, he said to me, 'Do you know what all these things are which you have seen?' I answered, I did not; and then he replied, 'That vale you saw so dreadful for consuming flames and cutting cold, is the place in which the souls of those are tried and punished, who, delaying to confess and amend their crimes, at length have recourse to repentance at the point of death, and so depart this life; but nevertheless because they, even at their death, confessed and repented, they shall all be received into the kingdom of heaven at the day of judgment; but many are relieved before the day of judgment, by the prayers, alms, and fasting, of the living, and more especially by masses. That fiery and stinking pit, which you saw, is the mouth of hell, into which whosoever falls shall never be delivered to all eternity. This flowery place, in which you see these most beautiful young people, so bright and merry, is that into which the souls of those are received who depart the body in good works, but who are not so perfect as to deserve to be immediately admitted into the kingdom of heaven; yet they shall all, at the day of judgment, see Christ, and partake of the joys of his kingdom; for whoever are perfect in thought, word and deed, as soon as they depart the body, immediately enter into the kingdom of heaven; in the neighbourhood, whereof that place is, where you heard the sound of sweet singing, with the fragrant odour and bright light. As for you, who are now to return to your body, and live among men again, if you will endeavour nicely to examine your actions, and direct your speech and behaviour in righteousness and simplicity, you shall, after death, have a place or residence among these joyful troops of blessed souls; for when I left you for a while, it was to know how you were to be disposed of.' When he had said this to me, I much abhorred returning to my body, being delighted with the sweetness and beauty of the place I beheld, and with the company of those I saw in it. However, I durst not ask him any questions; but in the meantime, on a sudden, I found myself alive among men."

Now these and other things which this man of God saw, he would not relate to slothful persons and such as lived negligently; but only to those who, being terrified with the dread of torments, or delighted with the hopes of heavenly joys, would make use of his words to advance in piety. In the neighbourhood of his cell lived one Hemgils, a monk, eminent in the priesthood, which he honoured by his good works: he is still living, and leading a solitary life in Ireland, supporting his declining age with coarse bread and cold water. He often went to that man, and asking several questions, heard of him all the particulars of what he had seen when separated from his body; by whose relation we also came to the knowledge of those few particulars which we have briefly set down. He also related his visions to King Alfrid, a man most learned in all respects, and was by him so willingly and attentively heard, that at his request he was admitted into the monastery above-mentioned, and received the monastic tonsure; and the said king, when he happened to be in those parts, very often went to hear him. At that time the religious and humble abbat and priest, Ethelwald, presided over the monastery, and now with worthy conduct possesses the episcopal see of the church of Lindisfarne.

He had a more private place of residence assigned him in that monastery, where he might apply himself to the service of his Creator in continual prayer. And as that place lay on the bank of the river, he was wont often to go into the same to do penance in his body, and many times to dip quite under the water, and to continue saying psalms or prayers in the same as long as he could endure it, standing still sometimes up to the middle, and sometimes to the neck in water; and when he went out from thence ashore, he never took off his cold and frozen garments till they grew warm and dry on his body. And when in the winter the half-broken pieces of ice were swimming about him, which he had himself broken, to make room to stand or dip himself in the river, those who beheld it would say, "It is wonderful, brother Drithelm (for so he was called), that you are able to endure such violent cold;" he simply answered, for he was a man of much simplicity and indifferent wit, "I have seen greater cold." And when they said, "It is strange that you will endure such austerity;" he replied, "I have seen more austerity." Thus he continued, through an indefatigable desire of heavenly bliss, to subdue his aged body with daily fasting, till the day of his being called away; and thus he forwarded the salvation of many by his words and example.

CHAPTER XIII

OF ANOTHER, WHO BEFORE HIS DEATH SAW A BOOK CONTAINING ALL HIS SINS, WHICH WAS SHOWED HIM BY DEVILS. [A.D. 704–709.]

IT happened quite the contrary with one in the province of the Mercians, whose visions and words, and also his behaviour, were neither advantageous to others nor to himself. In the reign of

Coenred, who succeeded Ethel-red, there was a layman in a military employment, no less acceptable to the king for his worldly industry, than displeasing to him for his private neglect of himself. The king often admonished him to confess and amend, and to forsake his wicked courses, before he should lose all time for repentance and amendment by a sudden death. Though frequently warned, he despised the words of salvation, and promised he would do penance at some future time. In the meantime, falling sick he was confined to his bed, and began to feel very severe pains. The king coming to him (for he loved the man), earnestly exhorted him, even then, before death, to repent of his offences. He answered, "He would not then confess his sins, but would do it when he was recovered of his sickness, lest his companions should upbraid him of having done that for fear of death, which he had refused to do in health." He thought he then spoke very bravely, but it afterwards appeared that he had been miserably deluded by the wiles of the Devil.

The distemper still increasing, when the king came again to visit and instruct him, he cried out with a lamentable voice, "What will you have now? What are ye come for? for you can no longer do me any good." The king answered, "Do not talk so; behave yourself like a man in his right mind."—"I am not mad," replied he, "but I have now all the guilt of my wicked conscience before my eyes."—"What is the meaning of that?" rejoined the king. "Not long since," said he, "there came into this room two most beautiful youths, and sat down by me, the one at my head and the other at my feet. One of them produced a very small and most curious book, and gave it me to read; looking into it, I there found all the good actions I had ever done in my life written down, and they were very few and inconsiderable. They took back the book and said nothing to me. Then, on a sudden, appeared an army of wicked and deformed spirits, encompassing this house without, and filling it within. Then he, who, by the blackness of his dismal face, and his sitting above the rest, seemed to be the chief of them, taking out a book horrid to behold, of a prodigious size, and of almost insupportable weight, commanded one of his followers to bring it to me to read. Having read it, I found therein most plainly written in black characters, all the crimes I ever committed, not only in word and deed, but even in the least thought; and he said to those men in white, who sat by me, 'Why do you sit here, since you most certainly know that this man is ours?' They answered, 'You are in the right; take and add him to the number of the damned.' This said, they immediately vanished, and two most wicked spirits rising, with forks in their hands, one of them struck me on the head, and the other on the foot. These strokes are now with great torture penetrating through my bowels to the inward parts of my body, and as soon as they meet I shall die, and the devils being ready to snatch me away I shall be dragged into hell."

Thus talked that wretch in despair, and dying soon after, he is now in vain suffering in eternal torments that penance which he refused to suffer during a short time, that he might obtain forgiveness. Of whom it is manifest, that (as the holy Pope Gregory writes of certain persons) he did not see these things for his own sake, since they availed him only for the instruction of others, who, knowing of his death, should be afraid to put off the time of repentance, whilst they have leisure, lest, being prevented by sudden death, they should depart impenitent. His having books laid before him by the good or evil spirits, was done by Divine dispensation, that we may keep in mind that our actions and thoughts are not lost in the wind, but are all kept to be examined by the Supreme Judge, and will in the end be shown us either by friendly or hostile angels. As to the angels first producing a white book, and then the devils a black one; the former a very small one, the latter one very large; it is to be observed, that in his first years he did some good actions, all which he nevertheless obscured by the evil actions of his youth. If, on the contrary, he had taken care in his youth to correct the errors of his more tender years, and to cancel them in God's sight by doing well, he might have been associated to the number of those of whom the Psalm says, "Blessed are those whose iniquities are forgiven, and whose sins are hid." This story, as I learned it of the venerable Bishop Pechthelm, I have thought proper to relate in a plain manner, for the salvation of my hearers.

CHAPTER XIV

OF ANOTHER, WHO BEING AT THE POINT OF DEATH, SAW THE PLACE OF PUNISHMENT APPOINTED FOR HIM IN HELL. [A.D. 704.]

I knew a brother myself, would to God I had not known him, whose name I could mention if it were necessary, and who resided in a noble monastery, but lived himself ignobly. He was frequently reproved by the brethren and elders of the place, and admonished to adopt a more regular life; and though he would not give ear to them, he was long patiently borne with by them, on account of his usefulness in temporal works, for he was an excellent carpenter; he was much addicted to drunkenness, and other pleasures of a lawless life, and more used to stop in his workhouse day and night, than to go to church to sing and pray, and hear the word of life with the brethren. For which reason it happened to him according to the saying, that he who will not willingly and humbly enter the gate of the church, will certainly be damned, and enter the gate of hell whether he will or no. For he falling sick, and being reduced to extremity, called the brethren, and with much lamentation, and like one damned, began to tell them, that he saw hell open, and Satan at the bottom thereof; as also Caiaphas, with the others that slew our Lord, by him delivered up to avenging flames. "In whose neighbourhood," said he, "I see a place of eternal perdition provided for me, miserable wretch." The brothers, hearing these words, began seriously to exhort him, that he should repent even then whilst he was in the flesh. He answered in despair, "I have no time now to change my course of life, when I have myself seen my judgment passed."

Whilst uttering these words, he died without having received the saving viaticum, and his body was buried in the remotest parts of the monastery, nor did any one dare either to say masses or sing psalms, or even to pray for him. How far has our Lord divided the light from darkness! The blessed martyr, Stephen, being about to suffer death for the truth, saw the heavens open, the glory of God revealed, and Jesus standing on the right hand of God. And where he was to be after death, there he fixed the eyes of his mind, that he might die with the more satisfaction. On the contrary, this carpenter, of a dark mind and actions, when death was at hand, saw hell open and witnessed the damnation of the Devil and his followers; the unhappy wretch also saw his own prison among them, to the end that, despairing of his salvation, he might die the more miserably; but might by his perdition afford cause of salvation to the living who should hear of it. This happened lately in the province of the Bernicians, and being reported abroad far and near, inclined many to do penance for their sins without delay, which we hope may also be the result of this our narrative.

CHAPTER XV

SEVERAL CHURCHES OF THE SCOTS, AT THE INSTANCE OF ADAMNAN, CONFORMED TO THE CATHOLIC EASTER; THE SAME PERSON WROTE A BOOK ABOUT THE HOLY PLACES. [A.D. 703.]

AT this time a great part of the Scots in Ireland, and some also of the Britons in Britain, through the goodness of God, conformed to the proper and ecclesiastical time of keeping Easter. Adamnan, priest and abbat of the monks that were in the isle of Hii, was sent ambassador by his nation to Alfrid, king of the English, where he made some stay, observing the canonical rites of the church, and was earnestly admonished by many, who were more learned than himself, not to presume to live contrary to the universal custom of the Church, either in relation to the observance of Easter, or any other decrees whatsoever, considering the small number of his followers, seated in so distant a corner of the world; inconsequence of this he changed his mind, and readily preferred those things which he had seen and heard in the English churches, to the customs which he and his people had hitherto followed. For he was a good and wise man, and remarkably learned in Holy Scripture. Returning home, he endeavoured to bring his own people that were in the isle of Hii, or that were subject to that monastery, into the way of truth, which he had learned and embraced with all his heart; but in this he could not prevail. He then sailed over into Ireland, to preach to those people, and by modestly declaring the legal time of Easter, he reduced many of them, and almost all that were not under the dominion of those of Hii, to the Catholic unity, and taught them to keep the legal time of Easter.

Returning to his island, after having celebrated the canonical Easter in Ireland, he most earnestly inculcated the observance of the Catholic time of Easter in his monastery, yet without being able to prevail; and it so happened that he departed this life before the next year came round, the Divine goodness so ordaining it, that as he was a great lover of peace and unity, he should be taken away to everlasting life before he should be obliged, on the return of the time of Easter, to quarrel still more seriously with those that would not follow him in the truth.

This same person wrote a book about the holy places, most useful to many readers; his authority, from whom he procured his information, was Arculf, a French bishop, who had gone to Jerusalem for the sake of the holy places; and having seen all the Land of Promise, travelled to Damascus, Constantinople, Alexandria, and many islands, and returning home by sea, was by a violent storm forced upon the western coast of Britain. After many other accidents, he came to the aforesaid servant of Christ, Adamnan, who, finding him to be learned in the Scriptures, and acquainted with the holy places, entertained him zealously, and attentively gave ear to him, insomuch that he presently committed to writing all that Arculf said he had seen remarkable in the holy places. Thus he composed a work beneficial to many, and particularly to those who, being far removed from those places where the patriarchs and apostles lived, know no more of them than what they learn by reading. Adamnan presented this book to King Alfrid, and through his bounty it came to be read by lesser persons. The writer thereof was also well rewarded by him, and sent back into his country. I believe it will be acceptable to our readers if we collect some particulars from the same, and insert them in our History.

CHAPTER XVI

THE ACCOUNT GIVEN BY THE AFORESAID BOOK OF THE PLACE OF OUR LORD'S NATIVITY, PASSION, AND RESURRECTION. [A.D. 704.]

HE wrote concerning the place of the nativity of our Lord, to this effect. "Bethlehem, the city of David, is seated on a narrow ridge, encompassed on all sides with valleys, being a thousand paces in length from east to west, the wall low without towers, built along the edge of the plain on the summit. In the east angle thereof is a sort of natural half cave, the outward part whereof is said to have been the place where our Lord was born; the inner is called our Lord's Manger. This cave within is all covered with rich marble, over the place where our Lord is said particularly to have been born, and over it is the great church of St. Mary." He likewise wrote about the place of his Passion and Resurrection in this manner. "Entering the city of Jerusalem on the north side, the first place to be visited, according to the disposition of the streets, is the church of Constantine, called the Martyrdom. It was built by the Emperor Constantine, in a royal and magnificent manner, on account of the cross of our Lord having been found there by his mother Helen. From thence, to the westward, appears the church of Golgotha, in which is also to be seen the rock which once bore the cross with our Saviour's body fixed on it, and now it bears a large silver cross, with a great brazen wheel hanging over it surrounded with lamps. Under the place of our Lord's cross, a vault is hewn out of the rock, in which sacrifice is offered on an altar for honourable persons deceased, their bodies remaining meanwhile in the street. To the westward of this is the Anastasis, that is, the round church of our Saviour's resurrection, encompassed with three walls, and supported by twelve columns. Between each of the walls is a broad space, containing three altars at three different points of the middle wall; to the north, the south, and the west, it has eight doors or entrances through the three opposite walls; four whereof front to the north-east, and four to the south-east. In the midst of it is the round tomb of our Lord cut out of the rock, the top of which a man standing within can touch; the entrance is on the east; against it is still laid that great stone. To this day it bears the marks of the iron tools within, but on the outside it is all covered with marble to the very top of the roof, which is adorned with gold, and bears a large golden cross. In the north part of the monument, the tomb of our Lord is hewed out of the same rock, seven feet in length, and three palms above the floor; the entrance being on the south side, where twelve lamps burn day and night, four within the sepulchre, and eight above on the right hand side. The stone that was laid at the entrance to the monument is now cleft in two; nevertheless, the lesser part of it stands as a square altar before the door of the monument; the greater part makes another square altar at the east end of the same church, and is covered with linen cloths. The colour of the said monument and supulchre appears to be white and red."

CHAPTER XVII

OF THE PLACE OF OUR LORD'S ASCENSION, AND THE TOMBS OF THE PATRIARCHS. [A.D. 704.]

CONCERNING the place of our Lord's ascension, the aforesaid author writes thus. "Mount Olivet is equal in height to Mount Sion, but exceeds it in breadth and length; bearing few trees besides vines and olive trees, and is fruitful in wheat and barley, for the nature of that soil is not calculated for bearing things of large or heavy growth, but grass and flowers. On the very top of it, where our Lord ascended into heaven, is a large round church, having about it three vaulted porches. For the inner house could not be vaulted and covered, because of the passage of our Lord's body; but it has an altar on the east side, covered with a narrow roof. In the midst of it are to be seen the last prints of our Lord's feet, the sky appearing open above where he ascended; and though the earth is daily carried away by believers, yet still it remains as before, and retains the same impression of the feet. Near this lies an iron wheel, as high as a man's neck, having an entrance towards the west, with a great lamp hanging above it on a pulley, and burning night and day. In the western part of the same church are eight windows; and eight lamps, hanging opposite to them by cords, cast their light through the glass as far as Jerusalem; this light is said to strike the hearts of the beholders with a sort of joy and humility. Every year, on the day of the Ascension, when mass is ended, a strong blast of wind is said to come down, and to cast to the ground all that are in the church."

Of the situation of Hebron, and the tombs of the fathers, he writes thus. "Hebron, once the city and metropolis of David's kingdom, now only showing what it was by its ruins, has, one furlong to the east of it, a double cave in the valley, where the tombs of the patriarchs are enclosed with a square wall, their heads lying to the north. Each of the tombs is covered with a single stone, worked like the stones of a church, and of a white colour, for three patriarchs. Adam's is of more mean and common workmanship, and lies not far from them at the farthest northern extremity. There are also some poorer and smaller monuments of three women. The hill Mamre is a thousand paces from the monuments, and is full of grass and flowers, having a flat plain on the top. In the northern part of it, Abraham's oak, being a stump about twice as high as a man, is enclosed in a church."

Thus much have we collected from the works of the aforesaid writer, keeping to the sense of his words, but more briefly delivered, and have thought fit to insert in our History. Whosoever desires to see more of the contents of that book, may see it either in the same, or in that which we have lately epitomised from it.

CHAPTER XVIII

THE SOUTH SAXONS RECEIVED EADBERT AND EOLLA, AND THE WEST SAXONS, DANIEL AND ALDHELM, FOR THEIR BISHOPS. OF THE WRITINGS OF THE SAME ALD- HELM. [A.D. 705.]

IN the year of the incarnation of our Lord 705, Alfrid, king of the Northumbrians, died just before the end of the twentieth year of his reign. His son Osred, a boy about eight years of age, succeeding him in the throne, reigned eleven years. In the beginning of his reign, Hedda, bishop of the West Saxons, departed to the heavenly kingdom; for he was a good and just man, and exercised his episcopal duties rather by his innate love of virtue, than by what he had gained from learning. The most reverend prelate, Pechthelm, of whom we shall speak in the proper place, and who was a long time either deacon or monk with his successor Aldhelm, is wont to relate that many miraculous cures have been wrought in the place where he died, through the merit of his sanctity; and that the man of that province used to carry the dust from thence for the sick, which, when they had put into water, the sprinkling or drinking thereof restored health to many sick men and beasts; so that the holy earth being frequently-carried away, there was a considerable hole left.

Upon his death the bishopric of that province was divided into two dioceses. One of them was given to Daniel, which he governs to this day; the other to Aldhelm, wherein he most worthily presided four years; both of them were well instructed, as well in ecclesiastical affairs as in the knowledge of the Scriptures.

Aldhelm, when he was only a priest and abbat of the monastery of Malmesbury, by order of a synod of his own nation, wrote a notable book against the error of the Britons, in not celebrating Easter at the proper time, and in doing several other things not consonant to the purity and the peace of the church; and by the reading of this book he persuaded many of them, who were subject to the West Saxons, to adopt the Catholic celebration of our Lord's resurrection. He likewise wrote a notable book on Virginity, which, in imitation of Sedulius, he composed double, that is, in hexameter verse and prose. He wrote some other books, as being a man most learned in all respects, for he had a clean style, and was, as I have said, wonderful for ecclesiastical and liberal erudition. On his death, Forthere was made bishop in his stead, and is living at this time, being likewise a man very learned in Holy Writ.

Whilst they were bishops, it was decreed in a synod, that the province of the South Saxons, which till then belonged to the diocese of the city of Winchester, where Daniel then presided, should also have an episcopal see, and a bishop of its own. Eadbert, at that time abbat of the monastery of Bishop Wilfrid, of blessed memory, called Selsey, was consecrated their first bishop. On his death, Eolla succeeded in the bishopric. He also died some years since, and the bishopric has been discontinued to this day.

CHAPTER XIX

COINRED, KING OF THE MERCIANS, AND OFFA, OF THE EAST SAXONS, ENDED THEIR DAYS AT ROME, IN THE MONASTIC HABIT. OF THE LIFE AND DEATH OF BISHOP WILFRID. [A.D. 709.]

IN the fourth year of the reign of Osred, Coinred, who had for some time nobly governed the kingdom of the Mercians, did a much more noble act, by quitting the throne of his kingdom, and going to Rome, where being shorn, when Constantine was pope, and made a monk at the relics of the apostles, he continued to his last hour in prayers, fasting and alms-deeds. He was succeeded in the throne by Coelred, the son of Ethelred, who had been king before Coinred. With him went the son of Sighere, king of the East Saxons above-mentioned, whose name was Offa, a youth of most lovely age and beauty, and most earnestly desired by all his nation to be their king. He, with like devotion, quitted his wife, lands, kindred and country, for Christ and for the Gospel, that he might "receive an hundredfold in this life, and in the world to come life everlasting." He also, when they came to the holy places at Rome, receiving the tonsure, and adopting a monastic life, attained the long wished-for sight of the blessed apostles in heaven.

The same year that they departed from Britain, the celebrated prelate, Wilfrid, died in the province of Undalum, after he had been bishop forty-five years. His body, being laid in a coffin, was carried to his monastery, called Ripon, and there buried in the church of the blessed Apostle Peter, with the honour due to so great a prelate. We will now turn back, and briefly mention some particulars of his life. Being a boy of a good disposition, and behaving himself worthily at that age, he conducted himself so modestly and discreetly in all respects, that he was deservedly beloved, respected, and cherished by his elders as one of themselves. At fourteen years of age he preferred the monastic to the secular life; which, when he had signified to his father, for his mother was dead, he readily consented to his heavenly wishes, and advised him to persist in his holy resolution. Accordingly he came to the isle of Lindisfarne, and there giving himself up to the service of the monks, he took care diligently to learn and to perform those things which belong to monastic purity and piety; and being of an acute understanding, he in a very short time learned the psalms and some books, before he was shorn, but when he was already become very remarkable for the greater virtues of humility and obedience: for which he was deservedly beloved and respected by his equals and elders. Having served God some years in that monastery, and being a clear-sighted youth, he observed that the way to virtue taught by the Scots was not perfect, and he resolved to go to Rome, to see what ecclesiastical or monastic rites were in use there. The brethren being made acquainted therewith, commended his design, and advised him to put it into execution. He then repaired to Queen Eanfled, to whom he was well known, and who had got him into that monastery by her advice and assistance, and acquainted her that he was desirous to visit the churches of the apostles. She, being pleased with the youth's resolution, sent him into Kent, to King Earconbert, who was her uncle's son, requesting that he would send him to Rome in an honourable manner. At that time, Honorius, one of the disciples of the holy Pope Gregory, and well instructed in ecclesiastical institutes, was archbishop there. Whilst he made some stay there, and, being a youth of an active spirit, diligently applied himself to learn those things which he undertook, another youth, called Biscop, or otherwise Benedict, of the English nobility, arrived there, being likewise desirous to go to Rome, of which we have before made mention.

The king gave him Wilfrid for a companion, with orders to conduct him to Rome. When they came to Lyons, Wilfrid was detained there by Dalfin, the bishop of that city; but Benedict hastened on to Rome. That prelate was delighted with the youth's prudent discourse, the gracefulness of his aspect, the alacrity of his behaviour, and the sedateness and gravity of his thoughts; for which reason he plentifully supplied him and his companions with all necessaries, as long as they stayed with him; and further offered to commit to him the government of a considerable part of France, to give him a maiden daughter of his own brother to wife, and to receive him as his adopted son. He returned thanks for the favour, which he was pleased to show to a stranger, and answered, that he had resolved upon another course of life, and for that reason had left his country and set out for Rome.

Hereupon the bishop sent him to Rome, furnishing him with a guide and plenty of all things requisite for his journey, earnestly requesting that he would come that way when he returned into his own country. Wilfrid arriving at Rome, by constantly applying himself to prayer and the study of ecclesiastical affairs, as he had before proposed to himself, gained the friendship of the most holy and learned Boniface, the archdeacon, who was also counsellor to the pope, by whose instructions he regularly learned the four Gospels, the true calculation of Easter, and many other things appertaining to ecclesiastical discipline, which he could not attain in his own country. When he had spent some months there, in successful study, he returned into France, to Dalfin; and having stayed with him three years, received from him the tonsure, and was so much beloved that he had thoughts of making him his heir; but this was prevented by the bishop's untimely death, and Wilfrid was reserved to be bishop of his own, that is, the English, nation; for Queen Baldhilda sent soldiers with orders to put the bishop to death; whom Wilfrid, his clerk, attended to the place where he was to be beheaded, being very desirous, though the bishop opposed it, to die with him; but the executioners, understanding that he was a stranger, and of the English nation, spared him, and would not put him to death with his bishop.

Returning to England, he was admitted to the friendship of King Alfrid, who had always followed the catholic rules of the Church; and therefore finding him to be a Catholic, he gave him land of ten families at the place called Stanford; and not long after, the monastery, of thirty families, at the place called Ripon; which place he had lately given to those that followed the doctrine of the Scots, to build a monastery upon. But, forasmuch as they afterwards, being left to their choice, would rather quit the place than adopt the catholic Easter, and other canonical rites, according to the custom of the Roman Apostolic Church, he gave the same to him, whom he found to follow better discipline and better customs.

At the same time, by the said king's command, he was ordained priest in the same monastery, by Agilbert, bishop of the West Saxons, above-mentioned, the king being desirous that a man of so much piety and learning should continue with him as priest and teacher; and not long after, having discovered and banished the Scottish sect, as was said above, he, with the advice and consent of his father Oswy, sent him into France, to be consecrated bishop, at about thirty years of age, the same Agilbert being then bishop of Paris, and eleven other bishops meeting at the consecration of the new bishop, that function was most honourably performed. Whilst he was yet beyond the sea, Chad, a holy man, was consecrated bishop of York, by command of King Oswy, as has been said above; and having ably ruled that church three years, he retired to govern his monastery of Lestingau, and Wilfrid was made bishop of all the province of the Northumbrians.

Afterwards, in the reign of Egfrid, he was expelled his bishopric, and others were consecrated bishops in his stead, of whom mention has been made above. Designing to go to Rome, to answer for himself before the pope, when he was aboard the ship, the wind blew hard west, and he was driven into Frisland, and honourably received by that barbarous people and their King Aldgist, to whom he preached Christ, and instructed many thousands of them in the word of truth, washing them from their abominations in the laver of salvation. Thus he there began the work of the Gospel which was afterwards finished by Wilbrord, a most reverend bishop of Jesus Christ. Having spent the winter there with his new converts, he set out again on his way to Rome, where his cause being tried before Pope Agatho and several bishops, he was by their universal consent, acquitted of what had been laid to his charge, and declared worthy of his bishopric.

At the same time, the said Pope Agatho assembling a synod at Rome, of one hundred and twenty-five bishops, against those that taught there was only one will and operation in our Lord and Saviour, ordered Wilfrid also to be summoned, and, when seated among the bishops, to declare his own faith and the faith of the province or island from whence he came; and they being found orthodox in their faith, it was thought fit to record the same among the acts of that synod, which was done in this manner: "Wilfrid, the beloved of God, bishop of the city of York, having referred to the Apostolic See, and being by that authority acquitted of every thing, whether specified against him or not, and having taken his seat in judgment, with one hundred and twenty-five other bishops in the synod, made confession of the true and catholic faith, and subscribed the same in the name of the northern part of Britain and Ireland, inhabited by the English and Britons, as also by the Scots and Picts."

After this, returning to Britain, he converted the province of the South Saxons from their idolatrous worship. He also sent ministers to the Isle of Wight; and in the second year of Alfrid, who reigned after Egfrid, was restored to his see and bishopric by that king's invitation. However, five years after, being again accused by that same king and several bishops, he was again expelled his diocese. Coming to Rome, together with his accusers, and being allowed to make his defence before a number of bishops and the apostolic Pope John, it was declared by the unanimous judgment of them all, that his accusers had in part laid false accusations to his charge; and the aforesaid pope undertook to write to the kings of the English, Ethelred and Alfrid, to cause him to be restored to his bishopric, because he had been falsely accused.

His acquittal was much forwarded by the reading of the synod of Pope Agatho, of blessed memory, which had been formally held when Wilfrid was in Rome, and sat in council among the bishops, as has been said before. For that synod being, on account of the trial, by order of the apostolic pope, read before the nobility and a great number of the people for some days, they came to the place where it was written, "Wilfrid, the beloved of God, bishop of the city of York, having referred his cause to the Apostolic See, and being by that power cleared," etc., as above stated. This being read, the hearers were amazed, and the reader stopping, they began to ask of one another, who that Bishop Wilfrid was? Then Boniface, the pope's counsellor, and many others, who had seen him there in the days of Pope Agatho, said, he was the same bishop that lately came to Rome, to be tried by the Apostolic See, being accused by his people, and who, said they, having long since been here upon such like accusation, the cause and controversy between both parties being heard and discussed, was proved by

Pope Agatho, of blessed memory, to have been wrongfully expelled from his bishopric, and so much honoured by him, that he commanded him to sit in the council of bishops which he had assembled, as a man of untainted faith and an upright mind. This being heard, the pope and all the rest said, that a man of such great authority, who had exercised the episcopal function near forty years, ought not to be condemned, but being cleared of all the crimes laid to his charge, to return home with honour.

Passing through France, on his way back to Britain, on a sudden he fell sick, and the distemper increasing, was so ill, that he could not ride, but was carried in his bed. Being thus come to the city of Meaux, in France, he lay four days and nights, as if he had been dead, and only by his faint breathing showed that he had any life in him; having continued so four days, without meat or drink, speaking or hearing, he, at length, on the fifth day, in the morning, as it were awakening out of a dead sleep, sat up in bed, and opening his eyes, saw numbers of brethren singing and weeping about him, and fetching a sigh, asked where Acca, the priest, was? This man, being called, immediately came in, and seeing him thus recovered and able to speak, knelt down, and returned thanks to God, with all the brethren there present. When they had sat awhile, and begun to discourse, with much reverence, on the heavenly judgments, the bishop ordered the rest to go out for an hour, and spoke to the priest, Acca, in this manner—

"A dreadful vision has now appeared to me, which I wish you to hear and keep secret, till I know how God will please to dispose of me. There stood by me a certain person, remarkable for his white garments, telling me he was Michael, the Archangel, and said, 'I am sent to save you from death: for the Lord has granted you life, through the prayers and tears of your disciples, and the intercession of his blessed mother Mary, of perpetual virginity; wherefore I tell you, that you shall now recover from this sickness; but be ready, for I will return to visit you at the end of four years. But when you come into your country, you shall recover most of the possessions that have been taken from you, and shall end your days in perfect peace." The bishop accordingly recovered, at which all persons rejoiced, and gave thanks to God, and setting forward on his journey, arrived in Britain.

Having read the letters which he brought from the apostolic pope, Bertwald, the archbishop, and Ethelred, who had been formerly king, but was then an abbat, readily took his part; for the said Ethelred, calling to him Coinred, whom he had made king in his own stead, he requested of him to be friends with Wilfrid, in which request he prevailed; but Alfrid, king of the Northumbrians, refused to admit him. However he died soon after, and his son Osred obtained the crown, when a synod was assembled, near the river Nidd, and after some contesting on both sides, at length, by the consent of all, he was admitted to preside over his church; and thus he lived in peace four years, till the day of his death. He died on the 12th of October, in his monastery, which he had in the province of Undalum, under the government of the Abbat Cuthbald; and by the ministry of the brethren, he was carried to his first monastery of Ripon, and buried in the church of Saint Peter the apostle, close by the south end of the altar, as has been mentioned above, with this epitaph over him—

Here the great prelate Wilfrid lies entomb'd,
Who, led by piety, this temple rear'd
To God, and hallow'd with blest Peter's name,
To whom our Lord the keys of heaven consign'd.
Moreover gold and purple vestments gave,
And plac'd a cross,—a trophy shining bright
With richest ore—four books o'erwrought with gold,
Sacred evangelists in order plac'd,
And (suited well to these) a desk he rear'd,
(Highly conspicuous) cas'd with ruddy gold.
He likewise brought the time of Easter right,
To the just standard of the canon law;
Which our forefathers fixed and well observ'd,
But long by error chang'd, he justly plac'd.

Into these parts a numerous swarm of monks
He brought, and strictly taught their founder's rules.
In lapse of years, by many dangers tossed;
At home by discords, and in foreign realms,
Having sat bishop five and forty years,
He died, and joyful sought the realms above;
That, blessed by Christ, and favour'd with his aid,
The flock may follow in their pastor's path.

CHAPTER XX

ALBINUS SUCCEEDED TO THE RELIGIOUS ABBAT HADRIAN, AND ACCA TO BISHOP WILFRID. [A.D. 709.]

THE next year after the death of the aforesaid father (Wilfrid), that is, in the first year of King Osred, the most reverend father, Abbat Hadrian, fellow labourer in the word of God with Theodore the archbishop of blessed memory, died, and was buried in the church of the blessed Mother of God, in his own monastery, this being the forty-first year from his being sent by Pope Vitalian with Theodore, and the thirty-ninth after his arrival in England. Of whose learning, as well as that of Theodore, one testimony among others is, that Albinus, his disciple, who succeeded him in the government of his monastery, was so well instructed in the study of the Scriptures, that he knew the Greek tongue to no small perfection, and the Latin as thoroughly as the English, which was his native language.

Acca, his priest, succeeded Wilfrid in the bishopric of the church of Hagulstad; being himself a most active man, and great in the sight of God and man, he much adorned and added to the structure of his church, which is dedicated to the Apostle St. Andrew. For he made it his business, and does so still, to procure relics of the blessed apostles and martyrs of Christ from all parts, to place them on altars, dividing the same by arches in the walls of the church. Besides which, he diligently gathered the histories of their sufferings, together with other ecclesiastical writings, and erected there a most numerous and noble library. He likewise industriously provided holy vessels, lights, and such like things as appertain to the adorning of the house of God. He in like manner invited to him a celebrated singer, called Maban, who had been taught to sing by the successors of the disciples of the blessed Gregory in Kent, for him to instruct himself and his clergy, and kept him twelve years, to teach such ecclesiastical songs as were not known, and to restore those to their former state which were corrupted either by want of use, or through neglect. For Bishop Acca himself was a most expert singer, as well as most learned in Holy Writ, most pure in the confession of the catholic faith, and most observant in the rules of ecclesiastical institution; nor did he ever cease to be so till he received the rewards of his pious devotion, having been bred up and instructed among the clergy of the most holy and beloved of God, Bosa, bishop of York. Afterwards, coming to Bishop Wilfrid in hopes of improving himself, he spent the rest of his life under him till that bishop's death, and going with him to Rome, learned there many profitable things concerning the government of the holy church, which he could not have learned in his own country.

CHAPTER XXI

ABBAT CEOLFRID SENT THE KING OF THE PICTS ARCHI-
TECTS TO BUILD A CHURCH, AND WITH THEM AN EPIS-
TLE CONCERNING THE CATHOLIC EASTER AND TONSURE.
[A.D. 710.]

AT that time, Naitan, king of the Picts, inhabiting the northern parts of Britain, taught by frequent meditation on the ecclesiastical writings, renounced the error which he and his nation had till then been under, in relation to the observance of Easter, and submitted, together with his people, to celebrate the catholic time of our Lord's resurrection. For performing this with the more ease and greater authority, he sought assistance from the English, whom he knew to have long since formed their religion after the example of the holy Roman Apostolic Church. Accordingly he sent messengers to the venerable Ceolfrid, abbat of the monastery of the blessed apostles, Peter and Paul, which stands at the mouth of the river Wear, and near the river Tyne, at the place called Jarrow, which he gloriously governed after Benedict, of whom we have before spoken; desiring, that he would write him a letter containing arguments, by the help of which he might the better confute those that presumed to keep Easter out of the due time; as also concerning the form and manner of tonsure for distinguishing the clergy; not to mention that he himself possessed much information in these particulars. He also prayed to have architects sent him to build a church in his nation after the Roman manner, promising to dedicate the same in honour of St. Peter, the prince of the apostles, and that he and all his people would always follow the custom of the holy Roman Apostolic Church, as far as their remoteness from the Roman language and nation would allow. The reverend Abbat Ceolfrid, complying with his desires and request, sent the architects he desired, and the following letter—

"To the most excellent lord, and most glorious King Naitan, Abbat Ceolfrid, greeting in the Lord. We most readily and willingly endeavour, according to your desire, to explain to you the catholic observance of holy Easter, according to what we have learned of the Apostolic See, as you, devout king, with a religious intention, have requested; for we know, that whenever the Church applies itself to learn, to teach, and to assert the truth, which are the affairs of our Lord, the same is given to it from heaven. For a certain worldly writer most truly said, that the world would be most happy if either kings were philosophers, or philosophers were kings. For if a worldly man could judge truly of the philosophy of this world, and form a correct choice concerning the state of this world, how much more is it to be wished, and most earnestly to be prayed for by the citizens of the heavenly country, who are travelling through this world, that the more powerful any persons are in this world,

the more they may labour to be acquainted with the commands of Him who is the Supreme Judge, and by their example and authority may induce those that are committed to their charge, as well as themselves, to keep the same.

"There are three rules in the Sacred Writings, on account of which it is not lawful for any human authority to change the time of keeping Easter, which has been prescribed to us; two whereof are divinely established in the law of Moses; the third is added in the Gospel by means of the passion and resurrection of our Lord. For the law enjoined, that the Passover should be kept in the first month of the year, and the third week of that month, that is, from the fifteenth day to the one-and-twentieth. It is added, by apostolic institution, in the Gospel, that we are to wait for our Lord's day in that third week, and to keep the beginning of the Paschal time on the same. Which threefold rule whosoever shall rightly observe, will never err in fixing the Paschal feast. But if you desire to be more plainly and fully informed in all these particulars, it is written in Exodus, where the people of Israel, being about to be delivered out of Egypt, are commanded to keep the first Passover, that the Lord said to Moses and Aaron, 'This month shall be unto you the beginning of months; it shall be the first month of the year to you. Speak ye unto all the congregation of Israel, saying, In the tenth day of this month, they shall take to them every man a lamb, according to the house of their fathers, a lamb for an house.' And a little lower, 'And he shall keep it until the fourteenth day of the same month; and the whole assembly of the congregation of Israel shall kill it in the evening.' By which words it most plainly appears, that thus in the Paschal observance mention is made of the fourteenth day, not that the Passover is commanded to be kept on that day: but the lamb is commanded to be killed on the evening of the fourteenth day; that is, on the fifteenth day of the moon, which is the beginning of the third week, when the moon appears in the sky. And because it was on the night of the fifteenth moon, when, by the slaughter of the Egyptians, Israel was redeemed from a long captivity, therefore it is said, 'Seven days shall ye eat unleavened bread.' By which words all the third week of the same month is decreed to be kept solemn. But lest we should think that those same seven days were to be reckoned from the fourteenth to the twentieth, God immediately adds, 'Even the first day ye shall put away leaven out of your houses; for whosoever eateth leavened bread, from the first day until the seventh day, that soul shall be cut off from Israel;' and so on, till he says, 'For in this selfsame day I will bring your army out of the land of Egypt.'

"Thus he calls that the first day of unleavened bread, in which he was to bring their army out of Egypt. But it is evident, that they were not brought out of Egypt on the fourteenth day, in the evening whereof the lamb was killed, and which is properly called the Passover or Phase, but on the fifteenth day, as is most plainly written in the book of Numbers. 'Departing therefore from Ramesse on the fifteenth day of the first month, the next day the Israelites kept the Passover with a high hand.' Thus the seven days of unleavened bread on the first whereof the people of God were brought out of Egypt, are to be reckoned from the beginning of the third week, as has been said, that is, from the fourteenth day of the first month, till the one-and-twentieth of the same month, that day included. But the fourteenth day is noted down separately from this number, by the name of the Passover, as is plainly made out by what follows in Exodus: where when it is said, 'For in this same day I will bring your army out of the land of Egypt;' it is presently added, 'You shall keep it a feast by an ordinance for ever. In the first month, on the fourteenth day of the month at even, ye shall eat unleavened bread, until the one-and-twentieth day of the month at even. Seven days shall there be no leaven found in your houses.' Now, who is there that does not perceive, that there are not only seven days, but rather eight, from the fourteenth to the one-and-twentieth, if the fourteenth be also reckoned in the number? But if, as by diligent study of Scriptures appears to be the truth, we reckon from the evening of the fourteenth day to the evening of the one-and-twentieth, we shall certainly find, that the same fourteenth day gives its evening for the beginning of the

Paschal feast; so that the sacred solemnity contains no more than only seven nights and as many days. By which our definition is proved to be true, wherein we said, that the Paschal time is to be celebrated in the first month of the year, and the third week of the same. For it is really the third week, because it begins on the evening of the fourteenth day, and ends on the evening of the one-and-twentieth.

"But since Christ our Paschal Lamb is slain, and has made the Lord's day, which among the ancients was called the first after the Sabbath, a solemn day to us for the joy of his resurrection, the apostolic tradition has so inserted it into the Paschal festivals as to decree, that nothing in the least be anticipated, or detracted from the time of the legal Passover; but rather ordains, that the same first month should be waited for, pursuant to the precept of the law, and accordingly the fourteenth day of the same, and the evening thereof. And when this day should happen to fall on the Sabbath, every one in his family should take a lamb, and kill it in the evening, that is, that all the churches throughout the world, composing one catholic church, should provide bread and wine for the mystery of the flesh and blood of the unspotted Lamb 'that took away the sins of the world;' and after the solemnity of reading the lessons and prayers of the Paschal ceremonies, they should offer up these things to the Lord, in hopes of future redemption. For that same night in which the people of Israel were delivered out of Egypt by the blood of the Lamb, is the very same in which all the people of God were, by Christ's resurrection, delivered from eternal death. Then, on the morning of the Lord's day, they should celebrate the first day of the Paschal festival; for that is the day on which our Lord, with much joy of pious revelation, made known the glory of his resurrection. The same is the first day of unleavened bread, concerning which it is distinctly written in Leviticus, 'In the fourteenth day of the first month, at even, is the Lord's Passover. And on the fifteenth day of the same month, is the feast of unleavened bread unto the Lord; seven days ye must eat unleavened bread; the first day shall be most solemn and holy.'

"If therefore it could be that the Lord's day should always happen on the fifteenth day of the first month, that is, on the fifteenth moon, we might always celebrate Easter at the very same time with the ancient people of God, though the nature of the mystery be different, as we do it with one and the same faith. But in regard that the day of the week does not keep pace exactly with the moon, the apostolical tradition, which was preached at Rome by St. Peter, and confirmed at Alexandria by Mark the Evangelist, his interpreter, appointed that when the first month was come, and in it the evening of the fourteenth day, we should also wait for the Lord's day, which falls between the fifteenth and the one-and-twentieth days of the same month. For on whichever of those days it shall fall, Easter will be properly kept on the same; as it is one of those seven days on which the unleavened bread is ordered to be kept. Thus it comes to pass that our Easter never deviates from the third week of the first month, but either observes the whole, or at least some of the seven legal days of unleavened bread. For though it takes in but one of them, that is, the seventh, which the Scripture so highly commends, saying, 'But the seventh day shall be more solemn and holy, ye shall do no servile work therein,' none can lay it to our charge, that we do not rightly keep our Lord's Paschal day, which we received from the Gospel, in the third week of the first month as the Law prescribes.

"The catholic reason of this observance being thus explained; the unreasonable error, on the other hand, of those who, without any necessity, presume either to anticipate, or to go beyond the term prescribed in the Law, is manifest. For they that think the Lord's day of Easter is to be observed from the fourteenth day of the first month till the twentieth moon, anticipate the time prescribed in the Law, without any necessary reason; for when they begin to celebrate the vigil of the holy night from the evening of the thirteenth day, it is plain that they make that day the beginning of their Easter, whereof they find no mention in the Law; and when they refuse to celebrate our Lord's Easter on the one-and-twentieth day of the month, they wholly exclude that day from their solemnity, which the Law often recommends as memorable for the greater festival; and thus, perverting the proper order, they place Easter day in the second week, and sometimes keep it entirely in the same, and never bring it to the seventh day of the third week. And again, because they rather think that Easter is to be kept on the sixteenth day of the said month, and so to the two-and-twentieth, they no less erroneously, though the contrary way, deviate from the right way of truth, and as it were avoiding to be shipwrecked on Scylla, they run on and are drowned in the whirlpool of Charybdis. For when they teach that Easter is to be begun at the rising of the sixteenth moon of the first month, that is, from the evening of the fifteenth day, it is manifest that they altogether exclude from their solemnity the fourteenth day of the same month, which the Law firstly and chiefly recommends; so that they scarcely touch upon the evening of the fifteenth day, on which the people of God were delivered from the Egyptian servitude, and on which our Lord, by his blood, rescued the world from the darkness of sin, and on which being also buried, He gave us hopes of a blessed repose after death.

"And the same persons, taking upon themselves the penalty of their error, when they place the Lord's day of Easter on the twenty-second day of the month, openly transgress and exceed the legal term of Easter, as beginning the Easter on the evening of that day in which the law appointed it to be finished and completed; and appoint that to be the first day of Easter, whereof no mention is anywhere found in the Law, viz. the first of the fourth week. And they are sometimes mistaken, not only in defining and computing the moon's age, but also in finding the first month; but this controversy is longer than can or ought to be contained in this letter. I will only say thus much, that by the vernal equinox, it may always be found, without the chance of an error, which is the first month of the year, according to the lunar calculation, and which the last. But the equinox, according to the opinion of all the Eastern nations, and particularly of the Egyptians, who exceed all other learned men in that calculation, usually happens on the twelfth day before the kalends of April, as we also prove by horological inspection. Whatever moon therefore is at the full before the equinox, being on the fourteenth or fifteenth day, the same belongs to the last month of the foregoing year, and consequently is not proper for the celebration of Easter; but that moon which is full after the equinox, or on the very equinox, belongs to the first month, and in it, without a doubt, the ancients were wont to celebrate the Passover; and we also ought to keep Easter when the Sunday comes. And that this must be so, there is this cogent reason, because it is written in Genesis, that 'God made two lights; a greater light to rule the day, and a lesser light to rule the night.' Or, as another edition has it, 'A greater light to begin the day, and a lesser to begin the night.' The sun, therefore, proceeding from the midst of the east, fixed the vernal equinox by his rising, and afterwards the moon, when the sun set in the evening, followed full from the midst of the east; thus every year the same first month of the moon must be observed in the like order, so that the full moon must be either on the very day of the equinox, as was done from the beginning, or after it is gone by. But if the full of the moon shall happen to be but one day before the time of the equinox, the aforesaid reason proves that such moon is not to be assigned to the first month of the new year, but rather to the last of the preceding, and that it is therefore not proper for the celebration of the Paschal festival.

"Now if it will please you likewise to hear the mystical reason in this matter, we are commanded to keep Easter in the first month of the year, which is also called the month of the new fruit, because we are to celebrate the mysteries of our Lord's resurrection and our deliverance, with our minds renewed to the love of heavenly things. We are commanded to keep it in the third week of the same month, because Christ, who had been promised before the Law, and under the Law, came with grace, in the third age of the world, to be slain as our Passover; and rising from the dead the third day after the offering of his passion, He wished this to be called the Lord's day, and the festival of his resurrection to be yearly celebrated on the same. For we also, in this manner only, can truly celebrate his solemnity, if we take care with Him to keep the Passover, that is, the passage out of this world to the Father, by faith, hope, and charity. We are commanded to observe the full moon of the Paschal month after the vernal equinox, to the end, that the sun may first make the day longer than the night, and then the moon may afford the world her full orb of light; inasmuch as first 'the sun of righteousness, in whose wings is salvation,' that is, our Lord Jesus, by the triumph of his resurrection, dispelled all the darkness of death, and so ascending into heaven, filled his Church, which is often signified by the name of the moon, with the light of inward grace, by sending down upon her his Spirit. Which plan of salvation the prophet had in his mind, when he said 'The sun was exalted and the moon stood in her order.'

"He, therefore, who shall contend that the full Paschal moon can happen before the equinox, deviates from the doctrine of the Holy Scriptures, in the celebration of the greatest mysteries, and agrees with those who confide that they may be saved without the grace of Christ forerunning them; and who presume to teach that they might have attained to perfect righteousness, though the true light had never vanquished the darkness of the world, by dying and rising again. Thus, after the equinoctial rising of the sun, and after the subsequent full moon of the first month, that is, after the end of the fourteenth day of the same month, all which, according to the law, ought to be observed, we still, by the instruction of the Gospel, wait in the third week for the Lord's day; and thus, at length, we celebrate our due Easter solemnity, to show that we do not, with the ancients, honour the shaking off of the Egyptian yoke; but that, with devout faith and affection, we worship the redemption of the whole world; which having been prefigured in the deliverance of God's ancient people, was completed in Christ's resurrection, to make it appear that we rejoice in the sure and certain hope of the day of our own resurrection, which we believe will happen on the same Lord's day.

"Now this calculation of Easter, which we show you is to be followed, is contained in a circle or revolution of nineteen years, which began long since, that is, in the very times of the apostles, especially at Rome and in Egypt, as has been said above. But by the industry of Eusebius, who took his surname from the blessed martyr Pamphilus, it was reduced to a plainer system; insomuch that what till then used to be sent about to all the several churches by the patriarch of Alexandria, might, from that time forward, be most easily known by all men, the course of the fourteenth day of the moon being regularly ordered. This Paschal calculation, Theophilus, patriarch of Alexandria, composed for the Emperor Theodosius, for a hundred years to come. Cyril also, his successor, comprised a series of ninety-five years in five revolutions of nineteen years. After whom, Dionysius Exiguus added as many more, in the same manner, reaching down to our own time. The expiration of these is now drawing near, but there is so great a number of calculators, that even in our churches throughout Britain, there are many who, having learned the ancient rules of the Egyptians, can with great ease carry on those revolutions of the Paschal times for any distant number of years, even to five hundred and thirty-two years, if they will; after the expiration of which, all that belongs to the question of the sun and moon, of month and week, returns in the same order as before. We therefore forbear to send you those revolutions of the times to come, because you only desired to be instructed respecting the Paschal time, and declared you had enough of those catholic tables concerning Easter.

"But having said thus much briefly and succinctly, as you required concerning Easter, I also exhort you to take care to promote the tonsure, as ecclesiastical and agreeable to the Christian faith, for concerning that also you desired me to write to you; and we know indeed that the apostles were not all shorn after the same manner, nor does the Catholic Church, though it agrees in the same Divine faith, hope, and charity, agree in the same form of tonsure throughout the world: in fine, to look back to remote times, that is, the times of the patriarchs, Job, the example of patience, when, on the approach of tribulation, he shaved his head, made it appear that he had used, in time of prosperity, to let his hair grow; and Joseph, the great practiser and teacher of chastity, humility, piety, and other virtues, is found to have been shorn when he was to be delivered from servitude; by which it appears, that during the time of servitude, he was in prison without cutting his hair. Now you may observe how each of these men of God differed in the manner of their appearance abroad, though their inward consciences were alike influenced by the grace of virtue. But though we may be free to confess, that the difference of tonsure is not hurtful to those whose faith is pure towards God, and their charity sincere towards their neighbour, especially since we do not read that there ever was any controversy among the Catholic fathers about the difference of tonsure, as there has been about the difference in keeping Easter, or in matters of faith; however, among all the tonsures that are to be found in the Church, or among mankind at large, I think none more worthy of being followed than that which that disciple had on his head, to whom, on his confession, our Lord said, 'Thou art Peter, and upon this rock I will build my Church, and the gates of hell shall not prevail against it, and to thee I will give the keys of the kingdom of heaven.' Nor do I think any more worthy to be abhorred and detested, by all the faithful, than that which that man used, to whom Peter, when he would have bought the grace of the Holy Ghost, said, 'Thy money be with thee to perdition, because thou thoughtest the gift of God to be purchased for money; there is no part or lot for thee in this speech.' Nor do we shave ourselves in the form of a crown only because Peter was so shorn; but because Peter was so shorn in memory of the passion of our Lord; therefore we also, who desire to be saved by the same passion, do with him bear the sign of the same passion on the top of our head, which is the highest part of our body. For as all the Church, because it was made a church by the death of Him that gave it life, is wont to bear the sign of his holy cross on the forehead, to the end, that it may, by the constant protection of his sign, be defended from the assaults of evil spirits, and by the frequent admonition of the same be instructed, in like manner, to crucify its flesh with its vices and con-cupiscences; so also it behoves those, who have either taken the vows of monks, or have any degree among the clergy, to curb them-selves the more strictly by continence.

"Every one of them is likewise to bear on his head, by means of the tonsure, the form of the crown which Christ in his passion bore of thorns, in order that Christ may bear the thorns and briars of our sins; that is, that He may remove and take them from us; and also that they may at once show that they, willingly and with a ready mind, endure scoffs and reproaches for his sake; to make it appear, that they always expect 'the crown of eternal life, which God has promised to those that love Him,' and that for the gaining thereof they despise both the adversities and the prosperities of this world. But as for the tonsure which Simon Magus is said to have used, what Christian will not immediately detest and cast it off together with his magic? Upon the top of the forehead, it does seem indeed to resemble a crown; but when you come to the neck, you will find the crown you thought you had seen so perfect cut short; so that you may be satisfied such a distinction properly belongs not to Christians but to Simoniacs, such as were indeed in this life thought worthy of a perpetual crown of glory by erring men; but in that life which is to follow this, are not only deprived of all hopes of a crown, but are moreover condemned to eternal punishment.

"But do not think that I have said this much, as judging those who use this tonsure, are to be damned, in case they favour the catholic unity in faith and actions; on the contrary, I confidently declare, that many of them have been holy and worthy of God. Of which number is Adamnan, the abbat and renowned priest of Columba, who, when sent ambassador by his nation to King Alfrid, came to see our monastery, and discovering wonderful wisdom, humility, and religion in his words and behaviour, among other things, I said to him in discourse, 'I beseech you, holy brother, who think you are advancing to the crown of life, which knows no period, why do you, contrary to the habit of your faith, wear on your head a crown that is terminated, or bounded? And if you aim at the society of St. Peter, why do you imitate the tonsure of him whom St. Peter anathematized? and why do you not rather even now show that you imitate to your utmost the habit of him with whom you desire to live happy for ever.' He answered, 'Be assured, my dear brother, that though I have Simon's tonsure, according to the custom of my country, yet I utterly detest and abhor the Simoniacal wickedness; and I desire, as far as my littleness is capable of doing it, to follow the footsteps of the most blessed prince of the apostles.' I replied, 'I verily believe it as you say; but let it appear by showing outwardly such things as you know to be his, that you in your hearts embrace whatever is from Peter the Apostle. For I believe your wisdom does easily judge, that it is much more proper to estrange your countenance, already dedicated to God, from resemblance to him whom in your heart you abhor, and of whose hideous face you would shun the sight; and, on the other hand, that it becomes you to imitate the outward resemblance of him, whom you seek to have for your advocate with God, as you desire to follow his actions and instructions.'

"This I then said to Adamnan, who indeed showed how much he had improved upon seeing the statutes of our churches, when, returning to Scotland, he afterwards by his preaching brought great numbers of that nation over to the catholic observance of the Paschal time; though he was not yet able to gain the consent of the monks that lived in the island of Hii, over whom he presided. He would also have been mindful to amend the tonsure, if his authority had extended so far.

"But I also admonish your wisdom, O king, that you endeavour to make the nation, over which the King of kings, and Lord of lords, has placed you, observe in all points those things which appertain to the unity of the Catholic and Apostolic Church; for thus it will come to pass, that after your temporal kingdom has passed away, the blessed prince of the apostles will lay open to you and yours the entrance into the heavenly kingdom, where you will rest for ever with the elect. The grace of the eternal King preserve thee in safety, long reigning, for the peace of us all, my most beloved son in Christ."

This letter having been read in the presence of King Naitan, and many more of the most learned men, and carefully interpreted into his own language by those who could understand it, he is said to have much rejoiced at the exhortation; insomuch that, rising from among his great men that sat about him, he knelt on the ground, giving thanks to God that he had been found worthy to receive such a present from the land of the English; and, said he, "I knew indeed before, that this was the true celebration of Easter, but now I so fully know the reason for observing of this time, that I seem convinced that I knew little of it before. Therefore I publicly declare and protest to you that are here present, that I will for ever continually observe this time of Easter, with all my nation; and I do decree that this tonsure, which we have heard is most reasonable, shall be received by all the clergy in my kingdom." Accordingly he immediately performed by his regal authority what he had said. For the circles or revolutions of nineteen years were presently, by public command, sent throughout all the provinces of the Picts to be transcribed, learned and observed, the erroneous revolutions of eighty-four years being everywhere suppressed. All the ministers of the altar and monks had the crown shorn, and the nation thus reformed, rejoiced, as being newly put under the direction of Peter, the most blessed prince of the apostles, and secure under his protection.

CHAPTER XXII

THE MONKS OF HII, AND THE MONASTERIES SUBJECT TO THEM, BEGIN TO CELEBRATE THE CANONICAL EASTER AT THE PREACHING OF EGBERT. [A.D. 716.]

NOT long after, those monks also of the Scottish nation, who lived in the isle of Hii, with the other monasteries that were subject to them, were by the assistance of our Lord brought to the canonical observation of Easter, and the right mode of tonsure. For in the year after the incarnation of our Lord 716, when Osred was slain, and Coenred took upon him the government of the kingdom of the Northumbrians, the holy father and priest, Egbert, beloved of God, and worthy to be named with all honour, whom we have often mentioned before, coming among them, was joyfully and honourably received. Being a most agreeable teacher, and devout in practising those things which he taught, and being willingly heard by all, he, by his pious and frequent exhortations, converted them from that inveterate tradition of their ancestors, of whom may be said those words of the apostle, "That they had the zeal of God, but not according to knowledge." He taught them to perform the principal solemnity after the catholic and apostolic manner, as has been said, under the figure of a perpetual circle; which appears to have been accomplished by a wonderful dispensation of the Divine goodness; to the end, that the same nation which had willingly, and without envy, communicated to the English people the knowledge of the true Deity, should afterwards, by means of the English nation, be brought where they were defective to the true rule of life. Even as, on the contrary, the Britons, who would not acquaint the English with the knowledge of the Christian faith, now, when the English people enjoy the true faith, and are thoroughly instructed in its rules, continue inveterate in their errors, expose their heads without a crown, and keep the solemnity of Christ without the society of the Church.

The monks of Hii, by the instruction of Egbert, adopted the catholic rites, under Abbat Dunchad, about eighty years after they had sent Aidan to preach to the English nation. This man of God, Egbert, remained thirteen years in the aforesaid island, which he had thus consecrated again to Christ, by kindling in it a new ray of Divine grace, and restoring it to the unity of ecclesiastical discipline. In the year of our Lord's incarnation 729, in which the Easter of our Lord was celebrated on the 24th of April, he performed the solemnity of the mass, in memory of the same resurrection of our Lord, and dying that same day, thus finished, or rather never ceases to celebrate, with our Lord, the apostles, and the other citizens of heaven, that greatest festival, which he had begun with the brethren, whom he had converted to the unity of grace. But it was a wonderful dispensation of the Divine Providence, that the venerable man not only passed out of this world to the Father, in Easter, but also when Easter was celebrated on that day, on which it had never been wont to be kept in those parts. The brethren rejoiced in the certain and catholic knowledge of the time of Easter, and rejoiced in the protection of their father, departed to our Lord, by whom they had been converted. He also congratulated his being so long continued in the flesh till he saw his followers admit, and celebrate with him, that as Easter day which they had ever before avoided. Thus the most reverend father being assured of their standing corrected, rejoiced to see the day of our Lord, and he saw it and was glad.

CHAPTER XXIII

OF THE PRESENT STATE OF THE ENGLISH NATION, OR OF ALL BRITAIN. [A.D. 725–731.]

IN the year of our Lord's incarnation 725, being the seventh year of Osric, king of the Northumbrians, who succeeded Coenred, Wictred, the son of Egbert, king of Kent, died on the 23rd of April, and left his three sons, Ethelbert, Eadbert, and Alric, heirs of that kingdom, which he had governed thirty-four years and a half. The next year died Tobias, bishop of the church of Rochester, a most learned man, as has been said before; for he was disciple to those teachers of blessed memory, Theodore, the archbishop, and Abbat Hadrian, by which means, as we have before observed, besides his erudition in ecclesiastical and general literature, he learned both the Greek and Latin tongues to such perfection, that they were as well known and familiar to him as his native language. He was buried in the porch of St. Paul the Apostle, which he had built within the church of St. Andrew for his own place of burial. After him Aldwulf took upon him the office of bishop, having been consecrated by Archbishop Bertwald.

In the year of our Lord's incarnation 729, two comets appeared about the sun, to the great terror of the beholders. One of them went before the rising sun in the morning, the other followed him when he set at night, as it were presaging much destruction to the east and west; one was the forerunner of the day, and the other of the night, to signify that mortals were threatened with calamities at both times. They carried their flaming tails towards the north, as it were ready to set the world on fire. They appeared in January, and continued nearly a fortnight. At which time a dreadful plague of Saracens ravaged France with miserable slaughter; but they not long after in that country received the punishment due to their wickedness. In which year the holy man of God, Egbert, departed to our Lord, as has been said above, on Easter day; and immediately after Easter, that is, on the 9th of May, Osric, king of the Northumbrians, departed this life, after he had reigned eleven years, and appointed Ceolwulf, brother to Coenred, who had reigned before him, his successor; the beginning and progress of whose reign were so filled with commotions, that it cannot yet be known what is to be said concerning them, or what end they will have.

In the year of our Lord's incarnation 731, Archbishop Bertwald died of old age, on the 9th of January, having held his see thirty-seven years, six months and fourteen days. In his stead, the same year, Tatwine, of the province of the Mercians, was made archbishop, having been a priest in the monastery called Briudun. He was consecrated in the city of Canterbury by the venerable men, Daniel, bishop of Winchester, Ingwald of London, Aldwin of Lichfield, and Aldwulf of Rochester, on Sunday, the 10th of June, being a man renowned for religion and wisdom, and notably learned in Sacred Writ.

Thus at present, the bishops Tatwine and Aldwulf preside in the churches of Kent; Ingwald in the province of the East Saxons. In the province of the East Angles, Aldbert and Hadulac are bishops; in the province of the West Saxons, Daniel and Forthere are bishops; in the province of the Mercians, Aldwin. Among those people who live beyond the river Severn to the westward, Walstod is bishop; in the province of the Wiccians, Wilfrid; in the province of the Lindisfarnes, Cynebert presides: the bishopric of the Isle of Wight belongs to Daniel, bishop of Winchester. The province of the South Saxons, having now continued some years without a bishop, receives the episcopal ministry from the prelate of the West Saxons. All these provinces, and the others southward to the bank of the river Humber, with their kings, are subject to King Ethelbald.

But in the province of the Northumbrians, where King Ceolwulf reigns, four bishops now preside: Wilfrid in the church of York, Ethelwald in that of Lindisfarne, Acca in that of Hagulstad, Pechthelm in that which is called the White House, which, from the increased number of believers, has lately become an episcopal see, and has him for its first prelate. The Picts also at this time are at peace with the English nation, and rejoice in being united in peace and truth with the whole Catholic Church. The Scots that inhabit Britain, satisfied with their own territories, meditate no hostilities against the nation of the English. The Britons, though they, for the most part, through innate hatred, are adverse to the English nation, and wrongfully, and from wicked custom, oppose the appointed Easter of the whole Catholic Church; yet, from both the Divine and human power withstanding them, can in no way prevail as they desire; for though in part they are their own masters, yet elsewhere they are also brought under subjection to the English. Such being the peaceable and calm disposition of the times, many of the Northumbrians, as well of the nobility as private persons, laying aside their weapons, rather incline to dedicate both themselves and their children to the tonsure and monastic vows, than to study martial discipline. What will be the end hereof, the next age will show. This is for the present the state of all Britain; in the year since the coming of the English into Britain about 285, but in the 731st year of the incarnation of our Lord, in whose reign may the earth ever rejoice; may Britain exult in the profession of his faith; and may many islands be glad, and sing praises in honour of his holiness!

CHAPTER XXIV

CHRONOLOGICAL RECAPITULATION OF THE WHOLE WORK: ALSO CONCERNING THE AUTHOR HIMSELF

I have thought fit briefly to sum up those things which have been related more at large, according to the distinction of times, for the better preserving them in memory.

In the sixtieth year before the incarnation of our Lord, Caius Julius Cæsar, first of the Romans, invaded Britain, and was victorious, yet could not gain the kingdom.

In the year from the incarnation of our Lord, 46, Claudius, second of the Romans, invading Britain, had a great part of the island surrendered to him, and added the Orkney islands to the Roman empire.

In the year from the incarnation of our Lord, 167, Eleutherius, being made bishop at Rome, governed the Church most gloriously fifteen years. Lucius, king of Britain, writing to him, requested to be made a Christian, and succeeded in obtaining his request.

In the year from the incarnation of our Lord, 189, Severus, being made emperor, reigned seventeen years; he enclosed Britain with a trench from sea to sea.

In the year 381, Maximus, being made emperor in Britain, sailed over into Gaul, and slew Gratian.

In the year 409, Rome was crushed by the Goths, from which time Roman emperors began to reign in Britain.

In the year 430, Palladius was sent to be the first bishop of the Scots that believed in Christ, by Pope Celestine.

In the year 449, Martian being made emperor with Valentinian, reigned seven years; in whose time the English, being called by the Britons, came into Britain.

In the year 538, there happened an eclipse of the sun, on the 16th of February, from the first to the third hour.

In the year 540, an eclipse of the sun happened on the 20th of June, and the stars appeared during almost half an hour after the third hour of the day.

In the year 547, Ida began to reign; from him the royal family of the Northumbrians derives its original; he reigned twelve years.

In the year 565, the priest, Columba, came out of Scotland, into Britain, to instruct the Picts, and he built a monastery in the isle of Hii.

In the year 596, Pope Gregory sent Augustine with monks into Britain, to preach the word of God to the English nation.

In the year 597, the aforesaid teachers arrived in Britain; being about the 150th year from the coming of the English into Britain.

In the year 601, Pope Gregory sent the pall into Britain, to Augustine, who was already made bishop; he sent also several ministers of the word, among whom was Paulinus.

In the year 603, a battle was fought at Degsastane.

In the year 604, the East Saxons received the faith of Christ, under King Sabert, and Bishop Mellitus.

In the year 605, Gregory died.

In the year 616, Ethelbert, king of Kent, died.

In the year 625, the venerable Paulinus was, by Archbishop Justus, ordained bishop of the Northumbrians.

In the year 626, Eanfleda, daughter to King Edwin, was baptized with twelve others, on Whit-Saturday.

In the year 627, King Edwin was baptized, with his nation, at Easter.

In the year 633, King Edwin being killed, Paulinus returned to Kent.

In the year 640, Eadbald, king of Kent, died.

In the year 642, King Oswald was slain.

In the year 644, Paulinus, first bishop of York, but now of the city of Rochester, departed to our Lord.

In the year 651, King Oswin was killed, and Bishop Aidan died.

In the year 653, the Midland Angles, under their prince, Penda, received the mysteries of the faith.

In the year 655, Penda was slain, and the Mercians became Christians.

In the year 664, there happened an eclipse of the sun; Earconbert, king of Kent, died; and Colman returned to the Scots; a pestilence arose; Ceadda and Wilfrid were ordained bishops of the Northumbrians.

In the year 668, Theodore was ordained bishop.

In the year 670, Oswy, king of the Northumbrians, died.

In the year 673, Egbert, king of Kent, died, and a synod was held at Hertford, in the presence of King Egfrid, Archbishop Theodore presiding; the synod did much good, and its decrees are contained in ten chapters.

In the year 675, Wulfhere, king of the Mercians, dying, when he had reigned seventeen years, left the crown to his brother Ethelred.

In the year 676, Ethelred ravaged Kent.

In the year 678, a comet appeared; Bishop Wilfrid was driven from his see by King Egfrid; and Bosa, Eata, and Eadhed were consecrated bishops in his stead.

In the year 679, Elfwine was killed.

In the year 680, a synod was held in the field called Hethfeld, concerning the Christian faith, Archbishop Theodore presiding; John, the Roman abbat, was also present. The same year also the Abbess Hilda died at Streaneshalch.

In the year 685, Egfrid, king of the Northumbrians, was slain.

The same year, Lothere, king of Kent, died.

In the year 688, Cædwalla, king of the West Saxons, went to Rome from Britain.

In the year 690, Archbishop Theodore died.

In the year 697, Queen Ostritha was murdered by her own people, that is, the nobility of the Mercians.

In the year 698, Berthred, the royal commander of the Northumbrians, was slain by the Picts.

In the year 704, Ethelred became a monk, after he had reigned thirty years over the nation of the Mercians, and gave up the kingdom to Coenred.

In the year 705, Alfrid, king of the Northumbrians, died.

In the year 709, Coenred, king of the Mercians, having reigned six years, went to Rome.

In the year 711, Earl Bertfrid fought with the Picts.

In the year 716, Osred, king of the Northumbrians, was killed; and Coenred, king of the Mercians, died; and Egbert, the man of

God, brought the monks of Hii to observe the Catholic Easter and ecclesiastical tonsure.

In the year 725, Withred, king of Kent, died.

In the year 729, comets appeared; the holy Egbert departed; and Osric died.

In the year 731, Archbishop Bertwald died.

The same year Tatwine was consecrated ninth archbishop of Canterbury, in the fifteenth year of Ethelbald, king of Kent.

Thus much of the Ecclesiastical History of Britain, and more especially of the English nation, as far as I could learn either from the writings of the ancients, or the tradition of our ancestors, or of my own knowledge, has, with the help of God, been digested by me, Bede, the servant of God, and priest of the monastery of the blessed apostles, Peter and Paul, which is at Wearmouth and Jarrow; who being born in the territory of that same monastery, was given, at seven years of age, to be educated by the most reverend Abbat Benedict, and afterwards by Ceolfrid; and spending all the remaining time of my life in that monastery, I wholly applied myself to the study of Scripture, and amidst the observance of regular discipline, and the daily care of singing in the church, I always took delight in learning, teaching, and writing. In the nineteenth year of my age, I received deacon's orders; in the thirtieth, those of the priesthood, both of them by the ministry of the most reverend Bishop John, and by the order of the Abbat Ceolfrid. From which time, till the fifty-ninth year of my age, I have made it my business, for the use of me and mine, to compile out of the works of the venerable Fathers, and to interpret and explain according to their meaning these following pieces—

On the Beginning of Genesis, to the Nativity of Isaac and the Reprobation of Ismaal, three books.

Of the Tabernacle and its Vessels, and of the Priestly Vestments, three books.

On the first Part of Samuel, to the Death of Saul, four books.

Of the Building of the Temple, of Allegorical Exposition, like the rest, two books.

Item, on the Book of Kings, thirty Questions.

On Solomon's Proverbs, three books.

On the Canticles, seven books.

On Isaiah, Daniel, the twelve Prophets, and Part of Jeremiah, Distinctions of Chapters, collected out of St. Jerome's Treatise.

On Esdras and Nehemiah, three books.

On the Song of Habacuc, one book.

On the Book of the blessed Father Tobias, one Book of Allegorical Exposition concerning Christ and the Church.

Also, Chapters of Readings on Moses's Pentateuch, Joshua, and Judges.

On the Books of Kings and Chronicles.

On the Book of the blessed Father Job.

On the Parables, Ecclesiastes, and Canticles.

On the Prophets Isaiah, Esdras, and Nehemiah.

On the Gospel of Mark, four books.

On the Gospel of Luke, six books.

Of Homilies on the Gospel, two books.

On the Apostle, I have carefully transcribed in order all that I have found in St. Augustine's Works.

On the Acts of the Apostles, two books.

On the seven Catholic Epistles, a book on each.

On the Revelation of St. John, three books.

Also, Chapters of Readings on all the New Testament, except the Gospel.

Also a book of Epistles to different Persons, of which one is of the Six ages of the world; one of the Mansions of the Children of Israel; one on the Words of Isaiah, "And they shall be shut up in the prison, and after many days shall they be visited;" one of the Reason of the Bissextile, or Leap-Year, and of the Equinox, according to Anatolius.

Also, of the Histories of Saints. I translated the Book of the Life and Passion of St. Felix, Confessor, from Paulinus's Work in metre, into prose.

The Book of the Life and Passion of St. Anastasius, which was ill translated from the Greek, and worse amended by some unskilful person, I have corrected as to the sense.

I have written the Life of the Holy Father Cuthbert, who was both monk and prelate, first in heroic verse, and then in prose.

The History of the Abbats of this Monastery, in which I rejoice to serve the Divine Goodness, viz. Benedict, Ceolfrid, and Huetbert, in two books.

The Ecclesiastical History of our Island and Nation in five books.

The Martyrology of the Birth-days of the Holy Martyrs, in which I have carefully endeavoured to set down all that I could find, and not only on what day, but also by what sort of combat, or under what judge they overcame the world.

A Book of Hymns in several sorts of metre, or rhyme.

A Book of Epigrams in heroic or elegiac verse.

Of the Nature of Things, and of the Times, one book of each.

Also, of the Times, one larger book.

A book of Orthography digested in Alphabetical Order.

Also a Book of the Art of Poetry, and to it I have added another little Book of Tropes and Figures; that is, of the Figures and Manners of Speaking in which the Holy Scriptures are written.

And now, I beseech thee, good Jesus, that to whom thou hast graciously granted sweetly to partake of the words of thy wisdom and knowledge, thou wilt also vouchsafe that he may some time or other come to thee, the fountain of all wisdom, and always appear before thy face, who livest and reignest world without end. Amen!

HERE ENDS, BY GOD'S HELP,

THE FIFTH BOOK

OF THE ECCLESIASTICAL HISTORY

OF THE ENGLISH NATION.

THE LIFE AND MIRACLES

OF SAINT CUTHBERT,

BISHOP OF LINDISFARNE

PREFACE

To the holy and most blessed Father Bishop Eadfrid, and to all the Congregation of Brothers also, who serve Christ in the Island of Lindisfarne, Bede, your faithful fellow-servant, sends greeting.

INASMUCH as you bade me, my beloved, prefix to the book, which I have written at your request about the life of our father Cuthbert, of blessed memory, some preface, as I usually do, by which its readers might become acquainted with your desire and my readiness to gratify it, it has seemed good to me, by way of preface, to recall to the minds of those among you who know, and to make known to those readers who were before ignorant thereof, how that I have not presumed without minute investigation to write any of the deeds of so great a man, nor without the most accurate examination of credible witnesses to hand over what I had written to be transcribed. Moreover, when I learnt from those who knew the beginning, the middle, and the end of his glorious life and conversation, I sometimes inserted the names of these my authors, to establish the truth of my narrative, and thus ventured to put my pen to paper and to write. But when my work was arranged, but still kept back from publication, I frequently submitted it for perusal and for correction to our reverend brother Herefrid the priest, and others, who for a long time had well known the life and conversation of that man of God. Some faults were, at their suggestion, carefully amended, and thus every scruple being utterly removed, I have taken care to commit to writing what I clearly ascertained to be the truth, and to bring it into your presence also, my brethren, in order that by the judgment of your authority, what I have written might be either corrected, if false, or certified to be true. Whilst, with God's assistance, I was so engaged, and my book was read during two days by the elders and teachers of your congregation, and was accurately weighed and examined in all its parts, there was nothing at all found which required to be altered, but every thing which I had written was by common consent pronounced worthy to be read without any hesitation, and to be handed over to be copied by such as by zeal for religion should be disposed to do so. But you also, in my presence, added many other facts of no less importance than what I had written, concerning the life and virtues of that blessed man, and which well deserved to be mentioned, if I had not thought it unmeet to insert new matter into a work, which, after due deliberation, I considered to be perfect.

Furthermore, I have thought right to admonish your gracious company, that, as I have not delayed to render prompt obedience to your commands, so you also may not be slow to confer on me the reward of your intercession; but when you read this book, and in pious recollection of that holy father lift up your souls with ardour in aspiration for the heavenly kingdom, do not forget to entreat the Divine clemency in favour of my littleness, in as far as I may deserve both at present with singleness of mind to long for and hereafter in perfect happiness to behold the goodness of our Lord in the land of the living. But also when I am defunct, pray ye for the redemption of my soul, for I was your friend and faithful servant; offer up masses for me, and enrol my name among your own. For you, also, most holy prelate, remember to have promised this to me, and in testimony of such future enrolment you gave orders to your pious brother Guthfrid, that he should even now enrol my name in the white book of your holy congregation. And may your holiness know that I already have written in heroic verse, as well as in this prose work, which I offer to you, the life of this same our father beloved by God, somewhat more briefly indeed, but nevertheless in the same order, because some of our brethren entreated the same of me: and if you wish to have those verses, you can obtain from me a copy of them. In the preface of that work I promised that I would write more fully at another time of his life and miracles; which promise, in my present work, I have, as far as God has allowed me, done my best to perform.

Wherefore it is my prayer for you, that Almighty God may deign to guard your holinesses in peace and safety, dearest brethren and masters of mine.—Amen!

CHAPTER I

HOW CUTHBERT, THE CHILD OF GOD, WAS WARNED BY A CHILD OF HIS FUTURE BISHOPRIC

THE beginning of our history of the life of the blessed Cuthbert is hallowed by Jeremy the prophet, who, in exaltation of the anchorite's perfect state, says, "It is good for a man, when he hath borne the yoke from his youth; he shall sit alone, and shall be silent, because he shall raise himself above himself." For, inspired by the sweetness of this good, Cuthbert, the man of God, from his early youth bent his neck beneath the yoke of the monastic institution; and when occasion presented itself, having laid fast hold of the anachoretic life, he rejoiced to sit apart for no small space of time, and for the sweetness of divine meditation to hold his tongue silent from human colloquy. But that he should be able to do this in his advanced years, was the effect of God's grace inciting him gradually to the way of truth from his early childhood; for even to the eighth year of his life, which is the first year of boyhood succeeding to infancy, he gave his mind to such plays and enjoyments alone as boys delight in, so that it might be testified of him as it was of Samuel, "Moreover Cuthbert knew not yet the Lord, neither had the voice of the Lord been revealed to him." Such was the panegyric of his boyhood, who in more ripened age was destined perfectly to know the Lord, and opening the ears of his mind to imbibe the voice of God. He took delight, as we have stated, in mirth and clamour; and, as was natural at his age, rejoiced to attach himself to the company of other boys, and to share in their sports: and because he was agile by nature, and of a quick mind, he often prevailed over them in their boyish contests, and frequently, when the rest were tired, he alone would hold out, and look triumphantly around to see if any remained to contend with him for victory. For in jumping, running, wrestling, or any other bodily exercise, he boasted that he could surpass all those who were of the same age, and even some that were older than himself. For when he was a child, he knew as a child, he thought as a child; but afterwards, when he became a man, he most abundantly laid aside all those childish things.

And indeed Divine Providence found from the first a worthy preceptor to curb the sallies of his youthful mind. For, as Trumwine of blessed memory told me on the authority of Cuthbert himself, there were one day some customary games going on in a field, and a large number of boys were got together, amongst whom was Cuthbert, and in the excitement of boyish whims, several of them began to bend their bodies into various unnatural forms. On a sudden, one of them, apparently about three years old, runs up to Cuthbert, and in a firm tone exhorts him not to indulge in idle play and follies, but to cultivate the powers of his mind, as well as those of his body. When Cuthbert made light of his advice, the boy fell to the ground, and shed tears bitterly. The rest run up to console him, but he persists in weeping. They ask him why he burst out crying so unexpectedly. At length he made answer, and turning to Cuthbert, who was trying to comfort him, "Why," said he, "do you, holy Cuthbert, priest and prelate! give yourself up to these things which are so opposite to your nature and rank? It does not become you to be playing among children, when the Lord has appointed you to be a teacher of virtue even to those who are older than yourself." Cuthbert, being a boy of a good disposition, heard these words with evident attention, and pacifying the crying child with affectionate caresses, immediately abandoned his vain sports, and returning home, began from that moment to exhibit an unusual decision both of mind and character, as if the same Spirit which had spoken outwardly to him by the mouth of the boy, were now beginning to exert its influence inwardly in his heart. Nor ought we to be surprised that the same God can restrain the levity of a child by the mouth of a child, who made even the dumb beast to speak when He would check the folly of the prophet: and truly it is said in his honour, "Out of the mouth of babes and sucklings hast thou perfected praise!"

CHAPTER II

HOW HE BECAME LAME WITH A SWELLING IN HIS KNEE, AND WAS CURED BY AN ANGEL

BUT because to every one who hath shall be given, and he shall have abundance; that is, to every one who hath the determination and the love of virtue, shall be given, by Divine Providence, an abundance of these things; since Cuthbert, the child of God, carefully retained in his mind what he had received from the admonition of man, he was thought worthy also of being comforted by the company and conversation of angels. For his knee was seized with a sudden pain, and began to swell into a large tumour; the nerves of his thigh became contracted, and he was obliged to walk lamely, dragging after him his diseased leg, until at length the pain increased, and he was unable to walk at all. One day he had been carried out of doors by the attendants, and was reclining in the open air, when he suddenly saw at a distance a man on horseback approaching, clothed in white garments, and honourable to be looked upon, and the horse, too, on which he sat, was of incomparable beauty. He drew near to Cuthbert, and saluted him mildly, and asked him as in jest, whether he had no civilities to show to such a guest. "Yes," said the other, "I should be most ready to jump up and offer you all the attention in my power, were I not, for my sins, held bound by this infirmity: for I have long had this painful swelling in my knee, and no physician, with all his care, has yet been able to heal me." The man, leaping from his horse, began to look earnestly at the diseased knee. Presently he said, "Boil some wheaten flour in milk, and apply the poultice warm to the swelling, and you will be well." Having said this, he again mounted his horse and departed. Cuthbert did as he was told, and after a few days was well. He at once perceived that it was an angel who had given him the advice, and sent by Him who formerly deigned to send his archangel Raphael to restore the eyesight of Tobit. If any one think it incredible that an angel should appear on horseback, let him read the history of the Maccabees, in which angels are said to have come on horseback to the assistance of Judas Maccabæus, and to defend God's own temple.

CHAPTER III

HOW HE CHANGED THE WINDS BY PRAYER, AND BROUGHT THE SCATTERED SHIPS SAFE TO LAND

FROM this time the lad becoming devoted to the Lord, as he afterwards assured his friends, often prayed to God amid dangers that surrounded him, and was defended by angelic assistance; nay, even in behalf of others who were in any danger, his benevolent piety sent forth prayers to God, and he was heard by Him who listens to the cry of the poor, and the men were rescued out of all their tribulations. There is, moreover, a monastery lying towards the south, not far from the mouth of the river Tyne, at that time consisting of monks, but now changed, like all other human things, by time, and inhabited by a noble company of virgins, dedicated to Christ. Now, as these pious servants of God were gone to bring from a distance in ships, up the above-named river, some timber for the use of the monastery, and had already come opposite the place where they were to bring the ships to land, behold a violent wind, rising from the west, carried away their ships, and scattered them to a distance from the river's mouth. The brethren, seeing this from the monastery, launched some boats into the river, and tried to succour those who were on board the vessels, but were unable, because the force of the tide and violence of the winds overcame them. In despair therefore of human aid, they had recourse to God, and issuing forth from the monastery, they gathered themselves together on a point of rock, near which the vessels were tossing in the sea: here they bent their knees, and supplicated the Lord for those whom they saw under such imminent danger of destruction. But the Divine will was in no haste to grant these vows, however earnest; and this was, without a doubt, in order that it might be seen what effect was in Cuthbert's prayers. For there was a large multitude of people standing on the other bank of the river, and Cuthbert also was among them. Whilst the monks were looking on in sorrow, seeing the vessels, five in number, hurried rapidly out to sea, so that they looked like five sea-birds on the waves, the multitude began to deride their manner of life, as if they had deserved to suffer this loss, by abandoning the usual modes of life, and framing for themselves new rules by which to guide their conduct. Cuthbert restrained the insults of the blasphemers, saying, "What are you doing, my brethren, in thus reviling those whom you see hurried to destruction? Would it not be better and more humane to entreat the Lord in their behalf, than thus to take delight in their misfortunes?" But the rustics, turning on him with angry minds and angry mouths, exclaimed, "Nobody shall pray for them: may God spare none of them! for they have taken away from men the ancient rites and customs, and how the new ones are to be attended to, nobody knows." At this reply, Cuthbert fell on his knees to pray, and bent his head towards the earth; immediately the power of the winds was checked, the vessels, with their conductors rejoicing, were cast upon the land near the monastery, at the place intended. The rustics blushing for their infidelity, both on the spot extolled the faith of Cuthbert as it deserved, and never afterwards ceased to extol it: so that one of the most worthy brothers of our monastery, from whose mouth I received this narrative, said that he had often, in company with many others, heard it related by one of those who were present, a man of the most rustic simplicity, and altogether incapable of telling an untruth.

CHAPTER IV

HOW, IN COMPANY WITH SHEPHERDS, HE SAW THE SOUL
OF BISHOP AIDAN CARRIED TO HEAVEN BY ANGELS

BUT whereas the grace of Christ, which is the directress of the life of the faithful, decreed that its servant should encounter the merit of a more rigid institution, and earn the glory of a higher prize, it chanced upon a time that he was tending a flock of sheep entrusted to his care on some distant mountains. One night, whilst his companions were sleeping, and he himself was awake, as he was wont to be, and engaged in prayer, on a sudden he saw a long stream of light break through the darkness of the night, and in the midst of it a company of the heavenly host descended to the earth, and having received among them a spirit of surpassing brightness, returned without delay to their heavenly home. The young man, beloved of God, was struck with the sight, and, stimulated to encounter the honours of spiritual warfare, and to earn for himself eternal life and happiness among God's mighty ones, he forthwith offered up praise and thanksgivings to the Lord, and called upon his companions, with brotherly exhortations, to imitate his example. "Miserable men that we are," said he, "whilst we are resigning ourselves to sleep and idleness, we take no thought to behold the light of God's holy angels, who never sleep. Behold, whilst I was awake and praying, during a moderate portion of the night, I saw such great miracles of God. The door of heaven was opened, and there was led in thither, amidst an angelic company, the spirit of some holy man, who now, for ever blessed, beholds the glory of the heavenly mansion, and Christ its King, whilst we still grovel amid this earthly darkness: and I think it must have been some holy bishop, or some favoured one from out of the company of the faithful, whom I saw thus carried into heaven amid so much splendour by that large angelic choir." As the man of God said these words, the hearts of the shepherds were kindled up to reverence and praise. When the morning was come, he found that Aidan, bishop of the Church of Lindisfarne, a man of exalted piety, had ascended to the heavenly kingdom at the very moment of his vision. Immediately, therefore, he delivered over the sheep, which he was feeding, to their owners, and determined forthwith to enter a monastery.

CHAPTER V

HOW, ON HIS WAY, HE WAS SUPPLIED WITH FOOD BY GOD

AND when he now began with care to meditate on his intended entrance to a more rigid course of life, God's grace was revealed to him, whereby his mind was strengthened in its purpose, and it was shown to him by the clearest evidence, that to those who seek the kingdom of God and his righteousness, the bounty of the Divine promise will grant all other things also, which are necessary for their bodily support. For on a certain day, as he was journeying alone, he turned aside at the fourth hour into a village which lay at some distance, and to which he found his way. Here he entered the house of a pious mother of a family, in order to rest himself a little, and to procure food for his horse rather than for himself, for it was the beginning of winter. The woman received him kindly, and begged him to allow her to get him some dinner, that he might refresh himself. The man of God refused, saying, "I cannot yet eat, for it is a fast-day." It was the sixth day of the week, on which many of the faithful, out of reverence to the Lord's passion, are accustomed to extend their fasting even to the ninth hour. The woman, from a motive of hospitality, persisted in her request. "Behold," said she, "on the way you are going there is no village, nor house; you have a long journey before you, and cannot get through it before sunset. Let me entreat you, therefore, to take some food before you go, or else you will be obliged to fast all the day, and perhaps even till to-morrow." But though the woman pressed him much, his love of religion prevailed, and he fasted the whole day until the evening.

When the evening drew near, and he perceived that he could not finish his intended journey the same day, and that there was no house at hand in which he could pass the night, he presently fell upon some shepherds' huts, which, having been slightly constructed in the summer, were now deserted and ruinous. Into one of these he entered, and having tied his horse to the wall, placed before him a handful of hay, which the wind had forced from the roof. He then turned his thoughts to prayer, but suddenly, as he was singing a psalm, he saw his horse lift up his head and pull out some straw from the roof, and among the straw there fell down a linen cloth folded up, with something in it. When he had ended his prayers, wishing to see what this was, he came and opened the cloth, and found in it half of a loaf of bread, still hot, and some meat, enough of both to serve him for a single meal. In gratitude for the Divine goodness, he exclaimed, "Thanks be to God, who of his bounty hath deigned to provide a meal for me when I was hungry, as well as a supper for my beast." He therefore divided the piece of bread into two parts, of which he gave one to his horse and kept the other for himself; and from that day forward he was more ready than before to fast, because he now felt convinced that the food had been provided for him in the desert by the gife of Him who formerly fed the prophet Elias for so long a time by means of ravens, when there was no man to minister unto him, whose eyes are upon those that fear Him, and upon those who trust in his mercy, that He may save their souls from death, and may feed them when they are hungry. I learnt these particulars from a religious man of our monastery of Weremouth, a priest of the name of Ingwald, who now, by reason of his extreme old age, is turning his attention, in purity of heart, to spiritual things rather than to earthly and carnal affections, and who said that the authority on which his relation rested was no less than that of Cuthbert himself.

CHAPTER VI

HOW, AS HE WAS COMING TO A MONASTERY, BOISIL, A HOLY MAN, BORE TESTIMONY TO HIM BY PROPHESYING IN SPIRIT

MEANWHILE this reverend servant of God, abandoning worldly things, hastens to submit to monastic discipline, having been excited by his heavenly vision to covet the joys of everlasting happiness, and invited by the food with which God had supplied him to encounter hunger and thirst in his service. He knew that the Church of Lindisfarne contained many holy men, by whose teaching and example he might be instructed, but he was moved by the great reputation of Boisil, a monk and priest of surpassing merit, to choose for himself an abode in the abbey of Melrose. And it happened by chance, that when he was arrived there, and had leaped from his horse, that he might enter the church to pray, he gave his horse and travelling spear to a servant, for he had not yet resigned the dress and habits of a layman. Boisil was standing before the doors of the monastery, and saw him first. Foreseeing in spirit what an illustrious man the stranger would become, he made this single remark to the bystanders: "Behold a servant of the Lord!" herein imitating Him who said of Nathaniel, when he approached Him, "Behold an Israelite indeed, in whom there is no guile!" I was told this by that veteran priest and servant of God, the pious Sigfrid, for he was standing by when Boisil said these words, and was at that time a youth studying the first rudiments of the monastic life in that same monastery; but now he is a man, perfect in the Lord, living in our monastery of Yarrow, and amid the last sighs of his fainting body thirsting for a happy entrance into another life. Boisil, without saying more, kindly received Cuthbert as he approached; and when he had heard the cause of his coming, namely, that he preferred the monastery to the world, he kept him near himself, for he was the prior of that same monastery.

After a few days, when Eata, who was at that time priest and abbot of the monastery, but afterwards bishop of Lindisfarne, was come, Boisil told him about Cuthbert, how that he was a young man of a promising disposition, and obtained permission that he should receive the tonsure, and be enrolled among the brethren. When he had thus entered the monastery, he conformed himself to the rules of the place with the same zeal as the others, and, indeed, sought to surpass them by observing stricter discipline; and in reading, working, watching, and praying, he fairly outdid them all. Like the mighty Samson of old, he carefully abstained from every drink which could intoxicate; but was not able to abstain equally from food, lest his body might be thereby rendered less able to work: for he was of a robust frame and of unimpaired strength, and fit for any labour which he might be disposed to take in hand.

CHAPTER VII

HOW HE ENTERTAINED AN ANGEL, AND WHILST MINISTERING TO HIM EARTHLY BREAD, WAS THOUGHT WORTHY TO BE REWARDED WITH BREAD FROM HEAVEN

SOME years after, it pleased King Alfred, for the redemption of his soul, to grant to Abbot Eata a certain tract of country called Inrhipum, in which to build a monastery. The abbot, in consequence of this grant, erected the intended building, and placed therein certain of his brother-monks, among whom was Cuthbert, and appointed for them the same rules and discipline which were observed at Melrose. It chanced that Cuthbert was appointed to the office of receiving strangers, and he is said to have entertained an angel of the Lord who came to make trial of his piety. For, as he went very early in the morning, from the interior of the monastery into the strangers' cell, he found there seated a young person, whom he considered to be a man, and entertained as such. He gave him water to wash his hands; he washed his feet himself, wiped them, and humbly dried them in his bosom; after which he entreated him to remain till the third hour of the day and take some breakfast, lest, if he should go on his journey fasting, he might suffer from hunger and the cold of winter. For he took him to be a man, and thought that a long journey by night and a severe fall of snow had caused him to turn in thither in the morning to rest himself. The other replied, that he could not tarry, for the home to which he was hastening lay at some distance. After much entreaty, Cuthbert adjured him in God's name to stop; and as the third hour was now come, prayer over, and it was time to breakfast, he placed before him a table with some food, and said, "I beseech thee, brother, eat and refresh thyself, whilst I go and fetch some hot bread, which must now, I think, be just baked." When he returned, the young man, whom he had left eating, was gone, and he could see no traces of his footsteps, though there had been a fresh fall of snow, which would have exhibited marks of a person walking upon it, and shown which way he went. The man of God was astonished, and revolving the circumstances in his mind, put back the table in the dining-room. Whilst doing so, he perceived a most surprising odour and sweetness; and looking round to see from what it might proceed, he saw three white loaves placed there, of unusual whiteness and excellence. Trembling at the sight, he said within himself, "I perceive that it was an angel of the Lord whom I entertained, and that he came to feed us, not to be fed himself. Behold, he hath brought such loaves as this earth never produced; they surpass the lily in whiteness, the rose in odour, and honey in taste. They are, therefore, not produced from this earth, but are sent from paradise. No wonder that he rejected my offer of earthly food, when he enjoys such bread as this in heaven." The man of God was stimulated by this powerful miracle to be more zealous still in performing works of piety; and with his deeds did increase upon him also the grace of God. From that time he often saw and conversed with angels, and when hungry was fed with unwonted food furnished direct from God. He was affable and pleasant in his character; and when he was relating to the fathers the acts of their predecessors, as an incentive to piety, he would introduce also, in the meekest way, the spiritual benefits which the love of God had conferred upon himself. And this he took care to do in a covert manner, as if it had happened to another person. His hearers, however, perceived that he was speaking of himself, after the pattern of that master who at one time unfolds his own merits without disguise, and at another time says, under the guise of another, "I knew a man in Christ fourteen years ago, who was carried up into the third heaven."

CHAPTER VIII

HOW CUTHBERT WAS RECOVERED FROM SICKNESS, AND BOISIL, ON HIS DEATH-BED, FORETOLD TO HIM HIS FUTURE FORTUNES

MEANWHILE, as every thing in this world is frail and fluctuating, like the sea when a storm comes on, the above-named Abbot Eata, with Cuthbert and the other brethren, were expelled from their residence, and the monastery given to others. But our worthy champion of Christ did not by reason of his change of place relax his zeal in carrying on the spiritual conflict which he had undertaken; but he attended, as he had ever done, to the precepts and example of the blessed Boisil. About this time, according to his friend Herefrid the priest, who was formerly abbot of the monastery of Lindisfarne, he was seized with a pestilential disease, of which many inhabitants of Britain were at that time sick. The brethren of the monastery passed the whole night in prayer for his life and health; for they thought it essential to them that so pious a man should be present with them in the flesh. They did this without his knowing it; and when they told him of it in the morning, he exclaimed, "Then why am I lying here? I did not think it possible that God should have neglected your prayers: give me my stick and shoes." Accordingly, he got out of bed, and tried to walk, leaning on his stick; and finding his strength gradually return, he was speedily restored to health: but because the swelling on his thigh, though it died away to all outward appearances, struck into his inwards, he felt a little pain in his inside all his life afterwards; so that, as we find it expressed in the Apostles, "his strength was perfected in weakness."

When that servant of the Lord, Boisil, saw that Cuthbert was restored, he said, "You see, my brother, how you have recovered from your disease, and I assure you it will give you no further trouble, nor are you likely to die at present. I advise you, inasmuch as death is waiting for me, to learn from me all you can whilst I am able to teach you; for I have only seven days longer to enjoy my health of body, or to exercise the powers of my tongue." Cuthbert, implicitly believing what he heard, asked him what he would advise him to begin to read, so as to be able to finish it in seven days. "John the Evangelist," said Boisil. "I have a copy containing seven quarto sheets: we can, with God's help, read one every day, and meditate thereon as far as we are able." They did so accordingly, and speedily accomplished the task; for they sought therein only that simple faith which operates by love, and did not trouble themselves with minute and subtle questions. After their seven days' study was completed, Boisil died of the above-named complaint; and after death entered into the joys of eternal life. They say that, during these seven days, he foretold to Cuthbert every thing which should happen to him: for, as I have said before, he was a prophet and a man of remarkable piety. And, moreover, he had three years ago foretold to Abbot Eata, that this pestilence would come, and that he himself would die of it; but that the abbot should die of another disease, which the physicians call dysentery; and in this also he was a true prophet, as the event proved. Among others, he told Cuthbert that he should be ordained bishop. When Cuthbert became an anchorite, he would not communicate this prophecy to any one, but with much sorrow assured the brethren who came to visit him, that if he had a humble residence on a rock, where the waves of the ocean shut him out from all the world, he should not even then consider himself safe from its snares, but should be afraid that on some occasion or other he might fall victim to the love of riches.

CHAPTER IX

HOW CUTHBERT WAS ZEALOUS IN THE MINISTRY OF THE WORD

AFTER the death of Boisil, Cuthbert took upon himself the duties of the office before mentioned; and for many years discharged them with the most pious zeal, as became a saint: for he not only furnished both precept and example to his brethren of the monastery, but sought to lead the minds of the neighbouring people to the love of heavenly things. Many of them, indeed, disgraced the faith which they professed, by unholy deeds; and some of them, in the time of mortality, neglecting the sacrament of their creed, had recourse to idolatrous remedies, as if by charms or amulets, or any other mysteries of the magical art, they were able to avert a stroke inflicted upon them by the Lord. To correct these errors, he often went out from the monastery, sometimes on horseback, sometimes on foot, and preached the way of truth to the neighbouring villages, as Boisil, his predecessor, had done before him. It was at this time customary for the English people to flock together when a clerk or priest entered a village, and listen to what he said, that so they might learn something from him, and amend their lives. Now Cuthbert was so skilful in teaching, and so zealous in what he undertook, that none dared to conceal from him their thoughts, but all acknowledged what they had done amiss; for they supposed that it was impossible to escape his notice, and they hoped to merit forgiveness by an honest confession. He was mostly accustomed to travel to those villages which lay in out of the way places among the mountains, which by their poverty and natural horrors deterred other visitors. Yet even here did his devoted mind find exercise for his powers of teaching, insomuch that he often remained a week, sometimes two or three, nay, even a whole month, without returning home; but dwelling among the mountains, taught the poor people, both by the words of his preaching, and also by his own holy conduct.

CHAPTER X

HOW CUTHBERT PASSED THE NIGHT IN THE SEA, PRAYING; AND WHEN HE WAS COME OUT, TWO ANIMALS OF THE SEA DID HIM REVERENCE; AND HOW THE BROTHER, WHO SAW THOSE THINGS, BEING IN FEAR, WAS ENCOURAGED BY CUTHBERT

WHEN this holy man was thus acquiring renown by his virtues and miracles, Ebbe, a pious woman and handmaid of Christ, was the head of a monastery at a place called the city of Coludi, remarkable both for piety and noble birth, for she was half-sister of King Oswy. She sent messengers to the man of God, entreating him to come and visit her monastery. This loving message from the handmaid of his Lord he could not treat with neglect, but, coming to the place and stopping several days there, he confirmed, by his life and conversation, the way of truth which he taught.

Here also, as elsewhere, he would go forth, when others were asleep, and having spent the night in watchfulness, return home at the hour of morning-prayer. Now one night, a brother of the monastery, seeing him go out alone, followed him privately to see what he should do. But he, when he left the monastery, went down to the sea, which flows beneath, and going into it, until the water reached his neck and arms, spent the night in praising God. When the dawn of day approached, he came out of the water, and, falling on his knees, began to pray again. Whilst he was doing this, two quadrupeds, called otters, came up from the sea, and, lying down before him on the sand, breathed upon his feet, and wiped them with their hair: after which, having received his blessing, they returned to their native element. Cuthbert himself returned home in time to join in the accustomed hymns with the other brethren. The brother, who waited for him on the heights, was so terrified that he could hardly reach home; and early in the morning he came and fell at his feet, asking his pardon, for he did not doubt that Cuthbert was fully acquainted with all that had taken place. To whom Cuthbert replied, "What is the matter, my brother? What have you done? Did you follow me to see what I was about to do? I forgive you for it on one condition,—that you tell it to nobody before my death." In this he followed the example of our Lord, who, when He showed his glory to his disciples on the mountain, said, "See that you tell no man, until the Son of man be risen from the dead." When the brother had assented to this condition, he give him his blessing, and released him from all his trouble. The man concealed this miracle during St. Cuthbert's life; but, after his death, took care to tell it to as many persons as he was able.

CHAPTER XI

HOW, WHEN THE SAILORS WERE PREVENTED FROM SAILING BY BAD WEATHER, HE PREDICTED THAT IT WOULD BE FINE ON A CERTAIN DAY, AND HOW HE OBTAINED FOOD BY PRAYER

MEANWHILE the man of God began to wax strong in the spirit of prophecy, to foretell future events, and to describe to those he was with what things were going on elsewhere. Once upon a time he left the monastery for some necessary reason, and went by sea to the land of the Picts, which is called Niduari. Two of the brethren accompanied him; and one of these, who afterwards discharged the priest's office, made known to several the miracle which the man of God there performed. They arrived there the day after Christmas-day, hoping, because the weather and sea were both tranquil, that they should soon return; and for this reason they took no food with them. They were, however, deceived in their expectations; for no sooner were they come to land, than a tempest arose, and prevented them from returning. After stopping there several days, suffering from cold and hunger, the day of the holy Epiphany was at hand, and the man of God, who had spent the night in prayer and watching, not in idleness or sloth, addressed them with cheerful and soothing language, as he was accustomed: "Why do we remain here idle? Let us do the best we can to save ourselves. The ground is covered with snow, and the heaven with clouds; the currents of both winds and waves are right against us: we are famished with hunger, and there is no one to relieve us. Let us importune the Lord with our prayers, that, as He opened to his people a path through the Red Sea, and miraculously fed them in the wilderness, He may take pity on us also in our present distress. If our faith does not waver, I do not think He will suffer us to remain all this day fasting—a day which He formerly made so bright with his heavenly majesty. I pray you, therefore, to come with me and see what provision He has made for us, that we may ourselves rejoice in his joy." Saying these words, he led them to the shore where he himself had been accustomed to pray at night. On their arrival, they found there three pieces of dolphin's flesh, looking as if some one had cut them and prepared them to be cooked. They fell on their knees and gave thanks to God. "You see, my beloved brethren," said Cuthbert, "how great is the grace of God to him who hopes and trusts in the Lord. Behold, He has prepared food for his servants; and by the number *three* points out to us how long we must remain here. Take, therefore, the gifts which Christ has sent us; let us go and refresh ourselves, and abide here without fear, for after three days there will most assuredly be a calm, both of the heavens and of the sea." All this was so as he had said: three days the storm lasted most violently; on the fourth day the promised calm followed, and they returned with a fair wind home.

CHAPTER XII

HOW HE FORETOLD THAT, ON A JOURNEY, AN EAGLE WOULD BRING HIM FOOD, AND HOW THIS TOOK PLACE ACCORDINGLY

IT happened, also, that on a certain day he was going forth from the monastery to preach, with one attendant only, and when they became tired with walking, though a great part of their journey still lay before them ere they could reach the village to which they were going, Cuthbert said to his follower, "Where shall we stop to take refreshment? or do you know any one on the road to whom we may turn in?"—"I was myself thinking on the same subject," said the boy; "for we have brought no provisions with us, and I know no one on the road who will entertain us, and we have a long journey still before us, which we cannot well accomplish without eating." The man of God replied, "My son, learn to have faith, and trust in God, who will never suffer to perish with hunger those who trust in Him." Then looking up, and seeing an eagle flying in the air, he said, "Do you perceive that eagle yonder? It is possible for God to feed us even by means of that eagle." As they were thus discoursing, they came near a river, and behold the eagle was standing on its bank. "Look," said the man of God, "there is our handmaid, the eagle, that I spoke to you about. Run, and see what provision God hath sent us, and come again and tell me." The boy ran, and found a good-sized fish, which the eagle had just caught. But the man of God reproved him, "What have you done, my son? Why have you not given part to God's handmaid? Cut the fish in two pieces, and give her one, as her service well deserves." He did as he was bidden, and carried the other part with him on his journey. When the time for eating was come, they turned aside to a certain village, and having given the fish to be cooked, made an excellent repast, and gave also to their entertainers, whilst Cuthbert preached to them the word of God, and blessed Him for his mercies; for happy is the man whose hope is in the name of the

Lord, and who has not looked upon vanity and foolish deceit.
After this, they resumed their journey, to preach to those among
whom they were going.

CHAPTER XIII

HOW HE FORESAW A VISION OF A FIRE COMING FROM THE DEVIL WHILST HE WAS PREACHING, AND HOW HE PUT OUT THE SAME

ABOUT the same time, as he was preaching the word of life to a
number of persons assembled in a certain village, he suddenly
saw in the spirit our old enemy coming to retard the work of salvation, and forthwith began by admonitions to prevent the
snares and devices which he saw were coming. "Dearest brethren,"
said he, "as often as you hear the mysteries of the heavenly kingdom preached to you, you should listen with attentive heart and
with watchful feelings, lest the devil, who has a thousand ways of
harming you, prevent you by superfluous cares from hearing
the word of salvation." As he said these words, he resumed the
thread of his discourse, and immediately that wicked enemy,
bringing supernatural fire, set light to a neighbouring house, so
that flakes of fire seemed to fly through the air, and a storm of
wind and thunder shook the sky. Nearly the whole multitude
rushed forward, to extinguish the fire, (for he restrained a few
of them himself,) but yet with all their real water they could not
put out the false flames, until, at Cuthbert's prayer, the author
of the deceit was put to flight, and his fictitious fires dispersed
along with him. The multitude, seeing this, were suffused with
ingenuous blushes, and, falling on their knees before him,
prayed to be forgiven for their fickleness of mind, acknowledg-
ing their conviction that the devil never rests even for an hour
from impeding the work of man's salvation. But he, encourag-
ing them under their infirmity, again began to preach to them
the words of everlasting life.

CHAPTER XIV

HOW, WHEN A HOUSE WAS REALLY SET ON FIRE, HE PUT OUT THE FLAMES BY PRAYER

BUT it was not only in the case of an apparition of a fire that his power was shown; for he extinguished a real fire by the fervency of his tears, when many had failed in putting it out with all the water they could get. For, as he was travelling about, preaching salvation, like the apostles of old, he one day entered the house of a pious woman, whom he was in the habit of often visiting, and whom, from having been nursed by her in his infancy, he was accustomed on that account to call his mother. The house was at the west end of the village, and Cuthbert had no sooner entered it to preach the word of God, than a house at the other end of the place caught fire and began to blaze most dreadfully. For the wind was from the same quarter, so that the sparks from the kindled thatch flew over the whole village. Those who were present tried to extinguish it with water, but were driven back by the heat. Then the aforesaid handmaid of the Lord, running to the house where Cuthbert was, besought him to help them, before her own house and the others in the village should be destroyed. "Do not fear, mother," said he; "be of good cheer; this devouring flame will not hurt either you or yours." He then went out and threw himself prostrate on the ground before the door. Whilst he was praying, the wind changed, and beginning to blow from the west, removed all danger of the fire assailing the house, into which the man of God had entered.

And thus in two miracles he imitated the virtues of two of the fathers. For in the case of the apparition of fire above mentioned, he imitated the reverend and holy father Saint Benedict, who by his prayers drove away the apparition of a fire like a burning kitchen, which the old enemy had presented before the eyes of his disciples: and, in the case of the real fire which he thus extinguished, he imitated that venerable priest Marcellinus of Ancona, who, when his native town was on fire, placed himself in front of the flames, and put them out by his prayers, though all the exertions of his fellow-countrymen had failed to extinguish them with water. Nor is it wonderful that such perfect and pious servants of God should receive power against the force of fire, considering that by their daily piety they enable themselves to conquer the desires of the flesh, and to extinguish all the fiery darts of the wicked one: and to them is applicable the saying of the prophet, [Is. xliii. 2.] "When thou walkest through the fire, thou shalt not be burned; neither shall the fire kindle upon thee." But I, and those who are, like me, conscious of our own weakness and inertness, are sure that we can do nothing in that way against material fire, and, indeed, are by no means sure that we shall be able to escape unhurt from that fire of future punishment, which never shall be extinguished. But the love of our Saviour is strong and abundant, and will bestow the grace of its protection upon us, though we are unworthy and unable in this world to extinguish the fires of vicious passions and of punishment in the world which is to come.

CHAPTER XV

HOW HE CAST OUT A DEVIL FROM THE PRÆFECT'S WIFE, EVEN BEFORE HIS ARRIVAL

BUT, as we have above related how this venerable man prevailed against the false stratagems of the devil, now let us show in what way he displayed his power against his open and undisguised enmity. There was a certain præfect of King Egfrid, Hildemer by name, a man devoted with all his house to good works, and therefore especially beloved by Saint Cuthbert, and often visited by him whenever he was journeying that way. This man's wife, who was devoted to almsgiving and other fruits of virtue, was suddenly so afflicted by a devil, that she gnashed her teeth, uttered the most pitiable cries, and, throwing about her arms and limbs, caused great terror to all who saw or heard her. Whilst she was lying in this state, and expected to die, her husband mounted his horse, and, coming to the man of God, besought his help, saying, "My wife is ill, and at the point of death: I entreat you to send a priest to visit her before she dies, and minister to her the sacrament of the body and blood of Christ; and, also, that when she is dead, she may be buried in this holy place." He was ashamed to say that she was out of her senses, because the man of God had always seen her in her right mind. Whilst the holy man was going to find out a priest to send to her, he reflected in his mind that it was no ordinary infirmity, but a visitation of the devil; and so, returning to the man who had come to entreat him in his wife's behalf, he said, "I will not send any one, but I will go myself to visit her."

Whilst they were going, the man began to cry, and the tears ran down his cheeks, for he was afraid lest Cuthbert, finding her afflicted with a devil, should think that she had been a false servant of the Lord, and that her faith was not real. The man of God consoled him: "Do not weep because I am likely to find your wife otherwise than I could wish; for I know that she is vexed with a devil, though you are afraid to name it: and I know, moreover, that, before we arrive, she will be freed, and come to meet us, and will herself take the reins, as sound in mind as ever, and will invite us in and minister to us as before; for not only the wicked but the innocent are sometimes permitted by God to be afflicted in body, and are even taken captive in spirit by the devil." Whilst he thus consoled the man, they approached the house, and the evil spirit fled, not able to meet the coming of the holy man. The woman, freed from her suffering, rose up immediately, as if from sleep, and, meeting the man of God with joy, held the bridle of his horse, and, having entirely recovered her strength, both of mind and body, begged him to dismount and to bestow his blessing upon her house; and ministering sedulously to him, testified openly that, at the first touch of the rein, she had felt herself relieved from all the pain of her former suffering.

CHAPTER XVI

HOW HE LIVED AND TAUGHT IN THE MONASTERY OF LINDISFARNE

WHILST this venerable servant of the Lord was thus, during many years, distinguishing himself by such signs of spiritual excellence in the monastery of Melrose, its reverend abbot, Eata, transferred him to the monastery in the island of Lindisfarne, that there also he might teach the rules of monastic perfection with the authority of its governor, and illustrate it by the example of his virtue; for the same reverend abbot had both monasteries under his jurisdiction. And no one should wonder that, though the island of Lindisfarne is small, we have above made mention of a bishop, and now of an abbot and monks; for the case is really so. For the same island, inhabited by servants of the Lord, contains both, and all are monks. For Aidan, who was the first bishop of that place, was a monk, and with all his followers lived according to the monastic rule. Wherefore all the principals of that place from him to the present time exercise the episcopal office; so that, whilst the monastery is governed by the abbot, whom they, with the consent of the brethren, have elected, all the priests, deacons, singers, readers, and other ecclesiastical officers of different ranks, observe the monastic rule in every respect, as well as the bishop himself. The blessed Pope Gregory showed that he approved this mode of life, when, in answer to Augustine, his first missionary to Britain, who asked him how bishops ought to converse with their clerks, among other remarks he replied, "Because, my brother, having been educated in the monastic rule, you ought not to keep aloof from your clerks: in the English Church, which, thanks be to God, has lately been converted to the faith, you should institute the same system, which has existed from the first beginning of our Church among our ancestors, none of whom said that the things which he possessed were his own, but they had all things common." When Cuthbert, therefore, came to the church or monastery of Lindisfarne, he taught the brethren monastic rules both by his life and doctrines, and often going round, as was his custom, among the neighbouring people, he kindled them up to seek after and work out a heavenly reward. Moreover, by his miracles he became more and more celebrated, and by the earnestness of his prayers restored to their former health many that were afflicted with various infirmities and sufferings; some that were vexed with unclean spirits, he not only cured whilst present by touching them, praying over them, or even by commanding or exorcising the devils to go out of them; but even when absent he restored them by his prayers, or by foretelling that they should be restored; amongst whom also was the wife of the præfect above mentioned.

There were some brethren in the monastery who preferred their ancient customs to the new regular discipline. But he got the better of these by his patience and modest virtues, and by daily practice at length brought them to the better system which he had in view. Moreover, in his discussions with the brethren, when he was fatigued by the bitter taunts of those who opposed him, he would rise from his seat with a placid look, and dismiss the meeting until the following day, when, as if he had suffered no repulse, he would use the same exhortations as before, until he converted them, as I have said before, to his own views. For his patience was most exemplary, and in enduring the opposition which was heaped equally upon his mind and body, he was most resolute, and, amid the asperities which he encountered, he always exhibited such placidity of countenance, as made it evident to all that his outward vexations were compensated for by the internal consolations of the Holy Spirit.

But he was so zealous in watching and praying, that he is believed to have sometimes passed three or four nights together therein, during which time he neither went to his own bed, nor had any accommodation from the brethren for reposing himself. For he either passed the time alone, praying in some retired spot, or singing and making something with his hands, thus beguiling his sleepiness by labour; or, perhaps, he walked round the island, diligently examining every thing therein, and by this exercise relieved the tediousness of psalmody and watching. Lastly, he would reprove the faintheartedness of the brethren, who took it amiss if any one came and unseasonably importuned them to awake at night or during their afternoon naps. "No one," said he, "can displease me by waking me out of my sleep, but, on the contrary, give me pleasure; for, by rousing me from inactivity, he enables me to do or think of something useful." So devout and zealous was he in his desire after heavenly things, that, whilst officiating in the solemnity of the mass, he never could come to the conclusion thereof without a plentiful shedding of tears. But whilst he duly discharged the mysteries of our Lord's passion, he would, in himself, illustrate that in which he was officiating; in contrition of heart he would sacrifice himself to the Lord; and whilst he exhorted the standers-by to lift up their hearts and to give thanks unto the Lord, his own heart was lifted up rather than his voice, and it was the spirit which groaned within him rather than the note of singing. In his zeal for righteousness he was fervid to correct sinners, he was gentle in the spirit of mildness to forgive the penitent, so that he would often shed tears over those who confessed their sins, pitying their weaknesses, and would himself point out by his own righteous example what course the sinner should pursue. He used vestments of the ordinary description, neither noticeable for their too great neatness, nor yet too slovenly. Wherefore, even to this day, it is not customary in that monastery for any one to wear vestments of a rich or valuable colour, but they are content with that appearance which the natural wool of the sheep presents.

By these and such like spiritual exercises, this venerable man both excited the good to follow his example, and recalled the wicked and perverse from their errors to regularity of life.

CHAPTER XVII

OF THE HABITATION WHICH HE MADE FOR HIMSELF IN THE ISLAND OF FARNE, WHEN HE HAD EXPELLED THE DEVILS

WHEN he had remained some years in the monastery, he was rejoiced to be able at length, with the blessing of the abbot and brethren accompanying him, to retire to the secrecy of solitude which he had so long coveted. He rejoiced that from the long conversation with the world he was now thought worthy to be promoted to retirement and Divine contemplation: he rejoiced that he now could reach to the condition of those of whom it is sung by the Psalmist: "The holy shall walk from virtue to virtue; the God of Gods shall be seen in Zion." At his first entrance upon the solitary life, he sought out the most retired spot in the outskirts of the monastery. But when he had for some time contended with the invisible adversary with prayer and fasting in this solitude, he then, aiming at higher things, sought out a more distant field for conflict, and more remote from the eyes of men. There is a certain island called Farne, in the middle of the sea, not made an island, like Lindisfarne, by the flow of the tide, which the Greeks call *rheuma*, and then restored to the mainland at its ebb, but lying off several miles to the East, and, consequently, surrounded on all sides by the deep and boundless ocean. No one, before God's servant Cuthbert, had ever dared to inhabit this island alone, on account of the evil spirits which reside there: but when this servant of Christ came, armed with the helmet of salvation, the shield of faith, and the sword of the Spirit, which is the word of God, all the fiery darts of the wicked were extinguished, and that wicked enemy, with all his followers, were put to flight.

Christ's soldier, therefore, having thus, by the expulsion of the tyrants, become the lawful monarch of the land, built a city fit for his empire, and houses therein suitable to his city. The building is almost of a round form, from wall to wall about four or five poles in extent: the wall on the outside is higher than a man, but within, by excavating the rock, he made it much deeper, to prevent the eyes and the thoughts from wandering, that the mind might be wholly bent on heavenly things, and the pious inhabitant might behold nothing from his residence but the heavens above him. The wall was constructed, not of hewn stones or of brick and mortar, but of rough stones and turf, which had been taken out from the ground within. Some of them were so large that four men could hardly have lifted them, but Cuthbert himself, with angels helping him, had raised them up and placed them on the wall. There were two chambers in the house, one an oratory, the other for domestic purposes. He finished the walls of them by digging round and cutting away the natural soil within and without, and formed the roof out of rough poles and straw. Moreover, at the landing-place of the island he built a large house, in which the brethren who visited him might be received and rest themselves, and not far from it there was a fountain of water for their use.

CHAPTER XVIII

HOW BY HIS PRAYERS HE DREW WATER FROM THE DRY GROUND, AND HOW HE GOT ON DURING HIS RETIREMENT

BUT his own dwelling was destitute of water, being built on hard and stony ground. The man of God, therefore, sent for the brethren, for he had not yet withdrawn himself entirely from the sight of visitors, and said to them, "You see that my dwelling is destitute of water; but I pray you, let us beseech Him who turned the solid rock into a pool of water and stones into fountains, that giving glory, not to us, but to his own name, He may vouchsafe to open to us a spring of water, even from this stony rock. Let us dig in the middle of my hut, and, I believe, out of his good pleasure, He will give us drink." They therefore made a pit, and the next morning found it full of water, springing up from within. Wherefore there can be no doubt that it was elicited by the prayers of this man of God from the ground which was before dry and stony. Now this water, by a most remarkable quality, never overflowed its first limits so as to flood the pavement, nor yet ever failed, however much of it might be taken out; so that it never surpassed or fell short of the daily necessities of him who used it for his sustenance.

Now when Cuthbert had, with the assistance of the brethren, made for himself this dwelling with its chambers, he began to live in a more secluded manner. At first, indeed, when the brethren came to visit him, he would leave his cell and minister to them. He used to wash their feet devoutly with warm water, and was sometimes compelled by them to take off his shoes, that they might wash his feet also. For he had so far withdrawn his mind from attending to the care of his person, and fixed it upon the concerns of his soul, that he would often spend whole months without taking off his leathern gaiters. Sometimes, too, he would keep his shoes on from one Easter to another, only taking them off on account of the washing of feet, which then takes place at the Lord's Supper. Wherefore, in consequence of his frequent prayers and genuflexions, which he made with his shoes on, he was discovered to have contracted a callosity on the junction of his feet and legs. At length, as his zeal after perfection grew, he shut himself up in his cell away from the sight of men, and spent his time alone in fasting, watching, and prayer, rarely having communication with any one without, and that through the window, which at first was left open, that he might see and be seen; but, after a time, he shut that also, and opened it only to give his blessing, or for any other purpose of absolute necessity.

CHAPTER XIX

HOW HE SOWED A FIELD WITH BARLEY, AND KEPT OFF THE BIRDS FROM THE CROP BY HIS MERE WORD

AT first, indeed, he received from his visitors a small portion of bread, and drank water from the fountain; but afterwards he thought it more fitting to live by the labour of his own hands, like the old fathers. He therefore asked them to bring him some instruments of husbandry, and some wheat to sow; but when he had sown the grain in the spring, it did not come up. At the next visit of the monks, he said to them, "Perhaps the nature of the soil, or the will of God, does not allow wheat to grow in this place: bring me, I beg of you, some barley: possibly that may answer. If, however, on trial it does not, I had better return to the monastery than be supported here by the labour of others." The barley was accordingly brought, and sown, although the season was extraordinarily late; and the barley came up most unexpectedly and most abundantly. It no sooner began to ripen, than the birds came and wasted it most grievously. Christ's holy servant, as he himself afterwards told it, (for he used, in a cheerful and affable manner, to confirm the faith of his hearers by telling them the mercies which his own faith had obtained from the Lord,) drew near to the birds, and said to them, "Why do you touch that which you have not sown? Have you more share than I in this? If you have received license from God, do what He allows you; but if not, get you gone, and do no further injury to that which belongs to another." He had no sooner spoken, than all the flock of birds departed, and never more returned to feed upon that field. Thus in two miracles did this reverend servant of Christ imitate the example of two of the fathers: for, in drawing water from the rock, he followed the holy St. Benedict, who did almost the same thing, and in the same way, though more abundantly, because there were more who were in want of water. And in driving away the birds, he imitated the reverend and holy father St. Antony, who by his word alone drove away the wild asses from the garden which he had planted.

CHAPTER XX

HOW THE CROWS APOLOGIZED TO THE MAN OF GOD FOR THE INJURY WHICH THEY DID HIM, AND MADE HIM A PRESENT IN COMPENSATION

I am here tempted to relate another miracle which he wrought in imitation of the aforesaid father St. Benedict, in which the obedience and humility of birds are a warning to the perversity and pride of mankind. There were some crows which had long been accustomed to build in the island. One day the man of God saw them, whilst making their nests, pull out the thatch of the hut which he had made to entertain the brethren in, and carry it away to build with. He immediately stretched out his hand, and warned them to do no harm to the brethren. As they neglected his command, he said to them, "In the name of Jesus Christ, depart as speedily as possible, and do not presume to remain any longer in the place, to which you are doing harm." He had scarcely uttered these words, when they flew away in sorrow. At the end of three days one of the two returned, and finding the man of God digging in the field, spread out its wings in a pitiable manner, and bending its head down before his feet, in a tone of humility asked pardon by the most expressive signs it could, and obtained from the reverend father permission to return. It then departed and fetched its companion; and when they had both arrived, they brought in their beaks a large piece of hog's lard, which the man of God used to show to the brethren who visited him, and kept to grease their shoes with; testifying to them how earnestly they should strive after humility, when a dumb bird that had acted so insolently, hastened by prayers, lamentation, and presents, to obliterate the injury which it had done to man. Lastly, as a pattern of reformation to the human race, these birds remained for many years and built their nests in the island, and did not dare to give annoyance to any one. But let no one think it absurd to learn virtue from birds; for Solomon says, "Go to the ant, thou sluggard, consider her ways, and be wise."

CHAPTER XXI

HOW EVEN THE SEA WAS SUBSERVIENT TO HIS WANTS

BUT not only did the animals of the air and sea, for the sea itself, as the air and fire, on former occasions which we have mentioned, exemplified their obedience to the venerable man. For it is no wonder that every creature should obey his wishes, who so faithfully, and with his whole heart, obeyed the great Author of all creatures. But we for the most part have lost our dominion over the creation that has been subjected to us, because we neglect to obey the Lord and Creator of all things. The sea itself, I say, displayed the most ready obedience to Christ's servant, when he had need of it. For he intended to build a little room in his monastery, adapted to his daily necessities; and on the side towards the sea, where the waves had scooped a hollow, it was necessary to put some support across the opening, which was twelve feet wide. He therefore asked the brethren, who came to visit him, when they returned the next time, to bring him a beam twelve feet long, to support his intended building. They readily promised to bring it, and having received his blessing, departed; but by the time they reached home they had entirely forgotten the matter, and on their next visit neglected to carry the timber which they had promised. He received them mildly, and giving them welcome in God's name, asked them for the wood which he had requested them to bring. Then they, remembering what they had promised, apologized for their forgetfulness. Cuthbert, in the most gentle manner, pacified them, and requested them to sleep there, and remain till the morning; "for," said he, "I do not think that God will forget my service or my necessities." They accepted his invitation; and when they rose in the morning, they saw that the tide had, during the night, brought on shore a beam of the required size, and placed it exactly in the situation where the proposed chamber was to be built. When they saw this, they marvelled at the holiness of the venerable man, for that even the elements obeyed him, and took much shame to themselves for their forgetfulness and sloth, who were taught even by the senseless elements what obedience ought to be shown to God's holy saints.

CHAPTER XXII

HOW HE GAVE SALUTARY ADMONITIONS TO MANY WHO CAME TO HIM, AND EXPOSED THE IMPOTENT SNARES OF THE OLD ENEMY

BUT many came to the man of God, not only from the furthest parts of Lindisfarne, but even from the more remote parts of Britain, led thither by the fame of his virtues, to confess the errors which they had committed, or the temptations of the devil which they suffered, or the adversities common to mortals, with which they were afflicted, and all hoping to receive consolation from a man so eminent for holiness. Nor did their hope deceive them. For no one went away from him without consolation, no one returned afflicted with the same grief which had brought him thither. For he knew how to comfort the sorrowful with pious exhortation; he could recal the joys of celestial life to the memory of those who were straitened in circumstances, and show the uncertainty of prosperity and adversity in this life: he had learnt to make known to those who were tempted the numerous wiles of their ancient enemy, by which that mind would be easily captivated which was deprived of brotherly or Divine love; whereas, the mind which, strengthened by the true faith, should continue its course, would, by the help of God, break the snares of the adversary like the threads of a spider's web. "How often," said he, "have they sent me headlong from the high rock! How many times have they thrown stones at me as if to kill me! Yea, they sought to discourage me by various trials of apparitions, and to exterminate me from this scene of trial, but were never able to affect my body with injury, or my mind with fear."

He was accustomed to relate these things more frequently to the brotherhood, lest they should wonder at his conversation as being peculiarly exalted, because, despising secular cares, he preferred to live apart. "But," said he, "the life of monks may well be wondered at, who are subjected in all things to the orders of the abbot, the times of watching, praying, fasting, and working, being all regulated according to his will; many of whom have I known far exceed my littleness, both in purity of mind and advancement in prophetic grace. Among whom must I mention, with all honour, the venerable Boisil, servant of Christ, who, when an old man, formerly supported me in my youth at Melrose Abbey, and while instructing me, he foretold, with prophetic truth, all things which would happen to me; and of all things which he foretold to me, one alone remains which I hope may never be accomplished." Cuthbert told us this was a prophecy of Boisil, that this, our holy servant of Christ, should attain to the office of a bishop; though he, in his eagerness after the heavenly life, felt horrified at the announcement.

CHAPTER XXIII

HOW ELFLED THE ABBESS AND ONE OF HER NUNS WERE CURED OF AN INFIRMITY BY MEANS OF HIS GIRDLE

BUT though our man of God was thus secluded from mankind, yet he did not cease from working miracles and curing those who were sick. For a venerable handmaid of Christ, Elfled by name, who, amid the joys of virginity, devoted her motherly care and piety to several companies of Christ's handmaids, and added to the lustre of her princely birth the brighter excellence of exalted virtue, was inspired with much love towards the holy man of God. About this time, as she afterwards told the reverend Herefrid, presbyter of the church of Lindisfarne, who related it to me, she was afflicted with a severe illness and suffered long, insomuch that she seemed almost at the gates of death. The physicians could do her no good, when, on a sudden, the Divine grace worked within her, and she by degrees was saved from death, though not fully cured. The pain in her inside left her, the strength of her limbs returned, but the power of standing and walking was still denied her; for she could not support herself on her feet, nor move from place to place, save on all fours. Her sorrow was, therefore, great; and she never expected to recover from her weakness, for she had long abandoned all hope from the physicians. One day, as she was indulging her bitter thoughts, she turned her mind to the holy and tranquil life of the reverend father Cuthbert; and expressed a wish that she had in her possession some article that had belonged to him; "for I know, and am confident," said she, "that I should soon be well." Not long after this, there came a person who brought with him a linen girdle from Saint Cuthbert: she was overjoyed at the gift, and perceiving that Heaven had revealed to the saint her wish, she put it on, and the next morning found herself able to stand upon her feet. On the third day she was restored to perfect health.

A few days after, one of the virgins of the same monastery was taken ill with a violent pain in the head; and whilst the complaint became so much worse that she thought she should die, the venerable abbess went in to see her. Seeing her sorely afflicted, she brought the girdle of the man of God to her, and bound it round her head. The same day the pain in the head left her, and she laid up the girdle in her chest. The abbess wanted it again a few days after, but it could not be found either in the chest or anywhere else. It was at once perceived that Divine Providence had so ordered it, that the sanctity of the man of God might be established by these two miracles, and all occasion of doubting thereof be removed from the incredulous. For if the girdle had remained, all those who were sick would have gone to it, and whilst some of them would be unworthy of being cured, its efficacy to cure might have been denied; whereas their own unworthiness would have been to blame. Whereof, as I said before, Heaven so dealt forth its benevolence from on high, that when the faith of believers had been strengthened, all matter for detraction was forthwith removed from the malice of the unrighteous.

CHAPTER XXIV

OF HIS PROPHECY IN ANSWER TO THE SAME ELFLED, CONCERNING THE LIFE OF KING EGFRID AND HIS OWN BISHOPRIC

AT another time, the same Elfled, who was a most holy virgin, and mother of the virgins of Christ, sent for the man of God, adjuring him in the name of our Lord that she might be allowed to see him and to speak about certain things of importance. He therefore entered with the brethren into a ship, and went over to an island which is situated in the mouth of the river Coquet, from which it received its name. The island was also remarkable for the number of its monks. The abbess, who had requested him to meet her in this island, when she had enjoyed his conversation for some time, and the man of God had answered many questions that she put to him; on a sudden, in the midst of his conversation, she fell at his feet and adjured him, by the terrible and sacred name of our heavenly King and his angels, that he would tell her how long her brother Egfrid would live and govern the English nation. "For I know," she said, "that you abound in the spirit of prophecy, and that, if you are willing, you are able to tell me even this." But he, shuddering at the adjuration, and yet not being willing openly to reveal the secret which she had asked him, replied, "It is a wonderful thing that you, being a wise woman and skilled in sacred Scriptures, should call long the duration of human life: the Psalmist says, that 'our years shall perish like a spider's web,' and Solomon advises, that if a man shall live many years, and shall have been prosperous in all of these, he ought to remember the gloomy time of many days, which when it shall come, the past is convicted of folly; how much more then ought that man, to whose life one year only is wanting, to be considered as having lived a short time when death stands at his door!"

On hearing these words she lamented the dreadful prophecy with many tears; but then having wiped her face, she with feminine boldness adjured him by the majesty of the Holy One, that he would tell her who would be the heir to the kingdom, seeing that Egfrid had neither sons nor brothers. After a short silence, he said, "Do not say that he is without heirs, for he shall have a successor, whom you shall embrace like Egfrid himself with the affection of a sister."—"But," said she, "I beseech you to tell me where he may be found." He answered, "You behold this great and spacious sea, how it aboundeth in islands. It is easy for God out of some of these to provide a person to reign over England." She therefore understood him to speak of Alfrid, who was said to be the son of her father, and was then, on account of his love of literature, exiled to the Scottish islands. But she was aware that Egfrid proposed to make him a bishop, and wishing to know if the effect would follow the intention, she began by inquiring in this manner: "Oh, with what various intentions are the hearts of men distracted! Some rejoice in having obtained riches, others always eager after them are still in want: but thou rejectest the glory of the world, although it is offered thee; and although thou mightest obtain a bishopric, than which there is nothing more sublime on earth, yet thou preferrest the recesses of thy desert to this rank."—"But," said he, "I know that I am not worthy of so high a rank; nevertheless, I cannot shun the judgment of the Supreme Ruler, who, if he decreed that I should subject myself to so great a burden, would, I believe, restore me after a moderate freedom, and perhaps after not more than two years would send me back to my former solitude and quiet. But I must first request you in the name of our Lord and Saviour that you do not relate to any one before my death the things which I have told you." When he had expounded to her the various things which she asked, and had instructed her concerning

345

the things which she had need of, he returned to his solitary island and monastery, and continued his mode of life as he had commenced it.

Not long after, in a full synod, Archbishop Theodore of blessed memory presiding in the presence of God's chosen servant, the holy King Egfrid, he was unanimously elected to the bishopric of the see of Lindisfarne. But, although they sent many messengers and letters to him, he could not by any means be drawn from his habitation, until the king himself, above mentioned, sailed to the island, attended by the most holy Bishop Trumwine, and by as many other religious and influential men as he could: they all went down on their knees before him, and adjured him by the Lord, with tears and entreaties, until they drew him away from his retirement with tears in his eyes, and took him to the synod. When arrived there, although much resisting, he was overcome by the unanimous wish of all, and compelled to submit to undertake the duties of the bishopric; yet the ordination did not take place immediately, but at the termination of the winter which was then beginning. And that his prophecies might be fulfilled in all things, Egfrid was killed the year afterwards in battle with the Picts, and was succeeded on the throne by his illegitimate brother Alfrid, who, a few years before, had devoted himself to literature in Scotland, suffering a voluntary exile, to gratify his love of science.

CHAPTER XXV

HOW, WHEN ELECTED TO THE BISHOPRIC, HE CURED A SERVANT OF ONE OF THE KING'S ATTENDANTS BY MEANS OF HOLY WATER

WHEN Cuthbert, the man of God, after having been elected to the bishopric, had returned to his island, and for some time had served God in secret with his accustomed devotion, the venerable Bishop Eata called him and requested him to come to an interview with him at Melrose. The conversation being finished, and Cuthbert having commenced his journey homewards, a certain attendant of King Egfrid met him, and besought him that he would turn aside and give a benediction at his house. When he had arrived there, and had received the grateful salutations of all, the man pointed out to him one of his servants who was infirm, saying, "I thank God, most holy father, that you have thought worthy to enter our house to see us, and, indeed, we believe that your arrival will afford us the greatest profit both of mind and body. For there is one of our servants tormented with the worst infirmity, and is this day afflicted with such great pain that he appears more like a man dying than sick. For his extremities being dead, he seems only to breathe a little through his mouth and nostrils." Cuthbert immediately blessed some water, and gave it to a servant whose name was Baldhelm, who is still alive and filling the office of presbyter in the bishopric of Lindisfarne, which he adorns by his good qualities. He also has the faculty of relating in the sweetest manner the virtues of the man of God to all who are desirous of knowing, and it was he that told me the miracle which I relate. The man of God, then, giving him the holy water, said, "Go and give it to the sick man to drink." In obedience to these words he brought the water to the sick man, and when he poured it into his mouth the third time, the sick man, contrary to his usual custom, fell asleep. It was now evening, and he passed the night in silence, and in the morning appeared quite well when his master visited him.

CHAPTER XXVI

OF HIS MANNER OF LIFE IN HIS BISHOPRIC

THE venerable man of God, Cuthbert, adorned the office of bishop, which he had undertaken, by the exercise of many virtues, according to the precepts and examples of the Apostles. For he protected the people committed to his care with frequent prayers, and invited them to heavenly things by most wholesome admonitions, and followed that system which most facilitates teaching, by first doing himself what he taught to others. He saved the needy man from the hand of the stronger, and the poor and destitute from those who would oppress them. He comforted the weak and sorrowful; but he took care to recal those who were sinfully rejoicing to that sorrow which is according to godliness. Desiring still to exercise his usual frugality, he did not cease to observe the severity of a monastic life, amid the turmoil by which he was surrounded. He gave food to the hungry, raiment to the shivering, and his course was marked by all the other particulars which adorn the life of a pontiff. The miracles with which he shone forth to the world bore witness to the virtues of his own mind, some of which we have taken care briefly to hand down to memory.

CHAPTER XXVII

HOW, THOUGH AT A DISTANCE, HE SAW IN SPIRIT THE DEATH OF KING EGFRID, AND THE END OF HIS WARFARE, WHICH HE HAD FORETOLD

Now, when King Egfrid had rashly led his army against the Picts, and devastated their territories with most atrocious cruelty, the man of God, Cuthbert, knowing that the time was now come, concerning which he had prophesied the year before to his sister, that the king would live only one year more, came to Lugubalia (which is corruptly called by the English Luel) to speak to the queen, who was there awaiting the result of the war in her sister's monastery. But the next day, when the citizens were leading him to see the walls of the town, and the remarkable fountain, formerly built by the Romans, suddenly, as he was resting on his staff, he was disturbed in spirit, and, turning his countenance sorrowfully to the earth, he raised himself, and, lifting his eyes to heaven, groaned loudly, and said in a low voice, "Now, then, the contest is decided!" The presbyter, who was standing near, in incautious haste answered, and said, "How do you know it?" But he, unwilling to declare more concerning those things which were revealed to him, said, "Do you not see how wonderfully the air is changed and disturbed? Who is able to investigate the judgments of the Almighty?" But he immediately entered in and spoke to the queen in private, for it was the Sabbath-day. "Take care," said he, "that you get into your chariot very early on the second day of the week, for it is not lawful to ride in a chariot on the Lord's day; and go quickly to the royal city, lest, perchance, the king may have been slain. But I have been asked to go to-morrow to a neighbouring monastery, to consecrate a church, and will follow you as soon as that duty is finished."

But when the Lord's day was come, whilst he was preaching the word of God to the brethren of the same monastery, the sermon being finished, he began again to teach his listening congregation, as follows:—"I beseech you, my beloved, according to the admonitions of the Apostle, to watch, remain stedfast in the faith, act manfully, and be comforted, that no temptation may find you unprepared, but rather that you may be always mindful of the precept of the Lord Himself, 'Watch and pray, lest ye enter into temptation.'" But some thought he said this because a pestilence had not long before afflicted them and many others with a great mortality, and that he spoke of this scourge being about to return. But he, resuming his discourse, said, "When I formerly lived alone in my island, some of the brethren came to me on the day of the Holy Nativity, and asked me to go out of my cabin and solemnize with them this joyful and hallowed day. Yielding to their prayers, I went out, and we sat down to feast. But, in the middle of the banquet, I suddenly said to them, 'I beseech you, brethren, let us act cautiously and watchfully, lest, perchance, through carelessness and a sense of security, we be led into temptation.' But they answered, 'We entreat you, let us spend a joyful day now, for it is the birthday of our Lord Jesus Christ!' To which I agreed. Some time after this, when we were indulging ourselves in eating, merriment, and conversation, I again began to admonish them that we should be solicitous in prayer and watchfulness, and ever prepared to meet all temptations. But they replied, 'You teach well; nevertheless, as the days of fasting, watching, and prayer are numerous, let us to-day rejoice in the Lord. For the angel manifested great joy to the shepherds when the Lord was born, and told them that it was a day to be celebrated by all people!' 'Well,' said I, 'let us do so.' But when I repeated the words of the same admonition the third time, they perceived that I would not have suggested this so earnestly for no purpose, and said to me in fear, 'Let us do as you teach, for it is incumbent on us to watch in spirit, armed against the snares and temptations of the devil.' When I said these things, I did not know any more than they that any new temptation would happen to us; but I was only admonished, as it were instinctively, that the state of the heart is to be always fortified against the storms of temptations. But when they returned from me to their own home, that is, to the monastery of Lindisfarne, they found that one of their brethren was dead of a pestilence; and the same disease increased, and raged so furiously from day to day, for months, and almost for a whole year, that the greater part of that noble assembly of spiritual fathers and brethren were sent into the presence of the Lord. Now, therefore, my brethren, watch and pray, that if any tribulation assail you, it may find you prepared."

When the venerable man of God, Cuthbert, had said these things, the brethren thought, as I have before stated, that he spoke of a return of the pestilence. But the day after, a man who had escaped from the war explained, by the lamentable news which he brought, the hidden prophecies of the man of God. It appeared that the guards had been slain, and the king cut off by the sword of the enemy, on the very day and hour in which it was revealed to the man of God as he was standing near the well.

CHAPTER XXVIII

HOW HE FORETOLD HIS OWN DEATH TO HEREBERT, THE HERMIT, AND BY PRAYERS TO GOD OBTAINED HIS ATTENDANCE

NOT very long afterwards, the same servant of God, Cuthbert, was summoned to the same city of Lugubalia, not only to consecrate priests, but also to bless the queen herself with his holy conversation. Now there was a venerable priest of the name of Herebert, who had long been united to the man of God, Cuthbert, in the bond of spiritual friendship, and who, leading a solitary life, in an island in the large marsh from which the Derwent rises, used to come to him every year, and receive from him admonitions in the way of eternal life. When this man heard that he was stopping in that city, he came according to his custom, desiring to be kindled up more and more by his wholesome exhortations in aspiring after heavenly things. When these two had drunk deeply of the cup of celestial wisdom, Cuthbert said, among other things, "Remember, brother Herebert, that you ask me now concerning whatever undertaking you may have in hand, and that you speak to me about it now, because, after we shall have separated, we shall see each other no more in this life. I am certain that the time of my death approaches, and the time of leaving my earthly tenement is at hand." Upon hearing these words, he threw himself at his feet with tears and lamentations, saying, "I beseech you by the Lord not to leave me, but be mindful of your companion, and pray the Almighty Goodness that, as we have served Him together on earth, we may at the same time pass to heaven to see his light. For I have always sought to live according to the command of your mouth; and what I have left undone through ignorance or frailty, I have equally taken care to correct, according to your pleasure." The bishop yielded to his prayers, and immediately learnt in spirit, that he had obtained that which he had sought from the Lord. "Arise, my brother," says he, "and do not lament, but rejoice in gladness, for his great mercy has granted us that which we asked of Him." The event confirmed his promise and the truth of the prophecy; for they never met again, but their souls departed from their bodies at one and the same moment of time, and were joined together in a heavenly vision, and translated at the same time by angels to the heavenly kingdom. But Herebert was first afflicted with a long infirmity, perhaps by a dispensation of holy piety, in order that the continual pain of a long sickness might supply what merit he had less than the blessed Cuthbert, so that being by grace made equal to his intercessor, he might be rendered worthy to depart this life at one and the same hour with him, and to be received into one and the same seat of everlasting happiness.

CHAPTER XXIX

HOW, THROUGH HIS PRIEST, HE CURED THE WIFE OF AN EARL WITH HOLY WATER

WHEN he was one day going round his parish to give spiritual admonitions throughout the rural districts, cottages, and villages, and to lay his hand on all the lately baptized, that they might receive the Holy Spirit, he came to the mansion of a certain earl, whose wife lay sick almost unto death. The earl himself, meeting him as he entered, thanked the Lord on his knees for his arrival, and received him with kind hospitality. When his feet and hands were washed, according to the custom of hospitality, and the bishop had sat down, the man began to tell him about the sickness of his wife, who was despaired of, and besought him to consecrate some water to sprinkle on her. "I believe," said he, "that by-and-by she will either, by the grace of God, be restored to health, or else she will pass by death to life eternal, and soon receive a recompense for so heavy and long-continued trouble." The man of God assented to his prayers, and having blessed the water which was brought to him, gave it to the priest, directing him to sprinkle it on the patient. He entered the bedroom in which she lay, as if dead, and sprinkled her and the bed, and poured some of the healing draught down her throat. Oh, wonderful and extraordinary circumstance! the holy water had scarcely touched the patient, who was wholly ignorant what was brought her, than she was so restored to health, both of mind and body, that being come to her senses she blessed the Lord and returned thanks to Him, that He thought her worthy to be visited and healed by such exalted guests. She got up without delay, and being now well, ministered to those who had been instrumental in curing her; and it was extraordinary to see her, who had escaped the bitter cup of death by the bishop's benediction, now the first of the nobleman's family to offer him refreshment, following the example of the mother-in-law of the Apostle Peter, who, being cured of a fever by the Lord, arose forthwith and ministered unto Him and his disciples.

CHAPTER XXX

HOW HE CURED A GIRL OF A PAIN IN THE HEAD AND SIDE BY ANOINTING HER WITH OIL

BUT the venerable Bishop Cuthbert effected a cure similar to this, of which there were many eye-witnesses, one of whom is the religious priest, Ethelwald, at that time attendant on the man of God, but now abbot of the monastery of Melrose. Whilst, according to his custom, he was travelling and teaching all, he arrived at a certain village, in which were a few holy women, who had fled from their monastery through fear of the barbarian army, and had there obtained a habitation from the man of God a short time before: one of whom, a sister of the above-mentioned priest, Ethelwald, was confined with a most grievous sickness; for during a whole year she had been troubled with an intolerable pain in the head and side, which the physicians utterly despaired of curing. But when they told the man of God about her, and entreated him to cure her, he in pity anointed the wretched woman with holy oil. From that time she began to get better, and was well in a few days.

CHAPTER XXXI

HOW HE CURED AN INFIRM MAN BY CONSECRATED BREAD

I must not here pass over a miracle which was told to me as having been worked by his holiness, though he himself was absent. We mentioned a prefect of the name of Hildemer, whose wife the man

of God freed from an unclean spirit. The same prefect afterwards
fell seriously ill, so that his malady daily increased, and he was confined to his bed, apparently near death. Many of his friends were
present who had come to console him in his sickness. Whilst they
were sitting by the bedside, one of them mentioned that he had
with him some consecrated bread which Cuthbert had given him:
"And I think," said he, "that if we were in faith to give him this to eat,
nothing doubting, he would be well." All present were laymen, but
at the same time very pious men, and turning to one another, they
professed their faith, without doubting, that by partaking of that
same consecrated bread he might be well. They therefore filled a
cup with water, and putting a little of the bread into it, gave it him to
drink: the water thus hallowed by the bread no sooner touched his
stomach than all his inward pain left him, and the wasting of his outward members ceased. A perfect recovery speedily ensued, and
both himself and the others who saw or heard the rapidity of this
wonderful cure were thereby stirred up to praise the holiness of
Christ's servant, and to admire the virtues of his true faith.

CHAPTER XXXII

HOW, BY PRAYER, HE RESTORED TO LIFE A YOUNG MAN
WHOM HE FOUND AT THE POINT OF DEATH ON A JOURNEY

As this holy shepherd of Christ's flock was going round visiting his
folds, he came to a mountainous and wild place, where many people had got together from all the adjoining villages, that he might
lay his hands upon them. But among the mountains no fit church
or place could be found to receive the bishop and his attendants.
They therefore pitched tents for him in the road, and each cut
branches from the trees in the neighbouring wood to make for himself the best sort of covering that he was able. Two days did the man
of God preach to the assembled crowds; and minister the grace of
the Holy Spirit by imposition of hands upon those that were regen-
erate in Christ; when, on a sudden, there appeared some women

bearing on a bed a young man, wasted by severe illness, and having placed him down at the outlet of the wood, sent to the bishop, requesting permission to bring him, that he might receive a blessing from the holy man. When he was brought near, the bishop perceived that his sufferings were great, and ordered all to retire to a distance. He then betook himself to his usual weapon, prayer, and bestowing his blessing, expelled the fever, which all the care and medicines of the physicians had not been able to cure. In short, he rose up the same hour, and having refreshed himself with food, and given thanks to God, walked back to the women who had brought him. And so it came to pass, that whereas they had in sorrow brought the sick man thither, he now returned home with them, safe and well, and all rejoicing, both he and they alike.

CHAPTER XXXIII

HOW, AT A TIME OF SICKNESS, HE RESTORED A DYING BOY IN HEALTH TO HIS MOTHER

AT the same time the plague made great ravages in those parts, so that there were scarcely any inhabitants left in villages and places which had been thickly populated, and some towns were wholly deserted. The holy father Cuthbert, therefore, went round his parish, most assiduously ministering the word of God, and comforting those few who were left. But being arrived at a certain village, and having there exhorted all whom he found there, he said to his attendant priest, "Do you think that any one remains who has need that we should visit and converse with him? or have we now seen all here, and shall we go elsewhere?" The priest looked about, and saw a woman standing afar off, one of whose sons had died but a little time before, and she was now supporting another at the point of death, whilst the tears trickling down her cheek bore witness to her past and present affliction. He pointed her out to the man of God, who immediately went to her, and, blessing the boy, kissed him, and said to his mother, "Do not fear nor be sorrowful; for your child shall be healed and live, and no one else of your household shall die of this pestilence." To the truth of which prophecy the mother and son, who lived a long time after that, bore witness.

CHAPTER XXXIV

HOW HE SAW THE SOUL OF A MAN, WHO HAD BEEN KILLED BY FALLING FROM A TREE, ASCEND TO HEAVEN

BUT now this man of God, foreseeing his end approaching, had determined to lay aside the duties of his pastoral office, and return to his former solitary life, that by shaking off the cares of this life he might occupy himself amidst unrestrained psalmody and prayer in preparing for the day of his death, or rather of his entrance into everlasting life. He wished first to go round his parishes, and visit the houses of the faithful in his neighbourhood; and then, when he had confirmed all with such consolatory admonitions as should be required, to return to the solitary abode which he so longed after. Meanwhile, at the request of the noble and holy virgin, the Abbess Elfleda, of whom I have before made mention, he entered the estate belonging to her monastery, both to speak to her and also to consecrate a church therein; for there was there a considerable number of monks. When they had taken their seats, at the hour of repast, on a sudden Cuthbert turned away his thoughts from the carnal food to the contemplation of heavenly things. His limbs being much fatigued by his previous duties, the colour of his face changed, his eyes became unusually fixed, and the knife dropped from his hands upon the table. The priest, who stood by and ministered to him, perceiving this, said to the abbess, "Ask the bishop what he has just seen: for I know there was some reason for his hand thus trembling and letting fall the knife, whilst his countenance also changed so wonderfully: he has surely seen something which we have not seen." She immediately turned to him and said, "I pray you, my lord bishop, tell me what you have just seen, for your tired hand did not let fall the knife just now without some cause." The bishop endeavoured to conceal the fact of his having seen any thing supernatural, and replied in joke, "I was not able to eat the whole day, was I? I must have left off some time or other." But, when she persisted in her entreaty that he would tell the vision, he said, "I saw the soul of a holy man carried up to heaven in the arms of angels."—"From what place," said she, "was it taken?"— "From your monastery," replied the bishop; upon which she further asked his name. "You will tell it me," said he, "to-morrow, when I am celebrating mass." On hearing these words, she immediately sent to the larger monastery to inquire who had been lately removed from the body. The messenger, finding all safe and well, was preparing to return in the morning to his mistress, when he met some men carrying in a cart the body of a deceased brother to be buried. On inquiring who it was, he found that it was one of the shepherds, a worthy man, who, having incautiously mounted a tree, had fallen down, and died from the bruise, at the same time that the man of God had seen the vision. He immediately went and told the circumstance to his mistress, who went forthwith to the bishop, at that time consecrating the church, and in amazement, as if she were going to tell him something new and doubtful, "I pray," said she, "my lord bishop, remember in the mass my servant Hadwald," (for that was his name,) "who died yesterday by falling from a tree." It was then plain to all that the holy man possessed in his mind an abundant spirit of prophecy; for that he saw before his eyes at the moment the man's soul carried to heaven, and knew beforehand what was afterwards going to be told him by others.

CHAPTER XXXV

HOW HE CHANGED WATER BY TASTING IT, SO THAT IT HAD THE FLAVOUR OF WINE

WHEN he had gone regularly through the upper districts, he came to a nunnery, which we have before mentioned, not far from the mouth of the river Tyne; where he was magnificently entertained by Christ's servant, Abbess Verca,—a woman of a most noble character, both in spiritual and temporal concerns. When they rose from their afternoon repose, he said he was thirsty, and asked for drink. They inquired of him what he would have, whether they should bring him wine, or beer. "Give me water," said he; and they brought him a draught from the fountain. But he, when he had given thanks and tasted it, gave it to his attendant priest, who returned it to the servant. The man, taking the cup, asked if he might drink out of the same cup as the bishop. "Certainly," said the priest, "why not?" Now that priest also belonged to the same monastery. He therefore drank, and the water seemed to him to taste like wine. Upon which he gave the cup to the brother who was standing near, that he might be a witness of so great a miracle; and to him also the taste seemed, without a doubt, to be that of wine. They looked at one another in amazement; and when they found time to speak, they acknowledged to one another that they had never tasted better wine. I give this on the authority of one of them, who stopped some time in our monastery at Weremouth, and now lies buried there.

CHAPTER XXXVI

HOW SOME OF THE BRETHREN, FOR DISOBEDIENCE TO HIM, WERE DETAINED BY A STORM AT SEA

WHEN Cuthbert had passed two years in the episcopal office, knowing in spirit that his last day was at hand, he divested himself of his episcopal duties and returned to his much-loved solitude, that he might there occupy his time in extracting the thorns of the flesh, and kindle up to greater brightness the flame of his former humility. At this time he was accustomed to go out frequently from his cell, and converse with the brethren, who came to visit him. I will here mention a miracle which he then wrought, in order that it may be more evident to all men what obedience should be rendered to his saints, even in the case of commands which they seem to have given with carelessness or indifference. He had one day left his cell, to give advice to some visitors; and when he had finished, he said to them, "I must now go in again; but do you, as you are inclined to depart, first take food; and when you have cooked and eaten that goose, which is hanging on the wall, go on board your vessel in God's name, and return home." He then uttered a prayer, and, having blessed them, went in. But they, as he had bidden them, took some food; but having enough provisions of their own, which they had brought with them, they did not touch the goose.

Now when they had refreshed themselves, they tried to go on board their vessel, but a sudden storm utterly prevented them from putting to sea. They were thus detained seven days in the island by the roughness of the waves, and yet they could not call to mind what fault they had committed. They therefore returned to have an interview with the holy father, and to lament to him their detention. He exhorted them to be patient, and on the seventh day came out to console their sorrow, and give them pious exhortations. When, however, he had entered the house in which they were stopping, and saw that the goose was not eaten, he reproved their disobedience with mild countenance and in gentle language. "Have you not left the goose still hanging in its place? What wonder is it that the storm has prevented your departure? Put it immediately into the caldron, and boil and eat it, that the sea may become tranquil, and you may return home."

They immediately did as he had commanded; and it happened most wonderfully that the moment the kettle began to boil, the wind began to cease, and the waves to be still. Having finished their repast, and seeing that the sea was calm, they went on board, and, to their great delight, though with shame for their neglect, reached home with a fair wind. Their shame arose from their disobedience and dulness of comprehension, whereby, amid the chastening of their Maker, they were unable to perceive and to correct their error. They rejoiced, because they now saw what care God had for his faithful servant, so as to vindicate him from neglect, even by means of the elements. They rejoiced, too, that the

Lord should have had so much regard to themselves, as to correct their offences even by an open miracle. Now this, which I have related, I did not pick up from any chance authority, but I had it from one of those who were present,—a most reverend monk and priest of the same monastery, Cynemund, who still lives, known to many in the neighbourhood for his years and the purity of his life.

CHAPTER XXXVII

OF THE TEMPTATIONS WHICH HE UNDERWENT IN HIS SICKNESS, AND HIS ORDERS CONCERNING HIS BURIAL

THE solemn day of the nativity of our Lord was scarcely over, when the man of God, Cuthbert, returned to his dwelling on the island. A crowd of monks were standing by as he entered into the ship; and one of them, an old and venerable monk, strong in faith but weak in body, in consequence of a dysentery, said to him, "Tell us, my lord bishop, when we may hope for your return." To this plain question, he replied as plainly, "When you shall bring my body back here." When he had passed about two months in the enjoyment of his rest, and had as usual subdued both his body and mind with his accustomed severity, he was suddenly seized with illness, and began to prepare for the joy of everlasting happiness, through pain and temporal affliction. I will describe his death in the words of him who related it to me, namely, his attendant priest Herefrid, a most religious man, who also at that time presided over the monastery of Lindisfarne, in the capacity of abbot.

"He was brought to the point of death," said he, "after having been weakened by three weeks of continued suffering. For he was taken ill on the fourth day of the week; and again on the fourth day of the week his pains were over, and he departed to the Lord. But when I came to him on the first morning after his illness began—(for I had also arrived at the island with the brethren three days before)—in my desire to obtain his blessing and advice as usual, I gave the customary signal of my coming, and he came to the window, and replied to my salutation with a sigh. 'My lord bishop,' said I, 'what is the matter with you? Has your indisposition come upon you this last night?'—'Yes,' said he, 'indisposition has come upon me.' I thought that he was speaking of an old complaint, which vexed him almost every day, and not of a new malady; so, without making any more inquiries, I said to him, 'Give us your blessing, for it is time to put to sea and return home.'—'Do so,' replied he; 'go on board, and return home in safety. But, when the Lord shall have taken my spirit, bury me in this house, near my oratory, towards the south, over against the eastern side of the holy cross, which I have erected there. Towards the north side of that same oratory is a sarcophagus under the turf, which the venerable Abbot Cudda formerly gave me. You will place my body therein, wrapping it in linen, which you will find in it. I would not wear it whilst I was alive, but for the love of that highly favoured woman, who sent it to me, the Abbess Verca, I have preserved it to wrap my corpse in.' On hearing these words, I replied, 'I beseech you, father, as you are weak, and talk of the probability of your dying, to let some of the brethren remain here to wait on you.'— 'Go home now,' said he; 'but return at the proper time.' So I was unable to prevail upon him, notwithstanding the urgency of my entreaties; and at last I asked him when we should return to him. 'When God so wills it,' said he, 'and when He Himself shall direct you.' We did as he commanded us; and having assembled the brethren immediately in the church, I had prayers offered up for him without intermission; 'for,' said I, 'it seems to me, from some words which he spoke, that the day is approaching on which he will depart to the Lord.'

"I was anxious about returning to him on account of his illness, but the weather prevented us for five days; and it was ordered so by God, as the event showed. For God Almighty, wishing to cleanse his servant from every stain of earthly weakness, and to show his adversaries how weak they were against the strength of his faith, kept him aloof from men, and put him to the proof by pains of the flesh, and still more violent encounters with the ancient enemy. At length there was a calm, and we went to the island, and found him away from his cell in the house where we were accustomed to reside. The brethren who came with me had some occasion to go back to the neighbouring shore, so that I was left alone on the island to minister to the holy father. I warmed some water and washed his feet, which had an ulcer from a long swelling, and, from the quantity of blood that came from it, required to be attended to. I also warmed some wine which I had brought, and begged him to taste it; for I saw by his face that he was worn out with pain and want of food. When I had finished my service, he sat down quietly on the couch, and I sat down by his side.

"Seeing that he kept silence, I said, 'I see, my lord bishop, that you have suffered much from your complaint since we left you, and I marvel that you were so unwilling for us, when we departed, to send you some of our number to wait upon you.' He replied, 'It was done by the providence and the will of God, that I might be left without any society or aid of man, and suffer somewhat of affliction. For when you were gone, my languor began to increase, so that I left my cell and came hither to meet any one who might be on his way to see me, that he might not have the trouble of going further. Now, from the moment of my coming until the present time, during a space of five days and five nights, I have sat here without moving.'—'And how have you supported life, my lord bishop?' asked I; 'have you remained so long without taking food?' Upon which, turning up the couch on which he was sitting, he showed me five onions concealed therein, saying, 'This has been my food for five days; for, whenever my mouth became dry and parched with thirst, I cooled and refreshed myself by tasting these;'—now one of the onions appeared to have been a little gnawed, but certainly not more than half of it was eaten;—'and,' continued he, 'my enemies have never persecuted me so much during my whole stay in the island, as they have done during these last five days.' I was not bold enough to ask what kinds of persecutions he had suffered: I only asked him to have some one to wait upon him. He consented, and kept some of us with him; amongst whom was the priest Bede the elder, who had always been used to familiar attendance upon him. This man was consequently a most faithful witness of every thing which he gave or received, whom Cuthbert wished to keep with him, to remind him if he did not make proper compensation for any presents which he might receive, that before he died he might render to every one his own. He kept also another of the brethren with him, who had long suffered from a violent diarrhœa, and could not be cured by the physicians; but, for his religious merit, and prudent conduct, and grave demeanour, was thought worthy to hear the last words of the man of God, and to witness his departure to the Lord.

"Meanwhile I returned home, and told the brethren that the holy father wished to be buried in his own island; and I added my opinion, that it would be more proper and becoming to obtain his consent for his body to be transported from the island, and buried in the monastery with the usual honours. My words pleased them, and we went to the bishop, and asked him, saying, 'We have not dared, my lord bishop, to despise your injunction to be buried here, and yet we have thought proper to request of you permission to transport your body over to the monastery, and so have you amongst us.' To which he replied, 'It was also my wish to repose here, where I have fought my humble battles for the Lord, where, too, I wish to finish my course, and whence I hope to be lifted up by a righteous Judge to obtain the crown of righteousness. But I think it better for you, also, that I should repose here, on account of the fugitives and criminals who may flee to my corpse for refuge; and when they have thus obtained an asylum, inasmuch as I have enjoyed the fame, humble though I am, of being a servant of Christ, you may think it necessary to intercede for such before the secular rulers, and so you may have trouble on my account.' When, however, we urged him with many entreaties, and asserted that such labour would be agreeable and easy to us, the man of God at length, after some deliberation, spoke thus:—'Since you wish to overcome my scruples, and to carry my body amongst you, it seems to me to be the best plan to bury it in the inmost parts of the church, that you may be able to visit my tomb yourselves, and to control the visits of all other persons.' We thanked him on our bended knees for this permission, and for his advice; and returning home, did not cease to pay him frequent visits.

CHAPTER XXXVIII

HOW, DURING HIS ILLNESS, HE CURED ONE OF HIS ATTENDANTS OF A DIARRHŒA

"His malady now began to grow upon him, and we thought that the time of his dissolution was at hand. He bade his attendants carry him to his cell and oratory. It was the third hour of the day. We therefore carried him thither, for he was too feeble to walk himself. When we reached the door, we asked him to let one of us go in with him, to wait upon him; for no one had ever entered therein but himself. He cast his eyes round on all, and, fixing them on the sick brother above mentioned, said, 'Walstod shall go in with me.' Now Walstod was the man's name. He went in accordingly, and stayed till the ninth hour: when he came out, and said to me, 'The bishop wishes you to go in unto him; but I have a most wonderful thing to tell you: from the moment of my touching the bishop, when I supported him into the oratory, I have been entirely free from my old complaint.' No doubt this was brought about by the effect of his heavenly piety, that, whereas in his time of health and strength he had healed many, he should now heal this man, when he was himself at the point of death, that so there might be a standing proof how strong the holy man was in spirit, though his body was at the lowest degree of weakness. In this cure he followed the example of the holy and reverend father and bishop, Aurelius Augustine, who, when weighed down by the illness of which he died, and lying on his couch, was entreated by a man to lay his hand on a sick person whom he had brought to him, that so he might be made well. To which Augustine replied, 'If I had such power, I should first have practised it towards myself.'

The sick man answered, 'I have been commanded to come to you: for some one said to me in a dream, Go to Bishop Augustine, and let him place his hand upon you, and you shall be well.' On hearing this, Augustine placed his hand upon him, gave him his blessing, and sent him home perfectly recovered.

CHAPTER XXXIX

OF HIS LAST INSTRUCTIONS TO THE BRETHREN; AND HOW, WHEN HE HAD RECEIVED THE VIATICUM, HE YIELDED UP HIS SOUL IN PRAYER

"I went in to him about the ninth hour of the day, and found him lying in one corner of his oratory before the altar. I took my seat by his side, but he spoke very little, for the weight of his suffering prevented him from speaking much. But when I earnestly asked him what last discourse and valedictory salutation he would bequeath to the brethren, he began to make a few strong admonitions respecting peace and humility, and told me to beware of those persons who strove against these virtues, and would not practise them. 'Have peace,' said he, 'and Divine charity ever amongst you: and when you are called upon to deliberate on your condition, see that you be unanimous in council. Let concord be mutual between you and other servants of Christ; and do not despise others who belong to the faith and come to you for hospitality, but admit them familiarly and kindly; and when you have entertained them, speed them on their journey: by no means esteeming yourselves better than the rest of those who partake of the same faith and mode of life. But have no communion with those who err from the unity of the Catholic faith, either by keeping Easter at an improper time, or by their perverse life. And know and remember, that, if of two evils you are compelled to choose one, I would rather that you should take up my bones, and leave these places, to reside wherever God may send you, than consent in any way to the wickedness of schismatics, and so place a yoke upon your necks. Study diligently, and carefully observe the

Catholic rules of the Fathers, and practise with zeal those institutes of the monastic life which it has pleased God to deliver to you through my ministry. For I know, that, although during my life some have despised me, yet after my death you will see what sort of man I was, and that my doctrine was by no means worthy of contempt.'

"These words, and such as these, the man of God delivered to us at intervals, for, as we before said, the violence of his complaint had taken from him the power of speaking much at once. He then spent the rest of the day until the evening in the expectation of future happiness; to which he added this also, that he spent the night in watchfulness and prayer. When his hour of evening service was come, he received from me the blessed sacrament, and thus strengthened himself for his departure, which he now knew to be at hand, by partaking of the body and blood of Christ; and when he had lifted up his eyes to heaven, and stretched out his hands above him, his soul, intent upon heavenly praises, sped his way to the joys of the heavenly kingdom.

CHAPTER XL

HOW, ACCORDING TO THE PREVIOUS WARNING OF THE PSALM WHICH THEY SANG AT HIS DEATH, THE BRETHREN OF LINDISFARNE WERE ASSAILED FROM WITHOUT, BUT BY THE HELP OF GOD WERE PROTECTED

"I immediately went out, and told the brethren, who had passed the whole night in watchfulness and prayer, and chanced at that moment in the order of evening service to be singing the 59th Psalm, which begins, 'O Lord, thou hast rejected us and destroyed us; thou hast been angry, and hast pitied us.' One of them instantly lighted two candles, and, holding one in each hand, ascended a lofty spot, to show to the brethren who were in the monastery of Lindisfarne, that the holy man was dead; for they had agreed beforehand that such a signal should be made. The brother, who had waited an hour on an opposite height in the island of

Lindisfarne, ran with speed to the monastery, where the brethren were assembled to perform the usual ceremonies of the evening service, and happened to be singing the above-named Psalm when the messenger entered. This was a Divine dispensation, as the event showed. For, when the man of God was buried, the Church was assailed by such a blast of temptation, that several of the brethren left the place rather than be involved in such dangers.

"At the end of a year, Eadbert was ordained bishop. He was a man of great virtues, learned in the Holy Scripture, and in particular given to works of charity. If I may use the words of Scripture, The Lord built up Jerusalem, *i.e.* the vision of peace, and gathered together the dispersion of Israel. He healed those who were contrite in heart, and bound up their bruises, so that it was then given openly to understand the meaning of the hymn which was then for the first time sung, when the death of the sainted man was known; namely, that after his death his countrymen should be exposed to be repulsed and destroyed, but after a demonstration of his threatening anger should again be protected by the Divine mercy. He who considers the sequel also of the above-named Psalm will perceive that the event corresponded to its meaning. The body of the venerable father was placed on board a ship, and carried to the island of Lindisfarne. It was there met by a large crowd of persons singing psalms, and placed in the church of the holy Apostle Peter, in a stone coffin on the right-hand side of the altar."

CHAPTER XLI

HOW A BOY, WHO WAS POSSESSED BY A DEVIL, WAS CURED BY SOME DIRT, FROM THE PLACE WHERE THE WATER IN WHICH HIS CORPSE HAD BEEN WASHED HAD BEEN THROWN

BUT even when the servant of Christ was dead and buried, the miracles which he worked whilst alive did not cease. For a certain boy, in the territory of Lindisfarne, was vexed so terribly by an evil spirit, that he altogether lost his reason, and shouted and cried aloud, and tried to tear in pieces with his teeth his own limbs, or whatever came in his way. A priest from the monastery was sent to the sufferer; but, though he had been accustomed to exorcise and expel evil spirits, yet in this case he could not prevail: he therefore advised the lad's father to put him into a cart and drive him to the monastery, and to pray to God in his behalf before the relics of the holy saints which are there. The father did as he was advised; but the holy saints, to show how high a place Cuthbert occupied amongst them, refused to bestow on him the benefit desired. The mad boy, therefore, by howling, groaning, and gnashing his teeth, filled the eyes and ears of all who were there with horror, and no one could think of any remedy; when, behold, one of the priests, being taught in spirit that by the aid of the holy father Cuthbert he might be cured, went privately to the place where he knew the water had been thrown, in which his dead body had been washed; and taking from thence a small portion of the dirt, he mixed it with some water, and carrying it to the sufferer, poured it into his open mouth, from which he was uttering the most horrible and lamentable cries. He instantly held his tongue, closed his mouth, and shutting his eyes also, which before were bloodshot and staring hideously, he fell back into a profound sleep. In this state he passed the night; and in the morning, rising up from his slumber, free from his madness, he found himself also, by the merits and intercession of the blessed Cuthbert, free from the evil spirit by which he had been afflicted. It was a marvellous sight, and delectable to all good men, to see the son sound in mind accompany his father to the holy places, and give thanks for the aid of the saints; although the day before, from the extremity of his madness, he did not know who or where he was. When, in the midst of the whole body of the brethren looking on and congratulating him, he had on his knees offered up before the relics of the martyrs praise to the Lord God and our Saviour Jesus Christ, he returned to his home, freed from the harassing of the foe, and confirmed in the faith which he before professed. They show to this day the pit into which that memorable water was thrown, of a square shape, surrounded with wood, and filled with little stones. It is near the church in which his body reposes, on the south side. From that time God permitted many other cures to be wrought by means of those same stones, and the dirt from the same place.

CHAPTER XLII

HOW HIS BODY AFTER NINE YEARS WAS FOUND UNDECAYED

Now Divine Providence, wishing to show to what glory this holy man was exalted after death, who even before death had been distinguished by so many signs and miracles, inspired the minds of the brethren with a wish to remove his bones, which they expected to find dry and free from his decayed flesh, and to put them in a small coffer, on the same spot, above the ground, as objects of veneration to the people. This wish they communicated to the holy Bishop Eadbert about the middle of Quadragesima; and he ordered them to execute this on the 20th of April, which was the anniversary of the day of his burial. They accordingly did so; and opening the tomb, found his body entire, as if he were still alive, and his joints were still flexible, as if he were not dead, but sleeping. His clothes, also, were still undecayed, and seemed to retain their original freshness and colour. When the brethren saw this, they were so astonished, that they could scarcely speak, or look on the miracle which lay before them, and they hardly knew what they were doing.

As a proof of the uncorrupted state of the clothes, they took a portion of them from one of the extremities,—for they did not dare to take any from the body itself,—and hastened to tell what they had found to the bishop, who was then walking alone at a spot remote from the monastery, and closed in by the flowing waves of the sea. Here it was his custom to pass the Quadragesima; and here he occupied himself forty days before the birthday of our Lord in the utmost devotion, accompanied with abstinence, prayer, and tears. Here, also, his venerable predecessor, Cuthbert, before he went to Farne, as we have related, spent a portion of his spiritual warfare in the service of the Lord. The brethren brought with them, also, the piece of cloth in which the body of the saint had been wrapped. The bishop thanked them for the gift, and heard their report with eagerness, and with great earnestness kissed the cloth as if it were still on the saint's body. "Fold up the body," said he, "in new cloth instead of this, and place it in the chest which you have prepared. But I know of a certainty that the place which has been consecrated by the virtue of this heavenly miracle will not long remain empty; and happy is he to whom the Lord, who is the giver of true happiness, shall grant to rest therein." To these words he added what I have elsewhere expressed in verse, and said,—

> "What man the wondrous gifts of God shall tell?
> What ear the joys of paradise shall hear?
> Triumphant o'er the gates of death and hell,
> The just shall live amid the starry sphere," &c.

When the bishop had said much more to this effect, with many tears and much contrition, the brethren did as he ordered them; and having folded up the body in some new cloth, and placed it in a chest, laid it on the pavement of the sanctuary.

CHAPTER XLIII

HOW THE BODY OF BISHOP EADBERT WAS LAID IN THE GRAVE OF THE MAN OF GOD, AND THE COFFIN OF THAT SAINT PLACED UPON IT

MEANWHILE, God's chosen servant, Bishop Eadbert, was seized by an illness, which daily grew more and more violent, so that not long after, that is, on the sixth of May, he also departed to the Lord. It was an especial mercy granted to his earnest prayers, that he left this life by a gradual, and not a sudden death. His body was placed in the grave of the blessed father Cuthbert, and upon it they placed the coffin in which the body of that saint lay. And to this day miracles are there wrought, if the faith of those who seek them admit of it. Even the clothes which had covered his blessed body, whether dead or alive, still possess a healing power.

CHAPTER XLIV

HOW A SICK MAN WAS CURED AT HIS TOMB BY PRAYER

LASTLY, there came from foreign parts a certain priest of the reverend and holy Wilbrord Clement, bishop of the Fresons, who, whilst he was stopping at the monastery, fell into a severe illness, which lasted so long, that his life was despaired of. Overcome with pain, he seemed unable either to live or die, until, thinking on a happy plan, he said to his attendant, "Lead me, I beg of you, to-day after mass," (for it was Sunday,) "to the body of the holy man of God, to pray: I hope his intercession may save me from these torments, so that I may either return whole to this life, or die, and go to that which is everlasting." His attendant did as he had asked him, and with much trouble led him, leaning on a staff, into the church. He there bent his knees at the tomb of the holy father, and, with his head stooping towards the ground, prayed for his recovery; when, suddenly, he felt in all his limbs such an accession of strength from the incorruptible body of the saint, that he rose up from prayer without trouble, and returned to the guests' chamber without the assistance of the conductor who had led him, or the staff on which he had leaned. A few days afterwards he proceeded in perfect health upon his intended journey.

CHAPTER XLV

HOW A PARALYTIC WAS HEALED BY MEANS OF HIS SHOES

THERE was a young man in a monastery not far off, who had lost the use of all his limbs by a weakness which the Greeks call paralysis. His abbot, knowing that there were skilful physicians in the monastery of Lindisfarne, sent him thither with a request that, if possible, he might be healed. The brethren, at the instance of their own abbot and bishop also, attended to him with the utmost care, and used all their skill in medicine, but without

371

effect, for the malady increased daily, insomuch that, save his mouth, he could hardly move a single limb. Being thus given over by all worldly physicians, he had recourse to Him who is in heaven, who, when He is sought out in truth, is kind towards all our iniquities, and heals all our sicknesses. The poor man begged of his attendant to bring him something which had come from the incorruptible body of the holy man; for he believed that by means thereof he might, with the blessing of God, return to health. The attendant, having first consulted the abbot, brought the shoes which the man of God had worn in the tomb, and having stripped the poor man's feet naked, put them upon him; for it was in his feet that the palsy had first attacked him. This he did at the beginning of the night, when bedtime was drawing near. A deep sleep immediately came over him; and as the stillness of night advanced, the man felt a palpitation in his feet alternately, so that the attendants, who were awake and looking on, perceived that the virtue of the holy man's relics was beginning to exert its power, and that the desired restoration of health would ascend upwards from the feet. As soon as the monastery bell struck the hour of midnight prayer, the invalid himself was awakened by the sound and sat up. He found his nerves and the joints of his limbs suddenly endowed with inward strength: his pains were gone; and perceiving that he was cured, he arose, and in a standing posture spent the whole time of the midnight or matin song in thanksgiving to God. In the morning he went to the cathedral, and in the sight of all the congratulating brethren he went round all the sacred places, offering up prayers and the sacrifice of praise to his Saviour. Thus it came to pass, that, by a most wonderful vicissitude of things, he, who had been carried thither weak and borne upon a cart, returned home sound in his own strength, and with all his limbs strengthened and confirmed. Wherefore it is profitable to bear in mind that this change was the work of the right hand of the Most High, whose mighty miracles never cease from the beginning of the world to show themselves forth to mankind.

CHAPTER XLVI

HOW THE HERMIT FELGELD WAS CURED OF A SWELLING
IN THE FACE BY MEANS OF THE COVERING OF THE WALL
OF THE MAN OF GOD'S HOUSE

Nor do I think I ought to omit the heavenly miracle which the Divine mercy showed by means of the ruins of the holy oratory, in which the venerable father went through his solitary warfare in the service of the Lord. Whether it was effected by the merits of the same blessed father Cuthbert, or his successor Ethelwald, a man equally devoted to the Lord, the Searcher of the heart knows best. There is no reason why it may not be attributed to either of the two, in conjunction with the faith of the most holy father Felgeld; through whom and in whom the miraculous cure, which I mention, was effected. He was the third person who became tenant of the same place and its spiritual warfare, and, at present more than seventy years old, is awaiting the end of this life, in expectation of the heavenly one.

When, therefore, God's servant Cuthbert had been translated to the heavenly kingdom, and Ethelwald had commenced his occupation of the same island and monastery, after many years spent in conversation with the monks, he gradually aspired to the rank of anchoritish perfection. The walls of the aforesaid oratory, being composed of planks somewhat carelessly put together, had become loose and tottering by age, and, as the planks separated from one another, an opening was afforded to the weather. The venerable man, whose aim was rather the splendour of the heavenly than of an earthly mansion, having taken hay, or clay, or whatever he could get, had filled up the crevices, that he might not be disturbed from the earnestness of his prayers by the daily violence of the winds and storms. When Ethelwald entered and saw these contrivances, he begged the brethren who came thither to give him a calf's skin, and fastened it with nails in the corner, where himself and his predecessor used to kneel or stand when they prayed, as a protection against the storm.

Twelve years after, he also ascended to the joys of the heavenly kingdom, and Felgeld became the third inhabitant of the place. It then seemed good to the right reverend Eadfrid, bishop of the church of Lindisfarne, to restore from its foundation the time-worn oratory. This being done, many devout persons begged of Christ's holy servant Felgeld to give them a small portion of the relics of God's servant Cuthbert, or of Ethelwald his successor. He accordingly determined to cut up the above-named calf's skin to pieces, and give a portion to each. But he first experienced its influence in his own person: for his face was much deformed by a swelling and a red patch. The symptoms of this deformity had become manifest long before to the monks, whilst he was dwelling among them. But now that he was living alone, and bestowed less care on his person, whilst he practised still greater rigidities, and, like a prisoner, rarely enjoyed the sun or air, the malady increased, and his face became one large red swelling. Fearing, therefore, lest he should be obliged to abandon the solitary life and return to the monastery; presuming in his faith, he trusted to heal himself by the aid of those holy men whose house he dwelt in, and whose holy life he sought to imitate. For he steeped a piece of the skin above mentioned in water, and washed his face therewith; whereupon the swelling was immediately healed, and the cicatrice disappeared. This I was told, in the first instance, by a religious priest of the monastery of Jarrow, who said that he well knew Felgeld's face to have been in the deformed and diseased state which I have described, and that he saw it and felt it with his hand through the window after it was cured. Felgeld afterwards told me the same thing, confirming the report of the priest, and asserting that his face was ever afterwards free from the blemish during the many years that he passed in that place. This he ascribed to the agency of the Almighty Grace, which both in this world heals many, and in the world to come will heal all the maladies of our minds and bodies, and, satisfying our desires after good things, crown us for ever with its mercy and compassion. AMEN.

THE LIVES OF THE HOLY ABBOTS

OF WEREMOUTH AND JARROW

BENEDICT, CEOLFRID, EASTERWINE, SIGFRID, AND HUETBERHT

THE pious servant of Christ, Biscop, called Benedict, with the assistance of the Divine grace, built a monastery in honour of the most holy of the apostles, St. Peter, near the mouth of the river Were, on the north side. The venerable and devout king of that nation, Egfrid, contributed the land; and Biscop, for the space of sixteen years, amid innumerable perils in journeying and in illness, ruled this monastery with the same piety which stirred him up to build it. If I may use the words of the blessed Pope Gregory, in which he glorifies the life of the abbot of the same name, he was a man of a venerable life, blessed (Benedictus) both in grace and in name; having the mind of an adult even from his childhood, surpassing his age by his manners, and with a soul addicted to no false pleasures. He was descended from a noble lineage of the Angles, and by corresponding dignity of mind worthy to be exalted into the company of the angels. Lastly, he was the minister of King Oswy, and by his gift enjoyed an estate suitable to his rank; but at the age of twenty-five years he despised a transitory wealth, that he might obtain that which is eternal. He made light of a temporal warfare with a donative that will decay, that he might serve under the true King, and earn an everlasting kingdom in the heavenly city. He left his home, his kinsmen and country, for the sake of Christ and his Gospel, that he might receive a hundredfold and enjoy everlasting life: he disdained to submit to carnal nuptials, that he might be able to follow the Lamb bright with the glory of chastity in the heavenly kingdoms: he refused to be the father of mortal children in the flesh, being foreordained of Christ to educate for Him in spiritual doctrine immortal children in heaven.

Having therefore left his country, he came to Rome, and took care to visit and worship in the body the resting-places of the remains of the holy Apostles, towards whom he had always been inflamed with holy love. When he returned home, he did not cease to love and venerate, and to preach to all he could the precepts of ecclesiastical life which he had seen. At this time Alfrid, son of the above-named King Oswy, being about to visit Rome, to worship at the gates of the holy Apostles, took him as the companion of his journey. When the king, his father, diverted him from this intention, and made him reside in his own country and kingdom; yet, like a youth of good promise, accomplishing the journey which he had undertaken, Biscop returned with the greatest expedition to Rome, in the time of Pope Vitalian, of blessed memory; and there having extracted no little sweetness of wholesome learning, as he had done previously, after some months he went to the island of Lerins, where he joined himself to the company of monks, received the tonsure, and, having taken the vow, observed the regular discipline with due solicitude; and when he had for two years been instructed in the suitable learning of the monastic life, he determined, in love for that first of the Apostles, St. Peter, to return to the city which was hallowed by his remains.

Not long after, a merchant-vessel arrived, which enabled him to gratify his wish. At that time, Egbert, king of Kent, had sent out of Britain a man who had been elected to the office of bishop, Wighard by name, who had been adequately taught by the Roman disciples of the blessed Pope Gregory in Kent on every topic of Church discipline; but the king wished him to be ordained bishop at Rome, in order that, having him for bishop of his own nation and language, he might himself, as well as his people, be the more thoroughly master of the words and mysteries of the holy faith, as he would then have these administered, not through an interpreter, but from the hands and by the tongue of a kinsman and fellow-countryman. But Wighard, on coming to Rome, died of a disease, with all his attendants, before he had received the dignity of bishop. Now the Apostolic Father, that the embassy of the faithful might not fail through the death of their ambassadors, called a council, and appointed one of his Church to send as archbishop into Britain. This was Theodore, a man deep in all secular and ecclesiastical learning, whether Greek or Latin; and to him was given, as a colleague and counsellor, a man equally strenuous and prudent, the abbot Hadrian. Perceiving also that the reverend Benedict would become a man of wisdom, industry, piety, and nobility of mind, he committed to him the newly ordained bishop, with his followers, enjoining him to abandon the travel which he had undertaken for Christ's sake; and with a higher good in view, to return home to his country, and bring into it that teacher of wisdom whom it had so earnestly wished for, and to be to him an interpreter and guide, both on the journey thither, and afterwards, upon his arrival, when he should begin to preach. Benedict did as he was commanded; they came to Kent, and were joyfully received there; Theodore ascended his episcopal throne, and Benedict took upon himself to rule the monastery of the blessed Apostle Peter, of which, afterwards, Hadrian became abbot.

He ruled the monastery for two years; and then successfully, as before, accomplished a third voyage from Britain to Rome, and brought back a large number of books on sacred literature, which he had either bought at a price or received as gifts from his friends. On his return he arrived at Vienne, where he took possession of such as he had entrusted his friends to purchase for him. When he had come home, he determined to go to the court of Conwalh, king of the West Saxons, whose friendship and services he had already more than once experienced. But Conwalh died suddenly about this time, and he therefore directed his course to his native province. He came to the court of Egfrid, king of Northumberland, and gave an account of all that he had done since in youth he had left his country. He made no secret of his zeal for religion, and showed what ecclesiastical or monastic instructions he had received at Rome and elsewhere. He displayed the holy volumes and relics of Christ's blessed Apostles and martyrs, which he had brought, and found such favour in the eyes of the king, that he forthwith gave him seventy hides of land out of his own estates, and ordered a monastery to be built thereon for the first pastor of his church. This was done, as I said before, at the mouth of the river Were, on the left bank, in the 674th year of our Lord's incarnation, in the second indiction, and in the fourth year of King Egfrid's reign.

After the interval of a year, Benedict crossed the sea into Gaul, and no sooner asked than he obtained and carried back with him some masons to build him a church in the Roman style, which he had always admired. So much zeal did he show from his love to Saint Peter, in whose honour he was building it, that within a year from the time of laying the foundation, you might have seen the roof on and the solemnity of the mass celebrated therein. When the work was drawing to completion, he sent messengers to Gaul to fetch makers of glass, (more properly artificers,) who were at this time unknown in Britain, that they might glaze the windows of his church, with the cloisters and dining-rooms. This was done, and they came, and not only finished the work required, but taught the English nation their handicraft, which was well adapted for enclosing the lanterns of the church, and for the vessels required for various uses. All other things necessary for the service of the church and the altar, the sacred vessels, and the vestments, because they could not be procured in England, he took especial care to buy and bring home from foreign parts.

Some decorations and muniments there were which could not be procured even in Gaul, and these the pious founder determined to fetch from Rome; for which purpose, after he had formed the rule for his monastery, he made his fourth voyage to Rome, and returned loaded with more abundant spiritual merchandise than before. In the first place, he brought back a large quantity of books of all kinds; secondly, a great number of relics of Christ's Apostles and martyrs, all likely to bring a blessing on many an English church; thirdly, he introduced the Roman mode of chanting, singing, and ministering in the church, by obtaining permission from Pope Agatho to take back with him John, the archchanter of the church of St. Peter, and abbot of the monastery of St. Martin, to teach the English. This John, when he arrived in England, not only communicated instruction by teaching personally, but left behind him numerous writings, which are still preserved in the library of the same monastery. In the fourth place, Benedict brought with him a thing by no means to be despised, namely, a letter of privilege from Pope Agatho, which he had procured, not only with the consent, but by the request and exhortation, of King Egfrid, and by which the monastery was rendered safe and secure for ever from foreign invasion. Fifthly, he brought with him pictures of sacred representations, to adorn the church of St. Peter, which he had built; namely, a likeness of the Virgin Mary and of the twelve Apostles, with which he intended to adorn the central nave, on boarding placed from one wall to the other; also some figures from ecclesiastical history for the south wall, and others from the Revelation of St. John for the north wall; so that every one who entered the church, even if they could not read, wherever they turned their eyes, might have before them the amiable countenance of Christ and his saints, though it were but in a picture, and with watchful minds might revolve on the benefits of our Lord's incarnation, and having before their eyes the perils of the last judgment, might examine their hearts the more strictly on that account.

Thus King Egfrid, delighted by the virtues and zealous piety of the venerable Benedict, augmented the territory which he had given, on which to build this monastery, by a further grant of land of forty hides; on which, at the end of a year, Benedict, by the same King Egfrid's concurrence, and, indeed, command, built the monastery of the Apostle St. Paul, with this condition, that the same concord and unity should exist for ever between the two; so that, for instance, as the body cannot be separated from the head, nor the head forget the body by which it lives, in the same manner no man should ever try to divide these two monasteries, which had been united under the names of the first of the Apostles. Ceolfrid, whom Benedict made abbot, had been his most zealous assistant from the first foundation of the former monastery, and had gone with him at the proper time to Rome, for the sake of acquiring instruction, and offering up his prayers. At which time also he chose priest Easterwine to be the abbot of St. Peter's monastery, that with the help of this fellow-soldier he might sustain a burden otherwise too heavy for him. And let no one think it unbecoming that one monastery should have two abbots at once. His frequent travelling for the benefit of the monastery, and absence in foreign parts, was the cause; and history informs us, that, on a pressing occasion, the blessed St. Peter also ordained two pontiffs under him to rule the Church at Rome; and Abbot Benedict the Great, himself, as Pope St. Gregory writes of him, appointed twelve abbots over his followers, as he judged expedient, without any harm done to Christian charity; nay, rather to the increase thereof.

This man therefore undertook the government of the monastery in the ninth year after its foundation, and continued it till his death four years after. He was a man of noble birth; but he did not make that, like some men, a cause of boasting and despising others, but a motive for exercising nobility of mind also, as becomes a servant of the Lord. He was the cousin of his own abbot Benedict; and yet such was the singleness of mind in both, such their contempt for human grandeur, that the one, on entering the monastery, did not expect any notice of honour or relationship to be taken of him more than of others, and Benedict himself never thought of offering any; but the young man, faring like the rest, took pleasure in undergoing the usual course of monastic discipline in every respect. And indeed, though he had been an attendant on King Egfrid, and had abandoned his temporal vocation and arms, devoting himself to spiritual warfare, he remained so humble and like the other brethren, that he took pleasure in threshing and winnowing, milking the ewes and cows, and employed himself in the bakehouse, the garden, the kitchen, and in all the other labours of the monastery with readiness and submission. When he attained to the name and dignity of abbot, he retained the same spirit; saying to all, according to the advice of a certain wise man, "They have made thee a ruler; be not exalted, but be amongst them like one of them, gentle, affable, and kind to all." Whenever occasion required, he punished offenders by regular discipline; but was rather careful, out of his natural habits of love, to warn them not to offend and bring a cloud of disquietude over his cheerful countenance. Oftentimes, when he went forth on the business of the monastery, if he found the brethren working, he would join them and work with them, by taking the plough-handle, or handling the smith's hammer, or using the winnowing machine, or any thing of like nature. For he was a young man of great strength, and pleasant tone of voice, of a kind and bountiful disposition, and fair to look on. He ate of the same food as the other brethren, and in the same apartment: he slept in the same common room as he did before he was abbot; so that even after he was taken ill, and foresaw clear signs of his approaching death, he still remained two days in the common dormitory of the brethren. He passed the five days immediately before his death in a private apartment, from which he came out one day, and sitting in the open air, sent for all the brethren, and, as his kind feelings prompted him, gave to each of them the kiss of peace, whilst they all shed tears of sorrow for the loss of this their father and their guide. He died on the seventh of March, in the night, as the brethren were leaving off the matin hymn. He was twenty-four years old when he entered the monastery; he lived there twelve years, during seven of which he was in priest's orders, the others he passed in the dignity of abbot; and so, having thrown off his fleshly and perishable body, he entered the heavenly kingdom.

Now that we have had this foretaste of the life of the venerable Easterwine, let us resume the thread of the narrative. When Benedict had made this man abbot of St. Peter's, and Ceolfrid abbot of St. Paul's, he not long after made his fifth voyage from Britain to Rome, and returned (as usual) with an immense number of proper ecclesiastical relics. There were many sacred books and pictures of the saints, as numerous as before. He also brought with him pictures out of our Lord's history, which he hung round the chapel of Our Lady in the larger monastery; and others to adorn St. Paul's church and monastery, ably describing the connexion of the Old and New Testament; as, for instance, Isaac bearing the wood for his own sacrifice, and Christ carrying the cross on which he was about to suffer, were placed side by side. Again, the serpent raised up by Moses in the desert was illustrated by the Son of Man exalted on the cross. Among other things, he brought two cloaks, all of silk, and of incomparable workmanship, for which he received an estate of three hides on the south bank of the river Were, near its mouth, from King Alfrid, for he found on his return that Egfrid had been murdered during his absence.

But, amid this prosperity, he found afflictions also awaiting his return. The venerable Easterwine, whom he had made abbot when he departed, and many of the brethren committed to his care, had died of a general pestilence. But for this loss he found some consolation in the good and reverend deacon, Sigfrid, whom the brethren and his co-abbot Ceolfrid had chosen to be his successor. He was a man well skilled in the knowledge of Holy Scripture, of most excellent manners, of wonderful continence, and one in whom the virtues of the mind were in no small degree depressed by bodily infirmity, and the innocency of whose heart was tempered with a baneful and incurable affection of the lungs.

Not long after, Benedict himself was seized by a disease. For, that the virtue of patience might be a trial of their religious zeal, the Divine Love laid both of them on the bed of temporal sickness, that when they had conquered their sorrows by death, He might cherish them for ever in heavenly peace and quietude. For Sigfrid also, as I have mentioned, died wasted by a long illness: and Benedict died of a palsy, which grew upon him for three whole years; so that when he was dead in all his lower extremities, his upper and vital members, spared to show his patience and virtue, were employed in the midst of his sufferings in giving thanks to the Author of his being, in praises to God, and exhortations to the brethren. He urged the brethren, when they came to see him, to observe the rule which he had given them. "For," said he, "you cannot suppose that it was my own untaught heart which dictated this rule to you. I learnt it from seventeen monasteries, which I saw during my travels, and most approved of, and I copied these institutions thence for your benefit." The large and noble library, which he had brought from Rome, and which was necessary for the edification of his church, he commanded to be kept entire, and neither by neglect to be injured or dispersed. But on one point he was most solicitous, in choosing an abbot, lest high birth, and not rather probity of life and doctrine, should be attended to. "And I tell you of a truth," said he, "in the choice of two evils, it would be much more tolerable for me, if God so pleased, that this place, wherein I have built the monastery, should for ever become a desert, than that my carnal brother, who, as we know, walks not in the way of truth, should become abbot, and succeed me in its government. Wherefore, my brethren, beware, and never choose an abbot on account of his birth, nor from any foreign place; but seek out, according to the rule of Abbot Benedict the Great, and the decrees of our order, with common consent, from amongst your own company, whoever in virtue of life and wisdom of doctrine may be found fittest for this office; and whomsoever you shall, by this unanimous inquiry of Christian charity, prefer and choose, let him be made abbot with the customary blessings, in presence of the bishop. For those who after the flesh beget children of the flesh, must necessarily seek fleshly and earthly heirs to their fleshly and earthly inheritance; but those who by the spiritual seed of the

Word procreate spiritual sons to God, must of like necessity be spiritual in every thing which they do. Among their spiritual children, they think him the greatest who is possessed of the most abundant grace of the Spirit, in the same way as earthly parents consider their eldest as the principal one of their children, and prefer him to the others in dividing out their inheritance."

Nor must I omit to mention that the venerable Abbot Benedict, to lessen the wearisomeness of the night, which from his illness he often passed without sleeping, would frequently call a reader, and cause him to read aloud, as an example for himself, the history of the patience of Job, or some other extract from Scripture, by which his pains might be alleviated, and his depressed soul be raised to heavenly things. And because he could not get up to pray, nor without difficulty lift up his voice to the usual extent of daily psalmody, the prudent man, in his zeal for religion, at every hour of daily or nightly prayer would call to him some of the brethren, and making them sing psalms in two companies, would himself sing with them, and thus make up by their voices for the deficiency of his own.

Now both the abbots saw that they were near death, and unfit longer to rule the monastery, from increasing weakness, which, though tending no doubt to the perfection of Christian purity, was so great, that, when they expressed a desire to see one another before they died, and Sigfrid was brought in a litter into the room where Benedict was lying on his bed, though they were placed by the attendants with their heads on the same pillow, they had not the power of their own strength to kiss one another, but were assisted even in this act of fraternal love. After taking counsel with Sigfrid and the other brethren, Benedict sent for Ceolfrid, abbot of St. Paul's, dear to him not by relationship of the flesh, but by the ties of Christian virtue, and with the consent and approbation of all, made him abbot of both monasteries; thinking it expedient in every respect to preserve peace, unity, and concord between the two, if they should have one father and ruler for ever, after the example of the kingdom of Israel, which always remained invincible and inviolate by foreign nations as long as it was ruled by one and the same governor of its own race; but when for its former sins it was torn into opposing factions, it fell by degrees, and, thus shorn of its ancient integrity, perished. He reminded them also of that evangelical maxim, ever worthy to be remembered,—"A kingdom divided against itself shall be laid waste."

Two months after this, God's chosen servant, the venerable Abbot Sigfrid, having passed through the fire and water of temporal tribulation, was carried to the resting-place of everlasting repose: he entered the mansion of the heavenly kingdom, rendering up whole offerings of praise to the Lord which his righteous lips had vowed; and after another space of four months, Benedict, who so nobly vanquished sin and wrought the deeds of virtue, yielded to the weakness of the flesh, and came to his end. Night came on chilled by the winter's blasts, but a day of eternal felicity succeeded, of serenity and of splendour. The brethren met together at the church, and passed the night without sleep in praying and singing, consoling their sorrow for their father's departure by one continued outpouring of praise. Others clung to the chamber in which the sick man, strong in mind, awaited his departure from death and his entry into eternal life. A portion of Scripture from the Gospels, appointed to be read every evening, was recited by a priest during the whole night, to relieve their sorrow. The sacrament of our Lord's flesh and blood was given him as a viaticum at the moment of his departure; and thus his holy spirit, chastened and tried by the lengthened gallings of the lash, operating for his own good, abandoned the earthy tenement of the flesh, and escaped in freedom to the glory of everlasting happiness. That his departure was most triumphant, and neither impeded nor delayed by unclean spirits, the psalm which was chanted for him is a proof. For the brethren coming together to the church at the beginning of the night, sang through the Psalter in order, until they came to the 82nd, which begins, "God, who shall be like unto thee?" The subject of the text is this; that the enemies of the

Christian name, whether carnal or spiritual, are always endeavouring to destroy and disperse the church of Christ, and every individual soul among the faithful; but that, on the other hand, they themselves shall be confounded and routed, and shall perish for ever, unnerved before the power of the Lord, to whom there is no one equal, for He alone is Most Highest over the whole earth. Wherefore it was a manifest token of Divine interposition, that such a song should be sung at the moment of his death, against whom, with God's aid, no enemy could prevail. In the sixteenth year after he built the monastery, the holy confessor found rest in the Lord, on the 14th day of January, in the church of St. Peter; and thus, as he had loved that holy Apostle in his life, and obtained from him admission into the heavenly kingdom, so also after death he rested hard by his relics, and his altar, even in the body. He ruled the monastery, as I have stated, sixteen years: the first eight alone, without any assistant abbot; the last eight in conjunction with Easterwine, Sigfrid, and Ceolfrid, who enjoyed with him the title of abbot, and assisted him in his duties. The first of these was his colleague four years; the second, three; the third, one.

The third of these, Ceolfrid, was a man of great perseverance, of acute intellect, bold in action, experienced in judgment, and zealous in religion. He first of all, as we have mentioned, with the advice and assistance of Benedict, founded, completed, and ruled the monastery of St. Paul's seven years; and, afterwards, ably governed, during twenty-eight years, both these monasteries; or, to speak more correctly, the single monastery of St. Peter and St. Paul, in its two separate localities; and, whatever works of merit his predecessor had begun, he, with no less zeal, took pains to finish. For, among other arrangements which he found it necessary to make, during his long government of the monastery, he built several oratories; increased the number of vessels of the church and altar, and the vestments of every kind; and the library of both monasteries, which Abbot Benedict had so actively begun, under his equally zealous care became doubled in extent. For he added three Pandects of a new translation to that of the old translation which he had brought from Rome; one of them, returning to Rome in his old age, he took with him as a gift; the other two he left to the two monasteries. Moreover, for a beautiful volume of the Geographers which Benedict had bought at Rome, he received from King Alfrid, who was well skilled in Holy Scripture, in exchange, a grant of land of eight hides, near the river Fresca, for the monastery of St. Paul's. Benedict had arranged this purchase with the same King Alfrid, before his death, but died before he could complete it. Instead of this land, Ceolfrid, in the reign of Osred, paid an additional price, and received a territory of twenty hides, in the village called by the natives Sambuce, and situated much nearer to the monastery. In the time of Pope Sergius, of blessed memory, some monks were sent to Rome, who procured from him a privilege for the protection of their monastery, similar to that which Pope Agatho had given to Benedict. This was brought back to Britain, and, being exhibited before a synod, was confirmed by the signatures of the bishops who were present, and their munificent King Alfrid, just as the former privilege was confirmed publicly by the king and bishops of the time. Zealous for the welfare of St. Peter's monastery, at that time under the government of the reverend and religious servant of Christ, Witmer, whose acquaintance with every kind of learning, both sacred and profane, was equally extensive, he made a gift of it for ever of a portion of land of ten hides, which he had received from King Alfrid, in the village called Daldun.

But Ceolfrid having now practised a long course of regular discipline, which the prudent father Benedict had laid down for himself and his brethren on the authority of the elders; and having shown the most incomparable skill both in praying and chanting, in which he daily exercised himself, together with the most wonderful energy in punishing the wicked, and modesty in consoling the weak; having also observed such abstinence in meat and drink, and such humility in dress, as are uncommon among rulers; saw himself now old and full of days, and unfit any longer, from his extreme age, to prescribe to his brethren the proper forms of spiritual exercise by his life and doctrine. Having, therefore, deliberated long within himself, he judged it expedient, having first impressed on the brethren the observance of the rules which St. Benedict had given them, and thereby to choose for themselves a more efficient abbot out of their own number, to depart, himself, to Rome, where he had been in his youth with the holy Benedict; that not only he might for a time be free from all worldly cares before his death, and so have leisure and quiet for reflection, but that they also, having chosen a younger abbot, might naturally, in consequence thereof, observe more accurately the rules of monastic discipline.

At first all opposed, and entreated him on their knees and with many tears, but their solicitations were to no purpose. Such was his eagerness to depart, that on the third day after he had disclosed his design to the brethren, he set out upon his journey. For he feared, what actually came to pass, that he might die before he reached Rome; and he was also anxious that neither his friends nor the nobility, who all honoured him, should delay his departure, or give him money which he would not have time to repay; for with him it was an invariable rule, if any one made him a present, to show equal grace by returning it, either at once or within a suitable space of time. Early in the morning, therefore, of Wednesday, the 4th of May, the mass was sung in the church of the Mother of God, the immaculate Virgin Mary, and in the church of the Apostle Peter; and those who were present communicating with him, he prepared for his departure. All of them assembled in St. Peter's church; and when he had lighted the frankincense, and addressed a prayer at the altar, he gave his blessing to all, standing on the steps and holding the censer in his hand. Amid the prayers of the Litany, the cry of sorrow resounded from all as they went out of the church: they entered the oratory of St. Laurence the martyr, which was in the dormitory of the brethren over against them. Whilst giving them his last farewell, he admonished them to preserve love towards one another, and to correct, according to the Gospel rule, those who did amiss: he forgave all of them whatever wrong they might have done him; and entreated them all to pray for him, and to be reconciled to him, if he had ever reprimanded them too harshly. They went down to the shore, and there, amid tears and lamentations, he gave them the kiss of peace, as they knelt upon their knees; and when he had offered up a prayer he went on board the vessel with his companions. The deacons of the Church went on board with him, carrying lighted tapers and a golden crucifix. Having crossed the river, he kissed the cross, mounted his horse, and departed, leaving in both his monasteries about six hundred brethren.

When he was gone, the brethren returned to the church, and with much weeping and prayer commended themselves and theirs to the protection of the Lord. After a short interval, having ended the nine o'clock psalm, they again assembled, and deliberated what was to be done. At length they resolved, with prayer, hymns, and fasting, to seek of the Lord a new abbot as soon as possible. This resolution they communicated to their brethren of St. Paul's, by some of that monastery who were present, and also by some of their own people. They immediately gave their consent, and both monasteries showing the same spirit, they all together lifted up their hearts and voices to the Lord. At length, on the third day, which was Easter Sunday, an assembly was held, consisting of all the brethren of St. Peter's and several of the elder monks from the monastery of St. Paul's. The greatest concord prevailed, and the same sentiments were expressed by both. They elected for their new abbot, Huetbert, who from his boyhood had not only been bred up in the regular discipline of the monastery, but had acquired much experience in the various duties of writing, chanting, reading, and teaching. He had been at Rome in the time of Pope Sergius, of blessed memory, and had there learnt and copied every thing which he thought useful or worthy to be brought away. He had also been twelve years in priest's orders. He was now made abbot; and immediately went with some of the brethren to Ceolfrid, who was waiting for a ship in which to cross the ocean. They told him what they had done, for which he gave thanks to God, in approbation of their choice, and received from his successor a letter of recommendation to Pope Gregory, of which I have preserved the few passages which follow.

"To our most beloved lord in the Lord of lords, and thrice blessed Pope Gregory, Huetbert, his most humble servant, abbot of the monastery of the holiest of the Apostles, St. Peter, in Saxony, Health for ever in the Lord! I do not cease to give thanks to the dispensation of Divine wisdom, as do also all the holy brethren, who in these parts are seeking with me to bear the pleasant yoke of Christ, that they may find rest to their souls, that God has condescended to appoint so glorious a vessel of election to rule the Church in these our times; and by means of the light of truth and faith with which you are full, to scatter the beams of his love on all your inferiors also. We recommend to your holy clemency, most beloved father and lord in Christ, the grey hairs of our venerable and beloved father Abbot Ceolfrid, the supporter and defender of our spiritual liberty and peace in this monastic retirement; and, in the first place, we give thanks to the holy and undivided Trinity, for that, although he hath caused us much sorrow, lamentation, and tears, by his departure, he hath nevertheless arrived at the enjoyment of that rest which he long desired; whilst he was in his old age devoutly returning to that threshold of the holy Apostles, which he exultingly boasted, that when a youth he had visited, seen, and worshipped. After more than forty years of care and toil, during his government of the monasteries, by his wonderful love of virtue, as if recently incited to conversation with the heavenly life, though worn out with extreme old age, and already almost at the gates of death, he a second time undertakes to travel in the cause of Christ, that the thorns of his former secular anxieties may be consumed by the fire of zeal blazing forth from that spiritual furnace. We next entreat your fatherly love, that, though we have not merited to do this, you will carefully fulfil towards him the last offices; knowing for certain, that though you may possess his body, yet both we and you shall have in his devout spirit, whether in the body or out of the body, a mighty intercessor and protector over our own last moments, at the throne of grace." And so on through the rest of the letter.

When Huetbert had returned to the monastery, Bishop Acca was sent for to confirm the election with his blessing. Afterwards, by his youthful zeal and wisdom, he gained many privileges for the monastery; and, amongst others, one which gave great delight to all, he took up the bones of Abbot Easterwine, which lay in the entrance porch of St. Peter's, and also the bones of his old preceptor, Abbot Sigfrid, which had been buried outside the Sacrarium towards the south, and placing both together in one chest, but separated by a partition, laid them within the church near the body of St. Benedict. He did this on Sigfrid's birthday, the 23rd of August; and on the same day Divine Providence so ordered that Christ's venerable servant Witmer, whom we have already mentioned, departed this life, and was buried in the same place as the aforesaid abbots, whose life he had imitated.

But Christ's servant Ceolfrid, as has been said, died on his way to the threshold of the holy Apostles, of old age and weakness. For he reached the Lingones about nine o'clock, where he died seven hours after, and was honourably buried the next day in the church of the three twin martyrs, much to the sorrow, not only of the English who were in his train, to the number of eighty, but also of the neighbouring inhabitants, who were dissolved in tears at the loss of the reverend father. For it was almost impossible to avoid weeping to see part of his company continuing their journey without the holy father, whilst others, abandoning their first intentions, returned home to relate his death and burial; and others, again, lingered in sorrow at the tomb of the deceased among strangers speaking an unknown tongue.

Ceolfrid was seventy-four years old when he died: forty-seven years he had been in priest's orders, during thirty-five of which he had been abbot; or, to speak more correctly, forty-three,—for, from the time when Benedict began to build his monastery in honour of the holiest of the Apostles, Ceolfrid had been his only companion, coadjutor, and teacher of the monastic rules. He never relaxed the rigour of ancient discipline from any occasions of old age, illness, or travel; for, from the day of his departure till the day of his death, *i.e.* from the 4th of June till the 25th of September, a space of one hundred and fourteen days, besides the canonical hours of prayer, he never omitted to go twice daily through the Psalter in order; and even when he became so weak that he could not ride on horseback, and was obliged to be carried in a horse-litter, the holy ceremony of the mass was offered up every day, except one which he passed at sea, and the three days immediately before his death.

He died on Friday, the 25th of September, in the year of our Lord 716, between three and four o'clock, in the fields of the city before mentioned, and was buried the next day near the first mile-stone on the south side of the city, in the monastery of the Twins, followed by a large number of his English attendants, and the inhabitants of the city and monastery. The names of these twin martyrs are Speusippus, Eleusippus, and Meleusippus. They were born at one birth, and born again by baptism at the same time: together with their aunt Leonella, they left behind them the holy remembrance of their martyrdom; and I pray that they may bestow upon my unworthy self, and upon our holy father, the benefit of their intercession and protection.

NOTES TO
THE HISTORY OF THE ENGLISH
CHURCH AND PEOPLE

PAGE

1. *Ceowulph.* King of Northumbria (729–737)
2. *Pope Gregory.* Gregory II. (715–731).
2. *Daniel.* He was bishop of Winchester.
4. Bede's account of Britain was taken from earlier authors; and his history of the Roman period from such writers as Orosius, who wrote in the fifth century, Eutropius, &c.
4. *Reptacestir* is now Richborough. *Gessoriacum* is Boulogne; it was the chief town of the Morini, who inhabited the later Artois.
4. *St. Basil.* That is, St. Basil the Great, who was bishop of Cæsarea in Cappadocia, and died in 379.
5. *Scythia.* In Bede, Scythia means Scandinavia, not Russia.
5. *Armorica.* A confusion caused probably by the fact that in Bede's time, Armorica was largely peopled by refugees from Britain. Armorica is the modern Brittany.
6. *"A very large gulf."* That is, the Firth of Clyde. *Alcluith* is the present Dumbarton.
7. *"The sixtieth year."* The date should be B.C. 55. Cæsar's second invasion was in B.C. 54.
7. *Cassibellaun:* or *Casivellaunus.* He was king of the Cassii, and ruled what is now Middlesex and the surrounding land. *Trinovatum* = (perhaps) London.
8. *"Cassibellaun's town."* Possibly on the site of St. Albans.
8. *"Wars and tumults . . . on every side."* The rebellion of Ambiorix.

8. *Orcades.* The Orkney and Shetland Islands. They were never really conquered by the Romans, though Julius Agricola ordered the circumnavigation of Britain.

9. *"Two most noble towns"* i.e. Camulodunum (Colchester) and London. They fell in the rising of Boadicea (A.D. 61), repressed by Suetonius Paulinus.

9. *Marcus Antoninus.* As it stands, there is much confusion in this chapter. Marcus Antoninus = Marcus Aurelius, who reigned from 161 to 180. Eleutherius was Pope from 177 to 193. The colleague of Marcus was first his adopted brother Verus, who died in 169. In 176 Marcus gave his son, Commodus, the title of Augustus. The error in the text may have arisen from the double association.

9. *"Civil wars."* Against Niger in the East, and Albinius in the West. The latter had been governor of Britain, and this partly led to the visit of Severus. Severus succeeded in 193.

10. *"A great ditch and strong rampart."* The Roman walls were four in number: (1) Julius Agricola built a wall from the Clyde to the Forth. (2) Hadrian built a second from the Solway Firth to the Tyne. (3) Severus repaired the wall of Hadrian. (4) Theodosius restored the line of Agricola's wall.

10. *Bassianus.* The emperor usually known as Caracalla.

10. *Carausius.* His title was "Count of the Saxon Shore," and he commanded a fleet and army on the east coast. Rebelled, 289; killed in 294.

15. *"Emperor of the Gauls."* Constantius was "Cæsar," an inferior title to "Augustus." His special province was the Prefecture of the Gauls, *i. e.* Britain, Gaul, Spain, and Mauritania. He was never, strictly speaking, emperor.

15. *Theodosius.* Theodosius the Great. The Valentinian is Valentinian II.

16. *Pelagius.* A Welshman; he denied the doctrine of original sin.

17. *"Two inlets"* *i. e.* the Firths of Clyde and Forth. *Giudi,* probably near Leith.

18. *Abercurnig.* Now Abercorn.

20. *Ætius.* The general of Valentinian III., who defeated Attila at Chalons (451).

22. *Angles.* Strictly the first settlers were Jutes. They came from Jutland, the Angles from Schleswig-Holstein, the Saxons from the banks of the Elbe, Wese, and Ems. In this account Bede follows Gildas, who wrote *De Calamitate et Conquestu Britanniæ,* sixth century.

23. *"Horsa . . . slain in battle."* At Aylesford.

24. *Ambrosius Aurelius.* Said to have been king of Devon and Cornwall.

24. *Baddesdewn-Hill.* The battle of Mt. Badon (Lansdown, Bath), won by Arthur.

25. *St. Germanus.* Bishop of Auxerre.

27. *"Tribune"* = a person of distinction merely; not a tribune in the classical sense.

29. *"Saxons and Picts."* The place of this battle is thought to have been Mold in Flint. There is a difficulty in the alleged presence of Saxons, who had hardly penetrated so far; either the battle was won over the Picts only or we must suppose another body of Saxons to have landed in Wales.

31. *"Valentinian was murdered."* His death is variously attributed to the followers of Ætius or to the private revenge of Maximus. The succession of emperors in the West actually continued some years longer, until 453.

32. Gregory (the Great) was Pope from 590 to 604. Augustine was a Benedictine and trained under Gregory at the monastery of St. Anthony, Rome.

34. Ætherius was really archbishop of Lyons.

35. Ethelbert reigned from 561 to 616. He is reckoned as the third "Bretwalda," = chief, among the Saxon kings; but the authority of such chief kings was rather nominal than real.

35. *Bertha.* Daughter of Charibert, king of Paris.

37. *St. Martin, i. e.* St. Martin of Tours, flourished in the fifth century.

38. *"They are to take wives."* St. Gregory the Great was the first to advocate celibacy of the clergy strongly.

51. *London and York.* London was a metropolitan see in Roman times; hence its equality with York here. The see of York was not refounded until twenty-four years later.

58. *Degsastan.* Probably near the modern Selkirk.

59. *Felix* = Pope Felix IV., A.D. 529.

60. *"Respondent"* = legate of the papal court; to the Emperor Maurice, A.D. 582–585.

61. *Eutychius.* Patriarch of Constantinople, A.D. 580.

65. *"The bishop"* = Pope Benedict I.

65 *Augustine's Oak.* Probably in Gloucestershire, near Aust.

66. *"Seven bishops."* Their sees are unknown and the number is itself doubtful.

66. *Bancornburg.* Bangor in Flint.

67. *Carlegion.* Chester.

72. *Mevanian Islands.* Anglesea and Man.

73. *"Wise persons."* The Witenagemot.

87. *Redwald.* King of East Anglia, reckoned as fourth Bretwalda.

93. *Cataract.* Catterick in Yorkshire. *Campodunum* = Doncaster. *Loidis* = Leeds.

95. *Dumnoc.* Dunwich (now under the sea).

96. *Pope Honorius.* Honorius I. (625–638) succeeded Boniface V.

98. 10*th of November.* About A.D. 630.

100. *John.* Afterwards Pope John IV., 640–642. *Severinus.* Pope in 639.

101. *Heathfield.* On the Don, near Doncaster.

101. *Cadwalla.* King of Strathclyde. The last Briton to bear the title of king.

103. *Deira* lay between the Tyne and Humber, *Bernicia* between the Tyne and the Finn of Forth; together they formed the kingdom of Northumbria.

104. *Denises-burn.* Site unknown.

105. *Heavenfield.* In the Lowlands on the Tweed. *Hagulstad* = Hexham.

107. *Lindisfarne* = Holy Island, off the coast of Northumberland. A new bishopric had to be created, since Paulinus still held the see of York theoretically.

107. *Hii* = Iona.

108. *Ninias* was a native of North Wales. *"The White House"* = Candida Casa. Whithern in Galloway.

112. *"The royal city"* = Bamborough.

112. *Gewissae* = "the West Folk," *i. e.* the West Saxons. *Cf.* Visigoths = the West Goths. *Dorcic* = Dorchester, near Oxford.

117. *Maserfield* = probably Oswestry, in Shropshire.

119. *Beardeneu* = Bardney in Lincolnshire; on which *Peartaneu* (p. 120) was dependent.

125. *Ingethlingum* = Gilling, in Yorkshire.

131. *"A school for youth."* Probably at Dunwich.

133. *Cnobher's Town* = Burgh Castle, in Suffolk.

136. *Clovis,* king of Neustria. One of the Rois Fainéants. *Latiniacum* = Lagny, near Paris.

136. *Girvii.* A district in Mercia.

137. *At the Wall.* Site not known certainly.

138. *"Bishop of the Middle Angles."* The see was first at Repton, and later at Lichfield.

144 *Heruteu* = Hartlepool.

147. *"Archbishop of France,"* rather, "metropolitan of the Franks."

147. *Rhypum* or *Inrhypum* = Ripon. *Streaneshalch* = Whitby.

152. *Tuda.* Bishop of Lindisfarne; the last sent from Scotland.

154. *"A sudden pestilence."* Known as the yellow plague.

154. *Pegnaleth* = Finchale, near Durham.

156. *"King of France."* Clothaire, king of Neustria.

158. *Vitalian.* Pope, 657–672.

163. *Ebrin.* Mayor of the palace in Neustria; the rival of the Pepins.

163. *Quentavic* = St. Quentin.

163. *"The emperor,"* *i. e.* the emperor of the East, who still held the Exarchate in Italy.

166. *Ad Barve*—Barton, in Lincolnshire. *Lichfield.* St. Chad was first bishop. The see was an archbishopric from 789 to 803.

171. *Inisbofinde.* An island off the N.W. coast of Galway.

174. *Medeshamstead* = Peterborough.

175. *Ceortesei* = Chertsey. *Bercingu* = Barking.

184. *Meanwara.* Part of Hampshire. *Wiccii.* A tribe on the left bank of the Severn.

184. *Bosanham* = Bosham, in Sussex.

188. *Ethelwalch.* Was king of the South Saxons, not of the West Saxons.

189. *At the Stone* = Stoneham. *Reodford* = Red bridge.

190. *Eutyches.* A presbyter of Constantinople, fifth century. He confused the two natures of Christ. *Heathfield* = Hatfield.

194. *"Apostle of the Gentiles."* The church was St. Paul's, London.

194. *Coludi* = Coldingham.

195. *Grantchester.* Near Cambridge.

202. *Calcacestir.* Site doubtful.

204. *Hackness.* Near Whitby. *Begu* = St. Bees

213. *Abercurnig* = Abercorn.

219. *Lugubalia.* In Cumberland.

223. *Dacore* = Dacre, Cumberland.

225. *John* = St. John of Beverley.

225. *Inderawood* = Beverley.

227. *Wetadun* = Walton, Yorkshire.

235. *Raculph* = Reculver. *Genlade* = the Inlade.

238. *Pepin* = Pepin d'Heristal, 687–714.

241. *Wiltaburg* = Wiltenburg; not Utrecht.

250. *Adamnan.* 624–704. It is doubtful if he really wrote the book *De Situ Terrae Sanctae* here quoted by Bede.

254. *Aldhelm.* Bishop of Sherborne. The see was afterwards removed to Salisbury.

256. *Undalum* = Oundle.

258. *Stanford* = Stamford, Lincolnshire.

263. *"His own monastery."* St. Augustine's, Canterbury.

278. *"Plague of Saracens."* This refers to the victory of Charles Martel over Abdulrahman at Tours, A.D. 732; and the passage must have been added after the rest of the History had been written.

SUGGESTED READING

BEDE. *Homilies on the Gospels, Vols. I–II.* Eds. Lawrence T. Martin and David Hurst. Kalamazoo, MI: Cistercian Publications, 1991.

BLAIR, PETER HUNTER. *The Work of Bede.* Cambridge: Cambridge University Press, 1990.

BROWN, GEORGE HARDIN. *Bede the Venerable.* Boston: Twayne, 1987.

COLGRAVE, BERTRAM, ED. AND TRANS. *Two Lives of St. Cuthbert.* Cambridge: Cambridge University Press, 1940.

DUCKETT, ELEANOR SHIPLEY. *Anglo-Saxon Saints and Scholars.* New York: Macmillan, 1947.

FARMER, DAVID H. *The Age of Bede.* London: Penguin, 1998.

LAPIDGE, MICHAEL. *Bede and His World: The Jarrow Lectures, 1958–1993, 2 Vols.* Aldershot: Variorum, 1994.

LEVISON, WIHELM. *England and the Continent in the Eighth Century.* New York: Oxford University Press, 1998.

MAYR-HARTING, HENRY. *The Coming of Christianity to Anglo-Saxon England: 3rd Edition.* University Park, PA: Penn State University Press, 1991.

MCCREADY, WILLIAM D. *Miracles and the Venerable Bede.* Toronto: Pontifical Institute, 1994.

RICHE, PIERRE. *Education and Culture in the Barbarian West: From the Sixth through the Eighth Century.* Trans. John Contreni. Columbia, SC: University of South Carolina Press, 1976.

SAWYER, PETER H. *From Roman Britain to Norman England, 2nd Ed.* London: Routledge, 1998.

SOUTHERN, RICHARD W. *Medieval Humanism and Other Studies.* New York: Harper & Row, 1970.

STENTON, FRANK. *Anglo-Saxon England.* Oxford: Clarendon, 1971.

WALLACE-HADRILL, J. M. *Bede's Ecclesiastical History of the English People: A Historical Commentary.* Oxford: Clarendon, 1988.

---. *Germanic Kingship in England and on the Continent.* Oxford: Clarendon, 1971.

YORKE, BARBARA. *Kings and Kingdoms of Early Anglo-Saxon England.* London: Seaby, 1990.